Alibris via
Amazon

Georg Meggle (Ed.)
Ethics of Humanitarian Interventions

PRACTICAL PHILOSOPHY

Herausgegeben von / Edited by

Heinrich Ganthaler • Neil Roughley
Peter Schaber • Herlinde Pauer-Studer

Band 7 / Volume 7

Georg Meggle (Ed.)

Ethics of Humanitarian Interventions

ontos verlag
Frankfurt • Lancaster

Bibliographic information published by Die Deutsche Bibliothek
Die Deutsche Bibliothek lists this publication in the Deutsche Nationalbibliographie; detailed bibliographic data is available in the Internet at http://dnb.ddb.de

North and South America by
Transaction Books
Rutgers University
Piscataway, NJ 08854-8042
trans@transactionpub.com

United Kingdom, Ire Iceland, Turkey, Malta, Portugal by
Gazelle Books Services Limited
White Cross Mills
Hightown
LANCASTER, LA1 4XS
sales@gazellebooks.co.uk

P.O. Box 15 41, D-63133 Heusenstamm
www.ontosverlag.com

ISBN 3-937202-58-7

2004

Printed on acid-free paper
ISO-Norm 970-6

Printed in Germany.

PRACTICAL PHILOSOPHY

Edited by
Heinrich Ganthaler • Neil Roughley
Herlinde Pauer-Studer • Peter Schaber

The aim of the series is to publish high-quality work that deals with questions in practical philosophy from a broadly analytic perspective. These include questions in meta-ethics, normative ethics and "applied" ethics, as well as in political philosophy, philosophy of law and the philosophy of action. Through the publication of work in both German and English the series aims to facilitate discussion between English- and German-speaking practical philosophers.

For
MIMA ANDJELKOVIC,
JOVAN BABIC,
MIROSLAV PROKOPIJEVIC,
and IVAN VUKOVIC
(Belgrade)

who first kindled the flame

CONTENTS

Preface

Humanitarian Interventions – that sounds nice; much nicer than *wars, battles* and *use of military force*. Foremost, the phrase makes you think of the delivery of sanitary goods, medication, of soup-kitchens. Here we are not supposed to think of interventions of this kind; we have to have *humanitarian interventions* in mind which are *humanitarian intervention-wars.*

(I) At exactly what point is the use of military force a humanitarian intervention? What is the humanitarian aspect of those interventions? Their occasion? Their motive? Their alleged as well as their actual consequences?

(II) At exactly what point are humanitarian intervention-wars morally justifiable? Are they justifiable even if they are wars of aggression breaching international law?

And finally:

(III) Was the war which was presented to us as the paradigmatic example of a humanitarian-intervention-war, that is: the war in Kosovo in the spring of 1999 (with over 37,000 bombing missions), really justifiable as a humanitarian intervention? Many of us wanted to believe so at the time. Does our *ex ante* judgement hold today in an *ex post* reflection? And which lessons for the future should we learn from the success or failure of this humanitarian war?

These are the questions proposed in this book; therefore, it is concerned with *problems of semantics* (part I), *problems of moral assessment* (part II) and with the moral, legal and political *conclusions* we draw from *our experiences* with the war in Kosovo, our primary example of a humanitarian intervention (part III).

International experts in the areas of philosophy, international law, sociology and peace studies debated these questions vigorously for several days. This is the resulting volume.

*

Will the arguments published here play a decisive role for the next humanitarian intervention-wars? According to all previous knowledge about human history, most likely not. Arguments, it seems, are not the definitive word on matters of war and peace.
But maybe something is gained with a volume like this if it contributes to a clearer distinction between comprehensible judgement and pure propaganda - for the next time/war, or the time/war after that. It helps clarify these distinctions *before* the next decisions are made; at least for those of us to whom this minimal, yet war-decisive difference still matters.

*

The discussions were held at the CENTER FOR INTERDISCIPLINARY RESEARCH (Zentrum für Interdisziplinäre Forschung, ZiF) at the University of Bielefeld in January 2002; the conference was partially funded by the DFG (DEUTSCHE FORSCHUNGSGEMEINSCHAFT). Many thanks to these institutions for their ongoing support. Thanks also to *Tobias Prüwer* and to *Andrea Busch* and *Katinka Schulte-Ostermann* who alertly helped me in completing this volume.

Leipzig, Summer of 2004 *Georg Meggle*

I. BASIC ISSUES

MICHAEL WALZER
The Argument about Humanitarian Intervention 21

I intend a "return" to the question of humanitarian intervention, in order to review, restate, and revise (there are in fact some important revisions) the argument about intervention that I first made in *Just and Unjust Wars (1977)* – and also to look more closely at some cases. What is the philosophical approach that my argument represents or applies? I start from Catholic just war theory, but at least some American Catholics arrive at conclusions very different from mine. So, I will represent a combination all my own: Catholic theory, Jewish anxiety, and left sensibility. And I will be looking back mainly to the Vietnamese intervention in Cambodia and reviewing a number of cases since.

SEUMAS MILLER
Collective Responsibility and Humanitarian Armed Intervention 37

One central question in relation to humanitarian intervention in contemporary armed conflict situations concerns the development by the international community of collective mechanisms to deal with the problem of large scale human rights violations within nation states. The moral justification for such a development would seem to rely on the notion of collective moral responsibility. In this paper I explore the notion of collective moral responsibility as it pertains to the development of such collective mechanisms. The paper draws on empirical and other literature on relevant institutional mechanisms, and on recent armed conflicts, including Bosnia and Kosovo.

OLAF L. MÜLLER
Reconstructing Pacifism. Different Ways of Looking at Reality 57

Pacifists and their opponents disagree not only about moral questions, but rather often about factual questions as well – as seen when looking at the controversy surrounding the crisis in Kosovo. According to my reconstruction of pacifism, this is not surprising since the pacifist, legitimately, looks at the facts in the light of her system of value. Her opponent, in turn, looks at the facts in the light of an alternative value system, and the quarrel between the two parties about supposedly descriptive matters never ceases, as there is no objective reality about the war in question that could settle the issue.
In my view, the pacifist's value-laden way of looking at reality implicitly obeys three epistemic imperatives. First, the *Epistemic Imperative concerning Human Nature* ("Resist demonizing the other side; always try to understand the case from the other point of view"). Second, the *Epistemic Imperative concerning Non-Violent Alternatives* ("Always search for non-violent alternatives to military action"). Third, the *Epistemic Imperative concerning Uncontrolled Escalation* ("Hone your senses to the uncontrolled, irreversible side effects of military action, particularly to the danger of military escalation leading to another world war"). Objective reality has no way of telling us how far we should go in following these imperatives. Rather, *we* have to make the decision about how far we are going to take them *ourselves*. In this way, the pacifist's epistemic imperatives are comparable to Kant's regulative principles.

UWE CZANIERA
How Far Shall We Go in Humanitarian Interventions? 81

One of the aims of a humanitarian intervention is a clear prospect of reintegration of the attacked country after the intervention has taken place. Now, if an alliance decides to attack a certain aggressor, should it not try to destroy the political structures of its target as far as possible? Otherwise, one might say, there would be decreasing prospects for the successful reintegration of the concerned country. If this is right, is there not a dilemma lurking for humanitarian interventions – in that heading for the (as I think) justifiable aim of reintegration does necessarily involve heading for the (at least) doubtful aim of extensive destruction of political structures?

The article distinguishes different forms of humanitarian interventions and proposes what may be called "legitimate aims" for each of them.

The main thesis of the essay is that the specific meaning and problems of humanitarian interventions are only intelligible if the basic dilemma structure is considered. The central idea is a conflict of principles which opposes the guarantee of state sovereignty with the protection of human rights. The essay starts with the definition of humanitarian interventions as resisted interference into another countries affairs supported by military forces. After locating the phenomenon of humanitarian intervention in the Westphalian system of plural states, a dilemma-continuum is proposed which helps to arrange the main theories according to their respective attitudes towards humanitarian interventions. The continuum includes different views which regard humanitarian interventions as exemptions, rights or duties. At the extremes there are the positions of state fetishism and global domestic politics which are prepared to negate the dilemma and therefore to get rid of the phenomenon of humanitarian intervention. The essay ends with considerations of the advantages of the dilemma analysis and the appropriate kind of balancing. Here, the second main thesis of the essay argues that every attempt to solve or circumvent the dilemma will either lose the phenomenon or distort the adequacy of the internal reasoning for or against humanitarian interventions.

I will try to answer three questions:
1. In which circumstances do we have a right to a humanitarian intervention and what are the moral constraints for such an action?
2. Do we as well have a duty to intervene where we have a right to do so?
3. If there is such a duty to assistance how shall we weigh it against other duties to help?

Were the NATO air strikes against Yugoslavia in 1999 morally justified? In my contribution I investigate a justification that played an important role, particularly in Germany: the idea that the military intervention was morally legitimate because it was an emergency aid (a 'humanitarian intervention'). It is a basic element of our ethical convictions that we are permitted or even obliged to help people in extreme need, i.e. when we are in what is called a Samaritan situation. In the first part of the paper I discuss Samaritan situations in more detail. In the second part I try to apply these considerations to the ethical situation of the corporate agent NATO in the Kosovo conflict. The result is that the military intervention was *not* justified as a Samaritan act. This leaves open the question whether it was legitimate on other grounds, e.g. as a just war.

A nationalist conflict is a violent conflict over the control of a territory between two or more national groups. In such a conflict, each group considers the very presence of the 'enemy' people on the contested territory, even if unarmed and otherwise harmless, a threat. As a result, the groups in conflict regard each other's civilians as an instrument of control and a threat and not as innocents.

A humanitarian military intervention is a case in which killing innocent people is justified by the saving of the lives of other innocent people. For a killing of innocents to be justified by the saving of lives of other innocents, it is necessary that there was no other way of saving these lives except the one that led to that killing; that there was no other morally unacceptable intention for that killing; and that the saving of lives in this way led to an over-all minimisation of deaths. The last condition requires that number of lives saved be greater than the number of lives lost through the killing of innocent.

In nationalist conflicts, military intervention in support of one nationalist group in conflict usually enables that group to kill and expel civilians of the unsupported group. Further, the intervening power kills conscript soldiers – innocent of any wrongdoing – who are simply resisting the invasion of their country or territory by an outside intervening power as well innocent civilians (usually by accident). An outside power, capable of military intervention, usually has sufficient influence and power to prevent or stop a nationalist conflict by means other than its military intervention. And in many cases the intervening powers use their military force in order to support an allied nationalist movement or in order to hide its illegal or denied support for such a movement. These motivations, however, cannot justify killing of any innocent people. Such military interventions clearly fail to satisfy the three conditions listed above.

In the case of NATO military intervention in Kosovo in 1999, illustrates well the difficulties in satisfying the above three necessary conditions for killing to be justified by the saving of innocent lives. On the evidence presented so far, it is not clear that the number of saved innocent lives exceeds the number of innocents (both conscripts and civilians of all nationalities) killed by NATO forces and its Kosovo Albanian ally, the Kosova Liberation Army (KLA), during or after the intervention. Further, in early 1999 in Rambuillet, France, NATO could have easily concluded an agreement with the Yugoslav government which would have led to the almost complete withdrawal of Yugoslav forces and administration from Kosovo. This would have saved lives of innocents without any killing of innocents. In short, NATO had an option other than killing innocents. Finally, there is some room to doubt that NATO intervention was motivated by the need to support the KLA and to hide the earlier undeclared support for that movement by the US and its allies: at the time of the intervention, the KLA was in danger of defeated and thus marginalized by the superior Yugoslav army forces.

In view of this, it is difficult to justify this and many other similar military interventions by reference to the lives of innocents it saved or even intended to save. Such interventions are not humanitarian and clearly stand in need of justifications better than this one.

MIROSLAV PROKOPIJEVIC
Humanitarian Intervention 189

Although many scholars consider humanitarian intervention (HI) as a duty to relieve a disaster, this paper is based on the conviction that HI cannot be a matter of duty, since there is no basis for such an obligation (Part A).

Two main troubles borne by HI are discussed in part B: the short supply of HI and the abuse of intervention. Part C is about condition(s) for HI: HI is considered to be a supererogatory act, and it may be employed when certain conditions are met. In order to be justified, an HI should necessarily satisfy the basic condition, and meet certain other conditions as much as possible. The basic condition (BC) is related to a massive and deep violation of vital human rights held by larger rather than smaller groups, over a longer period of time (or an explosive violation in a short period of time), which results in irrevocable harm for these groups. No HI is allowed if the BC is not fulfilled. All other conditions mentioned need not be fulfilled completely, but the more these conditions that are met, the better. Part D is about different types of humanitarian interventions.

II. INTERNATIONAL ETHICS & LAW

Humanitarian interventions are wars waged to counter government-supported threats to life, liberty or well-being of large groups of people in a foreign country. They are morally wrong, because they are wars. Wars are wrong, not because violence, or deadly violence, against human beings is always wrong. (To kill oneself is not always wrong.) Wars are wrong, or at least modern wars are wrong, because they entail grave harm done to innocents by innocents. Thus, waging war for humanitarian reasons is tantamount to taking third parties as hostages for a good purpose, and this is morally indefensible.

This paper wants to contribute to the discussion on humanitarian intervention by bringing the main legal and moral viewpoints together. First, it will briefly discuss public international law as it has developed within the setting of the Charter of the United Nations. After that, the current state of affairs within political philosophy will be displayed by paying attention to a number of leading theories, varying from the rejection of humanitarian intervention by Kant and Stuart Mill to the acceptance of a limited right of intervention by Walzer. Subsequently, assuming that such a right exists, I will ask what the corresponding duty should be. Here I will briefly discuss Hegel's critique on Kant and Habermas's hesitations regarding the Kosovo intervention. Finally, I will argue that a correct assessment of humanitarian intervention requires a new approach, and I suggest that Rawls's *The Law of Peoples* constitutes such an approach.

After the Kosovo war and at the possible outset of further NATO campaigns it is still controversial whether military interventions which lack UN-approval can be legitimate. With the Kosovo case in mind, it is often claimed that non-UN interventions are justified if they bring us closer to a just system of international law. For actual interventions, however, it is not easy to distinguish between progress towards a just system of international law and self-serving strategies of superpowers. Criteria for the legitimacy of non-UN interventions might enable us to distinguish between these possibilities more clearly. This paper suggests a set of three (necessary but not sufficient) criteria which all morally legitimate non-UN interventions should satisfy. The criteria concern (a) the implications of expert opinion about the lawfulness of an intervention, (b) the acceptance of independent international prosecution of war crimes regardless of the nationality of the perpetrators, and (c) attempts at the independent arbitration of crises that might evolve into intervention wars. NATO's intervention in Kosovo fails on all three points and therefore has not been legitimate.

This contribution discusses the benefits and shortcomings of the UNIC – known as the "Linz Appeal for a Policy of Peace". It has been widely supported by German and Austrian scientists and Austrian politicians, as well as figures of public life.

If for years multi-ethnic societies do not internally find a way to guarantee the cultural autonomy of their different communities, equal rights and equal treatment of all of their citizens before the law and in regards to distribution of labour and political office, as well as to political representation, the probability of armed conflict, even genocide, is high. The essay pleads for the right of intervention by the international community in these cases, yet exclusively with non-military means. Interventions of this sort, however, only have a prospect of success in very early stages of conflicts. An arbitrary intervention from the outside led by single states or alliances needs to be prevented. Therefor, a UN committee is suggested here which focuses on questions of prevention and works closely with already existing early-warning systems: if they indicate dangers of the sort outlined above, the committee has to be obliged to take action within a certain period of time. Since ethics aims at action, namely practice, the author – spurred by the events of the Kosovo-war – initiated a campain to institute such a committee, which resulted in the German-Austrian initiative of 2003.

VÉRONIQUE ZANETTI

International law treats the right to humanitarian intervention as a right belonging to the state or the community of states. It falls upon them to decide, unilaterally or multilaterally, if a case in which human rights are violated is severe enough to necessitate or justify intervention. At the same time, customary law shows a clear tendency to conceive the right to humanitarian intervention as an individual right. The right is then on the side of the victims and not on the side of the intervening powers, and hence constitutes a claim that individuals have on the international community when their basic rights are violated by the authority responsible for protecting them. I argue that this last interpretation is alone convincing according to the contractualist theory of rights, and then examine the implications this theory has for the obligations of the state.

III. KOSOVA / KOSOVO. THE MORAL COMBAT

Can the prevention of some crime ever justify military intervention? I argue that
(1) we can think of crimes the prevention of which justifies military intervention within the bounds of just war (ius in bello),
(2) there have been such crimes in human history, even in the recent one,
(3) the Serbian attack on the Albanian Kosovars belongs to such crimes,
(4) in spite of grave mistakes and violations of the rules of just war,
NATO intervention in Serbia was justified.

In spring 1999, NATO (Germany included) waged war against Yugoslavia/Serbia. In this war, NATO's hightech 'air-strikes' were backed up by two instruments of the utmost efficiency: *conceptual strategy* (e.g. "Humanitarian Intervention" instead of "War") and *morals* ("No more Auschwitz!"). As these two instruments are concerned, analytical philosophers are deemed to be experts. So, what do I think now – ex post – about NATO's (and the german majority's) use or misuse of these instruments? In particular: (i) Can Humanitarian Intervention Wars be morally justified? And: (ii) Did NATO's bombing policy in 1999 fulfill the relevant justification criteria? My position is YES to (i), but NO to (ii).

In contemporary democracies, the problem of ethical legitimization (or illegitimization) of war is, first of all, the contested subject of critical discussions in the public sphere. The hegemonic character of the Kosovo-war as well as the media covering of its emergence and enforcement, however, could make us doubt about liberal publics' general competence to judge and to decide upon the moral quality of a so called "humanitarian intervention" before its ruling proponents resort to armed force.

In the case of the Kosovo conflict, at least, my contribution raises weighty objections against fundamental reasons called on to justify war (the ius ad bellum) no less than against the way this war has been implemented (the ius in bello). In both regards, it seems more convenient to replace the dubious term 'humanitarian intervention' by another, more objective or neutral one, as for example 'collective protection', that might be more adequate even in the light of the law of nations. Ethically authorized are, for the time being, only interventions legitimized by the UN Security Council, the further development of which itself is under ethical reservation and requires an institutional-judicial renewal (e.g. a new position of human rights within the framework of UN purposes; reform of the Security Council;expansion of sanctions according to Chapter VII; possible creation of a court of interventions). It might be expected that the oppressing effects of the media system on the liberal public will be countered this way, in so far as the system has fatally interpreted the power asymmetry of the protagonists into a moral one.

JOHAN GALTUNG
Bombing Yugoslavia: Several Readings 335

There are many false alternatives in our Humanitarian Interventionism Discource. For example: "*Either* we do nothing and let things happen *or* we stop it and go in by means of military intervention." *Tertium datur*. Namely ... and now we have to TRANSCEND our ordinary ways of thinking. This paper is a radical destruction of the lies of official policy and of the main stream media – with respect to Humanitarian Interventionism in general and the Kosovo-war in particular. An analysis of the US military culture indicates that the US army is unfit for peacekeeping operations.

This contribution strongly opposes pursuing the idea of humanitarian intervention and also against the fact that it may be anchored in customary international law and not least against its political instrumentalization. In the case of the Kosovo War and on the basis of little known facts and status reports this Position is justified

- one of these is the lack of success in humanitarian interventions,
- and the other – moreover this is the predominant issue – is the danger of misuse this instrument holds (after all its implementation is a matter of life and death for innocent people).

If the case of Kosovo has been an ethical and moral lesson at all, then this is the fact that the humanitarian intervention à la Kosovo has not been a positive instrument whose use we should consider further. Rather, the lesson from the "case of Kosovo" is that this type of and similar types of intervention should in future and for all time be stopped completely. The alternative is a regional system of collective security ("legal system replaces intervention") as well as a Council for the Future as a "Third Chamber".

I

Basic Issues

MICHAEL WALZER

The Argument about Humanitarian Intervention

There is nothing new about human disasters caused by human beings. We have always been, if not our own, certainly each other's worst enemies. From the Assyrians in ancient Israel and the Romans in Carthage to the Belgians in the Congo and the Turks in Armenia, history is a bloody and barbaric tale. Still, in this regard, the 20th century was an age of innovation, first of all, and most importantly, in the way disasters were planned and organized and then, more recently, in the way they were publicized. I want to begin with the second of these innovations – the product of an extraordinary speed-up in both travel and communication. It may be possible to kill people on a very large scale more efficiently than ever before, but it is much harder to kill them in secret. In the contemporary world there is very little that happens far away, out of sight, or behind the scenes; the camera crews arrive faster than rigor mortis. We are instant spectators of every atrocity; we sit in our living rooms and see the murdered children, the desperate refugees. Perhaps horrific crimes are still committed in dark places, but not many; contemporary horrors are well-lit. And so a question is posed that has never been posed before – at least never with such immediacy, never so inescapably: What is our responsibility? What should we do?

In the old days, "humanitarian intervention" was a lawyer's doctrine, a way of justifying a very limited set of exceptions to the principles of national sovereignty and territorial integrity.[1] It is a good doctrine, because exceptions are always necessary, principles are never absolute. But we need to rethink it today, as the exceptions become less and less exceptional. The "acts that shock the conscience of humankind" – and, according to the nineteenth century lawbooks, justify humanitarian intervention – are probably no more frequent these days than they were in the past, but they are more shocking, because we are more intimately engaged by them and with them. Cases multiply in the world and in the media: Somalia, Bosnia, Rwanda, East Timor, Liberia, Sierra Leon, and Kosovo in only the past decade. The last of these has dominated the recent political debates, but it isn't the most illuminating case. I want to step back a bit, reach for a wider range of examples, and try to answer four questions about humanitarian intervention: first, what are its occasions? second, who are its preferred agents? third, how should the agents act to meet the occasions? and fourth, when is it time to end the intervention?

OCCASIONS

The occasions have to be extreme if they are to justify, perhaps even require, the use of force across an international boundary. Every violation of human rights isn't a justification. The common brutalities of authoritarian politics, the daily oppressiveness of traditional social practices – these are not occasions for intervention; they have to be dealt with locally, by the people who know the politics, who enact or resist the practices. The fact that these people can't easily or quickly reduce the incidence of brutality and oppression isn't a sufficient reason for foreigners to invade their country. Foreign politicians and soldiers are too likely to misread the situation, or to underestimate the force required to change it, or to stimulate a "patriotic" reaction in defense of the brutal politics and the oppressive practices. Social change is best achieved from within.

I want to insist on this point; I don't mean to describe a continuum that begins with common nastiness and ends with genocide but rather a radical break, a chasm, with nastiness on one side and genocide on the other. We should not allow ourselves to approach genocide by degrees. Still, on this side of the chasm, we can mark out a continuum of brutality and oppression, and somewhere along this continuum an international response (short of military force) is necessary. Diplomatic pressure and economic sanctions, for example, are useful means of engagement with tyrannical regimes. The sanctions might be imposed by some free-form coalition of interested states. Or perhaps we should work toward a more established regional or global authority that could regulate the imposition, carefully matching the severity of the sanctions to the severity of the oppression. But these are still external acts; they are efforts to prompt *but not to preempt* an internal response. They still assume the value, and hold open the possibility, of domestic politics. The interested states or the regional or global authorities bring pressure to bear, so to speak, at the border; and then they wait for something to happen on the other side.

But when what is going on is the "ethnic cleansing" of a province or country or the systematic massacre of a religious or national community, it doesn't seem possible to wait for a local response. Now we are on the other side of the chasm. The stakes are too high, the suffering already too great. Perhaps there is no capacity to respond among the people directly at risk and no will to respond among their fellow citizens. The victims are weak and vulnerable; their enemies are cruel; their neighbors indifferent. The rest of us watch and are shocked. This is the occasion for intervention.

We will need to argue, of course, about each case, but the list I've already provided seems a fairly obvious one. These days the intervening army will claim to be enforcing human rights, and that was a plausible and fully comprehensible claim in each of the cases on my list (or would have been, since intervention weren't attempted in all of them). We are best served, I think, by a stark and minimalist version of human rights here: it is life and liberty that are at stake. With regard to these two, the language of rights is readily available and sufficiently understood across the globe. Still, we could as easily say that what is being enforced, and what should be enforced, is simple decency.

In practice, even with a minimalist understanding of human rights, even with a commitment to nothing more than decency, there are more occasions for intervention than there are actual interventions. When the oppressors are too powerful, they are rarely challenged, however shocking the oppression. This obvious truth about international society is often used as an argument against the interventions that do take place. It is hypocritical, critics say to the "humanitarian" politicians or soldiers, to intervene in this case when you didn't intervene in that one – as if, having declined to challenge China in Tibet, say, the United Nations should have stayed out of East Timor for the sake of moral consistency.[2] But consistency isn't an issue here. We can't meet all our occasions; we rightly calculate the risks in each one. We need to ask what the costs of intervention will be for the people being rescued, and also for the rescuers, and for everyone else. And then we can only do...what we can do.

The standard cases have a standard form: a government, an army, a police force, tyrannically controlled, attacks its own people or some subset of its own people, a vulnerable minority, say, territorially based or dispersed throughout the country. (We might think of these attacks as examples of state terrorism and then consider forceful humanitarian interventions, such as the NATO campaign in Kosovo, as instances of the "war against terrorism", *avant la lettre*. But I won't pursue this line of argument here.) The attack takes place within the country's borders; it doesn't require any boundary crossings; it is an exercise of sovereign power. There is no aggression, no invading army to resist and beat back. Instead, the rescuing forces are the invaders; they are the ones who, in the strict sense of international law, begin the war. But they come into a situation where the moral stakes are clear: the oppressors or, better, the state agents of oppression, are readily identifiable; their victims are plain to see.

Even in the list with which I started, however, there are some nonstandard cases – Sierra Leon is the clearest example – where the state apparatus isn't the villain, where what we might think of as the administration of brutality is decentralized, anarchic, almost random. It isn't the power of the oppressors that interventionists have to worry about, but the amorphousness of the oppression. I won't have much to say about cases like this. Intervention is clearly justifiable but, right now at least, it's radically unclear how it should be undertaken. Perhaps there is not much to do beyond what the Nigerians did in Sierra Leon: they reduced the number of killings, the scope of the barbarism.

AGENTS

"We can only do...what we can do": who is this "we"? The Kosovo debate focused on the United States, NATO, and the UN as agents of military intervention.[3] These are indeed three political collectives capable of agency, but by no means the only three. The United States and NATO generate suspicion among the sorts of people who are called "idealists" because of their readiness to act unilaterally and their presumed imperial ambitions; the UN generates skepticism among the sorts of people who are called "realists" because of its political weakness and military ineffectiveness. The arguments here are overdetermined; I am not going to join them. We are more likely to understand the problem of agency if we start with other agents. The most successful interventions in the last 30 years have been acts of war by neighboring states: Vietnam in Cambodia, India in East Pakistan (now Bangla Desh), Tanzania in Uganda. These are useful examples for testing our ideas about intervention because they don't involve extraneous issues like the new (or old) world order; they don't require us to consult Lenin's, or any other, theory of imperialism. In each of these cases, there were horrifying acts that should have been stopped and agents who succeeded, more or less, in stopping them. So let's use these cases to address the two questions most commonly posed by critics of the Kosovo war: Does it matter that the agents acted alone? Does it matter that their motives were not wholly (or even chiefly) altruistic?

In the history of humanitarian intervention, unilateralism is far more common than its opposite. One reason for this is obvious: the great reluctance of most states to cede the direction of their armed forces to an organization they don't control. But unilateralism may also follow from the need for an immediate response to "acts that shock...." Imagine a case where the "shock" doesn't have anything to do with human evildoing: a fire in a neighbor's house in a new town where there is no fire department. It wouldn't make much sense to call a meeting of the block association, while the house is burning, and vote on whether or not to help (and it would make even less sense to give a veto on helping to the three richest families on the block). I don't think that the case would be all that different if, instead of a fire, there was a brutal husband, no police department, and screams for help in the night. Here too, the block association is of little use; neighborly unilateralism seems entirely justified. In cases like these, anyone who can help should help. And that sounds like a plausible maxim for humanitarian intervention also: who can, should.

But now let's imagine a block association or an international organization that planned in advance for the fire, or the scream in the night, or the mass murder. Then there would be particular people or specially recruited military forces delegated to act in a crisis, and the definition of "crisis" could be determined – as best it can be – in advance, in exactly the kind of meeting that seems so implausible, so morally inappropriate, at the moment when immediate action is necessary. The person who rushes into a neighbor's house in my domestic example and the political or military commanders of the invading forces in the international cases would still have to act on their own understanding of the events unfolding in front of them and on their own interpretation of the responsibility they have been given. But now they act under specified constraints, and they can call on the help of those in whose name they are acting. This is the form that multilateral intervention is most likely to take, if the UN, say, were ever to authorize it in advance of a particular crisis. And it seems preferable to the different unilateral alternatives, since it involves some kind of prior warning, an agreed-upon description of the occasions for intervention, and the prospect of overwhelming force.

But is it preferable in fact, right now, given the UN as it actually is? What makes police forces effective in domestic society, when they are effective, is their commitment to the entire body of citizens from which they are drawn and the (relative) trust of the citizens in that commitment. But the UN's General Assembly and Security Council, so far, give very little evidence of being so committed, and there can't be many people in the world today who would willingly entrust their lives to UN police. And so, if, in any of my examples, the UN's authorized agents or their domestic equivalents decide not to intervene, and the fire is still burning, the screams can still be heard, the murders go on – then unilateralist rights and obligations are instantly restored. Collective decisions to act may well exclude unilateral action, but collective decisions not to act don't have the same effect. In this sense, unilateralism is the dominant response when the common conscience is shocked. If there is no collective response, anyone can respond. If no one is acting, act.

In the Cambodia, East Pakistan, and Uganda cases, there were no prior arrangements and no authorized agents. Had the UN's Security Council or General Assembly been called into session, it would almost certainly have decided against intervention, probably by majority vote, in any case because of great power opposition. So, anyone acting to shut down the Khmer Rouge killing fields or to stem the tide of Bengalese refugees or to stop Idi Amin's butchery would have to act unilaterally. Everything depended on the political decision of a single state.

Do these singular agents have a right to act or do they have an obligation? I have been using both words, but they don't always go together: there can be rights where there are no obligations. In "good Samaritan" cases in domestic society, we commonly say that passersby are bound to respond (to the injured stranger by the side of the road, to the cry of a child drowning in the lake...); they are not, however, bound to risk their lives.[4] If the risks are clear, they have a right to respond; responding is certainly a good thing and possibly the right thing to do; still, they are not morally bound to do it. But military interventions across international boundaries always impose risks on the intervening forces. So perhaps there is no obligation here either; perhaps there is a right to intervene but also a right to refuse the risks, to maintain a kind of neutrality – even between murderers and their victims. Or perhaps humanitarian intervention is an example of what philosophers call an "imperfect" duty: someone should stop the awfulness, but it isn't possible to give that someone a proper name, to point a finger, say, at a particular country. The problem of imperfect duty yields best to multilateral solutions; we simply assign responsibility in advance through some commonly accepted decision procedure.

But perhaps, again, these descriptions are too weak: I am inclined to say that intervention is more than a right and more than an imperfect duty.[5] After all, the survival of the intervening state is not at risk. And then why shouldn't the obligation simply fall on the most capable state, the nearest or the strongest, as in the maxim I have already suggested: who can, should? Nonintervention in the face of mass murder or ethnic cleansing is not the same as neutrality in time of war. The moral urgencies are different; we are usually unsure of the consequences of a war, but we know very well the consequences of a massacre. Still, if we follow the logic of the argument so far, it will be necessary to recruit volunteers for humanitarian interventions; the "who" who can and should is only the state, not any particular man or woman; for individuals the duty remains imperfect. Deciding whether to volunteer, they may choose to apply the same test to themselves – who can, should – but the choice is theirs.

The dominance that I have ascribed to unilateralism might be questioned, commonly is questioned, because of a fear of the motives of single states acting alone. Won't they act in their own interests rather than in the interests of humanity? Yes, they probably will or, better, they will act in their own interests as well as in the interests of humanity; I don't think that it is particularly insightful, merely cynical, to suggest that those larger interests have no hold at all (surely the balance of interest and morality among interventionists is no different than it is among noninterventionists). In any case, how would humanity be better served by multilateral decision-making? Wouldn't each state involved in the decision process also act in its own interests? And then the outcome would be determined by bargaining among the interested parties – and humanity, obviously, would not be one of the parties. We might hope that particular interests would cancel each other out, leaving some kind of general interest (this is in fact Rousseau's account, or one of his accounts, of how citizens arrive at a "general will"[6]). But it is equally possible that the bargain will reflect only a mix of particular interests, which may or may not be better for humanity than the interests of a single party. Anyway, political motivations are always mixed, whether the actors are one or many. A pure moral will doesn't exist in political life, and it shouldn't be necessary to pretend to that kind of purity. The leaders of states have a right, indeed, they have an obligation, to consider the interests of their own people, even when they are acting to help other people. We should assume, then, that the Indians acted in their national interest when they assisted the secession of East Pakistan, and that Tanzania acted in its own interests when it moved troops into Idi Amin's Uganda. But these interventions also served humanitarian purposes, and presumably were intended to do that too. The victims of man-made disasters are very lucky if a neighboring state, or a coalition of states, has more than one reason to rescue them. It would be foolish to declare the multiplicity morally disabling. If the intervention is expanded beyond its necessary bounds because of some "ulterior" motive, then it should be criticized; within those bounds, mixed motives are a practical advantage.

MEANS

When the agents act, how should they act? Humanitarian intervention involves the use of force, and it is crucial to its success that it be pursued forcefully; the aim is the defeat of the people, whoever they are, who are carrying out the massacres or the ethnic cleansing. If what is going on is awful enough to justify going in, then it is awful enough to justify the pursuit of military victory. But this simple proposition hasn't found ready acceptance in international society. Most clearly in the Bosnian case, repeated efforts were made to deal with the disaster without fighting against its perpetrators. Force was taken, indeed, to be a "last" resort, but in an ongoing political conflict "lastness" never arrives; there is always something to be done before doing whatever it is that comes last. So military observers were sent into Bosnia to report on what was happening; and then UN forces brought humanitarian relief to the victims, and then they provided some degree of military protection for relief workers, and then they sought (unsuccessfully) to create a few "safe zones" for the Bosnians. But if soldiers do nothing more than these sorts of things, they are hardly an impediment to further killing; they may even be said to provide a kind of background support for it.[7] They guard roads, defend doctors and nurses, deliver medical supplies and food to a growing number of victims and refugees – and the number keeps growing. Sometimes it is helpful to interpose soldiers as "peace-keepers" between the killers and their victims. But though that may work for a time, it doesn't reduce the power of the killers, and so it is a formula for trouble later on. Peace-keeping is an honorable activity, but not if there is no peace. Sometimes, unhappily, it is better to make war.

In Cambodia, East Pakistan, and Uganda, the interventions were carried out on the ground; this was old-fashioned war-making. The Kosovo war provides an alternative model: a war fought from the air, with technologies designed to reduce (almost to zero!) the risk of casualties to the intervening army. I won't stop here to consider at any length the reasons for the alternative model, which have to do with the increasing inability of modern democracies to use the armies they recruit in ways that put soldiers at risk. There are no "lower orders", no invisible, expendable citizens in democratic states today, and in the absence of a clear threat to the community itself, there is little willingness even among political elites to sacrifice for the sake of global law and order or, more particularly, for the sake of Rwandans or Kosovars. But the inability and the unwillingness, whatever their sources, make for moral problems. A war fought entirely from the air, and from far away, probably can't be won without attacking civilian targets. These can be bridges and television stations, electric generators and water purification plants, rather than residential areas, but the attacks will endanger the lives of innocent men, women, and children nonetheless. The aim is to bring pressure to bear on a government acting barbarically toward a minority of its citizens by threatening to harm, or actually harming, the majority to which, presumably, the government is still committed. Obviously this isn't a strategy that would have worked against the Khmer Rouge in Cambodia, but it's probably not legitimate even where it might work – so long as there is the possibility of a more precise intervention against the forces actually engaged in the barbarous acts. The same rules apply here as in war generally: noncombattants are immune from direct attack and have to be protected as far as possible from "collateral damage"; soldiers have to accept risks to themselves in order to avoid imposing risks on the civilian population.

Any country considering military intervention would obviously embrace technologies that were said to be risk-free for its own soldiers, and the embrace would be entirely justified so long as the same technologies were also risk-free for civilians on the other side. This is precisely the claim made on behalf of "smart bombs": they can be delivered from great distances (safely), and they never miss. But the claim is, for the moment at least, greatly exaggerated. There is no technological fix currently available, and therefore no way of avoiding this simple truth: from the standpoint of justice, you cannot invade a foreign country, with all the consequences that has for other people, while insisting that your own soldiers can never be put at risk. Once the intervention has begun, it may become morally, even if it is not yet militarily, necessary to fight on the ground – in order to win more quickly and save many lives, for example, or to stop some particularly barbarous response to the intervention.

That's the moral argument against no-risk interventions. But there is also a prudential argument. Interventions will rarely be successful unless there is a visible willingness to fight and to take casualties. In the Kosovo case, if a NATO army had been in sight, so to speak, before the bombing of Serbia began, it is unlikely that the bombing would have been necessary; nor would there ever have been the tide of desperate and embittered refugees. Postwar Kosovo would look very different; the tasks of policing and reconstruction would be easier than they have been; the odds on success much better.

ENDINGS

Imagine the intervening army fully engaged: how should it understand the victory that it is aiming at? When is it time to go home? Should the army aim only at stopping the killings, or at destroying the military or paramilitary forces carrying them out, or at replacing the regime that employs these forces, or at punishing the leaders of the regime? Is intervention only a war or also an occupation? These are hard questions, and I want to begin my own response by acknowledging that I have answered them differently at different times.

The answer that best fits the original legal doctrine of humanitarian intervention, and that I defended in *Just and Unjust Wars*, is that the aim of the intervening army is simply to stop the killing.[8] Its leaders prove that their motives are primarily humanitarian, that they are not driven by imperial ambition, by moving in as quickly as possible to defeat the killers and rescue their victims and then by leaving as quickly as possible. Sorting things out afterwards, dealing with the consequences of the awfulness, deciding what to do with its agents – that is not properly the work of foreigners. The people who have always lived there, wherever "there" is, have to be given a chance to reconstruct their common life. The crisis that they have just been through should not become an occasion for foreign domination. The principles of political sovereignty and territorial integrity require the "in and quickly out" rule.

But there are three sorts of occasions when this rule seems impossible to apply. The first is perhaps best exemplified by the Cambodian killing fields, which were so extensive as to leave, at the end, no institutional base, and perhaps no human base, for reconstruction. I don't say this to justify the Vietnamese establishment of a satellite regime, but rather to explain the need, years later, for the UN's effort to create, from the outside, a locally legitimate political system. The UN couldn't or wouldn't stop the killing when it was actually taking place, but had it done so, the "in and quickly out" test would not have provided a plausible measure of its success; it would have had to deal, somehow, with the aftermath of the killing.

The second occasion is exemplified by all those countries – Uganda, Rwanda, Kosovo, and others – where the extent and depth of the ethnic divisions make it likely that the killings will resume as soon as the intervening forces withdraw. If the original killers don't return to their work, then the revenge of their victims will prove equally deadly. Now "in and quickly out" is a kind of bad faith, a choice of legal virtue at the expense of political and moral effectiveness. If one accepts the risks of intervention in countries like these, one had better accept also the risks of occupation.

The third occasion is the one I called nonstandard earlier on: where the state has simply disintegrated. It's not that its army or police have been defeated; they simply don't exist. The country is in the hand of paramilitary forces and war lords – gangs, really – who have been, let's say, temporarily subdued. What is necessary now is to create a state, and the creation will have to be virtually *ex nihilo*. And that is not work for the short term.

In 1995, in an article called "The Politics of Rescue", published in *Dissent* magazine,[9] I argued that leftist critics of protectorates and trusteeships needed to rethink their position, for arrangements of this sort might sometimes be the best outcome of a humanitarian intervention. The historical record makes it clear enough that protectors and trustees, under the old League of Nations, for example, again and again failed to fulfill their obligations; nor have these arrangements been as temporary as they were supposed to be. Still, their purpose can sometimes be a legitimate one: to open a span of time and to authorize a kind of political work between the "in" and the "out" of a humanitarian intervention. This purpose doesn't cancel the requirement that the intervening forces get out. We need to think about better ways of making sure that the purpose is actually realized and the requirement finally met. Perhaps this is a place where multilateralism can play a more central role than it does, or has done, in the original interventions. For multilateral occupations are unlikely to serve the interests of any single state and so are unlikely to be sustained any longer than necessary. The greater danger is that they won't be sustained long enough: each participating state will look for an excuse to pull its own forces out. An independent UN force, not bound or hindered by the political decisions of individual states, might be the most reliable protector and trustee – if we could be sure that it would protect the right people, in a timely way.[10] Whenever that assurance doesn't exist, unilateralism returns, again, as a justifiable option.

Either way, we still need an equivalent of the "in and out" rule, a way of recognizing when these longstanding interventions reach their endpoint. The appropriate rule is best expressed by a phrase that I have already used: "local legitimacy." The intervening forces should aim at finding or establishing a form of authority that fits or at least accomodates the local political culture, and a set of authorities, independent of themselves, who are capable of governing the country and who command sufficient popular support so that their government won't be massively coercive. And once such authorities are in place, the intervening forces should withdraw: "in and finally out."

But this formula may be as quixotic as "in and quickly out." Perhaps foreign forces can't do the work that I've just described; they will only be dragged deeper and deeper into a conflict they will never be able to control, gradually becoming indistinguishable from the other parties. That prospect is surely a great disincentive to intervention; it will often override not only the benign intentions but even the imperial ambitions of potential interveners. In fact, most of the countries whose inhabitants (or some of them) desperately need to be rescued offer precious little political or economic reward to the states that attempt the rescue. One almost wishes that the impure motivations of such states had more plausible objects, the pursuit of which might hold them to their task. At the same time, however, it's important to insist that the task is limited: once the massacres and ethnic cleansing are really over and the people in command are committed to avoiding their return, the intervention is finished. The new regime doesn't have to be democratic or liberal or pluralist or (even) capitalist. It doesn't have to be anything, except non-murderous. When intervention is understood in this minimalist fashion, it may be a little easier to see it through.

As in the argument about occasions, minimalism in endings suggests that we should be careful in our use of human rights language. For if we pursue the legal logic of rights (at least as that logic is understood in the US), it will be very difficult for the intervening forces to get out before they have brought the people who organized the massacres or the ethnic cleansing to trial and established a new regime committed to enforcing the full set of human rights.[11] If those goals are actually within reach, then, of course, it is right to reach for them. But intervention is a political and military process, not a legal one, and it is subject to the compromises and tactical shifts that politics and war require. So we will often need to accept more minimal goals, in order to minimize the use of force and the time span over which it is used. I want to stress, however, that we need, and haven't yet come close to, a clear understanding of what "minimum" really means. The intervening forces have to be prepared to use the weapons they carry, and they have to be prepared to stay what may be a long course. The international community needs to find ways of supporting these forces – and also, since what they are doing is dangerous and won't always be done well, of supervising, regulating, and criticizing them.

CONCLUSION

I have tried to answer possible objections to my argument as I went along, but there are a couple of common criticisms of the contemporary practice of humanitarian intervention that I want to single out and address more explicitly, even at the cost of repeating myself. A few repetitions, on key points, will make my conclusion. I am going to take Edward Luttwak's critical review of Michael Ignatieff's *Virtual War*[12] as a useful summary of the arguments to which I need to respond, since it is short, sharp, cogent, and typical. Ignatieff offers a stronger human rights justification of humanitarian warfare than I have provided, though he would certainly agree that not every rights violation "shocks the conscience of humankind" and justifies military intervention. In any case, Luttwak's objections apply (or fail to apply) across the board – that is, to the arguments I've made here as well as to Ignatieff's book.

First objection: the "prescription that X should fight Y whenever Y egregiously violates X's moral and juridical norms would legitimize eternal war." This claim seems somewhat inconsistent with Luttwak's further claim (see below) that the necessity of fighting not only forever but everywhere follows from the fact that there are so many violations of commonly recognized norms. But leave that aside for now. If we intervene only in extremity, only in order to stop mass murder and mass deportation, the idea that we are defending X's norms and not Y's is simply wrong. Possessive nouns don't modify morality in such cases, and there isn't a series of different moralities for each of the Xs and Ys in international society – the proof of this is the standard and singular lie told by all the killers and "cleansers": they deny what they are doing; they don't try to justify it by reference to a set of private norms.

Second objection: "Even without civil wars, massacres, or mutilations, the perfectly normal, everyday, functioning of armies, police forces, and bureaucracies entails constant extortion, frequent robbery and rape, and pervasive oppression" – all of which, Luttwak claims, is ignored by the humanitarian interveners. So it is, and should be, or else we would indeed be fighting all the time and everywhere. But note that Luttwak assumes now that the wrongness of the extortion, robbery, rape, and oppression is not a matter of X's or Y's private norms but can be recognized by anyone. Maybe he goes too far here, since bureaucratic extortion, at least, has different meaning and valence in different times and places. But the main actions on his list are indeed awful, and commonly known to be awful; they just aren't awful enough to justify a military invasion. I don't think the point is all that difficult, even if we disagree about exactly where the line should be drawn. Pol Pot's killing fields had to be shut down – and by a foreign army if necessary. The prisons of all the more ordinary dictators in the modern world should also be shut down – emptied and closed. But that is properly the work of their own subjects.

Third objection: "What does it mean", Luttwak asks, "for the morality of a supposedly moral rule when it is applied arbitrarily, against some but not others?" The answer to this question depends on what the word "arbitrarily" means here. Consider a domestic example. The police can't stop every speeding car. If they go after only the ones they think they will be able to catch without endangering themselves or anyone else, their arrests will be "determined by choice or discretion" which is one of the meanings of "arbitrary", but surely that determination doesn't undermine the justice of enforcing the speeding laws. On the other hand, if they only go after cars that have bumper stickers they don't like, and if their treatment of those drivers goes beyond what the law requires, so that traffic control becomes a pretext for the harrassment of political "enemies", then their actions "arise from will or caprice", another definition of "arbitrary", and are indeed unjust. It's the first kind of "arbitrariness" that ought to qualify humanitarian interventions (and often does). They are indeed discretionary, and we have to hope that prudential calculations shape the decision to intervene or not. Hence, as I have already acknowledged, there won't be an actual intervention every time the justifying conditions for it exist. But, to answer Luttwak's question, that acknowledgement doesn't do anything to the morality of the justifying rule. It's not immoral to act, or decline to act, for prudential reasons.

These three objections relate to the occasions for intervention, and rightly so. If no coherent account of the occasions is possible, then it isn't necessary to answer the other questions that I have addressed. My own answers to those other questions can certainly be contested. But the main point that I want to make is that the questions themselves cannot be avoided. Since there are in fact legitimate occasions for humanitarian intervention, since we know, roughly, what ought to be done, we have to argue about how to do it; we have to argue about agents, means, and endings. There are a lot of people around today who want to avoid these arguments and postpone indefinitely the kinds of action they might require. These people have all sorts of reasons, but none of them, it seems to me, are good or moral reasons.

NOTES

[1] See, for example W.E. Hall, *International Law* (5th ed., Oxford: Oxford University Press, 1904) p. 289ff.

[2] This is by far the most common criticism I have heard from both academic and political audiences as I have travelled and talked about humanitarian intervention over the last few years.

[3] For all the arguments, see William Joseph Buckley, ed., *Kosovo: Contending Voices on Balkan Interventions* (Grand Rapids: Eerdmans, 2000).

[4] See the useful essays in James M. Radcliffe, *The Good Samaritan and the Law* (Garden City, NY: Anchor Books, Doubleday, 1966).

[5] Cf. Daniel Statman, "Who Needs Imperfect Duties?" in *American Philosophical Quarterly* 33:2 (April, 1996), pp. 211-224.

[6] *The Social Contract*, Bk. II, ch. 3.

[7] This is the argument of David Rieff, *Slaughterhouse: Bosnia and the Failure of the West* (New York: Touchstone, Simon and Shuster, 1996).

[8] *Just and Unjust Wars* (New York: Basic Books, 1977), ch. 6.

[9] *Dissent*, Winter, 1995, pp. 35-40.

[10] On the possible role of the UN, see Michael Doyle, "The New Interventionism," in *Metaphilosophy*, 32:1/2 (January, 2001), pp. 212-235.

[11] For a strong argument along these lines, see Aryeh Neier, *War Crimes: Brutality, Genocide, Terror, and the Struggle for Justice* (New York: Times Books, Random House, 1998).

[12] "No-Score War," *Times Literary Supplement*, July 14, 2000, p. 11.

SEUMAS MILLER

Collective Responsibility and Humanitarian Armed Intervention

In recent times there have been a number of armed humanitarian interventions by nation states in relation to conflicts taking place within the borders of other nation states. Here one thinks of Bosnia, Kosovo, Somalia, Rwanda and East Timor. In some instances, such as Rwanda, armed intervention was evidently morally justified, however the armed forces deployed were inadequate and/or arrived far too late.[1] In other instances, such as Kosovo, armed intervention might have been justified and timely, but arguably the force deployed was excessive, or at least of the wrong form.[2]

The first general point to be made here is that at least *some* armed humanitarian interventions are morally justified. Consider the case of Rwanda. According to Fergal Keane, in Rwanda after the deaths in a plane crash of the Rwandan and Burundian Presidents in April 6th 1994 an orchestrated program of genocide took place: "In the ensuing 100 days up to one million people were hacked, straggled, clubbed and burned to death".[3] The genocide in Rwanda – and like cases – constitutes a decisive objection to the claim that armed humanitarian intervention is *never* morally justified. Moreover, cases such as East Timor appear to demonstrate that armed humanitarian intervention can be successful. On the other hand, the experience of cases such as Bosnia shows that even if armed intervention is justified, the situation on the ground needs to be adequately understood, if that intervention is to be successful. Evidently, the UN failed to understand that the war in Bosnia was in large part genocidal and directed at the civilian population. So interventionist methods aimed only at keeping groups of combatants from getting at one another were inadequate; such methods cannot and did not protect the civilian populations.[4]

The second general point concerns the nature of the justification. The fundamental justification for armed humanitarian intervention is that genocide, or other large scale human rights violations, are taking place, and armed intervention is the only way to put an end to it. This is a moral justification. Perhaps there can be decisive political or military justifications for armed interventions. Moreover, such non-moral justifications are not necessarily inconsistent with moral justifications; in some cases armed intervention might be politically expedient as well as being morally justified. In practice, armed interventions are likely to be motivated by a complex mix of moral, political, military, economic and other considerations. However, my point pertains to good and decisive justifications: I claim that the *fundamental* justification for armed humanitarian interventions is a moral justification.

Granted the existence of this general moral justification for armed humanitarian intervention, at least four further questions arise. First, should the armed intervention be undertaken by any nation state or states who happen to have the wherewithal to prosecute it successfully, or should it be undertaken only with the participation, or at least consent, of the international community? Second, should the notion of large scale human rights violations in question be a very narrow notion, and therefore restricted to, say, genocide, or should it be relatively wide, and embrace, say, authoritarian rule? Third, should the intervention go only so far as to terminate the rights violations that triggered it; or should it involve the taking of preventative measures in relation to possible future rights violations by the perpetrators, or indeed by the erstwhile victims?[5] Fourth, what form should the armed intervention take? For example, should aerial bombing – as opposed to, say, the use of ground troops – be the principal tactic?

My own view in relation to the first question is as follows. The moral responsibility to intervene is a collective moral responsibility – it is the collective responsibility of the members of the international community to combat large scale human rights violations taking place inside states whose governments are unwilling or unable to terminate those rights violations. (Indeed, the internal government might be the one perpetrating the rights violations.) Moreover, broad based, multilateral interventions are less likely to serve the interests of any one state, or small group of states, and therefore more likely to be motivated by genuine humanitarian, rather than purely political, considerations. Nevertheless, since the moral priority is to bring about the cessation of the rights violations – rather than merely determine who ought to be the one or ones to terminate it – then unilateral intervention may well be justified in cases in which the international community is unwilling to act.

In relation to the second question, I hold that the understanding of large scale human rights violations should be narrow in that it should involve only large scale human rights violations of the most morally despicable kind. Here I distinguish, firstly, between rights violations and injustice. Injustice does not provide an adequate justification for armed intervention. Secondly, I distinguish – admittedly somewhat arbitrarily – between violations of the right to life and the right to personal security, on the one hand, and violations of other rights, such as the right to political liberty, on the other hand. The former, but not the latter, justify armed intervention. So genocide, but not necessarily authoritarian governance, justifies armed intervention.

However, the appropriate notion of large scale human rights violations is wide in the sense that it should not be restricted to violations of so-called negative rights, such as the right not to be killed, but also some positive rights, such as the right to a basic subsistence. Consider the case of an autocrat such as Saddam Hussein, who for some political purpose is deliberately refraining from the provision of basic medicine and foodstuffs to some needy element of his community.[6] In such cases there might be an in-principle justification for armed intervention. Why armed intervention? Because the nation state in question is refraining from providing for the subsistence rights of its citizens.

In relation to the third question, I hold that interventions where possible should be preventative, and therefore should not necessarily be restricted to the termination of occurrent rights violations. I acknowledge the dangers attendant upon permitting intervention in relation to future, and therefore only potential, human rights violations. Nevertheless, where a process of large scale human rights violations has commenced, then intervention seems to me to be justified, at least in principle. Moreover, where it is clear, post-intervention, that the process of rights violations would recommence, were the intervening armed forces to retire, then the continued presence of the intervening armed forces – jointly acting with civilians engaged in a program of reconciliation and reconstitution of civil society – might also be justified.

I cannot here give a definitive answer to the fourth question beyond endorsing in general terms the ius in bello principles of just war theory. These principles are to the effect that: the armed force used should be the minimum necessary force; it should be proportionate, and; it should be effective. It has been argued that if NATO had used ground troops in Kosovo then some of these ground troops would have been killed, but the extent of the death of civilians and the destruction of property would have been much less. If so, by the lights of just war theory, NATO should have used ground troops – assuming armed intervention in some form was justified. For the lives of one's own soldiers do not have a greater moral value than the lives of the innocent people one's armed forces have been deployed to protect.

At any rate, in this paper I want to explore the notion of collective moral responsibility as it pertains both to nation states contemplating humanitarian armed intervention in a variety of settings involving states or groups perpetrating human rights violations. I do so on the assumption that such interventions are the collective moral responsibility of the community of nation states. I will further assume that humanitarian armed intervention is cross border use of armed forces, or the threat of such use, by a state or states for the purpose (though not necessarily the sole purpose) of protecting basic rights. Such intervention can be with or without the consent of the government of the state whose border is to be crossed, and it can include direct attacks on the armed forces of that government, as well as the deployment of armed forces to protect safe havens, ensure that food or other aid is distributed properly, and so on.

COLLECTIVE MORAL RESPONSIBILITY

For my purposes here I need to get to get clearer on the key notion of collective moral responsibility.

Collective moral responsibility for good or for evil has two main forms. First, there is collective moral responsibility for *actions*. Second, there is collective moral responsibility for *omissions*. Both actions and omissions can constitute rights violations. Moreover, rights violations, if they are sufficiently serious and on a sufficiently large scale, can generate a moral responsibility on the part of third parties to intervene to prevent or contain such violations. Moreover, where such third parties can or must act collectively to successfully intervene, the moral responsibility to intervene might be a *collective* moral responsibility.

The notion of collective responsibility is often given a collectivist, as opposed to an individualist, rendering.

There are a number of collectivist philosophical theories of collective responsibility. These include the theories of David Cooper[7] and Peter French.[8] On these views a collective entity can be morally responsible for some outcome, even though few, if any, of the individual members of the entity are individually morally responsible.

I am opposed to collectivist accounts of moral responsibility, and will defend an individualist account.

My suggestion is that collective moral responsibility can be regarded as a species of joint responsibility, or at least one central kind of collective moral responsibility can be so regarded.

Here we need to distinguish four senses of collective responsibility. In the first instance I will do so in relation to joint actions.

What is a joint action?[9] Roughly speaking, two or more individuals perform a joint action if each of them intentionally performs an individual action, but does so in the true belief that in so doing they will jointly realise an end which each of them has. Having an end in this sense is a mental state in the head of one or more individuals, but it is neither a desire not an intention. However, it is an end that is not realised by one individual acting alone. So we have called such ends, collective ends.

Consider the murder of 8,000 Muslim men by Serbian soldiers in the United Nations designated "safe area" of Srebrenica in Bosnia in July 1995.[10] The Serbian force bombed and then took the town of Srebrenica, after NATO had failed to support the UN force "protecting" the town. The Serbian soldiers then hunted down and murdered any Muslim men that they could find. Here was planned and orchestrated ethnic cleansing and mass murder in the service of ethnically pure territorial units and Serbian nationalism. There was joint action at a number of levels, but let us consider the actions of a group of soldiers on the ground who were dressed as UN peace-keepers, and were driving white UN vehicles. These Serbian soldiers guaranteed the Muslim's safety. They would then shoot them.[11] This is joint action. Some soldiers are driving the vehicle, another is looking for Muslims, then some of the Serbian soldiers are talking to the Muslims to convince them that they are safe. Finally, some of the Serbian soldiers shoot the Muslims dead. The soldiers coordinated their individual actions in the service of a collective end. Each performed a contributory action, or actions, in the service of the collective end of bringing about the death of the Muslim men.

Agents who perform a joint action are responsible for that action in the first sense of collective responsibility. Accordingly, to say that they are collectively responsible for the action is just to say that they performed the joint action. That is, they each had a collective end, each intentionally performed their contributory action, and each did so because each believed the other would perform his contributory action, and that therefore the collective end would be realised.

Here it is important to note that each agent is individually (naturally) responsible for performing his contributory action, and responsible by virtue of the fact that he intentionally performed this action, and the action was not intentionally performed by anyone else. Of course the other agents (or agent) *believe* that he is performing, or is going to perform, the contributory action in question. But mere possession of such a belief is not sufficient for the ascription of responsibility to *the believer* for performing the individual action in question. So what are the agents *collectively* (naturally) responsible for? The agents are *collectively* (naturally) responsible for the realisation of the (collective) *end* which results from their contributory actions.

Further, on my account to say that they are collectively (naturally) responsible for the realisation of the collective end of a joint action is to say that they are *jointly* responsible for the realisation of that end. They are jointly responsible because: (a) each relied on the other to bring about the state of affairs aimed at by both (the collective end), and; (b) each performed their contributory action on condition, and only on condition, the other(s) performed theirs. Here condition (b) expresses the *interdependence* involved in joint action.

Again, if the occupants of an institutional role (or roles) have an institutionally determined obligation to perform some joint action then those individuals are collectively responsible for its performance, in our second sense of collectively responsibility. Here there is a *joint* institutional obligation to realise the collective end of the joint action in question. In addition, there is a set of derived *individual* obligations; each of the participating individuals has an individual obligation to perform his/her contributory action. (The derivation of these individual obligations relies on the fact that if each performs his/her contributory action then it is probable that the collective end will be realised.)

The *joint* institutional obligation is a composite obligation consisting of the obligation each of us has to perform a certain specified action in order to realise that end. More precisely, I have the obligation to realise a collective end by means of doing some action, believing you to have performed some other action for that self-same end. The point about joint obligations is that they are not be discharged by one person acting alone.

Notice that typically agents involved in an institutional joint action will discharge their respective individual institutional obligations and their joint institutional obligation by the performance of one and the same set of individual actions. For example, if each of the members of a task force seeking out war criminals performs his individual duties having as an end the locating of a war criminal then, given favourable conditions, the task force will locate the war criminal. But one can imagine an investigating agent who recognises his individual institutional obligation, but not his jointly held obligation to realise the collective end in question. This investigator might have an overriding individual end to get himself promoted; but the head of the task force might be ahead of him in the queue of those to be promoted. So the investigator does not have locating the war criminal as a collective end. Accordingly, while he ensures that he discharges his individual obligation to (say) interview a particular suspect, the investigator is less assiduous than he might otherwise be because he wants the task force to fail to locate the war criminal.

There is a third putative sense of collective responsibility. This third sense of individual responsibility concerns those in authority. Here we need to distinguish two kinds of case. If the occupant of an institutional role has an institutionally determined right or obligation to order other agents to perform certain actions, and the actions in question are joint actions, then the occupant of the role is *individually* (institutionally) responsible for those joint actions performed by those other agents. This is our first kind of case; but it should be set aside, since it is not an instance of *collective* responsibility.

In the second kind of case it is of no consequence whether the actions performed by those under the direction of the person in authority were joint actions or not. Rather the issue concerns the actions of the ones in authority. In what sense are they collective? Suppose the members of NATO collectively decide to exercise their institutionally determined right to direct NATO forces to bomb Kosovo and not to use ground troops. The British wanted to use ground troops, the Americans and others do not. The Greeks did not want the bombing of Serbian civilian targets. At any rate, "there was a clear and powerful majority in favour of air strikes"[12]. Moreover, NATO ordered this action in the absence of a positive ruling from the UN Security Council. Accordingly, the NATO air forces bomb Kosovo. So the members of NATO are collectively responsible for the bombing of Kosovo. They are also collectively responsible for ignoring UN protocols.

There are a couple of things to keep in mind here. First, the notion of responsibility in question here is, at least in the first instance, institutional – as opposed to moral – responsibility.

Second, the 'decisions' of committees, as opposed to the individual decisions of the members of committees, need to be analysed in terms of the notion of a joint institutional mechanism that I have introduced elsewhere.[13] So the 'decision' of NATO can be analysed as follows. At one level each member of NATO voted for or against the bombing of Kosovo; and let us assume some voted in the affirmative, and others in the negative. But at another level each member of NATO agreed to abide by the outcome of the vote; each voted having as a collective end that the outcome with a majority of the votes in its favour would be pursued. Accordingly, the members of NATO were jointly institutionally responsible for the decision to order the NATO air forces to bomb Kosovo. So NATO was collectively institutionally responsible for bombing Kosovo; and the sense of collective responsibility in question is *joint* (institutional) responsibility.[14]

What of the fourth sense of collective responsibility, collective *moral* responsibility? Collective moral responsibility is a species of joint responsibility. Accordingly, each agent is individually morally responsible, but conditionally on the others being individually morally responsible; there is interdependence in respect of moral responsibility. This account of collective moral responsibility arises naturally out of the account of joint actions. It also parallels the account given of individual moral responsibility.

Thus we can the following claim about moral responsibility.

If agents are collectively responsible for the realisation of an outcome, in the first or second or third senses of collective responsibility, and if the outcome is morally significant then – other things being equal – the agents are collectively morally responsible for that outcome, and can reasonably attract moral praise or blame, and (possibly) punishment or reward for bringing about the outcome.

Here we need to be more precise about what agents who perform morally significant joint actions are collectively morally responsible for. Other things being equal, each agent who intentionally performs a morally significant *individual* action has *individual* moral responsibility for the action. So in the case of a morally significant joint action, each agent is *individually* morally responsible for performing *his contributory* action, and the *other* agents are *not* morally responsible for his individual contributory action. But, in addition, the contributing agents are *collectively* morally responsible for the outcome or *collective end* of their various contributory actions. To say that they are collectively morally responsible for bringing about this (collective) end is just to say that they are *jointly* morally responsible for it. So each agent is individually morally responsible for realising this (collective) end, but conditionally on the others being individually morally responsible for realising it as well. So in the Srebrenica example, a number of male Muslim villagers were lined up and shot by a number of Serbian soldiers. So Serbian soldier A might be individually morally responsible for shooting Muslim villagers X, Y and Z, soldier B for shooting villagers X, Y and Z, and so on for soldiers C, D. Suppose that while X, Y and Z were shot dead, no single soldier fired any shots which were sufficient to kill any villager. Nevertheless, A, B, C, and D are jointly morally responsible for the murder of villagers X, Y and Z.

Moreover, whatever the reason why each came to have the collective end in question, once each had come to have that collective end then there was interdependence of action. That is, each played his role in the massacre only on condition the others played their role. So the full set of actions performed by the individual members of the murderous group of Serbian soldiers can be regarded as *the means* by which the collective end was realised; and each individual contributory action was a *part of* that means. Moreover, in virtue of interdependence, each individual action is an integral part of the means to the collective end. Accordingly, I conclude that all of the members of the gang of soldiers are jointly – and therefore collectively – morally responsible for the massacre. For each performed an action in the service of that (collective) end, and each of these actions was an integral part of the means to that end.

Note the following residual points. First, it is not definitive of joint action that each perform his/her contributory action on the condition, and only on the condition, that *all* of the rest of the other perform theirs. Rather, it is sufficient that each perform his/her contributory action on the condition, and only on the condition, that *most* of the others perform theirs. So the interdependence involved in joint action is not necessarily *complete* interdependence. Nevertheless, if the action of one agent (or more than one agent) is not interdependent with *any* of the actions of the other agents, then the action of that first agent (or agents) is not part of the joint action. So if one (or more) of the members of the group of soldiers in fact performed his action independently of the rest, and if the rest performed their actions independently of that one agent, then the action of the latter would not be part of the joint action. The action of the latter agent would not be part of the means to the *collective* end; and the agent could not be said to have had the death of all the male Muslim villagers as a *collective* end.

Second, in my view, if an action is a means to some end, and if the action is sufficient for the realisation of that end, then the agent who performed the action has (natural) responsibility for bringing about the end. So the fact that the outcome in question might be overdetermined by virtue of the existence of some second action performed by some second agent, does not remove the responsibility of the first agent for the outcome in question.

Likewise we can conceive of two joint actions each of which is sufficient for the same outcome. Here there are two independent actions, albeit two joint actions performed by the members of two separate groups, respectively; and each of these (joint) actions is sufficient for some outcome. Just as the two individuals are both morally responsible for the outcome of their individual actions, so are the members of both of the two groups morally responsible for the two envisaged joint actions. The only difference is that in the former case each of the individuals is *individually* responsible for the outcome, whereas in the latter case the members of the first of the two groups are *jointly* responsible for the outcome in question, as are the members of the second group.

Third, an agent has moral responsibility if his action was intentionally performed in order to realise a morally significant collective end, and the action causally contributed to the end. The action does not have to be a necessary condition, or even a necessary part of a sufficient condition, for the realisation of the end.

Fourth, agents who intentionally make a causal contribution in order to realise a morally significant collective end, are not necessarily fully morally responsible for the end realised.

The second problem in relation to collective moral responsibility for actions arises in the context of the actions of large groups and organisations.

At this point the notion of, what I have elsewhere termed, a layered structure of joint actions needs to be introduced.[15] Suppose a number of 'actions' are performed in order to realise some collective end. Call the resulting joint action a *level two* joint action. Suppose, in addition, that each of the component individual 'actions' of this level two joint 'action', is itself – at least in part – a joint action with a second set of component individual actions. And suppose the member actions of this second set have the performance of this level two 'action' as their collective end. Call the joint action composed of the members of this second set of actions a *level one* joint action. An illustration of the notion of a layered structure of joint actions is in fact an army fighting a battle. At level one we have a number of joint actions. Consider the Croat forces attacking the Serbs in Knin in Croatia in Operation Storm in August 4th 1995. This was the turning point in the Croat/Serbian confrontation.[16] The Croat forces included artillery as well as ground troops. However, they were supported by NATO air forces who bombed Serbian communications systems, thereby greatly facilitating the progress of the Croat ground forces. So there are two level one joint actions. Now, each of these two (level one) joint actions is itself describable as an *individual* action performed (respectively) by the different military groups, namely, the action of bombing the communication systems, and the action of overrunning and occupying the town. However, each of these 'individual' actions is part of a larger joint action directed to the collective end of winning the battle against the Serbian force. For each of these individual attacks on the position is part of a larger plan coordinated by the NATO and Croat commands. So these 'individual' actions constitute a *level two* joint action directed to the collective end of winning the battle.

Accordingly, if all, or most, of the individual actions of the members of the NATO airforce squadron and of the Croat army were performed in accordance with collective ends, and the performance of each of the resulting level one joint actions were themselves performed in accordance with the collective end of winning the battle, then, at least in principle, we could ascribe joint moral responsibility for winning the battle to the individual pilots of the NATO air force and to the individual members of the Croat army.[17]

At any rate, the upshot of this discussion is that agents involved in complex cooperative enterprises can, *at least in principle*, be ascribed collective or *joint natural* responsibility for the outcomes aimed at by those enterprises, and in cases of morally significant enterprises, they can be ascribed collective or *joint moral* responsibility for those outcomes. This conclusion depends on the possibility of analysing these enterprises in terms of layered structures of joint action.

COLLECTIVE MORAL RESPONSIBILITY TO INTERVENE

Let us now turn to collective moral responsibility to intervene, and specifically to intervene in cases of large scale human rights violations.

Henry Shue has argued for the existence of what he terms, basic moral rights.[18] These include the right to security, and certain so called positive rights, such as the right to subsistence. Shue argues that these basic rights generate rights to protection and assistance. I accept Shue's arguments.

With the establishment of the nation state, and specifically of policing institutions, the responsibility for protecting and assisting those whose life or security is threatened from within a society has to a large extent devolved to the police. When these rights are externally threatened it is the military institutions of the state that bear the responsibility. So the state has a special responsibility to protect and assist its own citizens when there are either internal or external threats to their basic rights. So far so good, but what are we to say about cases in which the state is no longer willing or able to protect the rights to security of its citizens. Indeed, in some of these cases, the state is itself the source of the threat. The Rwandan genocide is one such case.

Henry Shue has persuasively argued that the state has obligations other than the obligation to promote the interests of its citizens.[19] Specifically, the state has an obligation not to unduly harm citizens of other states. Examples of such obligations include the obligation not to attack other states purely for economic gain, the obligation not to deplete the ozone layer by destroying forests, and so on. Here I want to go further and suggest that the state not only has moral obligations not to harm citizens of other states, it also has moral obligations to assist and protect the rights of citizens of other states. Specifically, it has these obligations when three general conditions are met: (I) the rights in question are basic moral rights, such as the right to security; (ii) the domestic state is not willing or able to protect these rights; (iii) the external state is able to protect these rights, whether by unilateral intervention, or by collective intervention with other states and/or internal social groups.

So basic moral rights generate moral responsibilities on the part of external nation-states. Earlier I suggested that such basic moral rights are not restricted to so-called negative rights; rather they include some so-called positive rights e.g. the right to subsistence. Accordingly, armed intervention might be justified in a case in which a state is refraining from providing for the basic material needs of its citizens, or more likely a section of its citizenry. Let us consider some simple examples to test our intuitions for this theoretical claim.

Consider the case of a drowning man who could easily be saved by one or other of three bystanders. Either one of the bystanders simply needs to throw the drowning man a life jacket, however each refuses to do so. But the drowning man has a gun and threatens to shoot one of the bystanders, if either he or one of his friends does not throw the jacket. They call his bluff and the drowning man shoots one of the bystanders dead. In fear of his life, the next bystander then throws the jacket.

Intuitively, the drowning man's action seems morally justified, given his action was the only way to preserve this life. For he had a positive right to be assisted, and the bystander was intentionally refraining from carrying out his duty to respect that right, and had no good reason to do so. So the case is analogous to those involving negative rights, such as the right not to be killed, or the right not to have one's freedom interfered with.

So deadly force can in principle be used to enforce positive rights, including presumably rights to subsistence, as well as to enforce negative rights.

Moreover, as is the case with negative rights, third parties – at least in principle – have rights, and indeed duties, to use deadly force to ensure that positive rights are respected.

This point has implications for governments who intentionally refrain from respecting the positive rights, including subsistence rights, of their citizens. Consider Saddam Hussein's refusal to distribute much needed food and medicine to his own citizens, albeit in the context of UN sponsored sanctions. The Iraqi citizens themselves, or third parties, are entitled to use deadly force against such a government. In such cases foreign governments capable of armed intervention are third parties. The justification for armed intervention is precisely the same as that used in relation to armed intervention to prevent genocidal slaughter in, say, Rwanda. The justification is that the such a government is engaged in large scale human rights violations, and the rights in question are basic rights. The fact that in some cases the rights are negative, and in other cases positive, is not a consideration of sufficient moral weight that armed intervention is justified in the former case, but not the latter.

In the light of this discussion, let us assume that under certain conditions large scale violations of basic rights, including violations of some so-called positive rights, generate a moral responsibility on the part of external states to intervene militarily to terminate those rights violations. Why is this moral responsibility a *collective* moral responsibility?

In so far as an external state contemplating armed intervention is a hierarchical complex comprised of a government and a military force then it's real and putative 'actions' can be understood as a layered structure of actions. (See the discussion above.) So in this sense the government and the military are collectively morally responsible for intervening or failing to intervene.

Naturally, given the hierarchical nature of such structures, some individuals have greater levels of moral responsibility. In particular, those in the lower echelons have diminished moral responsibility. And in so far as the upper echelons of the military are subordinate to the politicians, then even the upper echelons of the military might have diminished responsibility.

Moreover, the picture is further complicated when we consider the role of the citizenry of a democracy in relation to all this. It is conceivable that the citizenry of some democracy vote for an armed intervention to take place. If so, then they bear a degree of collective responsibility for the outcome. However, in a representative democracy it is much more likely that there will not be a popular vote in relation to military interventions, but rather the government alone will make the decision to intervene or not. This is not to say that the citizenry of a representative democracy does not have a collective moral responsibility to try to influence its government in favour of, or against, military intervention in an external state in which large scale human rights violations are taking place. The citizenry may well have such a collective responsibility, and might be able to exercise it in a variety of ways. For example, the citizenry might vote for or against the government on this issue. Or the citizenry might be able to influence their government's decision simply by virtue of their possession of a strong collective attitude in relation to armed intervention. Democratic governments can be very sensitive to strong collective attitudes, especially when they have reliable indicators of them e.g. as a result of market research. In this connections consider President Clinton's refusal to deploy ground troops in Kosovo because of the likely adverse response from the US public. They did not want to see another round of 'bodybags' containing US soldiers, as happened in Vietnam and Somalia.

At any rate, the upshot of the discussion on collective responsibility thus far, is that the moral responsibility of an external state to intervene in order to terminate large scale rights violations is a *collective* moral responsibility. Roughly speaking, it is a collective moral responsibility, because the notion of an external state in question is the notion of a collective agent.

However, a fundamental question remains unanswered. This is the question as to whether or not there is a collective responsibility to intervene in the sense that the set of external states – the community of nations, as we might say – has a collective moral responsibility to intervene.

In the light of our above analysis of collective responsibility, this question amounts to asking whether or not each member of the international community of nation states has an in principle moral responsibility to intervene militarily in cases of large-scale human rights violations, and this responsibility is possessed jointly with the other nation states.

Let us first take a closer look at the collective responsibility to intervene to terminate, reduce or prevent rights violations.

The failure to discharge such a collective responsibility constitutes a morally culpable act of omission. This is because the following two conditions obtain: (1) the wrong being done, or about to be done, is such that someone ought to intervene, and those on whom the collective responsibility to intervene falls are in a position to successfully intervene; (2) those who have the collective responsibility to intervene have that responsibility either by virtue of the nature and extent of the wrongdoing, or by virtue of an institutional obligation that they have, or by virtue of both of these considerations.

Moreover, the persons whose rights are being violated have a right to the collective action which it is the collective responsibility of the putative interveners to perform. Not only is the failure to intervene a morally culpable omission, but those who need the intervention to take place, have a moral right to intervention.

So far, so good. But here we need some theoretical account of culpable collective responsibility for omissions. Elsewhere I have elaborated such an account.[20]

According to that account, members of some group or community are collectively morally responsible for failing to intervene to halt or prevent some serious wrongdoing or wrongful state of affairs if: (1) the wrongdoing took place, or is taking place; (2) the members of the community intentionally refrained from intervening; (3) each or most of the members intervening having as a (collective) end the prevention of the wrongdoing probably would have prevented, or have a reasonable chance of halting, the wrongdoing; (4) each of the members of the community would have intentionally refrained from intervening – and intervening having as an end the prevention or termination of the wrongdoing – even if the others, or most of the others, had intervened with that end in mind. Note that on this account, if an agent would have intervened, but done so only because the others did ie not because he had as an end the prevention or termination of the wrong, then the agent would still be morally responsible, jointly with the others, for failing to intervene (given conditions (1)-(3)).

The first thing to note in relation to this account of collective moral responsibility for omissions is that it presupposes a community or group that could act together, if they chose to do so, in order to realise a collective end. I take it that the international community of nation states is such a community for the following reasons (at least).

First, there a high level of mutual awareness, including by way of the international mass media, and through the work of international groups, such as Amnesty International, that monitor human rights violations, of large scale human rights violations. So each nation state is aware of any episode of large scale human rights violations, and each is aware that everyone else is aware, and so on; there is mutual awareness.

Second, there is a high level of economic and political interdependence across nation states. They constitute a community in the sense that the interests, and therefore political and economic policies, of any one nation state are interdependent, and interdependent in the long term, with those of other nation states. As such, they have a raft of common problems, including the strength of the global economy, the quality of the environment, the preservation of international security (especially in the context of weapons of mass destruction), the reduction of international crime, and so on. In the contemporary setting national isolationism makes no sense.

Third, a set of international institutions have been developed in relation to the actions of nation states. These include the UN, the WTO and various pieces of international legislation and associated international courts. Indeed, there are rules and international institutional mechanisms for armed intervention in relation to genocide.

So in the contemporary world there is a *community* of nation states. The only question is what the moral standards governing the actions of that community ought to be. Is it to be a *moral* community? Protection of basic human rights constitutes the rock bottom minimum moral standards for human interaction. No political community, international or otherwise, can tolerate large scale human rights violations, and intelligibly conceive of itself as a moral community. But this is just to say that members of any political community have a collective moral responsibility to terminate or prevent large scale human rights violations, if they possibly can. It follows that the members of the international community of nation states have a collective moral responsibility to terminate or prevent large scale human rights violations, if they possibly can.

I take it to be self-evident that there are instances of large scale human rights violations that the actions of the members of the international community of nation states could terminate or prevent, if they acted together having as a (collective) end the termination or prevention of those rights violations. Therefore, there is a collective moral responsibility to do so.

Notice that the above account of collective moral responsibility does not presuppose that *any* individual nation state acting on its own could successfully intervene in relation to large scale human rights violations occurring in another nation state. Perhaps most nation states could not. On the other hand, it does not presuppose that *none* could successfully intervene on its own. Indeed, to do so would be clearly false. France, the US and others could have successfully unilaterally intervened in Rwanda, for example. Moreover, it may be the case that some nation state is so powerful that even all the others acting collectively could not successfully intervene in relation to massive human rights violations taking place in that very powerful nation state. If so, there might not be a collective responsibility to intervene.

Two final important points in relation to the above account. My account offers an elaboration and justification of the *collective* moral responsibility of nation states in relation to armed intervention in states in which large scale human rights violations are taking place. This account is consistent with two sorts of 'individual' moral responsibility.[21]

First, there is a prior moral responsibility on the part of the government and citizenry of the nation state in which the human rights violations are taking place, or are about to take place, to terminate or prevent those human rights violations. It is only if the government (or its citizenry) is unwilling or unable to discharge this responsibility that external intervention should be contemplated. In the presence of an internal solution there is no external collective responsibility to intervene (militarily or otherwise).

Second, the collective moral responsibility on the part of members of the international community to intervene in cases of large scale human rights violations is consistent with an individual moral responsibility on the part of some nation states who are able to do so. However, I have not sought to elaborate or justify this individual moral responsibility, and do not have the space to consider it here. However, I can say that individual moral responsibility would come into play in two sorts of case, namely, cases in which the collective moral responsibility has not been discharged, and cases in which the collective moral responsibility cannot be discharged. In the contemporary world there are few cases in which the collective moral responsibility *cannot* be discharged. There are quite a few cases in which the collective moral responsibility is not *in fact* discharged. But it is seldom a good idea to foist responsibilities on one individual or small group, because another individual, or the community at large, has failed to discharge theirs in the first place. Moreover, given the costs of armed intervention to the party or parties intervening, broad based, multilateral armed intervention is preferable to unilateral armed intervention. For one thing, the costs borne by a state intervening unilaterally are likely to be greater than if the burden is shared; so the individual state needs a greater incentive in terms of its self-interest, than it might if it were part of a broad based group engaged in multilateral intervention. For another thing, if a state intervenes unilaterally it might feel entitled, and have a greater capacity, to make peace more in conformity with its own interests, than the needs of the victims it has rescued. So broad based, multilateral humanitarian interventions are more likely to be motivated by humanitarian, rather than purely political, considerations.

NOTES

[1] See Seumas Miller "Collective Responsibility, Armed Intervention and the Rwandan Genocide" *International Journal of Applied Philosophy* vol.12 no.2 1998.

[2] For an argument to this effect see Georg Meggle "Is this war good?: An Ethical Commentary" In: Aleksandar Jokic (ed.), *Lessons of Kosovo. The Dangers of Humanitarian Interventions*, Broadview Press, 2003: 17-30.. See also Tony Weymouth and Stanley Henig *The Kosovo Crisis: The last American war in Europe?* (London: Pearson Education, 2001).

[3] Fergal Keane *Season of Blood: A Rwandan Journey* (London: Viking Press, 1995) p. 29. See also Miller "Collective Responsibility, Armed Intervention and the Rwandan Genocide" op.cit.

[4] See Mary Kaldor *New and Old Wars: Organised Violence in a Global Era* (Oxford: Polity Press, 1999) p. 64.

[5] Evidently in Kosovo the Albanians were the object of ethnic cleansing by the Serbs armed forces, but the Serbs themselves became the object of ethnic cleansing by some of Albanian armed forces (KLA). See Weymouth and Henig *The Kosovo Crisis* op. cit. p. 239.

[6] For an insight into Saddam Hussein's strategies and policies see Richard Butler *Saddam Defiant* (London: Phoenix, 2000).

[7] David Cooper "Collective Responsibility" *Philosophy* xliii July 1968.

[8] Peter French *Collective and Corporate Responsibility* (New York, 1984).

[9] See Seumas Miller *Social Action: A Teleological Account* (Cambridge University Press, 2001) Chapter 2.

[10] Laura Silber and Allan Little *Yugoslavia: Death of a Nation* (London: Penguin, 1997) pp. 345-350.

[11] Ibid. p. 350.

[12] Weymouth and Henig op. cit. p. 192.

[13] Miller *Social Action* op. cit. Chapter 5.

[14] This mode of analysis is also available to handle examples in which an institutional entity has a representative who makes an individual decision, but it is an individual decision which has the joint backing of the members of the institutional entity eg an industrial union's representative in relation to wage negotiations with a company. It can also handle examples such as the firing squad in which only one real bullet is used, and it is not know which member is firing the real bullet and which merely blanks. The soldier with the real bullet is (albeit unknown to him) *individually* responsible for shooting the person dead. However, the members of the firing squad are *jointly* responsible for its being the case that the person has been shot dead.

[15] Miller "Collective Responsibility, Armed Intervention and the Rwandan Genocide" op. cit.

[16] Silber and Little op. cit. p. 360.

[17] The cooperation between Croat land forces and NATO airpower against Serbian forces is in sharp contrast to what happened in Kosovo. NATO forces were in some sense in alliance with the Kosovo Liberation Army (KLA) who were engaged in fighting Serbian forces. The KLA were supposedly operating on behalf of the Albanian majority in Kosovo in their conflict with the Serbian forces controlled from Belgrade, but supposedly acting on behalf of the Serbian minority in Kosovo. However, NATO relied more or less exclusively on its own air power to destroy, or seek the capitulation of, the Serbian forces.

[18] Henry Shue *Basic Rights: Subsistence, Affluence and US Foreign Policy* (Princeton: Princeton University Press, 1996).

[19] Henry Shue "Eroding Sovereignty: The Advance of Principle" in (eds.) R. McKim and J. McMahan *The Morality of Nationalism* (Oxford: Oxford University Press, 1997).

[20] Miller *Social Action* op. cit. Chapter 8.

[21] These are individual moral responsibilities at one level of description ie at the level of the nation state conceived of as an individual entity. However, they are collective moral responsibilities in so far as nation states or their governments are thought of as groups of individual human persons. The latter description is ultimately the correct one. See Miller *Social Action* op. cit. Chapter 5.

OLAF L. MÜLLER

Reconstructing Pacifism. Different Ways of Looking at Reality

In this paper I aim to offer a reasonable reconstruction of pacifism. I shall neither attempt to *prove* pacifism, nor do I wish to provide arguments capable of convincing every reasonable person of pacifism and its merits. My aim is less ambitious. I wish to spell out a respectable version of pacifism, that is to say, a version of pacifism which is no longer vulnerable to the well-known suspicions of being hysterical, sentimental or blind to the hard facts.[1]

If I can prove my point that there is in fact a more attractive pacifist position than the positions usually associated with this title then this would be of great interest not only to declared pacifists but to their opponents as well. My result might even go so far as to help the pacifist's opponent see more clearly what position she has to make her case against. In short, my paper aims at contributing towards a better understanding of the very issue at stake between the pacifist and her opponent.

The main idea behind my reconstruction of pacifism stems from the metaethical insight that factual claims are often impossible to disentangle from claims about values.[2] I shall apply this insight to what appear to be factual disagreements about war; and I shall use the NATO intervention in Kosovo as my model example. If I am right, the pacifist has a specific way of looking at situations involving war. She looks at such situations *in the light of her system of value*, and in so doing arrives at descriptions differing from those of her opponent (who judges in the light of a competing system of value). None of the resulting descriptions have any legitimate claim to objectivity. And if it is true that the proponents of war are neither more nor less realistic than their pacifist opponents, then the claim that the pacifist way of looking at things is an objective illusion loses credence. In my view, it is impossible to overcome the limits of objectivity when describing conflicts such as the one in Kosovo. I find nothing alarming about this. Rather, I believe that we should learn to restrain our habitual appeal to objectivity and lead our moral lives in the face of value-laden facts. Whether this is easier for the pacifist or easier for her opponent, I shall not try to decide.

I. MORAL DISAPPROVAL OF WAR: SOME VARIETIES

Let us start by taking a look at different forms of pacifism that immediately appear ill-founded. First, there is the position fairly popular in post-war Germany (which of course is not to say that this position has not been tempting to people from other countries and epochs as well):

> Elitist Pacifism – for moral reasons *we* shall abstain from war; but alas, there have to be wars, which are, fortunately, carried out by others.

It should be obvious that this is quite a dubious position. It makes a moral difference between its proponents and all others – without providing any reason for making such a difference. Elitist Pacifism cannot be universalized, and thus, cannot claim to be a moral position at all.

If we extend the pacifist ban on war such that it addresses everyone, not only the pacifist elite, we obtain a position far stronger than Elitist Pacifism:

> Pacifist Rigorism – participation in any war is, *eo ipso*, morally wrong.

Apparently Pacifist Rigorism forbids too much. It runs counter to a conviction which most of us do not want to give up. It runs counter to the conviction that there was at least one war in history which was morally justified: the Allied war against Nazi Germany. And even if you do not happen to share this conviction (perhaps because you find that too many lives were sacrificed in the course of that war) you will nevertheless have to find a convincing response to the following thought experiment:

Let us imagine a counterfactual course of events from 1939 to 1945 in which the German side committed the same crimes against humanity as they did in actual history, but in which the Allied military action against Nazi Germany resulted in *far fewer* victims (on both sides). Would you insist that even this hypothetical war is morally wrong – simply because of its being a war? (And would you hold to this verdict even in the limiting case of an Allied military action producing almost no victims while at the same time putting an end to the human catastrophe which Nazi-Germany brought upon Poland, millions of Jews and the rest of Europe?)

You leave the grounds of Pacifist Rigorism as soon as you admit, at least in theory, that morally justified wars are conceivable. Of course, even then it is possible to insist that there are no real cases where the theoretical possibility (of *bellum iustum*) becomes actual. Nevertheless, it does not suffice to simply modify the Pacifist Rigorist's position and call all *actual* warfare morally wrong without further ado. We want to be told what it is that forbids all actual (but not all conceivable) war. This challenge cannot easily be met *tout court*. Rather it must be met by looking at the individual characteristics of actual cases.

If this is right, pacifism can be understood as generalizing about individual, actual cases, paying special tribute to the logical priority of the case's verdict. This version of pacifism is grounded in something like:

> Case-by-Case Pacifism – given the facts about the individual case at issue, this or that specific war is morally wrong,

and proceeds from there to generalizations such as:

> Pacifism of the Century – due to its actual characteristics, modern war is morally wrong. (But it is theoretically conceivable that even in modern times a just war might occur).

Of course, pacifism can be extended much further so as to cover, for example, all war from ancient times onwards.[3]

It should be noted that our characterization of Case-by-Case Pacifism (and all its various generalizations) is not yet complete. We still have to spell out what it is that makes a given war morally wrong. We have to annex a criterion for an individual war's being unjust. There are several reasonable alternatives; I want to mention only two of them.

> Example 1 (from a point of view in which consequentialist and humanitarian elements are essential): A war is morally wrong if it is not intended to put an end to crimes against humanity; and even if it is

intended to do this, it is still morally wrong if it risks sacrifices of such and such dimension.

Example 2 (from a utilitarian point of view): An individual war is morally wrong if it is likely to produce greater harm than its peaceable alternatives.

In the case of example 2, you may rightly ask: Is it not a little odd to speak of pacifism if nothing more is involved than, say, good old utilitarianism? (Couldn't the utilitarian be in favor of war now and then?)

If what I have said so far is right then the answer to this is that pacifism can be understood to consist of *two* claims – an evaluative claim and a factual claim. The pacifist's evaluative claim is the very criterion that differentiates between just and unjust war, for example the criterion of utilitarianism. And the pacifist's factual claim states in addition that non-military alternatives produce less harm than the war under consideration (Case-by-Case Pacifism); or than any war from our century (Pacifism of the Century); or than any war from ancient times onwards; or than any actual war whatsoever.[4]

Due to such factual claims, pacifism can no longer be accused of being silent about the facts. Our latest versions of pacifism are committed to certain factual claims; therefore they are vulnerable to empirical criticism and open to rational discussion. We have found options for the pacifist that are less dogmatic, and thus, more attractive than Elitist Pacifism or Pacifist Rigorism.

Unfortunately this achievement has a negative aspect. If you cease to be silent about the facts you can still be blind to the facts: It may well be the case that the factual claims in our latest versions of pacifism turn out to be *false*. And it seems quite risky indeed to be committed to factual claims of the sort I have been quoting. In the next section we'll take a first look at the risks and dangers involved in the pacifist's factual claims. Later (in sections III and IV) we'll see that it has been quite misleading to factorize the pacifist position into an evaluative and a factual component. My point will be that these two supposed components cannot be disentangled – neither in the pacifist's position nor in the position of her opponent.

II. A PROBLEM CONCERNING FACTS: THE CASE OF KOSOVO

Let us restrict our attention to Case-by-Case Pacifism. (Should it turn out that the difficulties concerning factual claims are already insuperable when

Case-by-Case Pacifism is at issue, then the situation would be far worse for its more ambitious cousins such as Pacifism of the Century). Let us look, for example, at NATO's Kosovo war. Below is a representative factual claim the pacifist must defend when applying Case-by-Case Pacifism to the case of Kosovo:

(*) If the Western countries had not bombed targets in Serbia and Kosovo, less Albanians and Serbs would have been killed, injured, or have lost their homes.[5]

Question: Is this claim about most recent history true? When you look at the furious disputes which our question has triggered again and again, it seems very hard to imagine an uncontroversial way of answering this question. Why is this so?

The influence of propaganda immediately comes to mind; truth is the first victim of war, says a well-known proverb. The critics of NATO's intervention in Kosovo tended at the time to be quite sensitive to the dangers of Albanian and Western propaganda[6] – but they were easy victims of Serbian propaganda (or so their opponents claimed). And the supporters of the intervention exhibited the same kind of bias, only the other way round. (I hasten to add that on both sides there were few people who were *considerably* freer from such biases).

Now you may say that with a little intellectual honesty and discipline it should be possible to free yourself of the biases stemming from your own side's propaganda. Naturally this leads to the proposal of withholding one's judgment concerning all controversial factual issues. Even so, some (undisputed) facts will remain in the game; couldn't we derive our moral verdict on the grounds of these? Sometimes this can be done. It may happen that one party can win the quarrel by appealing to facts which the other side does not dispute.[7]

In the quarrel over Kosovo, however, as in most other actual cases, we would not have come to any decision at all if we had simply suspended judgment on all controversial issues. And this is true not only from an *ex ante* perspective (the perspective we had to take during the process of Western decision making). It is also true from an *ex post* perspective. Although we now know, without a doubt that the greatest Serbian crimes against humanity in Kosovo – atrocities, mass deportations, destruction of whole villages and so forth – were mainly committed *after* the NATO had begun dropping bombs,[8] we still do not know what would have happened if the NATO had tried peaceable alternatives.

Critics of the war were claiming at the time that the increase in brutality on the Serbian side was a causal consequence of the NATO-intervention, while their opponents were claiming that the actual course of events proved what the Serbian authorities had been planning all along, and also, what "the" Serbian people were willing to do.[9]

Who is to decide what is true in this dispute and what not? Is this really a dispute that can be settled empirically, at least in principle? Is it a dispute which allows for scientific consensus? And if so, why are we not able to come to the projected consensus?

I submit that the lack of consensus we are facing here is not only to be blamed on propaganda and lack of knowledge about remote facts. The reasons for the disagreement are deeper. They are connected to the very nature of the contested claim, which (it will be recalled) is the following counterfactual:

(*) If the Western countries had not bombed targets in Serbia and Kosovo, less Albanians and Serbs would have been killed, injured or have lost their homes.

In the next section, I want to convince you that there is no objective, value-free reality which corresponds to such claims.

III. COUNTERFACTUALS

Let us observe first that it has been misleading to say that the pacifist's claim (*) is factual rather than evaluative. The claim is not a claim about the facts; it is a *counter*factual. Now there has been a lot of philosophical controversy as to the nature (and respectability) of counterfactuals. The radicals in this controversy want to forbid counterfactual idiom from serious speech altogether.[10] To follow these radicals, however, would not be a good idea in our context because it is difficult to see how reference to – counterfactual – alternatives of behavior can be avoided within moral discourse and because we certainly do not wish to put an end to our moral enterprise at the present juncture.

In our context it appears more attractive to listen to those who insist that counterfactuals do not have value-free content.[11] We do not have to wonder whether this is true *tout court* – even in the simplest, unsuspicious cases (such as "The bomb would not have exploded, had it been filled completely with cinnamon instead of dynamite"). For us it suffices to see that highly complex counterfactuals such as those which are at issue between the pacifist and her opponent, for example claim (*), do not have value-free content.

Let me elaborate. When proponents of the NATO-intervention in Kosovo dissent from the pacifist's counterfactual (*) they often appeal to quite general claims concerning Serbian or human nature. They say for example that the Serbian crimes against humanity, which were committed during the NATO-attacks, reveal an alarming readiness for brutality and cruelty; and they interpret such cruelty as a constant (or anyway, long-term) disposition of the Serbian population.

But it is simply not true that one can establish a certain Serbian readiness for brutality (already present prior to the Western intervention) by looking at the *actual* course of events. To the contrary, those who speak that way about the Serbian people express an interpretation or evaluation. For example, their claim might derive from looking at the actual course of events in the light of Anti-Serbian resentment. (Or should I say: in the *darkness* of Anti-Serbian resentment?)

One does not necessarily have to be prejudiced against the Serbian people to arrive at the belief that in the spring of 1999 the Serbs were prepared for the worst. Anti-Serbian resentment is perhaps the simplest but certainly not the only type of evaluation which could have led the war's proponents to believe in the Serbian readiness for cruelty against the Albanians. Another evaluation to the same effect may be grounded, more generally, in pessimism about human nature. The evaluation I have in mind flatters itself for being realistic, but of course, it cannot be meant to seriously constitute a branch of realism resting on all and only hard, objective facts. Rather it is a negative evaluation of these facts, presumably deriving from a one-sided simplification of human history.[12] According to a typical nuance of this negative world view, we should expect the worst from our fellow-humans – unless they are controlled by brute force.

I admit that I may be exaggerating in my characterization of the evaluations that I attribute to proponents of the NATO-intervention, in order to explain their dissent from the pacifist's counterfactual (*). Suffice it to say that, for the sake of clarity, I am characterizing a position at an extreme end of a certain scale which allows for less extreme positions similar in kind.

It is high time for another *caveat*. True, I have thus far spotted evaluations as one source of what made the war's proponent dissent from the pacifist's counterfactual. But I have been pointing out the impact of values not because I take this to be sufficient for criticizing the proponent of war. To the contrary, I have no objection to the impact of values when discussing counterfactuals such as (*). Only, I insist, we should be aware that we cannot determine the counterfactual's truth value independently of genuine evaluation. If this is right then the opponent of NATO's war in Kosovo must be committed to certain values as well – when she argues *in favor of* her counterfactual:

(*) If the Western countries had not bombed targets in Serbia and Kosovo, less Albanians and Serbs would have been killed, injured, or have lost their homes.

What values could be behind the pacifist's belief in this counterfactual? One possibility – which I only wish to mention before putting it aside – is Anti-American, Anti-Albanian, or Pro-Serbian prejudice. (I want to put this sort of evaluation aside because it becomes irrelevant as soon as the pacifist not only criticizes military action in the case of Kosovo but also extends her position into something more general, such as Pacifism of the Century).

Another possible type of evaluation, which may be involved in the pacifist's counterfactual (*), is optimism about human nature – the very mirror-image of the bellicose pessimism we sketched a short while ago.

You may ask: How can one earnestly keep an optimistic attitude about human nature when one looks at ethnic conflicts such as the one in Kosovo? My answer: One-sided simplification again (as much as in case of the pessimistic attitude we have ascribed to the pacifist's opponent). In the light of a typical pacifist's simplification, the ethnic conflict in Kosovo appears to be another example of an eruption of violence which *could have been avoided non-violently*. In this view it is, sadly, true that violence leads to still more violence (that much seems a proven fact from the war in Kosovo); but it is also true that the bloody circle of violence and counter-violence can be interrupted – at any moment! (And of course the pacifist can cite *well-chosen* examples from history in favor of her view).

IV. FACTS IN THE LIGHT OF VALUES

Where do we stand? The situation between the pacifist and her opponent seems symmetrical. Neither side can ground the verdict concerning counterfactual (*) on objective, value-free facts. The facts about human nature are too complicated and undecided to make an objective counterfactual possible; only in the light of values will we be able to simplify and decide the matter. As the values are controversial between pacifists and their critics, the counterfactual itself will remain so, too.

Couldn't we leave the facts complicated as they are, avoiding simplification in either direction, pessimist or optimist? Couldn't we just be *realistic*? We might, but we shouldn't. If we tried to look at the facts without evaluation and simplification, we would have to suspend judgment about all (or anyway, nearly all) counterfactuals relevant to our moral decision about the war in question. But typically we cannot suspend our decision. (If we do nothing we have made a decision as well).

Neither can we resort to tossing a coin in order to determine our moral decision about the war. Such procedure might be reasonable when gambling at the stock market, betting or playing poker. It is not a procedure to be recommended when it comes to matters of war and peace. To be sure, decisions about war are risky. But if we delegated decisions so important to an oracle of coins we would damage our self-understanding as moral agents.

Then what? I urge that we learn to lead our moral lives in the presence of value-laden counterfactuals – particularly when we are dealing with war and peace. As soon as we become fully aware of the values that inform our judgments on the relevant counterfactuals, we will be able to decide, consciously, in the light of which values we *want* to look at reality. And it may well be that the values behind the pacifist's counterfactuals are more attractive than the values her opponent appeals to when looking at reality.

You may wonder whether this won't lead us back to where we started; you may ask: When the pacifist decides to opt for values that support counterfactuals such as (*) – won't this be tantamount to a decision in favor of Pacifist Rigorism?

Not quite. The Pacifist Rigorist does not have to look at reality at all when she thinks about war; she can close her eyes and say: *No to war*, period. Such dogmatism does not seem attractive. And so we developed a position more sensitive to the facts. This was the juncture where Case-by-Case Pacifism and its generalizations (grounded for example in utilitarianism) entered the discussion. But these attempts went too far in the direction of the facts. They became hostage to "facts" that were beyond reach. To put it more perspicuously, the mistake in these attempts was to divide the pacifist position into an evaluative component and an unreachable factual component – two components separated by a canyon.

Now we see that there is a third option for the pacifist. Instead of *overlooking* the facts altogether, and instead of *overloading* her boat with facts totally independent of and, as it were, foreign to her values, she can sponsor an intimate wedding between facts and values: and then take the value-laden children on board. For a change of metaphor we may also say: When the pacifist follows my suggestion she must be in close contact with the facts – although this will be a different kind of contact than the one we know from the empirical sciences. In the sciences we try to look at reality without presupposing values that are controversial[13] – the pacifist and her opponent, by contrast, may look at reality in the light of controversial values.

Now looking at reality in the light of controversial values need not only lead to controversial counterfactuals such as claim (*); the phenomenon extends to other sorts of claims, which are also relevant to the moral decision about war. In the next sections I'll provide more examples of this. If I am right we can characterize the way pacifists look at reality by saying that they follow certain epistemic imperatives (which might be compared to Kant's regulative principles).

V. AN EPISTEMIC IMPERATIVE, AND KANT'S PRINCIPLE OF HOMOGENEITY

The pacifist's first epistemic imperative is connected to an issue which we have already touched on – the issue of human nature:

> Epistemic Imperative concerning Human Nature – resist against demonizing the other side; always try to understand the case from their point of view.

What does it mean in pacifist practice to follow this imperative? For example, what does it mean in the case of Kosovo? One way to follow the Epistemic Imperative concerning Human Nature is to try and learn as much as possible about the people and point of view of the country being targeted by military action. In the case of Kosovo this meant being informed about what Serbian citizens and members of their government were thinking about the conflict at the time. The proponents of war did not of course want to invest much effort into this. That explains, for example, why during the conflict there were almost no interviews with Milosevic in the Western mass media.[14]

To prevent misunderstandings, the Epistemic Imperative concerning Human Nature does not suggest that we believe everything Milosevic might have wanted to tell us; but according to the imperative we should have at least *listened* to him. And, still more important, we should have listened to critical Serbian intellectuals.

I think it is obvious that those who tried all this do not deserve to be called "blind to the facts". (If anyone is to be charged with this it should be the proponents of NATO's war, who typically did not know much about Serbian interpretations of the conflict).

What would have been the result of taking into account the Serbian point of view? I think one result would have been greater reluctance against hasty simplifications. Obeying her Epistemic Imperative concerning Human Nature, the pacifist might not have been so easily brought to abandon claims such as these:

> It is not yet proven that Milosevic is a monster.
>
> What the Serbian security forces were doing (prior to the NATO-attacks) may still be explained without saying that they are racists full of hatred.

How much evil has to happen before a revision of pacifist claims such as these becomes inevitable? My answer is that it never exactly becomes *inevitable*. It is a matter of personal decision, or evaluation, at what point you feel forced to revise such claims. The pacifist will resist the pressure to revise her claims much more persistently than her opponents. But she does not have to resist at any price; she does not have to resist *crazily*.

A comparison to a piece from Kant's philosophy of science might help to clarify the situation. According to Kant the scientist needs to follow certain epistemic imperatives – imperatives which he calls "regulative principles". These regulative principles play a role in the scientist's system of belief comparable to the one that our Epistemic Imperative concerning Human Nature plays in the pacifist's system of belief. Both sorts of imperative regulate the direction of further investigation.[15] One of Kant's examples is the Principle of Homogeneity:

> Do not rest satisfied with an excessive number of different original genera; always try to give an explanation of the manifold by detecting common *deep structure*.[16]

The motivation behind this Kantian principle is that even when the scientist has not yet found a common structure underlying the superficially manifold, it is still rational to orientate further research towards the assumption of such structure. One might say, slightly exaggerating matters, that scientists, who cease to follow Kant's Principle of Homogeneity, give up the scientific enterprise altogether. In the same fashion we might say, again slightly exaggerating, that pacifists, who cease to follow the Epistemic Imperative concerning Human Nature, give up the pacifist world view.

In Kant's system regulative principles lead to a certain branch of apriori knowledge. For example, in the light of his Principle of Homogeneity, the following judgment holds apriori:

> The manifold can be subsumed under higher genera;[17] differences in appearance (for example in chemistry) can be explained by appeal to one and the same sort of underlying structure (for example, to the number of electrons from the outermost orbit).

Kant does not claim to be able to *prove* this.[18] He claims that to *assume* the statement's truth is necessary for the very rationality of the scientific enterprise itself. The statement gives a direction to the scientific enterprise; without it, the scientific enterprise would lose its point. If this is so, the scientist is, by rationality, entitled to hold firm to the statement, no matter what recalcitrant experiences may tell against it. The statement is immune to scientific revision, which is just another way of attributing an apriori status to the statement – it is *prior* to the scientific enterprise. (Could it still be wrong? Yes, it could be wrong, should it ever turn out that what we call empirical science is impossible).

If there is a parallel between these pieces from Kant's system and our Epistemic Imperative concerning Human Nature then we should be able to develop it in two directions.

First, having spotted *apriori judgments* that derive from the scientist's obedience to the Principle of Homogeneity we should expect similar effects from the pacifist's obedience to our Epistemic Imperative concerning Human Nature. Here too we should expect to find something that we may grant an apriori status. And indeed, those who obey most persistently the

> Epistemic Imperative concerning Human Nature – resist demonizing the other side; always try to understand the case from their point of view,

can be said to hold firm to the following statement come what may:

> No human being is a monster, that is to say, morally degenerate through and through; it is always possible to understand a person from inside, as if that person were me.

The pacifist does not recommend sticking to these statements blindly. She recommends opening our eyes when evil seems present – and seeing the human inside.[19] Sometimes this is difficult, but it can be done. Call it a "focus imaginarius", if you will.[20]

So much for the first direction in which the parallel between pacifism and the sciences may be extended. The second direction leads to the question of values in the sciences. That we should be able to detect values in the sciences-à-la-Kant becomes plausible in the light of the following reasoning. If the pacifist's epistemic imperative can be seen to represent her system of value, and if her epistemic imperative can be compared to Kant's epistemic imperative for the scientist, then the latter imperative too has to be seen as representing values.

Which values? My answer is that when Kant's scientist orientates herself towards the Principle of Homogeneity, she does so because she values a certain property of scientific theory – the property of ontological economy: Everything else being equal, she prefers a scientific theory with the smallest number of independent entities and categories. According to contemporary philosophy of science this is just one of the criteria which guide the scientist's choice between competing theories. Other criteria appeal to values such as simplicity, elegance, generality, exactness[21]; and, of course, to empirical adequacy.

The value of empirical adequacy is responsible for the special claim to objectivity that the empirical sciences certainly deserve. The other values I mentioned appear more subjective because they seem to reflect, less about how reality exists independently of us, and more about how *we want* to look at reality. If I am not mistaken those values can be compared to certain pacifistic values, which also reflect certain wishes as to how one wants to look at reality.[22]

VI. NON-VIOLENT ALTERNATIVES

In the preceding section we saw that the pacifist's way of looking at the facts can be understood as obedience to what we have called the Epistemic Imperative concerning Human Nature. In the present and in the next section, I want to name two more epistemic imperatives that may also be taken to guide the pacifist's investigation of reality. They concern non-violent alternatives and the danger of uncontrolled escalation. (Although I shall not develop the argument, they too can be compared to Kant's regulative principles; they too yield certain judgments apriori). Our subject for the present section is the Epistemic Imperative concerning Non-Violent

Alternatives – always search for non-violent alternatives to projected military action.

We all know that pacifists tend to assign stronger emphasis than their opponents to the search for non-military alternatives. If they do so with good sense they have to look carefully at reality because in order to design alternative courses of action you need to know a lot. Now, the more desperate the search for non-violent alternatives becomes in a given situation, for example due to the alarming increase of brutality on all sides (as in Kosovo, March 1999), the less realistic that search will appear from a non-pacifist point of view; it will appear illusionary and hopelessly idealistic. But I want to stress that Reality Itself does not tell us when TINA's notorious words are in place:

There Is No (non-military) Alternative.

At what moment we submit ourselves to Margaret Thatcher's slogan depends not only on the objective situation but also on our personal decision, or more accurately, on our system of values. It is therefore legitimate, not a sign of objective illusion, when the pacifist orientates herself towards the Epistemic Imperative concerning Non-Violent Alternatives, and thus, dissents persistently from TINA's slogan. The slogan does not carry more realism than its pacifist counterpart – it carries different values (and I dare say, not the most attractive ones). What is worse, the slogan's adherent not only shows lack of political fantasy but, often, lack of contact to reality as well: If you do not see any alternative to military action then this might be because your eyes are closed. (Having said this I have not expressed an objective claim either; rather I have exhibited another example of what the pacifist may say, given her system of values).

In the case of Kosovo, the pacifist's system of values led to a number of concrete proposals for the non-violent de-escalation of an extremely dangerous situation. The most important among these proposals urged the strengthening and improvement of the Kosovo Verification Mission, KVM (that had been sent to the region by OSCE). It will be recalled that the opposite course of action was chosen: The evacuation of the KVM on March 20th, 1999, was a clear sign that the Western countries had decided in favor of war. Although there is some evidence – dating from the time when KVM was operating – that the presence of the mission in Kosovo would have been apt to relieve the tensions between the ethnic groups in the conflict,[23] we do not know objectively what *would have happened,* had the mission been continued in even more decided fashion.

Now we are led back to our earlier considerations concerning counterfactuals. And this is not a coincidence because those considerations are intimately connected to the present subject (to the Epistemic Imperative concerning Non-Violent Alternatives). If doing nothing is the only alternative to military action that comes to your mind you may well dissent from the pacifist's counterfactual in our earlier discussion:

(*) If the Western countries had not bombed targets in Serbia and Kosovo, less Albanians and Serbs would have been killed, injured or have lost their homes.

But the more non-violent and attractive alternatives to military action you have present in your mind, the more willingly you will agree on the counterfactual. The chances for the counterfactual being true will grow proportionally to the number of possibilities which make the antecedent true. When you are obedient to the Epistemic Imperative concerning Non-Violent Alternatives then you see many different possibilities for making the counterfactual's antecedent true; *ergo*, belief in the counterfactual and obedience to the epistemic imperative are both expressions of the very same system of values. (And this not only applies to the case of Kosovo; an equivalent nexus can be established in all other cases of projected war).

In the next section we'll unfold another epistemic imperative for pacifists. As we shall see, it is complementary to the Epistemic Imperative concerning Non-Violent Alternatives.

VII. THE DANGER OF UNCONTROLLED ESCALATION

The Epistemic Imperative concerning Non-Violent Alternatives (which was our subject in the previous section) was, optimistically, meant to sharpen our eyes for what could be done when we opt against war. To complement this the pacifist formulates her next epistemic imperative. Now she aims, pessimistically, at sharpening our eyes for what may happen when we wage war. The imperative in question is the

> Epistemic Imperative concerning Uncontrolled Escalation – hone your senses to the uncontrolled, irreversible side effects of military action, particularly to the danger of military escalation leading to another world war.

The pacifist's fright of *uncontrolled* escalation may appear hysterical to people with good nerves. It may remind them of Cassandra – tragically old-fashioned.[24] And indeed, doesn't the actual course of history, for example in Kosovo, provide an objective refutation of the pessimistic pacifist position, which predicted as much as the danger of the Third World War?[25]

Not quite. True, the NATO-intervention did not lead to another big European war; this much is objectively proven. But this does not tell us anything about the danger with which the NATO was gambling. A danger can exist even if it does not become actualized. (Think of a tiger sneaking into your children's room while they are happily playing in the bathroom). Again, it is a matter of personal attitude, or evaluation, a matter of the quality of nerves (if you prefer), at what point a situation is interpreted as being dangerous. Even if objective probabilities are given (which they are not, in the case of war), even if we know the likelihood of a certain evil happening, it is still not always a matter of objectivity whether a real danger in fact lurks. Pacifists are pacifists, partly because they find the prospects of another world war so disturbing that they see this danger earlier than others.

In the case of Kosovo they saw this danger alarmingly present in the night from May 6th to May 7th, 1999, when the Chinese embassy in Belgrade was bombed mistakenly. They claim, it was the sort of mishap whose consequences cannot be controlled vigorously enough. To speak of collateral damage in this context is in their view irresponsible because playing it down like that may well amount to overlooking the very possibility of a catastrophic chain reaction. China is an atomic power, after all, and its political elite has not always exhibited the desirable portion wisdom.

The possible effects of the situation on Russia were another source of alarm to pessimist pacifists. Following the Epistemic Imperative concerning Uncontrolled Escalation they were alarmed, and feared the worst, when on April 16th, 1999, the members of Russian parliament (led by pan-Slavic radicals) voted in favor of making Yugoslavia a third partner in the Treaty of Union between Russia and Belarus – by which they clearly intended to indicate that NATO's war against Serbia was considered a war against Russia as well. Luckily the Russian government proved more reasonable than that, but even so, another dangerous confrontation between Russia and the West lurked when their troops met at a surprising moment at the airport in Pristina, which had been captured by Russian troops on June 12th, 1999 without prior consultation with NATO.

How safe was all this, the pacifist wants to know, and this again is not a question concerning facts only – but a question connected to attitudes, evaluations, and quality of nerves. *All's well that ends well,* the pacifist's opponents will reply,[26] thus expressing *their* personal way of looking at things: a way which the pacifist finds preposterous when the danger of atomic confrontation is in the game.[27]

And so the quarrel between the two positions goes on and on. We'll have to leave it at that because we must try to come to some conclusions.

VIII. CONCLUSION

I have tried to reconstruct the pacifist world view by appealing to three epistemic imperatives: An imperative concerning human nature, an imperative concerning non-violent alternatives, and finally, an imperative concerning uncontrolled escalation. If you follow these imperatives you may be said to look at reality in the light of the pacifistic system of value. If you do not follow these imperatives you do not simply disagree about the so-called hard facts but exhibit adherence to an alternative system of value. Admittedly it often appears as if pacifists and their opponents disagree about factual claims. But if my diagnosis is right, these appearances are often misleading – often the disagreement about relevant claims, which are supposed to be factual, has its roots in controversial values.

Following the Epistemic Imperative concerning Human Nature, the pacifist will try much longer to find non-monstrous interpretations for enemy behavior than her opponent will; she will resist longer supposed factual claims such as

> This is a government full of racists and murderers.

Following the Epistemic Imperative concerning Non-Violent Alternatives, the pacifist will try much longer to find non-military courses of action for ending dangerous conflicts than her opponent will; she will resist longer supposed factual claims such as

> We have no other choice than to start a war.

And finally, following the Epistemic Imperative concerning Uncontrolled Escalation, the pacifist will be much more sensitive than her opponent to the slightest signs of escalation towards catastrophe; she will resist longer supposed factual claims such as

> Everything is under control; we have calculated all possible consequences of our military action, and although there will be some *collateral* damage, we can surely prevent the worst.

Three times over I have said now that the pacifist will resist longer than her opponent certain claims (which are used by her opponent to justify war). How, and particularly, how long does the pacifist have to resist these claims?

To the first part of this question I reply that the pacifist shouldn't resist with closed eyes. If she wants to avoid blind dogmatism, her negative reaction to the three bellicose claims should not come like the conditioned reflex of Pavlov's dog. ("Whenever anyone says something in favor of war, say no!") Rather she should try to look for good evidence, which speaks against the three bellicose claims. Our three epistemic imperatives are supposed to guide her scrutiny of reality; they give direction to the pacifist's search for evidence in favor of peace – a search that would not make much sense if it were not pursued under the assumption that the desired evidence can be found. When it comes to the worst, the assumption may fail. It may happen that the pacifist is no longer able to follow our three epistemic imperatives without betraying reason. In such a desperate case she will have to give up her resistance to the war in question (and also, of course, her resistance towards her former opponent's three claims).

How bad does a state of affairs have to become before the pacifist despairs of her position and ceases to follow our three epistemic imperatives? It will be recalled that this is the second part of our earlier question – to which I cannot give any general answer. I cannot give criteria, or a decision procedure, or an algorithm, which could take the question off the pacifist's shoulders. The only advice I can give is to use good judgment: The pacifist should follow the three imperatives persistently but not crazily.

From history we know an example where many declared pacifists – Bertrand Russell among them – felt forced to leave the path of peace: They supported England's and France's declaration of war against Hitler's Germany; and rightly so. But if we judge this (as I think we must judge it) to be the limiting case where obedience to our three imperatives would have been crazy, we have still not found an *objective* limit to the pacifist's world view. The judgment in question is not forced upon us by independent reality; rather it is a judgment which reflects – at one and the same moment – both our moral *self*-conception and our moral conception of an evil part of world history.[28]

Pacifists who do not subscribe to Pacifist Rigorism can embrace the judgment in favor of the war against Hitler's Germany. Such a judgment does not lead to giving up the pacifist world view altogether; when you open your eyes to other parts of reality, past, present, or future, you can still view events in the light of the pacifistic system of values – and you can do this most persistently.

No objective reality will be objective enough to refute your epistemic obedience to our three imperatives. The decision to follow these imperatives is no more irrational than the scientist's decision to look for common deep structure behind the chaotic differences in appearance. And it is no more irrational than the opposite decision to give up earlier: to give up the scientific enterprise in favor of non-scientific approaches to chaotic reality – or to give up the pacifist enterprise in favor of the chaos of war.

I have argued that in questions of war and peace we cannot avoid looking at reality in the light of some system of value or other. Different systems will yield controversial claims about the war in question. In this, I claimed, there is nothing irrational.

Does this mean that the pacifist's world view and the world view of her opponent are equally good? No. We can still compare the two opposing views to find out which is superior. For this we have to see whether the pacifist system (which consists of general claims, concrete claims about actual cases, epistemic imperatives, criteria of unjust war, rules of non-violent conduct, and so forth) will lead to an adequate moral life – that is, to a moral life more attractive than the one resulting from opposing world views. For lack of space we cannot even begin to engage ourselves in the details of such a comparison. Suffice it to say that this is an enterprise which calls for being in close contact with both reality and ourselves.[29]

NOTES

[1] Johan Galtung has suggested that I drop the word "pacifism" in order to free the debate from unhappy ideological associations. I am not sure, however, whether the word is really completely lost for serious discussion. There are indications that high-ranking politicians want to benefit from the word: Even some proponents of war try to claim that their position is truly pacifist. The most bizarre attempt of that sort was published by Ludger Volmer, Minister of State in the German Foreign Ministry. Volmer belongs to the Green Party (BUENDNIS 90 / DIE GRUENEN) which used to

be pacifist and which still wishes to be *called* so, come what may. See Volmer [WBvP].
[2] See Williams [ELoP]:140-141; Murdoch [IoP]:22-23, 42; McDowell [AMRH]:21; Putnam [RTH]:139-141; Putnam [CoFV].
[3] It would go beyond the scope of this discussion to look at the historical details of such options. – Notice that Pacifism of the Century can also be *limited* a little without losing the title of pacifism; for example we could restrict it to all war which was led in the 20th century, with the exception of the war against Hitler's Germany.
[4] And of course, a similar list can be produced by abandoning utilitarianism and appealing to other criteria for an unjust war, such as the one from example 1.
[5] I call this a *representative* claim because different versions of Case-by-Case Pacifism may employ different criteria for unjust war, see examples 1 and 2 from section I. The factual claim in the main text derives from the utilitarian criterion (example 2), but it can be taken to represent similar claims that enter the game when the Case-by-Case Pacifist chooses to ground her position in alternative criteria. Most (if not all) criteria of unjust war embrace at least consequentialist *elements*. (In the utilitarian criterion from example 2, section I, consequentialist considerations do the whole job – whereas in example 1 they do part of the job with additional appeal to humanitarian *intentions*).
[6] A good example for this are reports about well-organized Albanian lobbyism in the United States (see, e.g., *Die Woche*, April 23rd, 1999, p. 19).
[7] In my opinion, this would have been a promising strategy for critics of the 1991 US-war against Iraq, see Müller et al [LSGE].
[8] Here is what we read in the official report by the Kosovo Verification Mission (KVM): "*Further escalation after 24 March 1999.* Summary and arbitrary killing became a generalized phenomenon throughout Kosovo with the beginning of the NATO air campaign" (OSCE (ed.) [KKaS]: Chapter 5, p. 4/13; emphasis in the original). "Once the OSCE-KVM left on 20 March 1999 *and in particular after the start of the NATO bombing* of the FRY on 24 March, Serbian police and/or VJ [i.e., the armee of Yugoslavia – O.M.], often accompanied by paramilitaries, went from village to village and, in the towns, from area to area threatening and expelling the Kosovo Albanian population" (OSCE (ed.) [KKaS]: Chapter 14, p. 1/23; my emphasis).
[9] Which side you take in this quarrel will of course depend on your interpretation of what happened in Kosovo prior to NATO's intervention. I have argued elsewhere that there is no objective way to decide whether the Albanians were, already then, innocent victims of ethnic cleansing or whether they were fighting a civil war, perhaps even a terrorist war, against the Serbs. See Müller [WWSü], sections III – VI.
[10] See, for example, White [AS]:279, 284; Goodman [PoCC]. Skepticism about counterfactual idioms is just a part of skepticism about modality, whose champion was Quine; see, for example, Quine [RM].
[11] See, for example, Putnam [RP]:54-55.
[12] The nexus between simplification and evaluation is a general phenomenon. I say more about this in Müller [WWSü], section VI.
[13] The emphasis here is on "controversial", not on "values". As we'll see later, even in the sciences we have to presuppose certain values before we can start the scientific

enterprise. The point is that these values are not controversial among scientists. See section V, footnote 22.

[14] There was one exception: The interview of Milosevic to the American TV network CBS on April 22nd, 1999.

[15] See Kant [CoPR]:532 ff (A 642 ff / B 670 ff), particularly p. 533 (A 644 / B 672).

[16] The first half of my formulation is taken almost literally from Norman Kemp Smith's translation (Kant [CoPR]:543 (A 660 / B 688)); the second half is my attempt to assimilate Kant's principle to modern idiom. As our main point does not concern exegesis proper, I shall not elaborate on arguments in favor of my interpretation.

[17] See Kant [CoPR]:542 (A 657 / B 685).

[18] See Kant [CoPR]:535 (A 647 / B 675).

[19] This is a very special example of the perception of *aspects* which Wittgenstein was the first to philosophize about. See [PU]:518-533 (part II, section xi).

[20] Kant's expression, see [CoPR]:533 (A 644 / B 672).

[21] Duhem was one of the first philosophers who emphasized how crucial indeed criteria like these are in the development of the sciences. See [ASoP]:216-18 (chapter VI, §10). For a more recent discussion along similar lines, see Quine et al [WoB]:66-80.

[22] The values of simplicity, elegance, generality, exactness, and ontological economy are indispensable for the scientific enterprise; even there, then, the impression of *complete* objectivity rests on an illusion. For the sake of brevity, however, I shall continue to speak of "facts", "reality", "objectivity", and so forth, when I want to refer to respectable results from the sciences. This is less misleading than one might think, because with respect to objectivity there is still an important difference in degree between the scientific and the pacifistic enterprise. The values and imperatives which guide the scientist's scrutiny of reality are much less controversial than their counterparts on the pacifist's side. (Let me add a comment to philosophers who are defending what they call "moral realism": I do not intend here to make a decision against moral realism or against objectivity in ethics; rather my dialectical ambition is directed against those who believe in a strict science/ethics distinction and claim that ethical statements deserve less respect than scientific statements. I submit that the gap concerning objectivity between ethics and the sciences is far less serious than they claim. Since I do not see any reason as to why we should disrespect value-laden factuality, their opponents – including the moral realists – might welcome the observations from my discussion. By the way: Nothing what I am claiming in this paper is meant to preclude the very possibility of moral objectivity in areas where we are not concerned with war and peace. About this see my paper [FH]).

[23] See, for example, Loquai [KKiV]:56-67.

[24] See Wolf [K]. I shall say more about Cassandra's pessimism concerning atomic war in my paper [BB].

[25] In this paper I want to restrict attention to the danger of escalation to another world war because this is the worst danger I can think of. (I do not mean to indicate that the intervention in Kosovo did not carry the potential to any other escalation). By the way, not only pacifists were afraid of escalation to catastrophe. Even the conservative Minister President of Bavaria, Edmund Stoiber, referred to the danger of World War III when he warned the West against sending ground troops to Kosovo: "Der Einsatz

westlicher Bodentruppen würde zu einer Eskalation führen, die den dritten Weltkrieg heraufbeschwören könnte" (*Frankfurter Allgemeine Zeitung*, April 13th, 1999, p. 7).

[26] See, for example, the former German minister of defense, Rudolf Scharping, in [WDNW]:209.

[27] And to support her pessimism she will suggest to the optimist to study the transcripts of the presidential recordings of what the US-government was discussing, and risking, in the course of the Cuban Missile Crisis. (John F. Kennedy Library, Boston, President's Office Files, Presidential Recordings, Transcripts, Cuban Missile Crisis Meetings, October 27, 1962). These transcripts are partly published in Greiner [KK]:335-379, 383-391.

[28] I have tried to say more about the very function of this example in moral discourse, see Müller [WWSü], section IX.

[29] This paper includes in part considerations from my talk "Kosovo and Consequentialism, *or* How to Evaluate Humanitarian Interventions from a Non Consequentialist Perspective", presented at the Center for Interdisciplinary Research (ZiF), Bielefeld (Germany), on January 11th, 2002. (More considerations will follow under the title "Was wissen Sie über Kosovo? – Fallstudie über Pazifismus, Propaganda und die Verquickung von Fakten mit Werten" [WWSü]). I am grateful to Rüdiger Bittner, Dagmar Borchers, Uwe Czaniera, Anthony Ellis, Johan Galtung, Eckard Jantzen, Martina Herrmann, Dieter Lutz, Georg Meggle, Stephan Schlothfeldt, Thomas Schmidt, Matthias Schote, Rudolf Schüssler, Bojan Todosijevic, Sibylle Tönnies, Sylwia Trzaska, and Truls Wyller for criticism, discussion, and encouragement. Many thanks to Cynthia Myers, who helped me to improve the English of the text.

REFERENCES

Döring, Sabine / Mayer, Verena (eds.) [MG]: *Die Moralität der Gefühle*. (Berlin: Akademie-Verlag 2002. = *Deutsche Zeitschrift für Philosophie*. (Sonderband; 2002)).

Doetzer, Oliver / Motte, Jan (eds.) [G]: *Der Golfkrieg: Kalkül oder Kapitulation der Vernunft? Göttinger Positionen.* (Hannoversch Münden: Verlag in Volkmarshausen, 1992).

Duhem, Pierre [ASoP]: *The Aim and Structure of Physical Theory*. (Translated from the French by Philip P. Wiener. New York: Atheneum, 1962). [Appeared first 1954; first French edition appeared 1906].

Goodman, Nelson [FFF]: *Fact, Fiction, and Forecast*. (Cambridge / Mass.: Harvard University Press, fourth edition 1983). [Appeared first 1954].

Goodman, Nelson [PoCC]: "The Problem of Counterfactual Conditionals". In Goodman [FFF]:3-27. [Appeared first 1947].

Greiner, Bernd [KK]: *Kuba-Krise. 13 Tage im Oktober: Analysen, Dokumente, Zeitzeugen*. (Nördlingen: Greno, 1988).

Kant, Immanuel [CoPR]: *Critique of Pure Reason.* (Translated by Norman Kemp Smith. London: Macmillan, second impression 1933). [Appeared first 1929; the first German editions were published 1781 (A) and 1787 (B)].

Linsky, Leonard (ed.) [SPoL]: *Semantics and the Philosophy of Language*. (Urbana: University of Illinois Press, 1952).

Loquai, Heinz [KWiV]: *Der Kosovo-Konflikt – Wege in einen vermeidbaren Krieg. Die Zeit von Ende November 1997 bis März 1999.* (Baden-Baden: Nomos, 2000).

McDowell, John [AMRH]: "Are Moral Requirements Hypothetical Imperatives?" *Proceedings of the Aristotelian Society.* Supplementary Volume LII (1978), pp. 12-29.

Müller, Olaf [BB]: "Benign Blackmail. Cassandra's Plan, *or* What is Terrorism?" To appear in Georg Meggle (Ed.), *Ethics of Terrorism and Counter-Terrorism.* forthcoming.

Müller, Olaf [FH]: "Fühlen oder Hinsehen? Ein Plädoyer für moralische Beobachtungssätze". In Döring et al (eds.) [MG]:175-196.

Müller, Olaf [WWSü]: "Was wissen Sie über Kosovo? – Fallstudie über Pazifismus, Propaganda und die Verquickung von Fakten mit Werten". To appear in Georg Meggle (ed.) *Humanitäre Interventions-Moral. Was lehrt uns der Kosovo-Krieg?* (Paderborn: Mentis, 2004), pp. 53-90.

Müller, Olaf et al [LSGE]: "Lässt sich der Golfkrieg ethisch rechtfertigen? Erwiderung auf eine Rede von George Bush". (The final version of this paper was written in cooperation with Nelson Killius, Susanne Gahl, Marco Iorio, and Robert Castede). In Doetzer et al (eds.) [G]:37-44.

Murdoch, Iris [IoP]: "The Idea of Perfection". In Murdoch [SoG]:1-45.

Murdoch, Iris [SoG]: *The Sovereignty of Good.* (London: Routledge & Kegan Paul, 1970).

OSCE (ed.) [KKaS]: *Kosovo / Kosova as seen, as told. Part I (October 1998 to June 1999): The human rights findings of the OSCE Kosovo Verification Mission.* (http://www.osce.org/ kosovo/ documents/ reports/ hr/ part1/ p0cont.htm; visited on February 1st, 2002; a quotation such as "[KKaS]: Chapter 3, p. 8/16" refers to the 8th page (from 16 pages) in my printout, i.e., to a passage from the middle of the chapter in question.

Putnam, Hilary [CoFV]: *The Collapse of the Fact/Value Dichotomy.* (Cambridge / Mass.: Harvard University Press, 2002, Belnap Press 2004.

Putnam, Hilary [RP]: *Renewing Philosophy.* (Cambridge / Mass.: Harvard UP, 1992).

Putnam, Hilary [RTH]: *Reason, Truth and History.* (Cambridge: Cambridge UP, 1981).

Quine, Willard Van Orman [fLPo]: *From a Logical Point of View*. (Cambridge / Mass.: Harvard UP, second edition, revised, 1961). [Appeared first 1953].

Quine, Willard Van Orman [RM]: "Reference and Modality". In Quine [fLPo]:139-59.

Quine, Willard Van Orman / Ullian J.S. [WoB]: *The Web of Belief.* (New York: Random House, 2nd edition, 1978) [Appeared first 1970].

Scharping, Rudolf [WDNW]: *Wir dürfen nicht wegsehen. Der Kosovo-Krieg und Europa.* (München, Econ, aktualisierte Auflage 2001). [Appeared first 1999].

Volmer, Ludger [WBvP]: "Was bleibt vom Pazifismus. Die alten Feindbilder haben ausgedient / Warum militärische Mittel nicht ganz verzichtbar sind". *Frankfurter Rundschau* (7.1.2002), p. 6.

White, Morton G. [AS]: "The Analytic and the Synthetic: An Untenable Dualism". In Linsky (ed.) [SPoL]:272-286. [Appeared first 1950].

Williams, Bernard [ELoP]: *Ethics and the Limits of Philosophy.* (Cambridge / Mass.: Harvard University Press, 1985).

Wittgenstein, Ludwig [PU]: *Philosophische Untersuchungen.* In Wittgenstein [W]/1:225-618. [Appeared first 1953].

Wittgenstein, Ludwig [W]/1: *Werkausgabe Band 1.* (Frankfurt: Suhrkamp, 1984).

Wolf, Christa [K]: *Kassandra.* (Frankfurt / Main: Luchterhand, 1990).

UWE CZANIERA

How Far Shall We Go in Humanitarian Interventions?

[...] it still seems important to say of those
who die in war that they did not die in vain.
Michael Walzer

0 INTRODUCTION[1]

Many writers concerned with the ethical aspects of what is called "Humanitarian Intervention" focus on the question when – if ever – it is morally legitimate to *start* such an intervention. This paper addresses the opposite question – when the moment has come to *end* the operation. Of course, these two questions are closely interrelated. If you give an answer to the *first*, you also give an answer to the second (although, admittedly, a rather general one): Circumstances which gave rise to the intervention in the first place being removed, the aim of the intervention has to be conceived of as achieved and the operation should be stopped. If you answer the *second* question, you will have to mention certain circumstances *a*, *b*, *c* etc. whose attainment shall count as the morally legitimate conclusion of an intervention – in this case you hint that the lack of *a*, *b*, *c* etc. plays a role in the catalogue of criteria for its legitimate start. But two questions being interrelated does not mean that an exhaustive answer to the first does also provide an exhaustive answer to the second. It is therefore important to have a separate look at the criteria determining the right time to end a humanitarian intervention.

In what follows I will start with briefly *recalling the concept of humanitarian interventions*. I will then proceed by giving reasons for two convictions of mine, namely, that a) *there can be morally legitimate humanitarian interventions*, and b) *in this world, we will sometimes face occasions for launching them*. In determining the legitimate objectives of an intervention it is then advisable to *distinguish between overarching and specific objec-*

tives. Overarching objectives hold for every humanitarian intervention, whereas specific objectives can be regarded as adaptations of the overarching objectives to different kinds of intervention theatres. *Different kinds of theatres imply* (at least partially) *different legitimate objectives*. Unfortunately, all these kinds of theatres occurred in the world, and the story of their treatment testifies to the fact that it would have been no bad idea to spend some more effort on working out the aims and ends of humanitarian interventions.

1 HUMANITARIAN INTERVENTIONS: EXPLANATION AND JUSTIFICATION

1.1 Explanation

The concept of humanitarian interventions has already sufficiently been explained by others. Following Georg Meggle, I conceive of a humanitarian intervention as an *attempt to prevent or to intercept and end a certain process that harms beings capable of experiencing pain.*[2]

Such attempts may of course take on various forms – rescue operations to save people from volcanic eruptions, cases of neighbourhood emergency assistance (e. g. somebody rushing to help a fellow citizen threatened by a gang of youths) and even prayers. Usually, these examples are regarded as morally unproblematic.[3] You are free to pray or not to pray, and the villains are those who, without necessity, abstain from intervening for the benefit of the victims of volcano eruptions and youth violence.

In this paper I will confine myself to a subset of humanitarian interventions whose ethical assessment is usually regarded as being more problematic. These are the cases when the intervening agents are not merely providing help, but are themselves compelled to violate certain moral rules – through the use of force against some foreign person, group, organisation or state accused of having brought certain people into a condition that prompts nothing else but a humanitarian intervention.

1.2 Justification

Can such humanitarian interventions ever be morally legitimate? I think that they can. To be clear about this assumption, I do not pretend to have something like a proof of it. Moral convictions cannot be proven or turned into knowledge in some other way. So, if you do not agree with me on the possibility of morally legitimate humanitarian interventions, I will not be able to show that you have made a mistake in some serious epistemic sense. If it were possible to turn moral convictions into knowledge, moral problems would be much easier to solve (apart from the fact that we would presumably be much less interested in solving them). Assuming that it is not possible to attain moral knowledge, I am nevertheless convinced that an important principle of world policy should be that *those who commit large–scale crime against humanity must not get away with it.* So, humanitarian interventions may legitimately be started if…

a) *...they are aimed at preventing or intercepting and ending large–scale crime against humanity*; e. g. genocide, systematic massacre, mass rape, torture, mutilation, ethnic cleansing. Typically, such crimes are directed against certain religious or ethnic groups, and they are committed by organisations or groups that are somehow run, supported or at least tolerated by the government of the country where they are taking place. But this need not be the case. There could be a fairly tolerable newly established government that is merely still too weak to effectively demobilise some rival group devastating some region of the country.

b) *...there is no peaceful alternative that is likely to achieve the aim of the intervention at less expectable loss of life*. To conduct a humanitarian intervention means to wage war, and it should be clear that a peaceful and efficient alternative would be preferable. Such alternatives could consist of diplomatic pressure or economic sanctions.[4] They require a certain degree of vigilance on the side of the humanitarian–minded powers, since they are only likely to succeed if the crime has not yet started. *If* it has started, it is usually too late for peaceful alternatives: While the perpetrator's receptivity for diplomacy and sanctions is likely to decrease, the victims cannot wait. Note, however, that betting on the peaceful alternative is not *in principle* better than waging war. Wars are awful because of the suffering they lead to, but it may happen that a peaceful alternative causes even more suffering. In this case it should be chosen to intervene.

c) *...the humanitarian intervention is designed so as to achieve its aim with the least possible damage* to the intervening forces, the intervention's target and uninvolved parties. It seems fairly clear

> what is meant by "least possible damage": strike surgical, if possible; be considerate towards your POWs etc. Another point concerns the behaviour of the soldiers carrying out the intervention: Most of them will be no choir–boys, and they are likely to get exposed to situations where even the friendlier individuals might turn savage. It should therefore be ensured that the persons involved in a humanitarian intervention are held liable to international jurisdiction. It is less clear what is meant by the phrase "achieve its aim" and how this relates to what has to count as "least possible damage". I will address this question in section 2. Whether the design of an intervention meets condition c) or not has to be assessed in the light of the best available evidence. Therefore the ultimate judgement about whether or not condition c) is met can only be given *ex post*.

It is perhaps worth mentioning that the fulfilment of condition c) amounts to the fact that if a humanitarian intervention is justified, it is going to be a successful military operation (to be spoilt only by incompetence). Otherwise it simply could not be designed "so as to achieve its aim". Condition c) expresses the idea that a humanitarian intervention has to be an *efficient* device to end crimes such as those mentioned in a), and it seems clear that it will *not* be efficient if it is directed against some very strong or even superior military power.[5] Therefore it is no contradiction if one says, on the one hand, that one should launch an attack on Serbia, but, on the other hand, refrains from intervening in China. If you attack China, you are rather going to start the 3rd World War than to restore Tibet (which is of course no excuse for the current western policy of not even criticising China).

At this point, several criticisms will seem appropriate. Let me therefore give some counterarguments in advance.

Risk for soldiers: Whether humanitarian intervention wars are confined to militarily inferior enemies or not, the intervening soldiers are put to the risk of loosing their lives. Can this be morally justified? We seem to face a tragic choice here, since we either accept the risk for the soldiers or the death of the victims of terror. But we should not exaggerate: If the intervening soldiers have joined their army voluntarily and if they are well prepared, then to put them at risk is the better choice. If we contrast the *concrete* harm done to a defenceless people by murder, mutilation, torture etc.

with the *risk* for the soldiers of a well–prepared army fighting an inferior enemy, we should vote for putting the soldiers at risk.

Unavoidability of evil: It is clear that we would all be better off if it were never necessary to conduct a humanitarian intervention. But in the world *we* live in, we should be prepared to face atrocities that allow for only one answer – to wage war against them. There is of course a number of peaceful measures that might be brought to bear if a considerable deterioration of the human rights situation arises in some country. But it is not to be expected that these measures will always be implemented at the right moment. This is due to two properties of the *conditio humana*:

1. *Power radiates a certain temptation.* There will always be people who ruthlessly pursue the aim of gaining a most pervasive control of some region, its people and its resources. This fact can hardly be overlooked. It would seem at least ridiculous to base world policy on the assumption that nobody has an incentive to become like Adolf Hitler, Josef Stalin, Pol Pot, Idi Amin, or, to name some criminals less monstrous, Somali warlord Mohamed Farah Aideed, Rwandan rebel leader Foday Sankoh and Liberian president Charles Taylor.

2. *Reluctance is comfortable.* The beginnings of humanitarian catastrophes tend to be moderate. An attentive spectator will notice that some disaster is brewing, but she is likely to be regarded as irksome Jeremiah. This is understandable. The wrongfulness is at first not very spectacular, whereas the effort to provide a remedy would be quite tangible. It need not be very great, but it is the transition from zero effort to a certain positive amount where one has to force oneself in the highest degree. It is therefore not improbable that the period of time during which peaceful measures would be appropriate simply passes unused. Potential helpers remain passive until the crime has reached dimensions that can no longer be ignored – and then the peaceful measures are likely to be of no use anymore.

One may also think of global institutions that prevent such developments. But at present it still seems advisable to think about appropriate behaviour in a world where we have *no* such institutions.

Opacity of intentions and consequences: Another objection to the legitimacy of humanitarian interventions refers to the risks incurred by waging war. How can it be prevented that humanitarian interventions degenerate into an instrument of political power. And even if it can be prevented, doubts remain: Wars are enterprises of the utmost complexity. No–one really knows what is going on. Available information is not only scarce, but also likely to have been filtered according to the strategic interests of the conflicting parties. Nothing can guarantee that the intervening forces do not actually *worsen* the situation. They may lack not only the good intentions, but also the requisite information (resulting in bad organisation and then disaster). In the end, the intervention might have brought more harm into the world than it has removed. One might even suspect that it is simply *impossible* to acquire the knowledge necessary to conduct a truly successful humanitarian intervention. Should we not therefore confine ourselves to a policy of strict military abstinence?[6]

I cannot find such a kind of radical pacifism convincing. Again, if we contrast the *concrete* harm done to a defenceless people by murder, mutilation, torture etc. with the *possibility* of humanitarian interventions being misused for power politics, we should vote for ending the crime. An army efficiently preventing genocide in Rwanda in 1994 would have been preferable to the killings even if its country had thereby gained a powerful position in Rwanda. Beyond that, it seems altogether possible to acquire the knowledge that is necessary for the intervening agents to be successful. If we look, for example, at the studies provided by the *International Crisis Group*,[7] we find detailed and reliable accounts of the state of affairs in problematic regions of this world that could surely provide a reasonable basis for intervention war policy. These studies provide long–term coverage of the particular conflicts, and they are hardly to be suspected of partiality or superficiality. Therefore I think that this objection is not sound. It is certainly right to point out that the intervening agents should know as much as possible about the state of affairs in the intervention theatre. But that does not mean that they cannot acquire *sufficient* knowledge about it. We should rather read this argument as a call for paying more attention to the problematic regions of the world.

The real shame: Finally, it should be remarked that the humanitarian failures of Somalia, Rwanda and Sierra Leone (to name but a few) are not to be traced back to bad intentions or lacking information. What was lacking was *resolution*. Look, for example, at the UN mission for Rwanda (UNAMIR). Why did it fail? It failed because UNAMIR was not sufficiently backed by political and military resolution. It was poorly equipped and its whole design was much *too peaceable*.[8] The same holds for Somalia, where the UN went into grotesque cooperative relations with criminal warlords like General Aideed. On the other hand, the relative peace that has been achieved in Sierra Leone seems to have been made possible mainly by the *use of force* against the *Revolutionary United Front* (RUF).

I therefore propose the following procedure: If we have made the mistake of valuing "reluctance today" higher than "peace tomorrow" (conditions a) – c) are met), a humanitarian intervention may legitimately be started. *If* such an intervention is started, the intervening forces should act *resolutely*. It is a mistake to remain passive when the human rights situation in another country starts to deteriorate. It would be a parallel mistake if an intervention is designed so unobtrusively as to avoid any losses, since it is then likely that the whole enterprise fails. Acting that way amounts to choosing tomorrow's greater tragedy because it is today's more comfortable option.

Now, to assess whether an agent acts "resolutely" or not does obviously require a certain conception of what it would mean to "fulfil the mission". This is the question we are now going to address.

2 HUMANITARIAN INTERVENTIONS: OVERARCHING AND SPECIFIC OBJECTIVES

2.1 Overarching Objectives

In the introduction I distinguished between *overarching* and *specific* objectives; overarching ones holding for *every* humanitarian intervention, specific ones being their *adaptations* to different kinds of intervention theatres. Knowing these objectives is crucial for the evaluation of a humanitarian intervention both *ex ante* and *ex post*: Its legitimacy *ex ante* depends on the situation it responds to and its being *designed* in accordance with the objectives. Its legitimacy *ex post* has to be assessed by recording whether and how the objectives have been *achieved*.[9]

Which items belong to the overarching objectives (OO_i) every humanitarian intervention has to strive for? The first has already been mentioned at the beginning of 1.2:

OO_1: Prevention or interception and ending of large–scale crime against humanity; e.g. genocide, systematic massacre, mass rape, torture, mutilation, ethnic cleansing.

Achieving OO_1 may not be easy, but is not sufficient for the intervention to be legitimate *ex post*. If the intervening forces leave and the crime flares up again (perhaps, as has happened in the Kosovo, with the former victims as new offenders and vice versa), the intervention has stopped too early. We have to aim for...

OO_2: Termination of the crime has to be lasting (without a lasting presence of the intervention forces being necessary).

If OO_2 is not achieved, the intervention cannot be counted as legitimate *ex post*, although it may have been legitimate *ex ante*.[10] But even achieving OO_2 is not enough. Usually, the conflicts that legitimately prompt humanitarian interventions are marked by a multitude of interwoven interests. The group of the offenders as well as the group of the victims have presumably played a number of functional roles in the troubled country. At least to a certain degree, their ability to fulfil these roles is going to decrease, thereby generating a vacuum of power. This in turn might provide an incentive for predatory neighbours to rush in and attempt to seize control over what they deem valuable, thereby further destabilising the region.[11] Prevention of such destabilisation is the third overarching aim each humanitarian intervention should strive for:

OO_3: The period following the intervention must not induce a decay of peace and stability in the affected region.

OO_1–OO_3 specify states of affairs that may be approached via *different* routes. Here we may call on the minimum damage clause of 1.2 c) as a kind of *procedural* objective that holds for the manner in which OO_1–OO_3 are achieved. These objectives have to be kept in mind by the intervening powers from the very beginning of the planning phase. However, due to their overarching nature these objectives are formulated in a rather *general* way. It would therefore be welcome to have a more detailed account if one wants to know when the moment has to come to end an intervention. In the remainder I will try to put some more flesh on this skeleton of objectives.

2.2 Specific Objectives

Sketching more specific objectives of humanitarian interventions means adapting the overarching objectives to the possible states of affairs in the intervention theatres. We may distinguish between three different kinds of intervention theatres:

1. Crimes against humanity are not supported by the government of the country where they are committed. The government is not to be made responsible for the crimes except in the sense that it is too weak to hold the offenders in check. The case of the Kabbah administration in Sierra Leone provides an example: Tejan Ahmed Kabbah became president of Sierra Leone in a peaceful democratic election in 1996. But he did not manage to crush Foday Sankoh's RUF, a destructive movement of neither credibility nor legitimacy that is responsible for vast atrocities, among them an invasion of Sierra Leone's capital, Freetown, in January 1999 during which thousands of people were killed, mutilated and abducted. Although there is no reason to admire the Kabbah administration, it is surely to be conceived of as legitimate.
   Call this the Non–governmental Terror Intervention Theatre (NoGoTIT).

2. Crimes against humanity are supported or organised by the government of the country where they are committed. The government is to be made responsible for the crimes. The case of the Rwandan genocide in 1994 provides an example: The extremist members of the Hutu government did not live up to the terms of a power–sharing agreement with moderate Hutu politicians and the Tutsi minority. Local militias were armed and trained while at the same time all the Tutsi in Rwanda's capital Kigali were registered. When Rwandan President Habyarimana's plane was shot down on April 6, 1994, a systematic genocide started that has obviously been planned in advance. About 800.000 Tutsi and politically moderate Hutu were killed. UNAMIR did virtually nothing to contain the massacre.
   Call this the Political Terror Intervention Theatre (PoTIT).

3. Crimes against humanity are committed in a country where a central political power has ceased to exist. Various competing war-

lords and their militias are to be made responsible for the crimes. The stock example is, of course, the case of Somalia. Ethiopia and Somalia had been chosen as the theatre of a proxy war between the USSR and the USA, with Somalia's dictator Siad Barre propped up by the USA. Siad Barre subverted the traditional clan system and caused a decay of social values in Somalia. After he was overthrown in 1991, several militias, with General Aideed as one of their most prominent leaders, struggled for power and devastated the country. In 1992, a multinational intervention opened relief–supply routes and saved many lives. But since it failed to restore a political order to Somalia, it is now unanimously regarded as futile.
Call this the Chaos Intervention Theatre (CIT).

One could distinguish further subclasses of intervention theatres (e.g., by considering the political situation in neighbouring countries or the territory's suitability for guerrilla warfare), but for the present purposes it is sufficient to limit the classification to the aforementioned three kinds. What specific objectives should we strive for to achieve the overarching objectives of humanitarian interventions in these different kinds of intervention theatres?[12] I will start with some proposals for each kind of intervention theatre, and I will conclude with some general remarks on the importance of keeping these objectives in mind.

NoGoTIT Interventions: From the ethical point of view, the first kind of intervention theatre is perhaps the easiest case. Although the intervening forces will have to transgress the boundaries of a foreign state, and although they might get involved in serious combat situations, their mission is not war but more or less a kind of police help: It is not another *state* that is attacked but a certain *group* operating on the territory of that state and violating its law. Before the intervention actually starts, a last chance should be given to the lower–rank members of the criminal organisation – demobilisation in exchange for re–integration programs returning the former fighters to civilian life. Insofar as this offer is greeted with refusal, intervening forces should strive for...

...military defeat of the criminal organisation,
...collapse of its support from foreign powers (e. g., by imposing economic sanctions on them),
...disarmament and demobilisation of the criminal organisation,

...consolidating and fostering the economical and political structure of the country in a way that prevents revival of criminal organisations. It might be appropriate to hold new elections. In any case, UN–monitored efforts should be made that lead to...

...re–integration of lower–rank members of the criminal organisation into civil society,

...instigators of violence and key figures of the criminal organisation being put to trial,

...establishment of a kind of "Truth and Reconciliation Commission" that seeks "to produce a degree of healing between those who have committed crimes at a lower level, and their victims".[13]

CIT Interventions: It is much more complicated to determine the specific objectives for CIT cases. Adapting the requirement of resolution to CITs demands a serious commitment to flexibility. This is due to the much more complex situation. Neither are you going to have a clear picture of your enemy nor are you going to know whom to rely on. The enterprise will hardly turn out successful if you have not accumulated the maximum possible information about the CIT state of affairs. The intervening forces could easily cause a prolongation of the conflict by overestimating their capability of installing a peaceful state:

> "Desperate to put its seal on some kind of agreement, the UN has pinned its hopes on the warlords, failing to understand that their interests are served by prolonging the conflict. Worse, the UN is providing incentive for them to keep fighting. In the most violently contested areas, the UN's presence means jobs, contracts and money. The UN rents houses, hires trucks and issues millions of dollars in contracts and subcontracts to businessmen with close ties to the warlords. In addition, for two months some of the fiercest battles in Mogadishu have been around the airport as clan militias jockey to control the corridors through which the UN–imported food and equipment pass. Without the UN and those goods, the road wouldn't be worth fighting over. In contrast, areas without a UN presence have been relatively peaceful."[14]

To prevent outcomes like these, CIT interventions should be confined to a rather small range of specific objectives (although it will be difficult enough to attain them). Intervening forces should not strive for more than...

...opening and securing relief–supply for people in need of food, shelter and medical care,

...providing basic judicial functions (this might include measures like militia disarmament) until a group of persons has emerged that has sufficient authority[15] and popularity with the local people so that it can be handed over the task of restoring the country.

The restoration process should, of course, be supported by the UN; but to the degree that it makes headway, UN support should decrease.

PoTIT Interventions: PoTITs are usually regarded as providing the "classic" case of intervention wars. Since they exhibit the closest resemblance to non–intervention wars, this is hardly surprising. In contrast to CITs, a careful analysis of the situation should yield a reliable profile of perpetrators and victims. Now, if peaceful efforts to stop the crime have proven fruitless, how are the overarching objectives of humanitarian interventions best served in PoTIT cases? At least in my view, intervening forces should...

...fight the perpetrators until the crime has been stopped. Depending on the moment the attacked government is forced to refrain from committing further crimes, we may distinguish two main courses:

1. The attacked government succumbs relatively soon. In a certain sense, this is the more desirable case. Fighting may stop. The intervention forces should then establish a monitoring system that secures a lasting prevention of the crime's flaring up again in the future. As Michael Walzer has pointed out, a policy of "unconditional surrender" should only be pursued against enemies like the Third Reich.[16] Admittedly, this will lead to an unfriendly regime being left in office, but bringing about friendly conditions is not the task of humanitarian interventions.

2. The attacked government does not surrender until its ultimate defeat. This is certainly the worst case, and we must hope that the military superiority of the intervening forces (condition c) in 1.2) brings about this defeat without devastating the country. A period of occupation will be unavoidable, which should be used to

strengthen local democratic powers until they have gained enough authority so that they may take on the task of restoring the country. In any case, the installation of a puppet regime should be avoided.

Although this might cause some disagreement, I would even in PoTIT cases suggest that humanitarian interventions should be carried out by ground troops (after air sovereignty has been achieved). Deploying ground troops provides the most accurate opportunity to bring an end to the PoTIT atrocities. The deployment of ground troops allows for a minimum of non–combatant casualties. Beyond that, deploying ground troops makes it possible to leave the civilian economic structure of the country as far as possible intact. This might contribute to a fairly low degree of hostility on the side of the peaceable part of the invaded country's population. Moreover, this way facilitates the preparation of cooperative economical incentives which are likely to be necessary for the re–integration of the country into the peaceable part of the community of states.

3 CONCLUSION

Many of the aforementioned points may seem trivial, but they are not. The record of humanitarian interventions is bristling with failures to achieve the outlined objectives. In a sense, this is understandable: No country is very keen on putting its soldiers at risk, especially when it is not the country's own security that is at stake. One seems to think that if one takes the risk of going in, one may at least go out as soon as possible. Instead of being suspicious and vigilant until a stable peace is secured, those in charge of leading the intervention act with remarkable gullibility. Why? Because they *want* to think that the operation has been brought to a successful end and everybody may return home. These are the moments when the fox is set to keep the geese. Extensive amnesties for crimes of all kinds and appointments of rebel leaders as vice presidents (as has happened in Sierra Leone) will hardly turn out to be appropriate devices to secure peace and stability in intervention theatres. If the intervention powers are not *resolutely* inclined to head for the outlined objectives (at least in a reasonably modified version of our list), they should better stay at home, since otherwise we would have to say of those who die in war that they died in vain.

NOTES

[1] I am greatly indebted to the participants of the January 2002 ZiF conference "Humanitarian Interventions./.Ethics" in Bielefeld whose talks and discussions were most inspiring for me. My special thanks go to Georg Meggle and Matthias Hild.

[2] See §§ 2.1–2.5 of Georg Meggle's contribution to this volume. Usually, aiming at deliverance of human beings is regarded as rendering an intervention humanitarian. I would rather like to talk of "*sentient* beings" because I think that we should not rule out the possibility of humanitarian interventions for the benefit of non–humans; at least not on merely conceptual grounds.

[3] Of course, one might question the legitimacy of prayers if it is at the same time possible to provide help in a more tangible sense. I will not discuss this problem further.

[4] Being a peaceful alternative does not mean being unproblematic. Economic sanctions may miss their aim of preventing crimes against humanity, but may lead to a lasting destabilisation of a country's economy even *after* a humanitarian intervention has successfully taken place and the sanctions have been lifted. For some intelligent ideas concerning the peaceful prevention of crimes against humanity see Pogge 2001.

[5] Should I have recommended appeasement policy towards the Third Reich? No. I am convinced that it was right to declare war on Germany despite her being a superior military power in September 1939. This poses no problem for me since I would not regard the start of World War II as a case of humanitarian intervention.

[6] For a carefully developed version of this argument see Olaf Müller's contribution to this volume.

[7] See http://www.crisisweb.org; of course, a certain inclination to western political culture on the part of ICG can hardly be overlooked. But that does not diminish its reports' reliability.

[8] See Carlsson et al. 1999 and Power 2001.

[9] Some readers are likely to see my list of overarching objectives as incomplete. They may miss certain items, e.g. furthering a democratic world order, non–deterioration of the legal relationship between the states, deterrence effects on other potential offenders against human rights or the prevention of power policy on the pretext of humanity. I did not include these objectives in my list because I think that their achievement is certainly *desirable*, but *not necessary* for an intervention to count as legitimate.

[10] It is not really clear what is meant by "lasting" in this context. We would certainly demand too much if we said that the termination of the crime has to last *forever*. Perhaps what we need here is a clear description of the conflict the intervention addresses. We could then give a clear picture of what it would mean to *end this* conflict. If that state of affairs has been reached, we may say that OO_2 has been achieved. A later conflict has then to be conceived of as a *new* one, and the intervention in question cannot be blamed for this new conflict.

[11] Think of Liberian president Charles Taylor and the diamond deposits in neighbouring Sierra Leone. The example, however, does not work perfectly, since Taylor was actually fuelling the conflict in Sierra Leone, not just reacting to it.

[12] Since every single intervention theatre will show its own specific characteristics, it is impossible to figure out every aspect of an intervention in advance. Adapting the specific objectives to the real world is the task of politicians, strategists and commanders.
[13] International Crisis Group 2001a, p. 26.
[14] Maren 1994, p. 1f.
[15] The authority in question should, of course, not be based on superior strength and brutality.
[16] See Walzer 1977, p. 111ff.

REFERENCES

Carlsson, I. et al. (1999): "Bericht der Unabhängigen Untersuchungskommission vom 15. Dezember 1999 zum Verhalten der Vereinten Nationen während des Völkermords in Ruanda 1994"; in: *Blätter für deutsche und internationale Politik* 02/2000.

Finnegan, W. (1995): "A World of Dust"; in: *The New Yorker* March 20/1995.

International Crisis Group (2001a): "Sierra Leone: Time for a New Military and Political Strategy"; *ICG Africa Report* N° 28, Freetown/London/Brussels 11 April 2001.

— (2001b): "'Consensual Democracy' in Post–Genocide Rwanda. Evaluating the March 2001 District Elections"; *ICG Africa Report* N° 34, Nairobi/Brussels 09 October 2001.

— (2001c): "Sierra Leone: Managing Uncertainty"; *ICG Africa Report* N° 35, Freetown/London/Brussels 24 October 2001.

Maren, M. (1994): "Leave Somalia Alone"; in: *The New York Times* July 6/1994.

Parmelee, J. (1993): "Waltzing with Warlords. Will the West Make Martyrs of Thugs in Somalia?"; in: *The Washington Post* June 20/1993.

Pogge, Th. (2001): "Preempting Humanitarian Interventions"; in: Carter, I./Ricciardi, M. (eds.), *Freedom, Power and Political Morality. Essays for Felix Oppenheim*; London: Palgrave.

Power, S. (2001): "Bystanders to Genocide. Why the United States let the Rwandan Tragedy Happen"; in: *Atlantic Monthly* 09/2001.

Walzer, M. (1977): *Just and Unjust Wars*; New York: Basic Books ^{3}2000.

MARTIN FRANK

The Dilemmatic Structure of Humanitarian Interventions

1. NARROW CONCEPT OF HUMANITARIAN INTERVENTION

Humanitarian Intervention is an often used concept with a range of different meanings. It is therefore advisable to start with a definition which is widely accepted and useful for the purposses of this essay. Humanitarian Intervention is here seen as an intervention in the internal political affairs of another state with (military) force against the will of the government of that state for reasons of stopping gross human rights violations. This is not the only conception one can formulate, but with this conception the central normative problems of humanitarian intervention will become visible.

The main elements of this definition should briefly be explicated. First, the intervention consists of state action. The intervening party or parties are states and not private actors. Foreign governments may decide to support overtly or tacitly non-governmental powers in a civil war, but this does not count as an intervention in the defined sense. Second, not every actions of governments towards other governments should be regarded as interventions. The exchange of diplomatic notes or the criticism of political affairs in other states by state officials, for example, should not plausibly be seen as interventions in the strong and problematic sense. They should rather be interpreted as interferences which belong to the normal national and international administrative affairs.[1] The concerned government is not forced to believe or do something or to react in some way. Mostly, governments do not like this and say that one should not interfere with their internal affairs. Therefore, coercive state action is taken as a necessary condition of interventions. Third, in the case of coercive foreign action, governments will resist or try to resist that force.[2] In most cases the concerned goverments do not regard the foreign power as legitimized to that action, they do not approve of the effects of that action, and even if they see them as rather beneficial they will disapprove of the involved paternalism. Forth, for the coercive character of the action and the anticipated resistence the intervention is normally conducted by military forces.[3] The purpose of stopping human rights violations (mass killings, rapes or expulsions) provides a further reason for armed actions. It is essential to keep in mind that humanitarian interventions are not identified with war. For even if the military forces are the main intervening actors they need not be involved in armed combats. There may be no shooting or killing from the intervening side, since in some cases the mere presence of other forces is sufficient to stop the human rights violations. In other cases, armed forces are merely accompanying and securing technical or humanitarian stuff. Furthermore, the central problem of humanitarian interventions, which is the main topic of this essay, is not that combats and killings does occur in the course of the intervention. For humanitarian interventions are regarded as normatively problematic even if no deaths and human rights violations have to be deplored. Fifth, the reason for action must be mainly humanitarian. This humanitarian concern is here explicated as the stopping of human rights violations the amount and urgency of which justifies such extensive international action. This violations may be state-sponsered or government-approved. They may also be committed by private actors. But even then the state officials are responsible insofar as they missed their obligations to prevent harm from their citizens. Concerning the motivation of the intervening party, it would be too strong and unrealistic to require pure humanitarian motives. For the decision to intervene is a political one in which various interest have to be considered, there will almost always be a situation of mixed motives, so that the humanitarian reason is only one among many others. In principle, nothing is necessarily wrong with mixed motives as long as the motivation to help plays a salient role. What should be worried about, is the situation in which the humanitarian motive is but a marginal one.[4]

In order to distinguish humanitarian interventions from other kinds of international action for humanitarian reasons, one can produce a four-box matrix using two questions: Is military force involved or not? And is the intervention requested from the concerned goverment or not?

		requested +	requested –
military force	+	military support	intervention
military force	–	humanitarian help	sanctions

The matrix is a very rough one. Since the boundaries are usually blurred, there will always be actual cases and types of action that does not fit easily with the established criteria. But the distinctions are justified, as always, to the extent that clear cases could in principle be identified. If a government asks for military support of another state in order to fight an internal rebellion or an external enemy, it could mean the request for foreign troops or merely of weapons and equipment. Insofar as it is asked for, it does not fit the proposed definition of intervention. Peace keeping actions of third parties that are enacted by military forces also belong to this category. The line is transgressed if the foreign state provides weapons or funding for their acquisition for a rebellious group against the will of the government. This will clearly count as a case of interference in the internal affairs of another state, but insofar as the foreign government does not itself and directly take action within the other state, one should be reluctant to call it intervention. This further step towards the second box is done, if foreign troop transgress the borders of the other state against the will of the government of that state, for example to help a prosecuted minority. Here one form of boundary blurring is the difficult to establish small line between free request and pressed help and the mere factual impossibility of resist. Such cases as faked request (or ex post request), as e.g. was delivered by some Kuwait officials to justify the Iraqi invasion, will be excluded here.

Requested humanitarian help consist mainly of provision of food, medicine, tents and other infrastructural facilities. In the case of natural catastrophies, famines and extensive destructions through civil war most affected states ask for international help. In rare instances, such as Northern Corea, no support is requested. But since humanitarian help is expensive, there are almost no cases of pressed help against the will of the concerned government. In the paradigm examples no military forces are involved and necessary. So humanitarian help is in both criteria the opposite of humanitarian intervention. But the blurring can be exemplified by the Somalian case. While the humanitarian help was asked for or at least appreciated by the remaining officials and war lords, the later necessary securing of stuff and material through military forces was fiercly resisted. So what started as a humanitarian help action ended as the retreat from an military intervention.[5]

The distinction between interventions and sanctions is the most difficult one. Sanctions are one-sided imposed external action with the aim of motivating changes in the behavior of the concerned government. This can take the form of an embargo on certain goods, the blocking of bank accounts and monetary transfers, the prohibition of international air traffic or the exclusion from international institutions and contracts. All of this need not involve action that transgresses the borders to the affected state. Sanctions are almost always seen as negative goods and are therefore not asked for or appriciated by the target state. As limitations to the range of state actions sanctions typically are interferences with the internal affairs of other states, notwithstanding. But insofar as no transgression and military forces are directly involved, they should be distinguished from interventions. But sanctions can also be enforced with military means. Battle ships cruising in international sea, for example, can help to secure a boycott on oil exports. As a next step, foreign air forces can ensure a no-flight area within the territory of that state. This boundary thus is blurred insofar as the situation displays elements of both concepts. For it is resisted and disapproved of and military forces are playing some part, it resembles an intervention. And to the extent it is not intended directly to stop human rights violations but to give incentives, it also shows the indirect characteristic of sanctions.

2. BACKGROUND OF HUMANITARIAN INTERVENTIONS

Humanitarian intervention is a political notion that has its origins and meaning in the Westphalian system of plural states. With the establishment of the concept of state sovereignty there starts the discussion of its limits. The Westphalian state system is historically and conceptually a complicatd matter.[6] For the purposes of this essay, one can concentrate on the following key elements. First, the state system is primarily concerned with the external sovereignty of political communities. It starts from the concept of political independence and asks for the possible co-existence and relations of a plurality of externally independent states. Second, the main presupposition of at least co-existence is the mutual respect of their sovereignty. This implies, thirdly, the recognition of their equal status as parties within the system (equality). For states in fact are stratified according to political power, economic ability, size and prestige, the equality refers to their ascribed legal status. And it also implies, forth, the mutual assurance of non-interference with their internal political affairs (the doctrine of non-intervention). The equality condition points, fifth, to the anarchical character of the whole system, for it asserts that there is no legal hierarchy among states. That is, there is no authoritative force without the consent of the parties. Thus, the states retain their ultimate sovereignty in all international matters. In this context, the doctrine of non-intervention means the absence of juridical relations among states. No independent state is allowed to punish any other, and there are no punitive expeditions.[7] Sixth, while the state system is anarchical, it is not anomic. International law is an element of the Westphalian system, partly because it is agreed upon by the state parties, and partly because the mentioned features of the system as such function as procedural rules for international relations and the creation of new international law.

The corallary of the dependency on the Westphalian system is that the end of the state system will render the concept of humanitarian intervention meaningless. If there is no plurality of equally sovereign states, there will also be no cases of humanitarian interventions. It is not that humanitarian atrocities cannot occur, on the contrary they very likely will always happen. But it is interventions in other states which will be resisted on grounds of autonomy and sovereignty, that then cannot arise for conceptual reasons. The end of the Westphalian system in principle could come about in two ways. One the one hand, the currently existing states could loose its independence and thus their right to non-intervention on grounds of sovereignty. This is the case of a world state in which the formerly independent states are merely federative units without any international competences. On the other hand, the anarchical character of the system could change, and the now partially independent states could create a supra-national institution with the authority of "intervention". It may be some quasi-juridical agency in which the member states can be represented.[8] So the "intervention" will not be decided and enacted by other states. The quotation marks are used to indicate that the member states could no longer withstand the external stopping of human rights violations within their territory enacted by this agency refering to supposed rights of state independence and sovereignty. But since the member states will still have an equal status and partial independence, they will of course retain a right to non-intervention among them.

3. DILEMMATIC STRUCTURE

At the basis of every humanitarian intervention there is a constitutive dilemma. It originates from certain principles of the state system that pull sometimes in different directions. The dilemma is also entailed in the very expression of the concept: it is inter-vention and at the same time justified for humanitarian reasons. The opposing principles can be expressed in political, legal or moral terms. The claims of sovereignty stand against international duties. In international public law the prohibition of intervention stands against the declared norms of human rights.[9] And the principle of collective self-determination stands against the moral rights of individual human beings.

These are very rough and abstract formulations of the relevant principles. For the concepts admit of a considerable range of meanings there is no necessity of conflict involved. The term can be interpreted in such a way as to allow a certain reconciliation. Thus, it is sometimes argued that the consistency with recognized human rights is a condition of legitimacy for a reasonable concept of sovereignty. In this case, sovereignty cannot come into conflict with the claims of human rights. For in instances of state-sponsored or state-tolerated human right violations the government will loose its legitimacy and thus its rights of sovereignty. This argument is most plausible from the point of view of the victims of human rights violations and for the subject of internal sovereignty.[10] From the point of view of the concerned government other forms of reconciliation are possible. As indicated, the government can ask for foreign support and thus waive its right to non-intervention. Since non-intervention is a right, the government is free to cut it back or to reinterpret it in a more cooperative way. By contrast, the intervening party or parties cannot do this. From their perspective the dilemma is unavoidable and irreconcilable. When the intervention is started, it is normally clear for the intervening party that government of the target state has rejected the criticisms and offers, blocked interferences, refused mediation and threatened violent reaction. That is, the intervening parties do typically know, that they have to break the rule of non-intervention which they usually are prepared to respect.[11]

The dilemma asserts that both principles are valid and relevant, neither could be reduced or simply neglected. If the above account is sound, the intervening party would commit a political, legal and moral mistake, if it plainly discounts one principle. So what is asked for in considering humanitarian interventions is to weigh up the principles in the concrete situation and reach a certain balance or trade-off.

The dilemmatic structure helps to explain what is normatively problematic with humanitarian interventions. In this context, the question was raises whether the term "dilemma" is the appropriate one for this predicament.[12] For the term is misleading insofar as it hints at irreconcilability, the term "conflict" should be uses instead. Concerning the semantic issue, the difference could not be seen as a hard and fast one. Dilemmas are understood here as special cases of conflicts in general. While conflicts of interest, for example, mean the simultaneous confrontation of opposing interests or motives which cannot be satisfied at once, a dilemma additionally requires that both contradictory options are evils. The most simple definition of a dilemma is the choice between two evils. So whatever the party considering intervention does, intervening or refraining, it is caught in the trap of violation one of the two principles. And this unavoidability is an essential element of the classical dilemma concept. Concerning the irreconcilability topic, one should pay attention to the relevant perspective. The intervening party cannot unilaterally reinterpret the concept of sovereignty so as to fit the intervention purposes. As will described below, the common reinterpretation argues against an absolute, non-overridable conception of sovereignty and for an limited understanding. And in looking at the attitudes of the intervening parties in the course of an intervention, they typically do not assume that what they are doing is helping the victims of human rights violations simpliciter, but also overriding and breaking the rule of non-intervention. They do not think that the principle is not valid (in principle or in this case), but that they have sufficient reason to override it. Arguing for a humanitarian intervention is normally arguing within this dilemmatic structure.

4. DILEMMATIC CONTINUUM

The dilemmatic account allows for different attitudes towards humanitarian intervention, depending on the associated meanings and evaluations of the concerned principles. These attitudes – exemption, right, duty – can be placed on a continuum that extends between the extrem positions of outright general rejection (state fetishism) and outright general requirement (global domestic politics). But only the three mentioned attitudes lie on the d-interval for which the dilemmatic structure is constitutive. So the d-interval reaches from a more defensive to a more active estimation of humanitarian intervention.

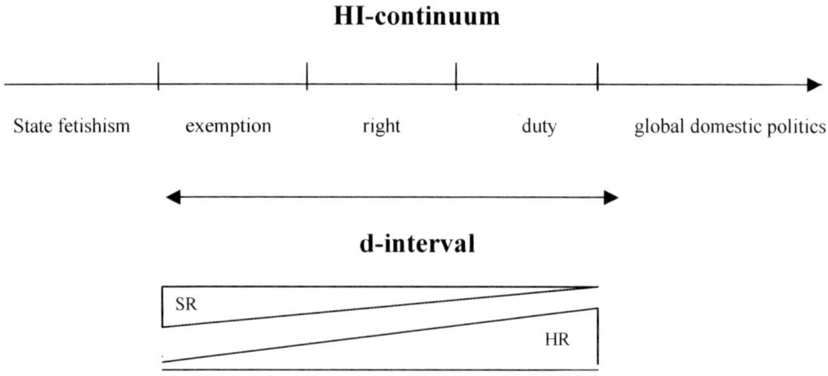

The exemption position lies on the defensive end of the interval. The principles of state rights are thought to be dominant. It considers humanitarian intervention as generally forbidden and only in very rare cases tolerable, but not as a general rule. Towards the left end of that segment the tendecy will increase not to interpret the very few cases of justified interventions as precedents for future actions. They rather should be viewed as specific and singular exceptions of a rule. The instances are then understood as extraodinary situations in international law. But as long es they remain within the segment the exemptions are justified on humanitarian grounds. Moving even further to the left side, the few cases of externally stopping human rights violations may still occur, even though their likelihood will decrease significantly, but they will be analysed in a fundamentally different way. Humanitarian reasons will no longer be an essential justificatory element. Towards the right end, the tendency will increase to see the few occuring cases as precedents. They then are either establishing a new rule or exemplifying an already existing one. With some simplification one can say, that the movement towards the right consists in a shift from rather political (power politics) to rather legal reasoning. Michael Walzer's original account of humanitarian intervention is perhaps best considered as laying somewhere on the border between the exemption and right position (see Walzer 1982).[13] For the restrictiveness and defensiveness of the conception and the fewness of cases he would allow displays more resemblance with the exemption position. Whereas the principled discussion and the interpretation of criteria as rules marks his position as rather reluctant right-oriented.

The right position lies in the centre of the interval. It is not decided between the defensive or active attitude. Compared with the exemption position the inclination of justifying humanitarian interventions will increase. In this context "right" does not mean "legal right".[14] It should only signify that humanitarian intervention are sometimes morally justifiable or legitimate (berechtigt). One is morally justified in intervening, if the considerations of state rights can be topped by more weightier human rights considerations. In the centre of the interval there is no clear general dominant consideration. This is the position of most commentators of the contemporary situation in international public law. The unconditional validity of the doctrine of non-intervention is as rejected as the simple negation of state rights altogether. The limited conception of sovereignty is a presupposition of the emerging dilemma. It is also taken for granted that human rights violations are prima facie sufficient reason for action. But it is still an open question what action is appropriate and justified in specific instances and who should and could when take care of the concerned duties.

This is more or less also the position the UN collective security system displays. The main difference is that the competence of identifying human rights violations as justificatory reasons resides with the security council. So the primary addressee of humanitarian duties is the security system as a whole which is unfortunately lacking any independent ability for effective action. But for the security council is the ultimate instance of interpreting and establishing international public law, it cannot be assumed to have a duty of intervention in humanitarian cases. The members of the security council should be concerned with humanitarian crises, but the UN charter (chapter VII) only ascribes the security council the authority to legitimize humanitarian interventions. That is, it can state the fact of threats to international peace and security and specify the range of actions that are appropriate and justified. But as can be seen in recent history, the security council has no duty to do so. Its competence is essentially to legitimize other member states to take the relevant actions. To sum up, the security council has the right (competence) to humanitarian interventions according to international public law and can delegate this right to other states which in turn cannot be forced to that decision. Those commentators who want to ascribe to the security council a duty to humanitarian intervention are rather thinking about future improvements of the security system than the actual state of affairs.

The duty position lies at the more active end of the interval. It takes therefore human rights considerations generally as more important than state rights. Stopping human rights violations is seen as a general collective international duty. The humanitarian duty translates thus in a duty to stop the violations with the means of external intervention. At the left end of the duty segment the element of obligation does little more than assert that if in a certain instance the intervention can be effectively justified on humanitarian reasons, then the states which are able and willing to intervene in good faith should do so. That is, able states worried about the situation in another country should feel obliged to act. Moving to the right end, the aspect of overriding international law decreases in significance. The humanitarian duties are seen as primary and in important cases as non-overridable. State rights considerations will still play some role in reasoning, but more in the sense of cautionary reasons that help to establish the limits and conditions in concrete instances. For even if a government feels obliged and justified to help, it is not thereby empowered to do everything it sees fit. The humanitarian task and the future of the target state set severe limits on aims, targets and means of intervention.[15] If even this minimal role is cancelled, then the dilemmatic structure is left and some form of global domestic politics is reached. Advocates of the duty position have to answer the question of which party is the main addressee of the duty. If they interpret it as a strict duty and prefer a collective system of international security as the primary instance, then they consequently are also inclined to do the last step towards global domestic politics. So without much exaggeration one can say that the telos of a consequent duty position is a certain form of global domestic politics.

5. EXTREME NON-DILEMMATIC POSITIONS

According to the preceding description there are two developments on the dilemma interval. Towards each end the main attitudes become more salient. The more defensive attitude at the left end starts from a presumption of the non-intervention priority. The proposed humanitarian reasons are confronted with the task of trumping this primary principle. At the right end the primary role is played by the humanitarian duties. But the presumptive priority does not (entirely) determine the specific weights the reasons have in certain situations. Thus, even at the extreme points on the dilemma interval there is always the possibility that the adverse reasons can in fact override the primary humanitarian principle, although the likelihood is rather small. The determination of the specific (absolute or relative) weights is a complicated matter that cannot be done in advance or a priori. So within the respective segments there are also systematic shifts of dominance of certain reasons. In short, while the priority is concerned with the question of how to argue (setting of judgemental burdens) the dominance rather refers to the actual performance and results of the argument.

In the non-dilemmatic attitudes the situation of a mix of principles with or without dominant importance is abandoned. They reduce the basic situation to one single principle. So the other principle simply does not matter, for it is seen as not valid or as irrelevant. Either they are state fetishists[16] and assert that there is only the important international rule of non-intervention, or they are scholars of global domestic politics (Weltinnenpolitik) and hold sovereignty rights for nothing or outdated.[17] For the first humanitarian intervention is nothing else than war or power politics. And for the second there will be no interventions any more, because there will be no plurality of sovereign states. So humanitarian interventions will transform into ordinary police action on a global scale. While the first views international relations as a thorough anarchy, the latter wants it to be a global state. Thus, for both positions there is no such thing as humanitarian intervention. And there is no humanitarian intervention, because they do not acknowledge the fundamental dilemmatic structure. In some sense one could say, they have a simple view of the world. For the first it always was as simple, while most others hope that the world will become simple.

It is surely a bit unfair to describe the positions in these terms. Almost no one is prepared to advocate state fetishism in this sense. But there are some commentators which argue with the help of a critique of ideology strategy for a certain variation of it.[18] It is asserted that humanitarian reasons are simply invoked to conceal other rather political and strategic reasons. Most defenders of global domestic politics on the other hand would like to recommend their position for other reasons. They are normally not worried about the possibility of loosing the phenomenon of humanitarian intervention, for viewed from their perspective, there is nothing valuable that should be deplored. They are rather concerned with the traditional normative problems associated with humanitarian interventions. Especially these are the problems of particularity and of selectivity. The first one is an aspect of the mixed motive difficulty, insofar as it highlights the probability that the intervening party is seldom disinterested and neutral, so that the intervention can also serve their particular interests. Apart from humanitarian motives neighbouring states can use the opportunity to influence the other state's policy, to weaken the disliked government or to impose one's own values and aims. The other and in some sense related problem of selectivity points to the empirical fact that not in every (similar) instance of human rights violations appropriate (similar) actions are taken. That is, equal cases are for reasons of political opportunity not treated equally. And the same intervening party that was able and willing to intervention in state A is reluctant to do the same in a similar case in state B. This inconsistency in action is particularly disturbing for a duty position. Therefore, advocates of the duty position has reason to shift consequently to global domestic politics. For as in domestic politics generally, there is a single and clear addressee of the humanitarian duties (administration, legal system and police) which is typically required to treat similar cases in a similar and impartial fashion. Therefore, it is mainly the problems of humanitarian interventions that motivate its advocates to a shift towards global domestic politics.[19]

6. ADVANTAGES

If this analysis is right, then today there is no such possibility as escaping the dilemma. Even the most affirmative duty attitude must take the basic evaluation as a balance or trade-off. And the fact that humanitarian interventions are sometimes justified or even required, does not mean that there are no opposing considerations. It merely means that the other reasons are in this case not strong enough. These reasons count, are morally or legally valid and are relevant. Therefore, the dilemmatic conception accounts for the defensive sense of humanitarian interventions as a necessary evil or burden. Using military force is an evil, and watching other people being killed is not good either. Thus, the dilemmatic conception helps to explain the ambivalent feelings accompanying most intervention decisions. In many cases humanitarian interventions are justifiable or tolerable, but they are not simply good actions.

Furthermore, the dilemmatic conception is helpful in elucidating the conditions and limits of humanitarian actions. The humanitarian purpose marks off interventions from war. Apart from the above mentioned differences, humanitarian interventions cannot be started with the aim of conquering territory or killing foreign population. Besides different purposes, humanitarian interventions can only have limited targets. The exchange of foreign governments (independent of the populations' will), the killing of tyrants or the destruction of great areas, for example, cannot be plausible and justifiable targets. For the targets have to be related to the humanitarian purpose, and the latter is restricted to the primary defensive concern of stopping of human rights violations. The two opposing dilemma principles also set constraints on the legitimate means (no mass destruction weapons), the kind and amount of intervention forces (no disproportionality or ineffectiveness), the lasting of the intervention (stopping human rights violations but not occupation or international administration of the area) and the non-modification or destruction of the political structures without the consent of the concerned population.[20] Since the doctrine of non-intervention was established to secure the self-determination of the citizens the humanitarian intervention cannot disregard this fundamental concern. So the doctrine can help to constrain the intervention to the necessary help for self-help, i.e. to one of the original meanings of humanitarian interventions.[21]

7. BALANCING

So even if one believes in a certain presumptive priority between the concerned principles, the balancing of reasons has to be considered as a weighing process. The proposition of a primary reason merely states the amount of the burdens of proof. The fact that the burden is severe does not mean that the primary reasons are in principle insurmountable. In order to determine the precise weight of the reasons one has to carefully look at the actual cases, for the dominance of reasons cannot be decided simply on conceptual grounds. The acknowledgment of the fundamental dilemma helps to understand this reasoning. For it is not required or meaningful to devalue the opposing principles or to argue that they are not valid or irrelevant. What is required, is to strike the balance in the appropriate way. For example, one has not to reason about the outdatedness of sovereignty or the meaningfulness of the principle of collective self-determination. One has only to consider their proper meaning and their importance in this concrete situation. In short, the justification of a humanitarian intervention should not try to dissolve or escape the dilemma, instead it should enter into a complicated reasoning process in a complex situation. To get no clear-cut or simple answers in such situations is not a sign of deficient reasoning or defective principles. It is a clear sign that one has arrived the muddeled grounds of social and political reality.

8. CONCLUSION

To sum up, the dilemmatic situation is the starting point of decisions of humanitarian interventions. To get rid of the dilemma is also to get rid of the concept of humanitarian intervention itself. The understanding of this dilemma is essential to the justification and implementation of humanitarian interventions. It is not necessary nor meaningful to try to dissolve the dilemma in justifying interventions. All what is needed is to strike a proper balance. And because the opposing principles are helpful in determining the appropriate limits, means and conditions of the humanitarian actions the normative dilemma should be kept in mind throughout the entire intervention. The dilemmatic structure can, thus, be seen as the expression of the ambivalent feelings associated with humanitarian interventions. If the so-called new interventionism is meant to indicate a change towards a simply positive attitude concerning humanitarian interventions, while this new evaluation also yields to an increase in instances, the constitutive dilemma will nonetheless insist on the fundamental normative mistake in this development.

NOTES

[1] See f.e. Czempiel/Link 1984; McMahan 1987.

[2] To be sure, it is the resistence of the concerned goverment, not necessarily also the resistence of the citizens. Contrary to Mill's suggestions (see Mill 1859), it is most unlikely that the victims will (or should for reasons of autonomy and self-respect) withstand humanitarian support.

[3] Since sometimes merely police forces are involved, the relevant generic term should be armend forces.

[4] Thus, Walzer's more realist position that the humanitarian motive need not even be the chief consideration, must be rejected (see Walzer 1982, 160f), for that motive will then be regarded merely as a fig-leaf. To be precise, the remark might also be interpreted as to refer to the ultimate effective reason for action. Then, the humanitarian motive need not be the most effective reason, but it should the central one. There is, of course, the problem of ideological uses of humanitarian reasons and the more complicated possibility of devaluations or contaminations of good normative reasons by bad strategic reasons.

[5] The mentioned actual examples should not be pressed to far, for empirical cases are rarely clear cases. Thus, the Somalia intervention is sometimes not regarded as an intervention at all because the utterly lack of a government.

[6] See Krasner 1999, chap. 1.

[7] See Walzer 1982, 151.

[8] Perhaps some modified security council. By the way, it is not unlikely that both ways will amount to the same.

[9] This confrontation appears even within certain declarations of the UN.

[10] Whether the government also looses its right to external sovereignty in relation to other states is a more complicated matter. For it is not clear what criteria of Westphalian sovereignty (see Krasner 1999, 20f) and of good governance are established. But if the other governments, the world community or the global public can in fact decide whether a government can loose its legitimacy and external sovereignty, then the currently prevalent notion of sovereignty has changed radically. To be sure, other governments can refuse to recognize governments for various reasons, they may not accept them as partners of contracts or as members of international organizations, but they currently lack any authority to decide of their sovereignty.

[11] The humanitarian principles on the other side are not to the same extent under the control of the parties. For simplicity's sake, it is assumed that they are generally (morally and legally) recognized. So the only question that has to be decided by the intervening parties is whether they are the appropriate subject to execute that duty. But in the course of the humanitarian intervention the obligations are in fact accepted.

[12] The question was raised by Thomas Schramme.

[13] Contrary to his own statement, Walzer's attitude has changed somewhat in his more recent writings (see Walzer 2002). Since he now focuses more on the urgentness of rescue action and is prepared to allow for preventive interventions, it seems justified to move his view more clearly to the right position on the continuum. Perhaps the conjecture can be ventured that this modification is partly due to his considering different and more recent examples which he takes as rather clear cases of stopping human rights violations. So the modification may be not a change of principled attitudes but a development towards a more comprehensive and differentiated account.
[14] See Kersting 2000, 207f.
[15] For this helpful distinction see Vincent 1974, 4ff.
[16] The term is uses for lack of a better one, but it hints a the relevant background view.
[17] There are certainly further extreme positions such as pacifists, but they typically do not use and totalize the mentioned principles.
[18] Perhaps one can cite in this context Carl Schmitt's remark that those speaking of humanity are lying. But there are also leftist and US-critical versions of it.
[19] In the german context see e.g. Höffe 1999; Senghaas 1992; Habermas 2000.
[20] The rules of the humanitarian international law is, of course, equally valid for war as for humanitarian interventions.
[21] See Walzer 1982.

REFERENCES

Czempiel, E.-O./Link, W. (ed.) 1984: Interventionsproblematik aus politikwissenschaftlicher, völkerrechtlicher und wirtschaftswissenschaftlicher Sicht. Kehl.

Habermas, J. 2000: "Bestialität und Humanität. Ein Krieg an der Grenze zwischen Recht und Moral." In: Merkel, R. (ed.): Der Kosovo-Krieg und das Völkerrecht. Frankfurt.

Höffe, O. 1999: Demokratie im Zeitalter der Globalisierung. München.

Kersting, W. 2000: "Bewaffnete Intervention als Menschenrechtsschutz?" in: Merkel, R.(ed.): Der Kosovo-Krieg und das Völkerrecht. Frankfurt.

Krasner, S. 1999: Sovereignty. Organized Hypocricy. Princeton.

McMahan, J. 1987: "The Ethics of International Intervention" in: Kipnis, K./Meyer, D.T. (ed.): Political Realism and International Morality. Ethics in the Nuclear Age. Boulder.

Mill, J.S. 1859: "A Few Words on Non-Intervention" in: Mill, J.S.: Collected Works. Vol. 21. Toronto. 1984.

Senghaas, D. 1992: "Weltinnenpolitik – Ansätze für ein Konzept" in: Europa-Archiv. 47/22.

Vincent, R.J. 1974: Nonintervention and International Order. Princeton.

Walzer, M. 1982: Gibt es den gerechten Krieg? Stuttgart.

Walzer, M. 2002: "Was heißt humanitär begründetes militärisches Eingreifen?" in: Frankfurter Rundschau 22.01.2002.

WALTER PFANNKUCHE

Humanitarian Interventions and Other Duties to Humanitarian Aid[1]

I. WHEN DO WE HAVE A RIGHT TO A HUMANITARIAN INTERVENTION?

What are, if there are any at all, the necessary conditions or circumstances for a legitimate humanitarian intervention? I don't want to investigate whether individuals – as those volunteering in the international brigades in the Spanish civil war, for example – have a right to intervene into internal affairs of other states. I am concerned with actions of states. The question is thus: When do states have a right to intervene into another state? By investigating whether or not there is such a right I do not mean to ask whether there is a legal right to do so. This is a highly disputed matter among professionals and I do not have the competence to contribute to this debate. However the legal point of view cannot by itself answer the question definitively. Even if there is no legal right to intervene for humanitarian purposes, this goal can in itself be strong enough to override the legal constraints. The overriding reasons would then be moral reasons and my goal is to investigate whether such reasons exist. Of course, if morality conflicts with legal norms the burden of proof is much higher since respect for the legal norms is a presupposition for peace and can thus be morally required even if the legal norms are not morally perfect.

The quest for moral reasons leads back to the fundamental question how we come to believe that we have any rights and duties at all. This again is widely disputed and controversial. In order to reach my concrete problems I will start from something that, as I hope, will not be very controversial and will nevertheless allow me to answer my questions – that is, a somewhat vague model of moral thinking and justification. I presuppose that rights and duties can be constructed as results of an impartial deliberation about what would be the most profitable general rules for a social cooperation. The impartiality required for moral thinking means that the fate and well-being of all affected by the rules has to be taken equally seriously. No one person is more important than another. Moral thinking, according to this approach, is consequentialistic in the sense that the impartial search for the best rules, must consider which consequences for the nonmoral interests of all people the rules would have.

This sketch of moral thinking is of course highly incomplete. It does not say what it means to take everybody equally seriously. Does that mean to look for rules which will make everybody equally happy, or for rules that maximize the total amount of happiness or for rules that make the worst position possible under their regime as good as possible? Nevertheless, I think I can get out of having to argue for one of these alternatives, since I believe that each of these alternatives will come to acknowledge a set of positive and negative rights and duties which are designed to protect the *basic interests* of human beings. The protected interests would then become the *human rights*.

And this is enough for my purpose, since I will limit my investigation to cases where people in a foreign state have to suffer from a massive and systematic violation of their human rights either by their government or by some group in their own state which to control the government is either unwilling or unable.

The right to a military humanitarian intervention can then be justified this way:

i The impartial moral consideration leads to an acknowledgement of universal and basic human rights.

ii To have a right includes to have a right to defend oneself against attacks on the original right.

iii A third party has at least the right to help the threatened person.

iv The primary objects and subjects of morality, those whose protection is central, are individuals.

v The existence and sovereignty of states is morally legitimate only in a secondary sense – only insofar they help to protect the individual rights.

vi It can therefore be morally justified to destroy temporarily the souvereignty of a state in order to end massive violations of human rights in this state.

This simple argument needs a lot of specification since humanitarian interventions do themselves produce serious evils. From the impartial point of view a humanitarian intervention can only be justified as long as it produces less evil than it prevents. This condition is easily pronounced but difficult to specify and it is even more difficult to find out whether or not it is fulfilled in a specific case. There are two main problems:

1. The evils we try to prevent as well as the evils originated by the intervention itself must be determined and measured. This will require a method to measure the badness of harms of different qualities done to different numbers of people.

2. The long-term consequences must be taken into consideration as well. Will a humanitarian intervention create a lasting peace at least in its area or will it rather endanger the peace in the world? These consequences are almost always hard to forsee, but of great importance especially if a humanitarian intervention violates the existing law of peoples.

Ad 1: Comparison of goods and evils

This problem has two aspects:

A fully developed comparison theory should, firstly, be able to weigh quantities of different qualities of evils. Consider that there is a form of slavery which is severe but does not aim at killing the slaves as long as they obey their suppressors – e.g. the slave system in the southern states of the US in the 19th century. Would it be morally correct to risk even one soldier's life in order to put an end to that system? Or would 10.000 killed soldiers be acceptable? Or as many as necessary to achieve that goal? I have no idea how to answer these and similar questions and I know no theory that does have an answer. In order to make at least some progress I will make my task easier and merely consider how we should act if we would have to think only about one kind of evil – the evil of being killed.

Even then we are confronted with the second aspect of the comparison problem: Since this evil can and will in the course of a military intervention be done to several parties how should the members of the parties count? It is important to see that the classical guidelines of the *ius in bello* are not very helpful here. These rules would demand that:

a) The means used in a humanitarian intervention must be *necessary* to end the human rights violations. That means they must not do more harm to the persecutor than is necessary to stop him.
b) Since in military action damages to third parties are unavoidable, these too must be as small as possible.
c) Finally the losses of the intervening party must be as small as possible.

These three imperatives of damage-minimization are plausible. The problem is that they notoriously conflict with each other. What we need is a theory of how to weigh (at least) the lives of the persecuted and the persecutors, of helpers and of bystanders.

Let me try to give at least a sketch of a solution:

(1) It seems to be clear that the lives of persecutors do not, in comparison, count for much. If you come home at night and see three people trying to kill your neighbor and if you can prevent this only by killing all three, this seems to be justified. It would be misleading to accuse you of having killed three people in order to save 'only' one life. This is justified from the consequentialist point of view since every reasonable consequentialist must look for general rules which will most likely make sure that the moral goal is reached – be that equality or maximization or maximin-distribution of well-being. It would simply be self-defeating if the enforcement of a moral rule would become morally wrong if only enough people decide to unjustly harm another person. It is not important how much good and evil is done in a single case. What counts is that obedience to the rules and their enforcement will in general make it possible to reach the goal of morality. Since the primary goal of morality is to protect the innocent, the lives of rule-breaking criminals, in comparison to lives of innocent people, do not count at all.

This needs some specification: Not all persecutors are guilty to the same degree. In particular, totalitarian regimes do normally have and use many possibilities of disinformation and indoctrination. They can furthermore threaten their citizens with severe sanctions for disobedience. The probably most awful combination of these possibilities is used in the transformation of children into soldiers. This shows that, from the impartial point of view, becoming a warrior for a bad regime is in some cases not much of an action the doers could be blamed for. This leaves, of course, untouched the reasons to stop them.

(2) More difficult is the weighing of lives of the other groups.

- What shall we do if we can save more lives among the persecuted if we do not only attack their immediate persecutors but many civilians in the country as well – given that the total number of lost innocent lives is still smaller?
- What shall we do if we can reduce the losses of the helping party by deciding to attack in a way that will kill more among the persecutors and/or the bystanders than would be killed by using another strategy? This was the question for the, so to say, 'morally correct' flight level of the NATO-bombers in the Kosovo war: Should the pilots attack from high above with little risk for themselves but with an increased risk of hurting innocent people or should we distribute the risks the other way around?

Before we try to deal with these as dreadful as unavoidable comparisons we face a fundamental problem. This is whether it can be permitted at all to hurt bystanders in order to save other innocent people. Aren't the bystanders then used as mere means even if they become means for the achievement of a noble goal? This is the question whether there are some moral rights which are absolute, not overridable by whatever might be at stake. From the impartial point of view, we must ask ourselves whether we want to have such absolute rights. I think the answer would be negative. The impartial-consequentialist answer will be this one: The lives of all innocent people count equally – be they helpers, bystanders or persecutees. Each of these roles is a role I might happen to play. The rational reaction to the possibility of losing my life in one of these roles can only be to reduce the probability of this terrible event as much as possible. And this is not done by endorsing rules that kategorically forbid risking the lives of bystanders. The reason is that it then might happen that more innocent people will be killed than would be killed if hurting outsiders would be allowed.[2] This means: If we can save the same number of persecutees only by either losing 20 helping soldiers and no bystanders or by losing 2 soldiers and 8 bystanders we should chose the latter course of action.

Some modification might become necessary if we look closer at how the soldiers fighting for the good side became soldiers. Is this a result of an impartial but coercive selection among those able to fight? Or are they members of an army of professionals they join voluntarily? In the latter case one might argue that the decision includes the readiness to take higher risks than the average citizen – as policemen do. But even then further problems arise: How much higher precisely is the risk-readiness we can expect from them? Do the soldiers get an approriate compensation for their readiness to risk their lives? Or do they predominantly belong to a social class, whose members do not have many other chances to earn a decent living? In order to avoid these problems I assume for the following that the soldiers of the good party will be recruited through a fair and coercive procedure.

Ad 2: Inclusion of long-term consequences

Such consequences are almost always hard to foresee and this opens a wide room for disagreement which is unsolvable. Philosophy cannot contribute much here. But the long-term consequences lead as well to two systematic and philosophical problems:

a) Which future events will count as consequences of a humanitarian intervention? Such large operations alter the causal chains which determine the future in countless ways. But it leads us nowhere if we try to take them all into account. – I cannot deal with this problem here, but will simply presuppose that the problem can be solved with some concept of immediate and forseeable consequences.

b) Which of the consequences that have to be taken into consideration will count as imputable and thus as an argument for or against the moral correctness of an humanitarian intervention? If a cruel dictator threatens the intervening forces with atomic weapons and does finally really use them is this a consequence the foreign forces can be blamed for or is it only the tyrant himself who is responsible for the resulting desaster?

This problem is expressed in two ways to understand the moral question:

* Do we have to search for rules and act according to rules which would have the best consequences if everybody *would* act accordingly or if there *would* at least be a powerful institution to insure almost universal obedience?

* Or must we take into account what others will *in fact* do if we start to act in a certain way? Must we consider that many people will *in fact* not act morally because there is no sanctioning power, and the right rules for our behaviour would then be those which would have the best consequences under these circumstances?

Both alternatives seem to be problematic: In the first case we would act according to rules which seem to be ignorant of the world for which our morality is after all supposed to be useful. That would be rules for an ideal world. In the latter case, if all real consequences of our acting are to be taken into consideration, we are exposing ourselves to all kinds of moral blackmailing.

I think a consequentialist cannot ignore the difference between an ideal world with almost universal compliance and the real world in which we, especially with respect to states, have no rule-enforcing super-power. He must try to improve the fate of the real world. For this reason we must try to combine both ways of thinking within the consequentialist model.

On a first level we impartially ask what would be the best rules for an ideal world, that is, for a world with almost universal rule-compliance. These would be the rules of an ideal world order, which would regulate the behaviour among individuals, among individuals and states, and finally among states. This ideal world would probably be a kind of world republic of states with limited sovereignty where the republic would hold a monopoly of power in order to guarantee international peace and the protection of human rights. For this republic it would be relatively easy to step in if human rights would be violated in one of its member states.

But the real world is not that way. It is not governed by a reasonable system of laws. In the real world we have well armed states and may be confronted with a tyrant who might even be an international pacifist, but nevertheless has for whatever reason the goal to extinguish some part of his people. What shall we do if declaring war on this state would result in the destruction of many more lives than letting the dictator execute his plans?

To deal with such problems the consequentialist must ascend to a second level of reflection. He must look for actions, which make it likely *to achieve the ideal world with the fewest possible costs and losses*. This may result in standing by and doing nothing while a powerful state massacres a part of its population. This can be the right thing to do if letting it happen will not likely encourage other dictators and thus become a major setback to the human project of building a world republic. The painful fact is that we in the most cases will not know which path to the world republic will be the less damaging one.

Nevertheless, one certainty remains: A result of this second-level deliberation is that we must take steps to establish an institution which will have the power to enforce moral rules everywhere in the world. And one step towards this government of reasonable laws must be the creation of a supranational institution that permanently shall and can intervene if a state violates the human rights of its members. As long as humanitarian interventions are dependent on ad-hoc coalitions of interested states we do not have a government of law and thus every future tyrant can speculate that no such coalition will come into existance in his case.

This has two important consequences:

As long as there is no permanent and powerful institution to stop and sanction human rights violations worldwide it is reasonable to expect that every single intervention undertaken by an ad-hoc coalition or even a single state must in itself satisfy the criterion that more good than evil results from it.

And second: States which are eager to conduct humanitarian interventions, but at the same time try to hinder the strengthening of supranational institutions lose their credibility.

These difficulties on the empirical as well as on the normative level are good reasons to be sceptic about the possibility of a meaningful ethics of humanitarian interventions. They therefore also deliver good reasons against the moral correctness of every specific such intervention. Nevertheless, in the following I will assume that all criteria for a justified humanitarian intervention are fulfilled in a case. The question is then:

II. IS THERE A DUTY TO INTERVENE IN CASES WHERE THERE IS A RIGHT TO INTERVENE?

The existence or non-existence of such a duty marks the crux of the problem. If large-scale violations of human rights are undertaken somewhere we do not ask whether this would be a good occasion for using our right to intervene. We rather think “There are people suffering. We could help them. Don’t we have an obligation to do so?”.

A duty to intervene would be a positve duty. One must give something – money or even one's life. From the moral-impartial point of view the question would be the following:

Is it better to live in a world where nobody has an obligation to help persecuted people in other states and in which there is subsequently not much hope of being helped? Or is it better to live in a world where every able person has the duty to help and where everybody can have some hope of being helped? And 'has the duty to help' would mean that a government would be entitled to recruit people fairly to become members of an intervention army.

For an impartial answer one would have to imagine being one of the inhabitants of this planet who could happen to be in one of the positions just described. And then the balance of risks is clearly in favour of a world with such a strong duty to help. Since it is already a requirement for a humanitarian intervention to be righteous, that the good exceed the evil, the duty to contribute to the helping forces will make it less likely to lose one's life in this world.

But there is a limit to this argument, which again stems from the moral imperfectness of the world. In the real world not every party and state will recruit soldiers in order to fight human rights violations somewhere in the world. But then the states, which do recruit soldiers will burden these with very high risks, if these soldiers would now have to become responsible for fighting the tyrants everywhere in the world. The risks they would have to take might even be higher than the risk – with reference to the entire world population – of becoming the victim of a human rights violation. It would then be irrational to shoulder this risk from the impartial point of view and therefore a recruitment forcing such high a risk on someone would be unfair.

Which risk would then be fair? Here again we are lost in the dark. We do not know how many human rights violations would occur in a generation if no military interventions would be made. Thus we do not know how high the risk for a member of this generation would be to die from such a violation. But we can use another method here: We can start from the strong criterion that every single humanitarian intervention must be allowed in itself, that is it must by itself reduce the total number of innocent lives lost. This being the case it would not be unfair to burden the helping forces with that degree of risk-taking that would be unavoidable if all able states would contribute to the intervening forces. As long as this is not the case the argument of unfair recruitment gives the few helping states a right to selective engagement.

III. THE WEIGHING OF POSITIVE DUTIES

I now assume that within the limits mentioned a positive duty to help persecuted persons out of their misery even with military force does exist. But moral thinking cannot stop here. It cannot since the same arguments which generate this duty will generate a duty to help in cases where the misery does not result from the intentional violation of human rights but from causes like poverty, malnutrition, overpopulation, poor medical standards, political corruption and so on.

From the impartial point of view it is just as rational to favour a non-military transfer of resources to prevent these terrible fates. This is even more evident, since it is less damaging for the inhabitants of relatively affluent states to, say, cut their income in half than it is to risk their health and life as a member of an intervention army. If there is a duty to help with military means there is as well a duty to help through a constant and effective transfer of resources, knowledge and experts.

One might reject this consequence by saying that there is a moral priority to fight *intentional* violations of human rights over the correction of mere unfortunate circumstances which happen to cause the same dreadful consequences. For this priority claim there are at least three reasonable arguments, which nevertheless cannot hold from an impartial point of view:

1. The protection against active wrongdoings should have priority because this protection is constitutive for the very existence of a legal system. Where negative rights are not protected, there is no government of law at all. The intentional murder of 30.000 people a year in some state combined with a crime-solving-rate close to zero is a much more potent reason to question whether this state is governed by law than the avoidable starvation and death of 30.000 poor people would be. – This maybe true, but it is insufficient to prove the priority-thesis. Such a high murder rate would of course invade the entire lives of all citizens and threaten all feelings of security and protectedness by law. But this does not imply that the avoidance of being killed deserves an unchallenged priority over avoiding other possible threats. From the impartial point of view being

killed is as terrible an event as being forced to die from starvation because nobody is willing to share his food. It will be rational to have universal moral principles designed to avoid both fates. And it is by no means rational to first consume huge resources to hire more police officers in order to reduce the murders to zero before considering the use of resources to prevent starvation because of unemployment or to prevent death from cancer. All these are terrible threats and the rational reaction must be to reduce the overall sensation of threat as far as possible. The argument loses even more power when we turn to the international case. In a domestic case a high murder-rate will indeed undermine the government of law in general. But at the international level even genocide in some country will not endanger the government of law in other parts of the world.

2. The priority claim could be true because we have to include the long-term consequences. Thus even if in a single case the balance of good and evil might speak against a military intervention compared to a non-military humanitarian intervention, the deterrence effect might tip the balance. – But this again is not sufficient to establish a general priority of this type of action since the good long-term consequences can be claimed on the other side as well. Non-military humanitarian intervention can stimulate economic growth, raise the educational level and reduce the birth rate, which might in turn help avoid situations from which many ethnic conflicts arise.

3. The deepest source of resistance against the model of weighing threats will probably be a scepticism about the underlying consequentialist model of constructing rights and duties. Murder, you might think, is simply in itself a greater evil than the omission to prevent a preventable death. He who kills, denies the human dignity of his victim. But he who lets die does not deny the dignity of the suffering. And people, so the argument, do not simply want to stay alive they even more urgently want to see their dignity respected. – It is certainly true that dignity matters for people. But why then is the dignity of the starving man not denied? As soon as my starvation is avoidable by a transfer of resources, it is no longer a bad fate that unfortunately has befallen me, but it is a consequence of the inactivity and unwillingness to help of other human beings. Their inactivity wounds my human dignity as much as the bullet from the racist does. My dignity is hurt whenever the rules I would accept from the impartial point of view are broken. Dignity can thus be added on all sides of the morally protected goods. It cannot in itself alter the primary weighing of which of the basic goods should be protected by moral rules to which degree.

If the priority claim is not convincing we have to face a final problem: If we – the rich and powerful – happen to have all these duties to help, we will pretty soon first reach the limits of our willingness to fulfil them and even if we can manage to overcome these we will reach the limits of our ability to help. This makes it necessary to rank our duties. The argument is then:

- i If fighting intentional violations of human rights has no moral priority over helping others out of life-threatening miseries stemming from other causes and
- ii if we, due to scarce resources, cannot help everywhere at the same time and
- iii if it is a rational requirement to use our resources where they can provide the most good and
- iv if it is likely that civil aid is more effective than military help,
- v then we must be very reluctant with respect to military humanitarian interventions in our time and circumstances.

I find it quite obvious that military interventions are the most expensive and often at the same time the most uncertain method of helping people out of desperate need. I would therefore propose that we take our duties to help more seriously and focus on non-military forms of help. I do not mean to say that this would in short time obviate all occasions which might call for military action. It is true, most of the massive human rights violations are triggered by scarcity of basic resources. Nevertheless, there will surely remain other cases in which ideological or religious delusions provide the impetus. But again: It is probably more effective to react to these cases with all kinds of sanctions below the threshold of war and save the resources for other types of help. This would at the same time save us from the painful business of comparing the killing of different people in complex circumstances. And it would probably diminish our wealth to a level where no resources are left for military actions.

NOTES

[1] For the english version I am highly indebted to Susan Hechler whose help made a difference.

[2] This will not convince someone who believes in absolute rights. But this position is hard to defend if one accepts that every morality must be able to deal with the distribution of risks. And this is unavoidable since societies create countless artificial risks and expose their members to them. Thousands of people including pedestrians could be saved if only car traffic would be forbidden. Even some attempts to rescue people will result in killing some bystanders each year – as does the permission for ambulances to drive at high speed (this example was given by Thomas Pogge). Can those coming into the path of these cars claim that it was morally wrong to allow high-speed driving? If not, it seems to be permissible to risk harming bystanders in order to save more lives.

RALF STOECKER

Help, Intervention and Involvement

"To retreat home within the safety of my four walls instead of intervening, while those outside are slaughtering each other, is not an attitude that I regard as political [...]"
German Foreign Minister Joschka Fischer
according to "Die Zeit" 5/2002

"And it's one, two, three,
What are we fighting for?
Don't ask me, I don't give a damn,
Next stop is Vietnam [...]"

Country Joe and The Fish,
Woodstock 1969

For eleven weeks, from March 24 to June 9, 1999, NATO jets bombed targets in the territory of the Federal Republic of Yugoslavia (FRY). This war was from the onset controversial: There were doubts concerning the wisdom behind the military and political intervention, its legality, but first and foremost concerning its moral legitimacy. Was NATO really allowed to attack Yugoslavia, and if so, was it perhaps also obliged to do so? Answering these questions depends on two factors: first, on the many facts about the historical development preceding and accompanying the bombings, and secondly, on the preconditions that may morally permit a state to wage war against another state. In both respects there is still a great deal of ambiguity and disagreement. In this paper, I shall first concentrate on the second, ethical aspect in order to form an argumentative basis for assessing the war in Kosovo in the second part.

1 JUSTIFYING THE CENTRAL QUESTION

Were the NATO air strikes on Yugoslavia morally justified? Not only the answer but also the question is suspect. We are acquainted with moral judgements primarily through our interpersonal relationships. What we evaluate, in terms of moral judgements, is what human beings do and do not do. But neither NATO itself, nor the states that took part in the attacks, are human beings; rather, they are much more abstract objects, so-called 'corporative agents', and hence, one might very well ask whether it is at all sensible to apply our moral criteria to them.

These concerns are basically justified. Of course, one might easily blame or praise institutions such as NATO, or *regard* them as good or evil, but in a sense these judgements do not hit their target as they would do if they were directed at us personally. Due to the abstract, almost virtual character of these agents, accusations and acclamations lose their moral adhesiveness, because, after all, institutions cannot feel morally afflicted; they feel neither shame nor pride, nor possess a good or bad conscience, nor are they capable of feeling joy or sorrow. Only human beings are capable of this. Given that it is essential for a real moral agent, a *moral subject*, to exhibit these kinds of attitudes and sensibilities, corporations are not moral subjects.

It may therefore be deemed recommendable not to demand a moral evaluation of NATO's actions but to consider formulating a moral assessment of the politicians and soldiers as well as the citizens of the states involved in these actions. Was it morally justified what Bill Clinton, Javier Solana, Rudolf Scharping and many ordinary pilots did during the spring of 1999? No doubt, this is a pertinent question. But the problem remains that the actions of these people in turn could not be assessed apart from their relationship to the NATO attacks *and* without a moral evaluation of these attacks. Succinctly stated, since human agency frequently involves participation in corporative action, we have no choice but to assess the moral worth of corporative action as well, although a moral evaluation of corporative agents is in itself not our fundamental concern.

Yet the initial question of whether the attacks on Yugoslavia were justified is not only suspect on the part of the agent but also on the part of the persons affected by the actions of the agents, i.e., the victims of the attacks. Is it really possible to act against Yugoslavia, whether right or wrong? Answers to this question might be, among others, that its sovereignty has been violated or that its infrastructure destroyed. But who was targeted, and who was harmed? The problem is not that you cannot damage, in one sense or another, Yugoslavia, but that it is morally irrelevant whether you do so or not. In contrast to human beings (and presumably animals) states have no moral status of their own. We need not pay them moral respect. (They share this fate with almost everything in the world: greenhouses, bushfires, gross national products, etc.)[1] The people living in Yugoslavia, though, do possess a moral status. Hence, the crucial question is not whether NATO did something wrong to Yugoslavia but whether it did something wrong to the people living there.

In summary, there are no definitive ethical grounds that preclude the question of the moral worth of the NATO attacks from the onset, but one has to bear in mind that the only relevant victims are the people affected by the attacks, not the abstract corporation of Yugoslavia, and that in the end the only interesting agents committing these attacks are humans too.

The primacy of human agency is not simply a matter of defining victim and perpetrator, but also in establishing the criteria for making moral judgements. That is, deciding whether what NATO and its member states did was morally legitimate is to be measured on the same basis as all interpersonal behaviour. This ethical stance of relying on individual morals was taken to be particularly important by the politicians concerned at the time, who repeatedly emphasized the emergency situation, which would not allow them to "look away" (as the German minister of defence, Rudolf Scharping, has put it in the title of his book "Wir dürfen nicht wegsehen"). According to this approach, the NATO states were free to aid the endangered Kosovo Albanian people, quite as everyone else has the right to help a person in existential need. In Germany, this kind of moral justification took precedent, particularly in the debate between the veterans and heirs of diverse peace movements, and proved to be important for NATO as a whole, because it allowed for a legal argument to be constructed that the military attacks, though not vindicated by a UN mandate, did not contradict international law; further, that when judged to be illegal, the attacks could still be considered legitimate.[2]

It is the aim of this paper to pursue this basic ethical idea.[3] I shall therefore work with the assumption that in order to understand the moral situation of NATO in the spring of 1999, one should first ask how an individual alone should have behaved in a similar situation. After discussing this question I shall then try to transform its results, in spite of the great differences between corporations and human beings, into an assessment of the NATO mission. Accordingly, the rest of the paper is divided into two parts: §§ 2-4 discuss the individual situation as an instance of the so-called Samaritan Situation; §§ 5-7 apply these considerations to the war in Kosovo.

2 THE PROBLEM OF THE SAMARITAN

In moral philosophy, situations developing out of interpersonal relationships, which could possibly lend justificatory support to the NATO attacks, are usually discussed with reference to the biblical *parable of the Good Samaritan*. Jesus, in reply to the question of how to understand God's commandment to love thy neighbour as thyself, tells the story of a man who "fell among robbers, who stripped him and beat him, and departed, leaving him half dead" (Lk. 30). A priest and then a Levite pass by the man, ignoring him, but then a citizen of Samaria arrives, who takes pity on the poor victim, bandages his wounds, transports him to an inn, provides for his care and makes sure the man is well attended. The ethical question is how to evaluate the respective behaviour of these three passers-by.[4]

In general, the situation with which the three man were confronted has five crucial features, which can easily be extracted from the biblical tale:

(1) The agent *A* must be confronted with
(2) a stranger *S*,
(3) who is in serious danger or need,
(4) from which *A* believes that he could rescue *S*,
(5) while there are no other agents present whose duty it is to help (e.g., close relatives, doctors, etc.) and who are moreover willing to perform their duty.

A situation in which these five conditions are fulfilled I shall call a *Samaritan Situation.*

How are we to evaluate the different options an agent faces in such a situation? One answer is already obvious from the biblical story: It was morally right that the Samaritan rescued the victim and cared for him. So far, nobody would doubt this assessment, but it only entails that it is *sometimes* right to act as a good Samaritan, leaving open three additional, more difficult questions, which together form what one might call the *Problem of the Samaritan*:

(R) Is it *always morally right* to help in Samaritan Situations?
(W1) Is it *sometimes morally wrong* not to help in Samaritan Situations?
(W2) Is it *always morally wrong* not to help in Samaritan Situations?

I shall start with (W1), which appears to be the easiest question. The biblical answer, once again, is clear: The priest and the Levite, who unscrupulously leave the victim to his fate, are not right in their behaviour. They should have helped him; more so, it was their duty to rescue him. At least with respect to paradigmatic instances of Samaritan situations, there seems to be a clear *duty to assist and rescue* the victim. This view gains support through the consideration of other fictional examples, where it seems to be even more obvious that such a duty exists: Someone sitting in a lounge chair next to a swimming pool watches a small child falling into the water and drowning just a few inches away. He could simply reach down and pull the child out of the water, but he does not. Could there be any doubt that he had the duty to rescue the child?[5]

The view that the man in the lounge chair has a duty to help is also in accord with certain ethical conceptions, foremost, of course, with Christian charity, but also with utilitarian views, according to which we are obliged to maximize the well-being of all people. In the example, the benefit accrued by the victim of being rescued (staying alive) obviously is much greater than the damages suffered by the rescuer (a wet sleeve); therefore, he must save the child.

Yet two problems develop out of the application of both of these ethical conceptions to Samaritan Situations. First, we usually regard the Samaritan's behaviour not simply as righteous or good, but as particularly *praiseworthy*, as a 'good deed'. Accordingly, the rescued victim will not feel that the Samaritan has acted merely for the sake of duty. The victim will be grateful and feel deeply indebted to his rescuer. But neither reaction corresponds well with the assumption that assistance in an emergency is nothing more than the performing of a duty.

The second problem is a general one, due to the impersonality of such duty-based ethical theories. People are not simply distant executors and beneficiaries of the good. It is much more plausible to trace back their duties to their specific, individual ethical situation, particularly to the *moral rights* they possess and others possess with respect to them.[6] But given the notion that all duties should be based on moral rights, Samaritan Situations create a difficulty, in that it is not easy to find a right corresponding to the duty to help. This can be demonstrated from the following survey of *different ways a duty can be grounded on rights* at all.

Firstly, duties can arise from rights which are intrinsic to a *special relationship* between the agent and the recipient of the action. Those who take the wedding vows to stand by each other in good times and in bad, enjoy, then, a right, because of the mutual promise made through the wedding ceremony, to expect help in an emergency from their spouse, and the spouse has the corresponding duty. But in a Samaritan Situation the person in need is, by definition, a 'stranger'. That is, there is no pre-existing special relationship which exists between the persons involved guaranteeing a special right and corresponding duty.

Duties can also, secondly, be based on *universal human rights*, as example, the right not to be killed, tortured or enslaved. But what these rights usually have in common is their negative quality: they only oblige people to abstain from doing something. My right not to be killed entails a duty for everyone else not to kill me. A human right to be rescued from danger or need, on the other hand, would, instead, be a *positive* right. It would commit all people to be active in a certain way. But according to many moral philosophers, especially from the liberal tradition, it is inconceivable that a person enjoys the right that every other person should do something for him.

Moreover, such a universal right of being guaranteed rescue or assistance in emergency situations would entail that none of us in most cases are able to fulfil our moral duties. There are plenty of people in the world who live in urgent need and whom we could help, but we do not. So, if we have the obligation to help them, then the way we usually behave is wrong. This may be already a refutation of the view that we have a positive duty to help everyone in the world who is in existential need, but it may also be argued that this is a refutation too rashly made and that we could indeed be, morally considered, far from behaving decently. More importantly though, even if it is granted that we have a duty to help these people, the problem of the Samaritan would not be solved, since it is ultimately implausible to assume that such a general duty, whether we have it or not, could be the sole basis of the man's duty to rescue the drowning child. If this were the case, the mere ethical difference between us and him would be that while all of us neglect our duties with respect to countless starving people in the world he also neglects his duty to one additional person, namely the drowning child. And this description certainly is inadequate. What the man by the pool is guilty of is something far more severe than allowing himself to feel a general indifference to the world.

There is also a third way in which duties can arise from an agent's particular situation. They can exist through a special *responsibility*, as for example, when one has promised to take care of a child or when one is employed as a swimming pool attendant. In contrast to the obligation arising through the recitation of the wedding vows, such a special responsibility may not entail a corresponding right on the side of the person one is responsible for (e.g., the child), but may be based on rights of a third party (e.g., the parents). But such a pre-existing responsibility is also excluded by definition from the Samaritan Situation. The biblical Samaritan was not an ambulance driver who was responsible for aiding wounded travellers. Again, there seems to be no basis for a duty to rescue.

These difficulties of incorporating the duty of aid and rescue into a right-based moral framework have given rise to a lively debate in ethics as well as in the philosophy of law. This is not surprising since there is a tendency to extend the insights of a moral right for aid and rescue to the need of establishing a *legal right for the same*. Such a legal right would find accord with many European laws, but it would be in conflict with the Anglo-Saxon legal system, where the priest and the Levite presumably would have provoked public disdain but would not have taken the risk of being put on trial. This legal tolerance could only be justified in turn either by doubts concerning the codification of this particular moral right, or by doubts concerning the existence of the right – which then immediately leads us into the ethical debate.

Is there any way out of the seemingly absurd claim that in situations as the biblical one there is no duty to help the needy? One possible response is to be found in the already mentioned fact that we usually praise good Samaritans for their deeds. Our praise suggests that what the Samaritan has done was more than what his duty required of him, that helping the victim was a *supererogatory* act. From this perspective, helping was not morally obligatory but only morally desirable. It was good that he has done it although it would not have been wrong not to do it. We praise the Samaritan not for fulfilling his duty but for his generosity, and we expect the victim to be grateful, because we believe that he his indebted to his helper. Accordingly, although the behaviour of the hard-hearted passers-by who do not help would not be in breach of their duties, it would still be considered *offensive*. We blame them for their lack of generosity and kindness, not for a shirking of their duties.

With respect to the exemplary biblical Samaritan, this assessment is quite plausible. He was not bound by duty to care for the victim of the robbery as fully as in fact he did (e.g., paying the bill at the inn); hence, he has done more than he was obliged to do. But it does not follow that the Samaritan had no duty at all to help the man. One can still ask the question whether he would also have acted supererogatorily if he had not been a good, but merely a 'minimally decent' Samaritan.[7]

The main problem, though, with the above-formulated assessment rests in the case of the other two, hard-hearted passers-by. To refuse to help a person in an extreme emergency situation does not fit within the category of standard instances one would call offensive. No one is required to bathe now and then, or to be polite; it is only offensive not to behave so. Yet, to let a baby drown and remain unmoved or to ignore a dying traveller seem to be misdeeds on quite another scale.

The plausible nature of the above-proposed ethical argument would need to incorporate not only the offensiveness of the non-deed, but the shirking of a duty itself. I will explore a more sound solution to the ethical problem in the following section.

3 A PROPOSAL FOR A SOLUTION

To my mind, the key to an adequate understanding of the problem of the Samaritan is already to be found in the biblical story itself, with the question who is meant as our 'neighbour' in the Old Testament commandment to love thy neighbour (3 Mose 19,18). This is an interesting question, since on the one hand 'neighbour' usually is an expression characterizing specific interpersonal relationships. The neighbour is someone nearby, such as a brother, a tribal comrade or someone from the neighbourhood; on the other hand, according to Christian doctrine, the commandment to love thy neighbour as thyself is the highest, most general of all commandments (Mt. 12,31); 'neighbour' could therefore hardly be restricted to a person's relatives. The tale of the Good Samaritan solves this tension and specifies who our 'neighbour' is: Even a complete stranger is someone to whom I stand in the special relationship from which I am committed to care for him; I am not only responsible for him, because we are friends, belong to the same family or live nearby one another. I am also responsible for him, given that he is just someone I happen to come across.

This solution may be read as the claim that we are responsible for all people in general, but then we are back to the problems already mentioned created by an ethics of universal responsibility and a corresponding general positive duty to help everyone in the world. But it is also possible to read the biblical story differently, avoiding the inference that responsibility for the stranger corresponds to a responsibility for everyone in the world. According to such an alternative interpretation, it is the *encounter* which creates the responsibility. The Samaritan is not responsible for the needy of the world, but the circumstances of his encounter with the stranger create a special relation between them. His being confronted (condition 1) with the stranger's plight creates the responsibility of caring for him. It is this immediacy that makes them 'neighbours'.

Underlying this idea is the observation that responsibility is not always based on an explicit agreement. There are other ways leading to responsibility. One possibility is to take over responsibility one-sidedly (as in the case of someone who decides, for example, to care for the tidiness of the local playground or for the future of German philosophy). But there is also a second possibility of how responsibility is assumed. Life itself places the burdens of many types of responsibility upon us. It already happens when one is born into a family, and it happens if one forms his own family, too. Our relationships to parents, children, brothers and sisters give rise to responsibilities that we do not assume with regard to other people, at least not without having made the conscious decision to do so. It is a difficult question how far these responsibilities go (and how much they are dependent on one's social context), but every plausible ethical theory must incorporate the fact that duties may stem from such domains of responsibility that we could not shape at will. Presumably, these duties could not entirely be grounded on moral rights, but they do preserve the basic idea that moral agents are no distant benefactors and that moral duties arise depending on the individual circumstances of the agent. We are 'our brother's keeper' not because we are shepherds of a flock consisting of everyone but because we stand in a special relationship to a particular person, a relationship that we have not chosen (in contrast to the one to our friends and business partners).

If it is accepted that there are responsibilities that we do not assume, but that simply fall to us, then it is plausible to accept that this is what happens in Samaritan Situations as well. It is the fate of the three biblical travellers to walk along that path exactly at the time when the victim of the robbery is in existential need of aid, and therefore to become responsible for his staying alive. This is why they have the duty to help him.

Nonetheless is it appropriate for the victim to be grateful to his helper, even if the help were confined to the bare essentials (instead of the supererogatory aid given by the actual biblical Samaritan). In contrast to a duty based on a corresponding right in Samaritan Situations, the victim has no special claim on the bearer of the duty; he has merely the same claim that all of us have to assert, that other people should behave morally.

I therefore conclude that under the assumption that persons may need to take on a responsibility simply by arriving at situations to find someone in great danger or need, we can incorporate a duty defined by such assistance into a plausible ethical theory and hence solve the Problem of the Samaritan. What remains unanswered is the question why, except from its initial plausibility, we should accept this assumption and believe that in these situations there is in fact the possibility that responsibility increases.

A possible reason for the increase would be to work with the assumption that we always are responsible for things that we could make better, but, as I have stated repeatedly, such an ever-expanding responsibility would be much too demanding. Another possible reason would be to deduce this special responsibility from the harm principle, according to which we should never harm people; but at least prima facie the hard-hearted travellers do not harm the needy victim, they simply fail to do anything for his benefit.

Much more convincing, to my mind, is a third approach, which is the attempt to trace the responsibility of the Samaritan to human dignity, not to the dignity of the victim but to the *dignity of the helper* himself. It is beneath one's own dignity to be so callous as not to help in such situations, as for example, to let the victim of a robbery perish unaided or to let a child drown instead of pulling it out of the pool. A person who acts in such a manner would be "moral slime", as it was put, curiously enough, by an opponent of a duty to rescue,[8] and slime is not human. Such behaviour as letting others suffer and die while remaining unmoved falls outside the scope of what defines humanity. Hence, everyone who behaves as such damages his own dignity. He discredits himself when faced with the other's need he refuses to help.

This is just a brief synopsis of how to support the assumption that people necessarily take on responsibility when they are confronted with situations where one is found in desperate need. But this assumption has the advantage of making clear why in cases where providing aid is justified (as perhaps in the Kosovo debate), it is rightly emphasized that after all *one could not simply stand by and watch and do nothing*. To be sure, this feeling may only be due to a pang of conscience, when one feels obliged to help, but I am convinced that there is more to it. It illustrates the point that a person, in not responding to a situation of need, does harm to herself. She would be unable to look at herself in the mirror in the morning if she had simply turned away from such a situation and not tried to help.

It is therefore beneath our dignity as humans to refuse coolly to help those in need; more so and yet similarly, it also does injury to our *honour*, where honour is a specific kind of individual dignity, bound to the social role that a person plays or wants to play. The point that needs to be made here is that our sense of honour moves us to help, and this desire to help based on honour not only explains *why*, but also *how* we act. It opens up the possibility that there may be *honourable and dishonourable ways of helping*. If it is, for example, a point of honour for a "real man" to aid a woman who is molested by a lout, this could hardly be done by handing out one hundred Euro to the lout to make him go away. That would not be manly. In contrast to the obligation to respect human dignity, demands of honour are not by themselves moral duties. But in cases where a moral duty is based on a threat to our own dignity, as in the Samaritan cases, it is easy to confuse dignity and honour and to have the feeling that one is in the right when one is following one's particular sense of honour, independent even of any moral consideration. (This point will later prove to be important for the discussion of military intervention.)

Given these considerations about the ethical basis of our responsibility for people in need, we can now answer (W1), the first of the three questions, whether it is sometimes morally wrong not to help in Samaritan Situations. In the biblical tale, as well as in the example of the drowning child, a responsibility falls to the agent simply due to the special situation in which he finds himself, which gives him the duty to rescue the child. If he does not perform his duty, he does something wrong.

It is also possible to answer the more specific question (W2), whether it is *always* wrong not to help. There is no reason to assume that the responsibility one attains in a Samaritan Situation is stronger or even as strong as other responsibilities, which are based on other interpersonal relationships. It is, for example, unobjectionable that an agent saves his child first, before caring for another child, even where the need of his own child is somewhat lower than that of the other child. And there is no reason to assume that the helper has the duty to make sacrifices in order to rescue a stranger. It is not beneath our dignity when we do not behave as heroes or saints, though sometimes it would be nice if we did.

4 SPECIAL SAMARITAN SITUATIONS

This leaves us with question (R), whether we always have a *right*, if not a duty, to help the needy, or if it sometimes could be morally wrong to do so. In the biblical case, the Samaritan obviously had the right to help the injured victim and in the case of the drowning child the man in the lounge chair certainly has the right to rescue the baby. But the circumstances are not so clear in other Samaritan Situations. There are situations in which it is more difficult to decide how to act, and others in which it is even obviously morally wrong to help.

An initial aspect, making things more complicated, is that some acts of rescue result in side effects developing for the saved person or that the rescue itself creates a certain risk. Even persons who are in real danger or real need can suffer additional harm, for example, when hostages get killed by a measure that was meant to rescue them. A right to rescue therefore presupposes a calculation of possible consequences. Only if the balance of this calculation is in the positive, with all things considered, should one attempt to help another, and even then the helper is obliged to employ the most mild and inexpensive measures necessary.

This leads immediately to the problem of how to evaluate the possible consequences developing out of an attempt to help, since it is not always clear that the calculation will look similar from the perspective of the people in need as from the perspective of the agent doing the assisting. A man who tries to prevent a rape by firing with his machine gun, knowing that he will probably also hit the woman in danger but believing it better for her to be dead than to be dishonoured, behaves paternalistically. In cases like this the agent may only have the choice between not helping or forcing the person in need to pay a price for his assistance, regardless of whether he knows whether the person would agree to pay this price or not. And then sometimes, particularly if the price is very high, the agent has no right to help.

Moreover, the supportive action may not only have side effects for the people in need but also for third parties. In the first place, it may infringe on the rights claimed by third parties due to their special relationship to the person capable of lending assistance. If two children are drowning, it is not only the father's right to save his own child first, but his child also has the right to assume his father will save him first; hence, the father has a duty to save his child and has no right to save the other child until his own is in safety.

As illustrated above, each individual has several negative rights with regard to the potential helper: the helper must respect one's privacy, property, dignity, bodily integrity and especially one's right to life. If an emergency measure threatens to violate such rights, the potential helper has to weigh the danger that may be involved against the plight of the person in need and the chances he has of actually helping him. By such a calculation, of course, not every right carries the same weight. One may obviously smash an antique vase on the head of a madman in order to prevent him from stabbing a child, even if the vase is owned by someone else. It may even be permitted to risk the life and well-being of third party individuals in order to help, otherwise police cars and ambulances could not be allowed to travel at high speeds in emergencies, with the risk of causing severe accidents. But again it does not follow that one may simply off set the costs paid by third party individuals against the benefits accrued by the persons in need, as for example, to kill one person to save the lives of five. The intuition which plays a role in the moral debate on the difference between killing and letting one die tells us that such an act is wrong. Even if, with respect to every right, there may be circumstances under which a right may be violated, such a violation is certainly not permissible on the basis of a simple cost-benefit calculation.

In Samaritan Situations there is sometimes the additional difficulty in weighing the costs paid by third parties against the costs paid by the agent himself. Basically, one can assume that in cases of doubt the helper should carry the burden himself instead of shifting it off onto others. If one has the option of breaking his own vase or that belonging to someone else, he should smash his own. Only when the weighed risks prove highly imbalanced may it be justified to spare oneself and shift the burden onto others.

As I have demonstrated, under certain circumstances within Samaritan Situations, deciding whether one has a right to help, to help at all or to help in specific ways proves difficult, when weighed against the special rights claimed by individuals in a particular situation or against the so-called negative rights existing on the part of the agent, the person in need, or third party individuals.

But some Samaritan Situations have another, special feature that gives rise to further ethical considerations. These are situations in which helping consists of an *intervention* into a conflict. Not every kind of help is an intervention. Neither the good deed of the biblical Samaritan nor the rescue of a drowning child are interventions. Interventions presuppose a *conflict* between different agents into which a third agent interferes who has not been involved yet. Nor is every intervention an act of helping, not even when the intervention is justified. (A mother may, e.g., intervene in a conflict between her children in order to make them finish their homework.) But in many instances of Samaritan Situations, help would still consist of an intervention, and if so, the agent has to consider two further ethical aspects. Firstly, interventions frequently entail costs for the threatening party of the conflict (e.g., if one prevents a man from beating his wife through the use of brute force). So one may ask how the possible harm that may be done to the threatening side of a conflict should enter into the decision to help. Secondly, conflicts usually continue even after an intervention has removed the actual danger or need, so the question becomes how far the helper's interference involves him morally in the ongoing conflict.

The answer to the first question seems to be easy. A person who threatens or torments someone else should pay the consequences when others step in to help his victim, at least up to some limits. (One does not automatically forfeit one's right to life if one is cruel or humiliating with regard to others.) This is plausible, providing that the threatening person has no right at all to behave as he does. It is more complicated, though, when he is somewhat justified in how he approaches his victim, or at least if his behaviour is understandable. To rescue a hostage from his place of captivity may, for example, be justified under circumstances that would not justify freeing a convicted prisoner from his cell. If someone is beaten because he is small and weak, we are strongly inclined to intervene, but not so in a case where he is beaten because he has deceived his subsequent aggressor beforehand (even if such revenge is not morally just). Conflicts not always, but sometimes, have a history, which has to be taken into consideration when one asks whether and how to intervene.

Moreover, conflicts also frequently lead to repercussions. The relationship between the conflicting parties does not necessarily come to an end when the emergency is removed. Neighbours still live nearby, even when the one is not able to harass the other one any longer. Couples are not divorced just because the man is prevented from beating his wife. This is where the second question comes in, in examining how far the intervention changes the moral involvement of the helper. The answer is that, since interventions consist in interfering within a conflict, the intervening agent himself thereby becomes a party in the conflict, and is, therefore, still involved in these relationships, even when there is no longer an emergency. But interpersonal relationships necessitate the forming of responsibilities, which the helper would not have had if he had not intervened. As things are, he is involved, and it is reasonable to expect from him that he continues to act within the situation. That does not mean that he is not free to relinquish this responsibility at some point, but unlike in the situation where he does not interfere at all, in that moment when he in fact does interfere, he takes on the responsibility. To relinquish his responsibilities is a new step, which is in need of its own moral justification.

How far the helper's responsibility goes and how easy it should be for him to relinquish it again, depends essentially on the costs entailed through his aid, particularly for the persons in need and for third party individuals. This is due to the genuinely paternalistic and consequentialistic character of a decision that burdens others with the fruits of our actions, although they neither have incurred guilt nor explicitly asked for the action. When we feel entitled to let others suffer in order to do something which is decidedly good as a whole, we commit ourselves to the obligation of taking care that everything will work further.[9]

Samaritan situations that are interventions into a conflict are therefore more complicated to assess ethically than classical Samaritan situations, in which someone is saved from an impersonal danger. These non-classical situations can result in further obligations on the part of the helper. What may render the assessment even more difficult is that one has to consider still another ethical aspect apart from the obligation to help. When someone places another person in the threat of danger, this behaviour is usually considered morally wrong in itself. Hence, the intervening helper does not direct his help simply against a danger, but against a culprit. His action is not only to act in such a way as to wipe out the threat of danger, but to serve justice by doing so. As with respect to honour, this aspect could speak in favour of some ways and against others for intervening. Giving one hundred Euro to the lout in order to stop him from molesting the woman would not only be lacking in chivalry but would also be unjust, because it would reward him for his wicked behaviour. Accordingly, to give him a blow instead, in addition to saving the woman and revealing one's manliness, would give him what he deserves.

It is precisely this impulse for justice that renders the moral evaluation of rescue interventions so difficult. After all, it is not only the plight of others that we do not want to let continue but also blatant injustice. This is particularly so in situations where we are involved, where we hold responsibility, as is characteristic for interventions. Unfortunately, help and justice are not always compatible. The lout in the above-mentioned example could be stronger than I am, which leaves me with the decision either to bribe him or to expose the woman to his rudeness. Presumably, in most of these cases we have no choice but to help the needy. To leave someone in the lurch for the sake of justice would be a dubious form of moral egoism. But it is a further reason to feel responsible for any future course of events: One should better act to alleviate any injustice brought on through one's own actions (even if these actions were carried out unwillingly).

There is one final aspect of the moral evaluation of help, whether with regard to classical Samaritan Situations or to interventions: the helpers' *intentions*. Is every act of assistance, which is in accord with one's duties, morally good, or is it necessary that the assistance should be done from the point of 'good will'? This is a general question in ethics and not confined to assistance, but in Samaritan cases it is particularly tricky, first because assistance usually demands gratitude, which only seems to be appropriate for actions undertaken out of responsibility for the needy, and secondly, because frequently the costs accumulated through the assistance must be paid by others, and it does not seem appropriate that a malicious agent should have the right to harm others in order to pursue his dubious intentions. Nonetheless, I am afraid that in the end what matters morally is only that one relieves the plight of others by acceptable means, even if one does it through dishonest motives. Someone who knocks down a madman who tries to stab a child is doing the right thing, even if he does it in the hope of a reward or to settle an old score. Saving the child is the right thing to do, though doing it for the wrong reasons does not mean doing good is necessarily being good.

5 WAS NATO IN A SAMARITAN SITUATION IN 1999?

It is the aim of my paper to answer the question whether the NATO bombings of Yugoslavia in the spring of 1999 were morally justified. I began with the assumption that they could only be justified if they were humanitarian interventions, which in turn should be assessed with analogy to individual, interpersonal help offered in a time of need. We therefore have to apply the considerations of the previous sections about the ethics of Samaritan Situations to the NATO air strikes.

The question, whether these air strikes were justified reactions to a Samaritan Situation, presupposes that Nato actually was in such a situation on March 24, 1999. Is this assumption true? That depends on whether the five conditions for Samaritan Situations outlined above are satisfied.

What is beyond doubt is that at the beginning of 1999 the Albanian population of Kosovo (which was about 90% of the total population) lived under extremely unpleasant circumstances. For ten years they had already borne a system of apartheid implemented by a regime of Serbian nationalists, against which they had built up a self-organized parallel society alongside the Serbian moulded state institutions. When their hopes for a better, more autonomous future were dashed in the Dayton agreement of 1995, the UCK gained influence, and since February 1998 at the latest (when a major Serbian offensive in the Drenica region took place) a civil war was raging in Kosovo, under which the whole population suffered.[10] During one year, up to March 1999, considerably more than 1,000 of the 2.2 Million people who lived in Kosovo had been killed, many others had been injured, raped and humiliated, while more than 400,000 people had temporarily fled or had been expelled from their homes.[11]

In the autumn of 1998, after a violent earlier phase in the spring and summer of that year, the situation had eased up considerably. Following a number of increasingly sharper toned international protests, NATO had resolved on an activation order for air strikes against Yugoslavia on October 13, which immediately, on the same day, led to a cease fire agreement between Richard Holbrook, representative of the international Yugoslavia Contact Group, and the Yugoslavian president Slobodan Milosevic, committing him to troop reduction and permitting the stationing of 2,000 OSCE controllers (the Kosovo Verification Mission KVM). Yet, by the end of 1998 the fighting flared up again, not least because the UCK took advantage of the situation and attempted to win back terrain which they had lost in earlier stages of the civil war and to attack governmental and military targets. In reaction to this development, the Yugoslavia Contact Group attempted to persuade the fighting parties to come to an agreement again, first in February in Rambouillet, France, and then in mid-March in Paris. The Albanian side eventually agreed, the Yugoslavian side did not. As a result the KVM personnel was removed from Kosovo and, following a last, futile meeting between Holbrook and Milosevic, the air raids began on March 24, 1999.

As I have said, there is no doubt that at the beginning of 1999 the people from Kosovo were in desperate straits, what is questionable is *how* desperate their situation was. In any case, until the KVM controllers left, their situation was no worse than it was a year before. There was no dramatic change, no intensification, until the OSCE retreated and the air strikes began.[12] Nonetheless there was an emergency situation, and help was urgently needed. When large parts of a population have emigrated or are internally displaced, when anyone from the region need be prepared he or she might fall victim to violence, when basic civil rights are ignored, then the people are certainly in existential danger and in need, from which they should be rescued if possible. This demonstrates that the third condition for Samaritan Situations was satisfied.

The same is true for the first condition that we were confronted with their need. Our confrontation with the events of Kosovo was possible through the modern reality of mass media, which saturate us daily with images and news at an international scope. Scharping's appeal "We dare not look away" was so plausible, because thanks to television it would be difficult to do that and look away. Moreover, the audience in Western Europe, particularly in Germany, had even more direct access to what was unfolding in Kosovo. Since the beginning of the Serbian policy of suppression launched in the early nineties, Kosovo Albanians began fleeing west, and this stream of refugees dramatically increased in 1998 due to the civil war. (According to statistics put out by the German Minister of the Interior, in 1998 thirty-five thousand citizens of Yugoslavia had fled their country seeking asylum, while in 1997 only fifteen thousand had done so.) In such a matter as this, their plight was brought home to us, too. And finally, Kosovo is spatially nearby, only a few minutes flight time from our favourite beaches in Italy and Greece. Whatever happens in Kosovo, therefore, happens in our immediate neighbourhood.

What about condition 5, that there had not been any other agents who were in charge and willing to help? No doubt, the governments of the FRY and of the Republic of Serbia had the obligation to prevent the Kosovo population from being exposed to danger and from facing oppression. This is in accord with the Yugoslavian constitution, as well as with § VII of the CSCE Final Act of Helsinki. But obviously these governments not only did not perform their duty, but rather were seen as the instigators of the threat, from the point-of-view of the persons in need.

One could also ask, whether the United Nations or the Security Council had a special obligation to protect the Kosovar population.[13] On the one hand, in the preamble of the UN Charta, the United Nations commits itself to the aim of protecting human rights. On the other hand, its Declaration of Human Rights from 1948 only has an advisory status, which is not binding for the member states. Even subsequent and more definite UN-agreements only ground entitlements between the member states of the UN, not between states and individual persons. Consequently, the victims of human rights violations can not claim the right to receive aid from the UN. Nor is it the task of the Security Council to provide aid. Its function is confined to safeguarding peace and international security (§ 24 UN Charta). Hence, the Kosovar population indeed was on its own, and condition 5 was satisfied.

The same is true of condition 2. There was no pre-existing special obligation between those who offer assistance and people in need. To be sure, there have been special relationships between Western countries and the FRY, for example, the CSCE contracts and the Dayton agreement. But with regard to the latter, the Kosovo problem is explicitly excluded as being a domestic problem of Serbia. The Western states in no way felt responsible for the fate of the Kosovar people. This can also be observed from the shared practice of the Schengen states of enforced repatriation of Kosovo-Albanian refugees immediately after Dayton. At that time about 130,000 Kosovo-Albanians were expelled from Germany alone, although it was well known that widespread, ethically motivated discrimination and suppression existed in Kosovo.[14] Obviously in the mid-nineties most Western governments regarded the Kosovar population as outsiders whose fate was not a matter of concern.

This observation is perfectly compatible with the claim that these Western states could have prevented the disaster in Kosovo (as well as other disasters in former Yugoslavia), if after the end of the Cold War they had been sufficiently far-sighted and had invested more into the future of this region.[15] In international affairs, the protagonists of Samaritan Situations are never so alien to each other as their biblical forerunners. States do not simply find themselves confronted with an emergency without any former pretext; the world is much too small and transparent for that. An alien relationship between states is more comparable to the artificial distance between the individuals in an apartment building: the personal interests of the tenants rather than the spatial distance between them create the boundaries between them. To keep out of Kosovo until the situation there escalated, was just like a neighbour ignoring the shouting and beating next-door, only until he could not absolutely mistake the screams any longer.

Finally, one has to ask whether condition 4 for Samaritan Situations was fulfilled, that of the appropriateness of the help. In order to answer this question, one has to specify in more detail what was the assistance that NATO was willing to offer. Up until now I went on the assumption that the relevant actions were the air raids in the springtime of 1999, but the intervention certainly began earlier than March 1999; the air strikes were only the final act in an escalating process that had already been set in motion a year earlier. At the latest, serious international intervention into the civil war began with the arms embargo by the UN Security Council on March 31, 1998, and then reached its initial climax in October 1998 with NATO's activation order, before the Holbrook-Milosevic agreement had led to an interim détente. As this agreement shows, these earlier interventions were quite successful. Forceful diplomatic pressure, supported by the embargo and, finally, by a military threat, diminished the urgent need (although these effects presumably could have been strengthened if the UCK would have been bound into the agreement more tightly and if the KVM had been implemented faster and had been better equipped).

The NATO officials, therefore, had good reason to believe that a repetition of their threat in the spring of 1999 would prove to be effective again. And even when immediate success was not forthcoming, they could reasonably have expected to possess enough military power for imposing their will on the Yugoslavian government. After all, NATO is by far the world's most powerful military alliance. Even the limitation of their military attacks to air strikes, without using ground troops, was not per se insufficient in exerting pressure on the Yugoslavian government. Hence, it appears that the fourth condition was also satisfied. In March 1999 NATO was confronted with a Samaritan Situation, where the civilian population of Kosovo was in a severe emergency situation, which was caused by the repressive conduct of state institutions and irregular Serbian fighters. As in the case of any Samaritan Situation, there was a consequent obligation for NATO to intervene and help. The only question is whether the manner in which NATO carried out its duty was morally correct.

6 WAS THE BOMBING OF YUGOSLAVIA BY NATO A MORALLY JUSTIFIED ACT OF ASSISTANCE?

As I have mentioned, a number of states and international organisations had already intervened into the Kosovo conflict in 1998. NATO was involved at the latest when it issued its activation order, which led to the Holbrook-Milosevic agreement. It sheds some light on the evaluation of the later decisions to ask first, how does one morally evaluate the threat from October 1998. Prima facie the attempt to intimidate the Yugoslavian ruler was unobjectionable. It had the desired effect of de-escalating the conflict without causing any negative side-effects. But moral value is not simply a matter of actual success; it also depends on the risks the agent has taken. (If you wager the life of your child on a racehorse, you are not excused for your action when you win the bet.) That the NATO states indeed ran a risk when they threatened Yugoslavia with military attacks in October 1998 became clear the following March, when Milosevic refused to surrender and thus forced upon the NATO states the alternative of either carrying out their threat and launching the air raids or exposing themselves as paper tigers.

The evaluation of the NATO threat exemplifies a general problem that emerges in all threats of violence. If these threats turn out to be successful, then they are a relatively inexpensive means. The threatening party need not actually do anything, the threatened party is not harmed (except for a certain loss of face). Difficulties arise if the threat does not succeed, because then the threatening party only has the alternative either to act upon the threat, which usually is quite costly, or to do nothing and risk a severe loss of credibility. In short, threatening with violence is a cheap but risky form of intervention. It should not be employed without a serious calculation of the costs it may create. The NATO states certainly knew the risks and already in October 1998 were quite obviously willing to put their threat into action if necessary. Hence, it can be concluded that in the end the moral assessment of the first NATO intervention in October 1998 is dependent on the evaluation of the later military attack in March.

I have already demonstrated that in March 1999 the NATO states were confronted with a Samaritan Situation, which prima facie obliged them to intervene. The question is, whether the way they carried out their duty was morally acceptable. This in turn is dependent on two other questions: firstly, whether such measures could be *morally justified at all* (given the burden placed on the people involved, and not, as I have stated, on abstract agents such as the FRY); secondly, whether there were *less costly alternatives* available to achieve the intended aim.

Every military attack creates adverse effects on the people living in the targeted country. First of all, it destroys the life or health of many of them. In response to the parliamentary question of the PDS party (based on a report of the International Tribunal for Former Yugoslavia), the German Bundesregierung has estimated that the NATO air strikes killed about 500 civilians and wounded 820.[16] In addition, an unknown number of soldiers were killed or wounded.[17] Moreover, the bombings damaged personal property and the environment (although the Bundesregierung felt unable to quantify the extent of destruction). All in all it has to be stated that in spite of all the high tech weaponry employed, the NATO air strikes created many more civilian victims than the Serbian attacks in Kosovo for the same period before (military victims left out again).

Part of these collateral damages presumably could have been avoided, if NATO had been willing to place their soldiers at a higher risk by letting them drop the bombs from lower altitudes. So, one might ask, whether such a more dangerous strategy would have been morally superior. This is a difficult question, since on the one hand, as I have already mentioned, it is generally plausible that the aggressor, not the helper, should carry the burden of the costs ensued through intervention. On the other hand, in Kosovo the aggressor has been the FRY (or the Serbian Republic) and not individual Serbs. It is a central insight of modern laws of war that not every citizen is an enemy. Hence, it might be necessary to regard the civilian Serbian population as a third party in the conflict, and usually it is not right to place the costs of one's assistance onto third parties. One has to smash one's own vase instead of the one belonging to someone else. Still, pilots are not vases. They are moral subjects in their own right, too, and moreover they stand in a special relationship to the helping agent: As soldiers they are presumably obliged to run higher risks; but their home country, in turn, carries a special responsibility of providing for their welfare. In the end, these divergent considerations do not fit into a clear-cut ethical picture. The responsibility to its own soldiers speaks in favour of the defensive NATO strategy, but there certainly is a kind of Haut gout in the fact that NATO has waged a war without losing any soldiers at all for the price of causing the collateral damage of hundreds of killed civilians. How much one is, nonetheless, willing to approve this strategy is presumably dependent on how much one is inclined to blame *all* Serbian people for the suppression and mistreatment of the local population in Kosovo (as well as in Bosnia and Croatia before). That is, how far the Kosovo-Albanians had to be defended against 'the Serbs' themselves, and not just the Serbian rulers.

The most serious consequences of the air strikes, though, were felt most adversely not by NATO, nor by the Serbians , but by the people in Kosovo itself. The NATO air raids gave rise to an excessive and unrestrained backlash against the Kosovo Albanians, carried out by the Yugoslavian army, police, illegal fighters and a Serbian mob. According to an estimation by the Independent Kosovo Research Commission, between March and June 1999 about 10,000 people were killed in Kosovo and 1.45 Million were expelled.[18] If injuries, rapes and humiliations are taken into account as well, along with the sheer terror of becoming the victim of such violence, practically every Kosovo Albanian has lived in a situation of danger and distress that is scarcely imaginable for most of us. In short, the supposed aid had increased the need of the victims dramatically instead of removing it.

This fact, though, does not entail that the attacks were morally wrong. The moral value of an action is not simply drawn from its consequences. Bad luck might turn even an entirely praiseworthy act into a catastrophe. Yet, the more incalculable and dangerous an action is, the higher are the demands placed upon the agent to act cautiously and the less likely it is for the agent to claim bad luck as a force which shaped the outcome. Waging war certainly is a risky enterprise; one should demand a careful cost-benefit-calculation, and the warrior has to accept that he gets credited even for those consequences of war that he did not intend but could have foreseen.

So, the question is whether the atrocities that occurred during the war were foreseeable for NATO. The German Bundesregierung has quite explicitly denied that they were: "An expulsion on a scale that actually happened was not regarded as possible."[19] But what was the scale of possibilities? Noam Chomsky, in his book *The New Military Humanism*, offers a great deal of evidence that the Western governments were afraid that the withdrawal of the OSCE verificationists and the Serbian feelings of being powerless against the air raids would dramatically worsen the repression in Kosovo. In this light it is much more probable that the NATO governments had accepted these risks as possible side-effects of their measures.

But there is another, more pertinent justification for the NATO attack, despite the risks involved for the already suffering people of the region. It was particularly emphasized by the German government, regardless of a certain inconsistency with regard to the supposed unforeseeability of the atrocities.[20] According to this justification, the Serbian, or Yugoslavian, rulers had planned the violent expulsion of the Kosovo Albanians beforehand. The air strikes were only the welcome trigger to setting these plans into motion, which sooner or later would have been implemented without the NATO bombings. In that sense the NATO attack was not the cause of the atrocities but at best the reason why they took place right then. This analysis of the situation proposed by the Bundesregierung was confirmed by secret service material, the so-called 'Horseshoe Plan', which was supposed to have proven that a concrete military plan had already been conceived for the expulsion of the Kosovo Albanians.[21]

It is difficult to assess the soundness of this second justification, in particular from a distant philosophical perspective. To me it seems to be obvious yet that there would not have been such a sudden, widespread escalation of expulsions if the KVM had stayed in Kosovo and if no air strikes had been undertaken. It also seems to be obvious, though, that as the situation appeared at the beginning of 1999, there was no possibility for a peaceful state of affairs which would not have caused a massive loss of face for one of the parties in the civil war. A repetition of the Holbrook-Milosevic agreement would have been as tenuous as the original one, except if it were guaranteed by strong international military forces present in Kosovo. But in this case, Kosovo would have been separated from Serbia, quite as it is today after the war, which would have been unacceptable for Milosevic. Given his definite intention that Kosovo, despite its overwhelming Albanian majority, had to remain a Serbian dominated and Serbian oriented part of Serbia, the Yugoslavian president had no other choice but to expel many Kosovo Albanians and to occupy Kosovo (regardless of how advanced these plans already were when the NATO attacks began). The governments of the other countries, therefore, were presumably right to assume that such measures had to be expected anyway, irrespective of how much the documents proved. Furthermore, the international expectations were certainly influenced by Serbian conduct during the wars in Croatia and Bosnia, where foreign air raids had not led to ethnic cleansing and excessive human rights violations. It was not far off to expect that sooner or later the Kosovo Albanians would be treated similarly. And given that the member states were already assuming the worst, a victorious NATO after the war would be able to put an end to the atrocities and could undo many of the expulsions. This appears to be the lesser evil, even more so if the war also could put to an end the many years of nationalist suppression.

Moreover, one has to ask whose standards should be applied here. As I have said, helpers tend to make decisions paternalistically, over the heads of the needy. It is therefore important to take the attitudes of the Albanians themselves into account, especially the willingness of the UCK to sacrifice their lives and the lives of others in order to fight the Serbian oppressors, and their the support granted to them by the Kosovo Albanians, who were disappointed by the failure of their long-standing non-violent resistance. For the UCK, the air attacks and the following escalation of the war were welcomed. One can perhaps assume a certain willingness on the part of the Kosovo Albanians to accept the militaristic way of liberating their homeland, despite the heavy losses which would then ensue.[22]

In order to complete the calculation, another cost factor had to have been taken into account, which would then have to be paid when the NATO attacks were successful: the fate of the Non-Albanian Kosovars after the end of the war. According to the Bundesregierung, from the end of war until the end of 2000 389 people were killed, 3,714 people injured, 287 people kidnapped, 899 houses were burned down to the ground and about 220,000 non-Albanian refugees were expelled from the region.[23] This means, if we only look at the number of expelled people, the war had not changed anything, except for the ethnic origin of the victims. There was still roughly the same amount of refugees in Kosovo.

Now that the various effects of the NATO attacks have been named, how do they add up into an ethical judgement? To my mind, the situation of the Kosovo Albanians in advance of the air raids was so desperate that it was not principally wrong to intervene with military force, even if this meant the death of Serbian civilians. It is less clear to me, though, that NATO was justified in laying the burden of the war on the Serbian people, as was in fact done. With respect to the situation in Kosovo, I have no doubt that NATO had accepted beforehand that the attacks would lead to increased suffering for the Kosovo Albanian people, although perhaps not on such a large scale. Whether the attacks were nonetheless justified depends on how things would have developed if NATO had not intervened. It seems to me that it was neither probable that the persecutions and atrocities would have been as severe as the actual ones, nor that without NATO intervention the conditions for the Albanians would have become even modestly decent. Presumably, the civil war with all of its horrors would have continued undiminished.

All in all, these aspects do not create a clear picture which would illustrate a definitive argument for or against the NATO attacks; it remains open whether these attacks were right or wrong. But there are two more considerations that have to be taken into account which change the picture significantly: first, an appraisal of the long-term and broader effects of the attacks, beyond Kosovo, and secondly, the question of whether the NATO attacks were not only a suitable, but also the best and least harmful, means for the intended result. I shall begin with the second consideration, which will eventually lead to a discussion of the first one.

Was it really impossible to stop the civil war and the resulting misery without waging war and hence without risking excessive expulsion and large-scale atrocities? I believe it may have been possible. The international community could have instead supported the Yugoslavian rulers in their attempts to restore the situation to the time before the civil war. If their governments would have been willing to cut the ground from under the feet of the UCK, to block their supply of arms, and disarm them, to restore the undiminished authority of the Serbian republic in Kosovo and to secure it for the future, the Yugoslavian government in turn probably would have granted the people in Kosovo a right to stay and the minimal protection they had enjoyed before 1998. In this way it would have been possible to reduce the plight caused by the civil war without military intervention and presumably with far fewer casualties. This would mean that there has been a much less costly alternative available to NATO other than the bombing, which would have been suitable in relieving the suffering of the population. If NATO had been merely interested in providing emergency relief, then the above-mentioned alternative would have been the best option; NATO would not have had the right to carry out military missions. The attacks would have been morally wrong.

But the answer is not so simple. It is much more plausible to react as in the case of the guy who is bullying a woman. One would not like to bribe him to stop his offensive behaviour, even if it were to be the most effective and cheapest means, since, firstly, it would offend our sense of honour, and secondly, it would be utterly unjust. I am sure that both aspects played an important role in the actual decision-making process to begin the bombings, and they are both relevant for the ethical evaluation.

That the Kosovo war was primarily a matter of preserving one's honour, if not also a matter of even less respectable motives, is the argument presented by Noam Chomsky. He considers the air raids to be yet another example of proof illustrating the ruthlessness of the policy of the US and US-dominated NATO.[24] According to Chomsky, the US was not interested in whether people were suffering in Kosovo but in its own status as the one and only world super power, which possibly would have been marred, if, in the year of NATO's 50th anniversary, Milosevic could have triumphed over it. Chomsky supports his claim that the plight of the people of Kosovo played a marginal role at best in how decisions were made by the US government by providing an impressive list of countries where the US government not only tolerates but actively supports a treatment of citizens that is not better and even worse than what the Kosovo Albanians had to endure. But as I have said before, the moral value of an action is not tied to the honest intentions of the agent. At least from the German perspective, it is still a pertinent question whether the less costly alternative of supporting

Milosevic against the UCK could have proven the air strikes to be morally wrong.

This is where the second objection begins to unfold, in that it would have been unjust, and unfair, to support Milosevic instead of fighting him. The way in which the Serbs treated the Kosovo Albanians after they had repealed their autonomy was utterly reprehensible; hence, the legitimate right to fight was to be rightly claimed by the Albanian side of the civil war, not by the side of the Serbs. If NATO would have tried to appease Milosevic at the expense of the Kosovo Albanians, it would have made itself an accomplice to the actions of the Serbian government and it would then be responsible for a desperately unjust situation in Kosovo. The NATO states were not willing to offer such support. Instead, they readily accepted that their emergency measures in assistance to the Kosovo-Albanians could also, as a welcome side-effect, lead to more justice, lawfulness, democracy and liberty for the population. Or, the NATO states already were actively intending this outcome through their assistance.

Justice, lawfulness, democracy and liberty are valuable moral commodities, and to promote them is prima facie right and good. It may well be discussed if it could be right or even obligatory to employ military means to pursue these ends. (With respect to guerrilla and freedom fighters, this question was readily discussed even within the peace movements of the sixties, seventies and eighties.) But these commodities are not in congruence with the aims of helping the needy. The legitimacy of pursuing moral aims by waging war is not to be found in the ethics of Samaritan Situations, but in the traditional question of what is a *just war* – including all the difficulties associated with that topic. For me, this result is unavoidable: If the NATO attack was morally justified at all, it was not merely because it was an instance of a justified Samaritan act but because it was an instance of a just war for several excellent, 'just' reasons, only one of which was saving the people from their existential danger.

This is the answer to the initial question in my examination: The needs of the endangered and tormented people alone could not justify the military attack, since they could have been aided more readily by strengthening Milosevic. Whether the attacks nonetheless could be justified as an instance of a just war is beyond the scope of this paper. Without such an additional justification, though, the air attacks were essentially morally wrong.

Before concluding my argument, I want to point out the slippery slope of NATO's own justification for attacking FRY (which is to be taken into account regardless of what kind of ethical justification we have in mind). The three years since the Kosovo air strikes have already made clear that the danger of war has increased. I doubt that it would have been so easy for the US government after September 11 to regard fighting a war against Afghanistan just as a matter of course if there had not been the wars in Kosovo and in Kuwait beforehand, which smoothed the way for open military campaigns in response to evil international acts, and Bush would presumably be less frank in threatening (and perhaps soon pursuing) military aggression against Iraq and other countries as well. Within a short period of time, the recourse to a minimal right for helping those in desperate need has turned into a universal claim to enforce law and order as one wishes and to activate military power against whatever one regards as a 'rogue state'.[25] But as soon as a claim to such a right is generally accepted, the demands for a coherent and explicit justification for military actions are immediately reduced into mere public propaganda pronouncements.[26]

Perhaps the most conspicuous feature of the developments over the last three years is the almost indissoluble entanglement between morals and honour, which was already mentioned as a problem for the ethics of Samaritan interventions. Although politicians frequently talk about morals, what they actually try to display are virtues of a quite different quality: strength, serenity, self-control, the ability to assert oneself. These are not typical characteristics of morally grounded behaviour; at best they can be regarded as characteristics of a man of honour and pride; rather, they are associated with behaviour linked to self-righteousness and hypocrisy. Their importance for politicians makes obvious that we should not expect them to care much about morally impeccable action. Politicians might all too easily take the renaissance of ethics in international affairs as a welcome opportunity for a revival of hypocritical chivalry or a mendacious Wild West codex, which usually is no more than a disguise of a tough egoistic policy of self-interest.

7 CONCLUSION

How shall we asses the NATO attack against the FRY ethically? In general, to help others in need is frequently permitted and sometimes even mandatory. The people in Kosovo in 1998/99 doubtlessly were in a desperate situation and had to rely on external aid. The way of helping them with the least amount of loss of life and of health would have consisted in supporting Milosevic's attempt to restore his illegitimate power in Kosovo. The immense costs the Kosovo Albanian people had to pay instead, due to the air raids that actually took place, are only justifiable if the aims of the war are taken to be more extensive, consisting of promoting justice, liberty, and civil rights. How far these aims suffice to make these particular military actions morally legitimate depends on whether there are just wars to begin with and whether this war was such a war.

But even if military actions are just, waging a war lends itself to accepting a considerable amount of resulting costs. First, as with every intervention, one becomes responsible for the further course of events. In the beginning, the intervening states have accepted this aspect of their intervention more fervently than in many other cases, by accepting responsibility for administering to the political and policing forces in the region, signing the Stability Pact for South Eastern Europe, just to mention a few examples. Secondly, everyone who finds himself on a slippery slope has to take care that things don't get out of control. The members of the German Bundesregierung and parliament who have proclaimed that they have considered their approval of the NATO attacks very carefully, should now be judged by the same standards whenever they have to decide again whether to engage in military actions.

Finally, the self-critical question remains, what am I as a moral philosopher doing, when I sit at my desk in Germany and write under what circumstances is it justified for people somewhere else in the world to wage war. I am confident that I have addressed the ethical deliberations and arguments in this context appropriately. With regard to the facts, I hope to have been careful enough not to overstate my positions in lieu of my limited capabilities. Still, a sense of inappropriateness remains. After all, in the end it is not the moral philosopher or the foreign minister who ultimately, in the words of Joschka Fischer, decides not to retreat to the safety within his four walls but intervenes where people are slaughtering each other; that is, it is the more-or-less voluntary soldier. And were I to land in Pristina, Kabul, or Baghdad, I could not be sure that when confronted with the basic question of this paper I would not simply answer with the old slogan from Woodstock: "Don't ask me, I don't give a damn."[27]

NOTES

[1] I have examined the moral status of corporations in my "Metaphysische und moralische Personen".

[2] The contention that the right to assistance in an emergency, as a prepositive right, could not be unlawful is defended by Reinhard Merkel, "Das Elend der Beschützten", sec. 2. The weaker claim that the NATO attacks were illegal but nonetheless legitimate has been made explicitly by the Independent International Kosovo Commission: "The Commission concludes that the NATO military intervention was illegal but legitimate" ("The Kosovo Report", p. 4).

[3] In this respect I am following Georg Meggle's strategy in his article "Ist dieser Krieg gut?".

[4] Cf. the extended discussion of the topic in Joel Feinberg "Harm to Others", Chapt. 4.

[5] The example is from Jeffrie Murphy, "Blackmail: A Preliminary Inquiry", p. 168.

[6] The basic notion that ethics should rely on moral rights instead of duties or utility is to be found in John Mackie, "Can There Be a Right-Based Moral Theory?".

[7] The expression "minimally decent Samaritan" is from J.J. Thomson, "A Defense of Abortion", p. 15.

[8] Murphy, op. cit.

[9] This does not imply though that the assisted parties are obliged to accept our care. As we might have the right to refuse responsibility for any unfolding future events, the victims have the right to say farewell to us after the end of our initial assistance.

[10] According to Hans Loquai, in his very extensive study *Der Kosovo-Konflikt – Wege in einen vermeidbaren Krieg,* the civil war had already begun in November 1997 (p. 22).

[11] The number of those killed is based on the Kosovo-Report by the International Kosovo Commission (p. 82 f). The authors report more than a thousand persons killed for the period between March and August 1998, including UCK fighters though. According to the authors, the toll of lives was considerably smaller in the remaining period until March 1999. The German government also used these figures in their response to a 'Große Anfrage' of the parliamentary party PDS [henceforth: "Anfrage"]. A detailed account of many individual attacks and infringements is to be found in the report of the Kosovo Verification Mission *Kosovo/Kosova As Seen, As Told*", part III.

[12] Cf. Loquai, op. cit. p. 44, who also discusses the alleged exception, the so-called Racak massacre on January 15, 1999.

[13] Cf. for the following Otto Kimminich, *Einführung in das Völkerrecht*, Chapt. 13.

[14] Cf. *The Kosovo Report*, p. 59.

[15] Cf. Horst Grabert, "Die Kriegslogik durchbrechen".

[16] "Anfrage", answers to questions 5 and 6. This estimation is supported by a report of Human Rights Watch from February 2000 "Civilian Deaths in the NATO Air Campaign," Principal Findings).

[17] According to Serbian information at least 600 soldiers were killed, half of them by the UCK ("The Kosovo Report," S. 94).

[18] "The Kosovo Report", p. 2.

[19] Anfrage, answer to question 102 (my translation).
[20] Cf. "Anfrage", answer to question 82.
[21] Cf. Loquai, op. cit. Chp. 8, "Anfrage", answer to question 89. The claim that the expulsion was systematically planned beforehand was supported by the OSCE report: "Most tellingly, the analysis of some of the most prevalent human rights and humanitarian law violations, as well as the analysis of their geographical organization and their impact on communities, demonstrate how the violations inflicted on the Kosovo Albanian population after 20 March were a continuation of actions by Yugoslav and Serbian military and security forces that were well rehearsed, insofar as they were already taking place in many locations in Kosovo well before 20 March." ("Kosovo/Kosova – As Seen, As Told" Executive Summary). Yet it has to be taken into account that such an important international organization as the OSCE is hardly free from political considerations.
[22] Cf. Loquai, op. cit. p. 44.
[23] "Anfrage", answers to questions 5, 6, 13, 14
[24] Cf. his *The New Military Humanism.*
[25] That this is what the US officials always had in mind was made very explicit by senator John McCain at the Konferenz für Sicherheitspolitik in Munich 2002: "Several years ago, I and many others argued that the United States, in concert with willing allies, should work to undermine from within and without outlaw regimes that disdain the rules of international conduct and whose internal dysfunction threatened other nations. Since then, two rogue regimes have fallen after military intervention by American-led allied coalitions: Slobodan Milosevic's Serbia and the Taliban's Afghanistan. In both countries, liberal reformers are now in power, and the threat each nation posed to its neighbors ended with the downfall of the tyrants who ruled them." (Speech text taken from the conference internet page).
[26] An excellent example for this tendency is provided by the ubiquitous talk about fighting terrorism as an obvious justification of military violence, despite the fact that these days it is almost arbitrary whom to call a terrorist and whom not. Milosevic was perfectly right to emphasize in his speech for the defence in the Hague that he fought the UCK as terrorists. None of that alters the fact that his fighting was illegitimate, but the statement makes clear how absurd the present 'alliance against terrorism' is and how easily the moral language may degenerate in the mouths of politicians.
[27] I want to thank Toni Koch, Jens Kulenkampff, Lorenz Lorenz-Meyer and Charlie Prankel for their helpful comments and discussion. I am also very grateful to Diane Kerns who has corrected and improved my English considerably.

REFERENCES

Chomsky, Noam, *The New Military Humanism*, Monroe 1999.
Feinberg, Joel, *Harm to Others*, Oxford 1984.
Grabert, Horst, "Die Kriegslogik durchbrechen", in: F. Leidenmühler, R. Steinweg (eds.), *Kosovo und die Folgen*, Idstein 2000: 61-71.

Human Rights Watch, Civilian Deaths in the Nato Air Campaign, Internetsource: http://www.hrw.org/reports/2000/nato/

Ignatieff, Michael, *Die Zivilisierung des Krieges*, Hamburg 2000.

Kimminich, Otto, *Einführung in das Völkerrecht*,. Tübingen, Basel [6]1997.

Loquai, Heinz, *Der Kosovo-Konflikt – Wege in einen vermeidbaren Krieg*, Baden-Baden 2000.

Mackie, John, "Can There Be a Right-Based Moral Theory?", in: Mackie, *Persons and Values*, Oxford 1985: 105-119.

Meggle, Georg, "*Ist dieser Krieg gut*?", in: R. Merkel (ed.), *Der Kosovo-Krieg und das Völkerrecht*, Frankfurt/M. 2000: 138-159.

Merkel, Reinhard, "Das Elend der Beschützten", in: R. Merkel (ed.), *Der Kosovo-Krieg und das Völkerrecht*, Frankfurt/M. 2000: 66-98.

Murphy, Jeffrie, "Blackmail: A Preliminary Inquirie", *The Monist* 63 (1980).

OSZE Kosovo Verification Mission, Kosovo/Kosova As Seen, As Told, Internetsource: http://www.osce.org/kosovo/documents/reports/hr/

Stoecker, Ralf, "Metaphysische Personen als moralische Personen", *Allgemeine Zeitschrift für Philosophie* 22 (1997): 245-271.

Thomson, Judith Jarvis, "A Defense of Abortion", in: Thomson, *Rights, Restitution and Risk*, Cambridge (Mass.), London 1986: 1-19.

Unabhängige Internationale Kosovo-Kommission, The Kosovo Report, Internetsource: *http://www.kosovocommission.org/reports/index.html*

ALEKSANDAR PAVKOVIĆ

Saving Lives in Nationalist Conflicts: A Few Moral Hazards[1]

1. HUMANITARIAN INTERVENTION: SAVING LIVES BY KILLING PEOPLE

Humanitarian military interventions are usually or even primarily justified by reference to their principal aim: to save the lives of unarmed civilians which would have otherwise been lost. Unlike humanitarian non-military interventions, the military ones are meant to use deadly force in the process of saving lives. The use of deadly force in modern 'high tech' wars or interventions still has the unintentional but predictable effect of killing other unarmed and non-threatening civilians.

In consequence, any justification of humanitarian military intervention which refers to the saving of innocent lives faces the following question: Could the saving of innocent lives justify killing other people who are not threatening anyone, that is, who are equally innocent? And if so, how could saving innocent lives justify acts of war, which involve killing people who are not threatening anyone? This essay will address these two questions in the context of military interventions in nationalist conflicts such as the one in Kosovo.

In our attempt to answer these two related questions let us start with an imaginary but realistic example in which the act of killing innocent people is justified by the saving of lives.

> Due to an accident, a passenger ship starts taking water on one side and is in danger of rolling over. In order to prevent this and save the lives of hundreds of passengers, the captain has no other option but to flood the compartments on the other side, knowing that this act is likely to (or will) kill dozens of trapped crew and passengers.

In order for this killing to be justified by the saving of lives, it is, I believe, necessary:

(1) that the action leading to the killing of the innocent be the only available action which could have saved the endangered lives. It is not *only* a less risky or a less costly option than other available actions but the only action that could have been undertaken to save these lives. In our example, the captain decided to flood the compartments *not* because any other attempts to right the ship and save the passengers were less likely to succeed. He decided to do this *not* because he regarded the death of a dozen crew and third class passengers as less costly than the death of the equal, or greater, number of the first class passengers whose lives were in danger. He decided to do this because to the best of his knowledge at the time, there was no other way of saving the threatened passengers. We can call this condition the *No Other Option condition.*

(2) that the causing the death (or killing) of the innocent people be an action of the kind that can be justified by reference to its consequences in the saving of lives. Some types of killing cannot, I believe, be justified in this way. In our example, the captain ordered that the compartments be flooded *not* because he wanted to kill the members of the crew in those compartments because they had witnessed his complicity in some criminal acts (e.g. of extortion or blackmail): his action was not a murder of potential witnesses against him. If it were, that action could not justified by reference to the lives saved by its performance. Probably there is no generally accepted list of actions which cannot be justified in this way – but the murder of witnesses of one's own criminal acts is surely one of those. This condition will be called the *Justifiability condition.*

(3) that the action leading to the death of the innocents may reasonably be expected to save more lives than it terminates. The captain ordered the flooding of the compartments knowing that they held a much smaller number of crew and passengers than the total number of passengers and crew threatened by the rollover of the ship. Had that not been the case, and the number of those killed

had been greater than the number of those saved, he (and we) would have considered his action irrational and senseless (if not devious). As in (2) above, there is no generally accepted formula of proportionality, stating that one killed person could, in such emergencies, justify the saving of *X* number of lives. This condition we shall name the *Death Minimization Condition*.

The No Other Option condition in (1) could be justified by the humanist principle of equal and paramount value of each human life. This principle asserts that no human life is less or more valuable than any other and that an individual's life is not comparable in value to anything else but another human life.

The Death Minimization condition in (3) follows from the same principle, and the description of the action as that of saving innocent lives. If the saving of lives is expected to lead to more deaths than those saved, either this was not intended to be an action of saving lives or else the principle of the equality of human lives was intentionally breached in the belief that the lives of those killed were less valuable than those saved.

The Justifiability condition in (2) is, however, more controversial. Some – those usually inclined towards deontological ethical views – would argue that no non-accidental or intentional killing (or perhaps no action whatsoever) can be justified by its beneficial consequences, while others – usually the consequentialists of various kinds – would argue that every type of action, however wrong it may appear to be, could be justified, at least to some extent, by its beneficial consequences. The position I take here is a pluralist one, according to which actions, in general, can be justified both by their intrinsic moral characteristics and by their beneficial consequences. In some cases, however, I hold that the intrinsic moral characteristics of an action cancel any justification by its beneficial consequences; in such cases the beneficial consequences following from such an action are considered irrelevant to its justifiability. Some cases of killing for specific self-interested reasons, I believe, fall into this category. Thus any beneficial consequences of a killing committed to prevent the disclosure of other immoral or criminal acts of the killer or his associates, are irrelevant for the moral judgment on, or justification of, that act. In other words, any other description of that act which would make it morally neutral or morally permissible (such as 'killing for the sake of saving other lives') is incompatible with the initial and true description of that act as a case of killing for specific self-interested reasons. In contrast, killing for altruistic reasons, for example, killing a terminally ill relative or friend who is in great pain, may also be truly described as a mercy-killing; under that description the act is morally permissible and justifiable by its consequences.

There are at least two arguments in support of my view that some acts of killing are not justifiable by their beneficial consequences. First, one can point to harmful or unacceptable consequences of the policy which would allow individuals to commit irreversibly harmful acts, such as killing, provided that these also have beneficial consequences. The policy of permitting killing provided it saved some lives would encourage people to kill for self-interested reasons in such circumstances where this would save someone's life. For example, killing of witnesses of one's criminal acts could be justified by the fact that his donated organs would save the lives of many ill people. The general policy advice would be: if you kill anyone, be sure that as a consequence of his death, at least some lives are saved. This is not the kind of policy advice consequentialists would endorse or give. Quite independently of this, a policy prescription which would allow killing for self-interested reasons, provided specific beneficial consequences were to follow, would threaten the rule of law at least as it is understood in modern liberal democracies: the monopoly on the use of deadly force would be taken from the state and 'privatized'. Second, this policy would breach the principle of equal value of each human life: some lives would, in accordance with this policy, be less valuable and thus become expendable. Some innocent people could be justifiably killed for the personal gain of others, provided that their deaths saved lives. While these two arguments are not, necessarily, conclusive they provide at least some reasons for accepting the Justifiability condition.[2]

Having thus outlined three necessary (but not sufficient) conditions for justifying killing by the saving of lives it causes, I can now address the question: How could the saving of lives justify the waging of war against another state? A core activity of war consists in killing people; thus, one could argue, the killing of people is one of the main instruments of war. This makes war a rather poor candidate as a means of saving lives. In spite of this, each side in the First and Second World War argued that its waging of war was justified by its intent to save peoples' lives. Some of those justifications were often so transparently deceptive that, after the wars ended, they could not be taken seriously. In the next section we shall not consider the justifications offered for any war in the past but rather consider a very narrow category of wars, those waged in order to stop the killing of non-threatening and unarmed civilians, people who are in this essay called 'innocents'.

2. SAVING LIVES BY WAGING WAR

A state or group of states may wage war against another state with the intention of stopping the systematic killing of innocents taking place in that state. In such a case, from the fact that the systematic killing is taking place, it is obvious that the state in question is pursuing a policy of killing innocent civilians or a policy of condoning such killing by non-governmental agencies. In view of this systematic killing and the underlying governmental policy, a victorious war waged to replace this government, or to stop this pursuit of its murderous policies would, in all likelihood, save innocent lives. Yet, like any other war, this would result in killing of innocents as well. It is for this reason that such a war would need to satisfy the three conditions which are based on the three necessary conditions outlined in the preceding section:

First, waging war against the allegedly murderous government or state must be the only way to stop the killing of innocents. In some cases, the killing will be organised by the state and carried out by state agents for ideological reasons. The best known example in recent history is the Khmer Rouge killing of Cambodian civilians. Between 1975 and 1979 the revolutionary Khmer Rouge government in Cambodia forced most urban dwellers out of the cities and towns into countryside where they were put to work under extremely brutal conditions. As a result, several hundred thousand civilians died or were intentionally killed.[3] If all diplomatic efforts (including threats and sanctions) to induce the government to stop or prevent such killing have failed, and the government's ideological commitment to that kind of killing indicates that no further efforts of this kind would succeed, then the No Other Option condition appears to be satisfied.

Second, waging war in such circumstances must be justifiable by reference not only to broadly defined beneficial consequences but, specifically, to the saving of lives. For example, various oppressed groups wage liberation wars against their conquerors or oppressors and justify the killing and destruction caused by the intended beneficial consequences of such wars – the liberation of their group from an unjust or oppressive rule. This broadly defined beneficial consequence is not equivalent to the saving of innocent lives. Unjust and oppressive (foreign or domestic) governments do not, necessarily and as a matter of policy, kill their non-threatening and unarmed subjects. The removal of such a government by war cannot, therefore, always be justified by the saving of lives of innocents. The converse, however, does hold: a government which organizes or condones killing of its non-threatening unarmed subjects is certainly an oppressive and unjust government. Thus, those wars which stop the killing of innocents may also lead to the removal of oppressive and unjust governments. Even so, the justification by reference to the first beneficial consequence differs from the one which refers to the second.

There are also wars which are waged with the intention of gaining control over a people, and the territory on which they live against the wishes of that people. Any such war is a war of conquest (where 'conquest' is broadly interpreted as any imposition of control over a territory) and is the very opposite of a war of liberation. These wars also result in the end of violence and killing. Are these wars then justified by the saving of lives? Among philosophers, Michael Walzer appears to think some such wars are: the Vietnamese invasion of Cambodia in December 1978 which removed the Khmer Rouge government from power and replaced it with a Vietnamese-controlled regime also ended the systematic killing of innocent civilians by the Khmer Rouge. This result justifies the war the Vietnamese waged against the Khmer Rouge government – although it does not justify their imposing a government of their choosing on Cambodia.

This example is not meant to demonstrate that waging wars of conquest is, in general, justifiable by the saving of lives, only that in some cases such wars can be so justified. Is there also a kind of war – like killing for self-interested reasons – which cannot be so justified? At times, governments wage wars to cover up evidence of their own incompetence or malfeasance or to distract the attention of their constituencies from unacceptable or dubious aspects of their rule. If a war of this kind leads to killing of innocents, then it resembles killing carried out in order to remove evidence of criminal acts in at least one way: in both cases people are killed in order that the evidence of wrongdoing be covered up. Further, governments sometimes wage wars of conquest (broadly defined) in order to enable their individual members or their associates to exploit the resources of the conquered territory for personal gain. This kind of war resembles killing for the purpose of robbery; such a murder (and any resembling war) is not, in my opinion, justifiable by the saving of lives. This indicates that there are some kinds of war which are not justifiable by the fact that they save lives; these examples, however, do not provide the necessary or sufficient conditions for such unjustifiable wars.

Third, if a war turns out to have caused a larger number of deaths than it saved, it cannot be justified by reference to the lives saved; therefore, in order to be justifiable by the saving of lives, war needs to be waged with the reasonable expectation of saving more lives than causing deaths. Various aspects of modern warfare make it quite difficult to satisfy this requirement. For example, if a life-saving government uses any modern weapons of mass destruction, it may cause, unintentionally but predictably, a larger number of deaths than lives saved. Likewise, a life-saving government cannot control the way its enemy will fight back – the enemy may choose to expose its own side to the greatest possible number of casualties. If a government intent on going to war is to justify the waging of its war by reference to the lives saved, it would need to wage this war in the way which avoid predictable but unintended casualties among the non-threatening civilians.

Such a problem arises in any war in which saving lives is dependent on a military victory over a resisting enemy. Military victory can be achieved only by the use of appropriate or proportionate force against the enemy forces. But the use of appropriate force (in particular, weapons of mass destruction) to this end, in the face of a strongly resisting enemy, may indeed lead to more deaths than saved lives. Thus, the means required to achieve victory may be incompatible with a death minimization strategy which aims to minimize the deaths of all warring parties. In such a case, the fulfilment of the Death Minimisation condition is conceptually incompatible to the requirement of military victory: in order to satisfy the condition, the life-saving government would have to give up victory in a war that would be too costly in human lives.

From time immemorial military commanders and political leaders have, however, adopted a *partial* death minimization strategy: in their pursuit of military victory, they often strive to minimize, both for prudential and for ethical reasons, only the number of deaths of their own co-nationals and their allies. In some circumstances a partial death minimization strategy of this kind is incompatible with the above Death Minimization condition, requiring, as a reasonable expectation, that the war will cause less deaths than lives saved. For example, one's own military personnel can be protected by using weapons of mass destruction against a technologically inferior enemy. For example, high altitude aerial bombing or long-range artillery or missile bombardment of a technologically inferior enemy effectively minimizes death among the military personnel of its technologically superior adversary. But the use of unguided weapons of this kind poses a greater risk of death to innocent civilians than the use of ground forces and their close support aircraft targeting military facilities (the latter, however, increases the death toll among the life-saving military personnel). It is also difficult to estimate and to control the death toll among the civilians exposed to weapons of the kind; and, unless the estimate of lives to be saved is very large, it is difficult to reasonably expect that the use of the weapons of mass destruction is to lead to a smaller number of deaths than lives saved.

Unlike the life-threatening disasters caused by accidents or by natural phenomena (floods, earthquakes and the like) war is an intentional activity whose main instrument is the use and the threat of use of deadly force. If its use is to be justified by the saving of lives, as we have seen above, one needs to restrict its scope and aim. This may not only reduce its effectiveness as an instrument of war but may also change the nature of the war waged for that purpose. If so, the wars waged with the intention of saving the lives of enemy subjects are specially restricted wars in so far as the use of deadly force in them is restricted to minimize deaths. In their aim, these specially restricted wars resemble humanitarian interventions such as the operations launched to assist the victims of large scale natural disasters such as famines, earthquakes and the like. The aim of any humanitarian intervention, apart from providing assistance to the victims, is to remove either the potential causes of death and injury or the individuals from the area in which they are exposed to the risk of being killed. Specially restricted wars of this kind also aim to remove the potential causes of death and to protect the endangered individuals from violence and death. This gives some ground for the argument, readily espoused by the politicians and media in the interventionist countries, that specially restricted wars for the sake of saving lives of innocents are a species of humanitarian intervention.

However, in non-violent humanitarian interventions, the principal aim – the saving of lives – is achieved by the use of means other than the deadly military force or the threat of such force. As a result, in non-violent humanitarian interventions, interventionist personnel are not exposed to the risk of being intentionally killed by those who resist their intervention – and, of course, those whose lives are to be saved (the victims) are not exposed to the same risk of being killed, unintentionally, by those who were supposed to save their lives. In non-violent interventions, the interventionist personnel can thus safely seek to minimize both the deaths in their own group and of the victims without bringing into question their humanitarian aim – the saving of the lives. In violent humanitarian interventions, a partial death minimization strategy, aiming to minimize the deaths *only* among the interventionist personnel, and allowing as many deaths among innocent people of the opposing side as required for a military victory, may bring into the question the intervention's over-all aim of saving the lives of innocents. Humanitarian interventions in which the risk of death is minimized only for the interventionist personnel may turn out not to be that humanitarian, after all. This becomes quite apparent in cases of military interventions in nationalist conflicts.

But in spite of all these difficulties facing humanitarian military interventions, one may still argue that the war by Vietnam against the Khmer Rouge government in 1978/1979 fulfilled the above three conditions necessary for such an intervention. One could argue that the war caused fewer deaths than it saved, partly because the Khmer Rouge military resistance to the Vietnamese military was weak, the Vietnamese did not resort to indiscriminate bombing of any targets close to civilian centres and the Cambodian civilian population mostly welcomed the Vietnamese forces. Apart from the war, there was no other way of stopping the Khmer Rouge government from pursuing its policy of killing civilians; and, during the ten years of occupation, the Vietnamese officials did not, systematically or otherwise, exploit Cambodia's resources for their own personal gain.[4] Nationalist conflicts, as we shall see, create conditions which are quite unlike those under which the Vietnamese intervention was carried out.

3. SAVING LIVES IN NATIONALIST CONFLICTS

A nationalist conflict is a war between two or more national groups over political control of a single territory. Each national group is mobilized to support the use of violence against the other national group(s). The very presence of members of a national group on the contested territory is considered by its opponent(s) as an obstacle to their political control of the territory. In consequence, each member of the opposing national group on the contested territory is considered to be a threat of some kind. Hence, members of the war-mobilized national groups do not, in general, consider the non-threatening and unarmed civilians of the opposing national group as 'innocents'. This view explains, at least in part, the intentional mass killing of unarmed civilians, including women and children, by any party in such a conflict.

A stronger warring party in a nationalist conflict would resist any outside military intervention aiming to save the lives of innocents because it would regarding the saving lives of the enemy population as aiding their enemies' war effort. By protecting war-mobilized civilian population of the weaker party, such an intervention could enable that party to hold or to conquer the territory which the stronger party considers its own. For the same reason the weaker party or parties would welcome such an intervention.

Irrespective of this contest over territory, a military intervention against one warring party, with the intention of saving the lives of its enemies, may enable members of the 'enemy' group(s) to kill innocent members of the group against which the military intervention is directed. Since the former do not consider the latter as innocents, they would not consider this impermissible and there would be no effective constraint to prevent them from doing so.

In the context of a nationalist conflict, an interventionist war for the sake of saving lives may, therefore, lead to the deaths of the innocents in at least three ways:

First, as in any war, military action aiming to defeat or subdue the military forces may, unintentionally – and unnecessarily – lead to the death of innocents among all warring groups.

Second, interventionist military action may lead to the death of the conscripts, belonging to the resisting group, who are resisting the interventionist force simply because the latter is attacking their group and its territory. These conscripts are not engaged in killing or threatening to kill innocents of the enemy group and are, therefore, innocent themselves.

Third, military actions against one group may enable the members of the other, adversary, group to kill innocents from the group against which the action is directed.

In a nationalist conflict with the already established inter-group hostility and violence, one can expect that a military action against one group will enable the other, adversary, group to proceed to kill members of the group exposed to this action. Therefore, in such a case the interventionists would have at least to share responsibility for the deaths of these innocents: without their military intervention, it is unlikely that these murders of members of one party to the conflict would have been committed.

In a war waged to save one group of innocents from a murderous and unpopular government, such as Vietnam's war against the Khmer Rouge regime, the interventionist force, targeting a relatively small and isolated group of people and its military force, may find it easier to avoid inflicting civilian casualties; and the conscripts may find safer to surrender to the interventionist forces than to fight for a government which they do not support. During their invasion of Cambodia, the Vietnamese forces found it relatively easy to avoid civilian casualties as the towns have been evacuated before their arrival, the civilians welcomed their invasion, and many members of the Khmer Rouge conscript force surrendered or fled. In cases of nationalist conflicts, evacuating one's own civilians from any territory is considered a defeat and is avoided by all costs – thus exposing the civilians to military action. For soldiers, conscripted or volunteers, to surrender to the enemy or its allies is considered highly risky – and this is only one reason why they are not likely to surrender. And, for the reasons mentioned above, civilian population of the opposing side is seen as a threat and is therefore exposed to selective or mass killing. An outside military intervention in such a conflict faces a wider range of ways of causing deaths to innocents than a military intervention against a murderous and unpopular government. This makes it less likely that the Death Minimization condition would be satisfied in a nationalist conflict.

But an outside military intervention in such a conflict may face additional difficulties of satisfying the No Other Option as well as the Justifiability condition. Let us start with the No Other Option condition. Nationalist conflicts are a result of a series of decisions made by political and community leaders of the national groups inhabiting one and the same territory. The latter at some points decide to use force or to condone the use of force against members of other national groups. In the present scenario of an impending life-saving military intervention by outside powers, these leaders have also decided to at least condone mass murder of innocents from the enemy national group

At each stage, these leaders had options other than the use of force and condoning mass murder. This is a major difference between natural disasters resulting in mass deaths and human-engineered mass killing. Since the warring parties have other options than to participate in mass killing, the interventionist party has also other options than to intervene by force to stop the mass killing. In most natural disasters, there are no options, of any kind, for preventing or avoiding mass deaths. If the interventionist party has the military power to intervene in the conflict, it is likely that it also has (or is capable of gaining influence) over the warring parties in the conflict. If the interventionist party has an option to influence the warring parties to desist from the use of force and from killing, then that military intervention is not the only option it has to stop the killing.

In order for the No Other Option to be fulfilled, the interventionist party must have exercised all other options at its disposal to stop or prevent killing, including that of using all the influence it has on any warring parties in the conflict. While it is often difficult for outside observers to establish whether all the options of this kind have been exercised, if it is shown that the interventionist party, before its military intervention, failed to exercise an option it had to prevent or stop the killing, that would make clear that in this case the No Other Option condition has not been fulfilled.

Military powers capable of effective intervention in nationalist conflicts often (but not always) support, politically and militarily, one of the warring parties in the conflict. In cases in which no warring party is supported by a major military power, such as that of Rwanda in 1994, the outside military powers usually fail to intervene, in spite of a huge losses of innocent lives. But if a potential (life-saving) interventionist power is already supporting the territorial claims of one warring party and provides it with military support in its armed struggle, it has already opted for the use of force as a way of resolving this conflict. In doing so, the potential interventionist party may have already forgone the option of using its influence on one of the warring parties to desist from the use of force. The former may have good reasons for doing so; for example, it may have good reasons for believing that the other warring party(or parties) in this conflict would kill innocents, regardless of whether the party it supports desists from its use of force or not. But, in such a case, regardless of its reasons for forgoing this option, a military intervention is not the only option the interventionist party had in its attempt avoid or stop mass killing.

This kind of support for one of the warring parties in the conflict may make it difficult for the eventual military intervention to satisfy the Justifiability condition as well. In many cases, military support to one of the warring parties – in weapons, training, and logistic support – is hidden from the public because it is not legally authorised; in order to keep it hidden, the potential interventionist government publicly (and falsely) denies giving any such support. If the supported party is defeated, this would probably lead to the disclosure of the support and of the accompanying lies and so in order to prevent such an exposure, the implicated government intervenes in the conflict, thus winning the war for its almost defeated ally, and justifies its intervention by reference to the innocent lives it saved.

This scenario has obvious and intentional similarities with a case in which the captain orders compartments of his listing ship flooded with the intention of killing a few crew members in them who witnessed his extortion or blackmail (and also of righting his ship as described in the original scenario). By flooding the compartments he succeeds in saving many more lives, but the saving of lives was not his primary or only intention. Similarly, in the above scenario, while the military intervention saved innocent lives, the interventionist government would not have ordered it, had it not been threatened by the disclosure of its lies and its illegal military support. Under these conditions, one could argue, its military intervention, which led to (unintentional) killing of innocents, cannot be justified by the saving of innocent lives: under these conditions, killing innocents cannot be justified by the saving of (other) innocent lives.

No doubt, an interventionist power can surmount difficulties such as these and thus satisfy both the No Other Option and Justifiability condition. For example, if a potential interventionist power remains neutral in a nationalist conflict and if all or some warring parties reject all non-military attempts by the interventionist and other parties to make them desist from using force, military intervention may indeed be the only option for stopping mass killing. However, in such a situation the life-saving interventionist force may face resistance from all or most warring parties and from their war-mobilized populations; this resistance in turn may increase the death toll on all sides, including the interventionist military personnel. Satisfying these two conditions in this way may make it more difficult to satisfy the Death Minimization condition.

A good illustration of how these difficulties in satisfying the above condition in may arise is provided by NATO's military intervention, in 1999, in the nationalist conflict in the province of Kosovo (or Kosova) in Yugoslavia.

4. SAVING LIVES IN KOSOVO?

The war NATO waged against the Federal Republic of Yugoslavia, from March to May 1999 has been justified by reference to the saving of lives of Yugoslav citizens of Albanian nationality in the province of Kosovo who were, it was alleged, exposed to mass killing by the special forces and paramilitaries of the Yugoslav government. NATO politicians and journalists often referred to this military action as a humanitarian intervention. Let us now see whether this military action satisfies the three conditions for justification of killing by reference to saving lives.

The Death Minimisation condition. In keeping with their proclaimed aim, the NATO military followed a death minimization strategy: NATO aircraft did not target the areas inhabited by civilians and flew at high altitude to avoid the exposure of its aircraft crews to the anti-aircraft fire. These two policies failed to achieve the desired minimization of deaths: in pursuing the second, the aircraft had to fly so high as to make it very difficult to distinguish military from civilian targets; this led to the bombing of civilian residential quarters, hospitals, civilian traffic and even Albanian refugee groups. Further, the NATO command did not seek to minimize deaths of the Yugoslav army conscripts who were not engaged in killing or threatening to kill innocents. For example, they systematically bombed the defensive positions of the Yugoslav army which was attempting to prevent the Albanian military forces from crossing into the territory of Yugoslavia from Albania.[5]

Upon the mutually agreed deployment of its ground forces in Kosovo in June 1999, NATO command pursued a policy of restricted protection of the non-Albanian population of Kosovo – Serbs, Montenegrins, the Roma and the Turks – from the Kosovo Albanian forces. In pursuit of this policy, NATO forces prevented Albanian access to several enclaves populated by non-Albanians including Serbs but studiously avoided any confrontation with the Kosovo Albanian armed forces or individuals who were expelling, kidnapping, killing or threatening to kill the non-Albanian inhabitants or the alleged Albanian collaborators outside these protected areas. During the first few months of its occupation of the province, the NATO forces failed to prevent the murder and kidnapping (involving suspected murder) of several thousands of non-Albanian civilians (as well as the expulsion from Kosovo of over 100 thousand non-Albanians). They also failed to find and bring to justice the great majority of the perpetrators of those murders and kidnappings.[6]

This indicates that NATO's strategy was at its core a traditional partial minimization of deaths, primarily restricted to its own personnel and that of its ally, the Albanian Kosova Liberation Army (the KLA). The saving of lives of the non-Albanian population or the Albanian inhabitants accused of past collaboration with the Serb government was throughout the war and in its immediate aftermath a secondary concern, which was not allowed to interfere with the primary purpose of minimizing the deaths among its own forces and its allies.

Whatever the strategy, did NATO military intervention satisfy the Death Minimization condition – did it save more lives than it caused deaths? There are two distinct questions here: Was the NATO military intervention intended and carried out so as to save more lives than it caused deaths? Did that military intervention in fact save more lives than it caused deaths?

The major difficulty for any attempt to answer the second question is the absence of any reliable evidence as to how many lives the intervention in fact saved. To find that out one would have to discover the plans of the Serbian and Yugoslav government, under Slobodan Milosevic, as well as the plans of paramilitary organizations operating in Kosovo to carry out the mass killing of Albanian innocents, prior to the NATO attack in March 1999. There is no evidence advanced so far[7] that, prior to that attack, Milosevic's government carried out any mass killing of innocents outside of immediate areas of fighting between its forces and the KLA. Neither the Yugoslav forces nor the KLA pursued a policy of saving the lives of innocents in the area of their military operations.[8]

In view of these policies of the two warring parties, had they continued to fight and had the area of their clashes continued to widen, many more innocents would have been killed in the course of their fighting: this would have happened, even if the Yugoslav government (or the KLA) had no plans for the mass killing of innocents. But given the steady advance of the Yugoslav military and its obvious military superiority over the KLA, it was likely that the former would confine the area of the KLA's activity to a few sparsely populated mountainous areas. Had that happened, the death toll among innocent civilians from the military operations would have, in fact, decreased. In order to save the lives of innocents in this way – by limiting their exposure to violent conflict and fighting – a military intervention by NATO was not necessary. In the absence of evidence of planned mass or systematic killings of Albanian civilians prior to the NATO attack, it is not possible to establish that NATO military intervention in fact saved more innocent lives than it caused deaths.

In spite of this, it is still possible to argue that NATO governments, on the basis of the previous evidence of mass killings carried out by the Serb forces in Bosnia-Hercegovina, had good reason to expect a similar policy to be pursued in Kosovo. According to this argument, NATO's military intervention was intended and carried out to prevent mass killings of the kind which took place in Bosnia-Hercegovina. The Serb forces which carried out mass killings in Bosnia-Hercegovina, were most often volunteer paramilitaries (often recruited from among persons with criminal records) or special policy/military forces and not ordinary conscripts of the Bosnian Serb military. To prevent such mass killings in Kosovo, NATO aircraft would have had to attack the units and their command posts which are most likely to carry them out. But these units and their command posts could not have been successfully targeted from the safe altitude at which NATO aircraft had to fly to avoid anti-aircraft fire. The initial bombing of Yugoslav army military installations and troops all over Yugoslavia from this altitude could not have been intended to stop or prevent mass killings; according to the commanding officer of the NATO operation,[9] they were not intended to do so. Had not been engaged in killing of the innocents. In fact the bombing did nothing to prevent those mass killings of Albanians, carried out by paramilitaries or special police units, which followed the air attacks on Yugoslavia. The effective prevention of the mass killings of innocents would not have been possible under NATO's partial death minimization strategy in which the highest priority was assigned to saving the lives of NATO personnel.

NATO's partial death minimization strategy was compatible not with a military operation which would effectively prevent mass killings of innocents in Kosovo but with a military operation aimed at securing control over Kosovo for NATO's ally, the KLA and its political leaders. In answer to the first question above then one can say that the way NATO's military operation was carried out did not indicate that its overriding aim was to save the lives of innocents; if so, it is doubtful that NATO's primary or overriding intention was to minimize the death toll of innocents. Even if evaluated only from the point of view of its intention, NATO's military intervention in Kosovo does not appear to satisfy the Death Minimization condition.

No Other Option. The NATO attack on Yugoslavia was preceded by a series of negotiations aimed at reaching a peaceful settlement between the Yugoslav government and the Kosovo Albanian political parties.[10] Prior to and during the negotiations, NATO government leaders repeatedly and publicly threatened the Yugoslav government with a military action unless it signed a peace agreement prepared and proposed by NATO governments. The attack ensued after the Yugoslav government, and its leader Milosevic, refused to sign this peace agreement. A major reason for their refusal was article 8 of the proposed agreement which allowed the deployment of NATO forces throughout Yugoslavia without the Yugoslav government's permission.[11] The attack was thus launched upon the Yugoslav government's refusal to allow the NATO forces to be deployed throughout Yugoslavia.

This indicates that NATO's war against Yugoslavia was not the only option available to NATO governments for preventing the expected mass killings of Kosovo Albanians. Another option, which NATO governments failed to pursue, was a mutually agreed deployment of NATO forces, under the mandate of the UN Security Council, in the province of Kosovo alone. Such a deployment – and the withdrawal of most of the Yugoslav military forces from Kosovo – would have been sufficient to prevent any action by the Serb paramilitary or professional police units against Kosovo Albanian civilians. Since the Yugoslav government agreed to such a deployment, the effective prevention of mass killings of Kosovo Albanians could have been achieved without any war against Yugoslavia. In fact, after 78 days of bombing Yugoslavia, NATO governments accepted a similar arrangement allowing NATO's deployment of forces in the province of Kosovo alone under the UN Security Council mandate. From this it follows that there were other options apart from waging of war and killing innocents: NATO's war against Yugoslavia thus fails to satisfy the No Other Option condition.

Justifiability. It appears that the US government and its NATO allies started to support the KLA in its armed struggle against the Yugoslav government in the early 1998. However, in spite of their help, by mid-1998 the KLA lost large areas it had previously controlled and failed to hold on to any towns. Its attempts to establish itself as an alternative or replacement government of Kosovo had thus largely failed. Moreover, the probable defeat of the KLA as an effective fighting force would have also ended its political effectiveness as well. It is still an open question whether and to what extent NATO's war against Yugoslavia was used to cover up the failure of its earlier policy of support for the KLA and to prevent its removal as an effective military and political force in Kosovo. If it turns out that NATO governments waged this war to cover up for the failure of their earlier policies, its justifiability in terms of the saving of lives would be, as I have argued above, questionable.[12]

Thus NATO's war against Yugoslavia fails to satisfy the No Other Option condition and, on the available evidence, it does not appear to satisfy the Death Minimisation condition. There is also some room for doubt as to whether it satisfies the Justifiability condition. In short, this war, at least on the available evidence, failed to save more innocent lives than it caused deaths – and those lives which were saved could have been saved by peaceful means, through a UN-supervised withdrawal of the Yugoslav forces and administration from Kosovo.

There are two obvious reasons why it fails to do so. First, the partial death minimization strategy aiming at saving the lives of NATO personnel and its allies first, under the conditions of the nationalist conflict, led to an increased number of civilian deaths of all national groups. Second, NATO's commitment to the victory of its ally among the warring parties, the KLA, prevented it from pursuing other options at its disposal for stopping or preventing the mass killing of innocents. In short, NATO's political and military goals – the victory of its preferred ally in the nationalist conflict at the lowest possible cost in human lives to its own personnel – were incompatible with the policy of saving innocent lives from all national groups involved in the conflict.

Let us now consider two alternative approaches that NATO could have taken in its military intervention in Kosovo. First, NATO could have taken a neutral stance in this conflict and intervened not in support of the KLA but only to save innocent lives from any national group. As pointed out in the preceding section, such a military intervention would have in all probability satisfied the No Other Options and the Justifiability conditions, but it is unlikely that it would have satisfied the Death Minimization condition. But NATO military intervention, using primarily air strikes, against all warring parties might have led to a greater number of killed innocents than the lives saved; a deployment of its ground troops, if resisted by all sides, would have also led to a substantial number of deaths among its personnel.

The second alternative, a NATO intervention without its partial death minimization strategy (aiming to protect the lives of its personnel) would assume that the NATO personnel engaged in it would have a duty to sacrifice their lives in a war waged in order to save the lives of threatened innocents in Kosovo. This raises two interrelated questions: First, are the citizens of NATO countries under any moral obligation to sacrifice their lives for the sake of saving the lives of non-citizens? And, second, would a protracted military operation aiming to save the lives of non-citizens, leading to a large number of deaths among NATO personnel, find electoral support in NATO constituencies?

A full discussion of these questions is beyond the scope of this paper. Here I can only state, without any elaboration, my preferred answers. As for the first question, I do not believe that NATO citizens had any general or special duties to sacrifice their lives for the sake of saving the lives of innocents in Kosovo. I do not believe that there is a general duty of every individual to sacrifice his or her life, if need be, for the sake of the saving lives of others, however those may be threatened. Further, the citizens and governments of NATO states at the time did not have any special duties towards the citizens of Kosovo and of Yugoslavia which could justify such a sacrifice. The citizens and governments of NATO bear no responsibility for the nationalist conflict in Kosovo and had not participated in the decision-making which led to the war between the KLA and the Yugoslav forces in the first place. The responsibility for the conflict is born, I believe, principally by the national leaders and on their constituencies in that region. Moreover, these leaders and their constituencies were, at the time when NATO attacked Yugoslavia, still in a position to end the conflict and thus to save the innocents without sacrificing any lives. If so, NATO citizens were not obliged to sacrifice their lives for the sake of saving the lives of non-citizens which could have been saved without their (or anyone else's) sacrifice.

If so, NATO electoral constituencies would be right not to support any policies willingly sacrificing their co-citizens' lives for the sake of saving lives which could have been saved without that sacrifice. The partial death minimization policy pursued by NATO was, I take it, meant to avoid any sacrifice of NATO personnel's lives. In so far as this was its aim, I believe it was justifiable both by prudential political considerations and by broader considerations of their citizens' duties towards non-citizens.

In short, I have tried to argue, first, that NATO's war against Yugoslavia in 1999 cannot be justified by the saving of innocent lives and, second, that NATO governments had no alternative ways of waging war or of military intervention at their disposal which would be so justified. This suggests – although it does not entail – that one should not attempt to justify a military intervention in a nationalist conflict by reference to the saving of innocent lives. Let us see whether (or how) this suggestion can be resisted.

5. SAVING LIVES REGARDLESS OF THE ABOVE THREE CONDITIONS

The above argument against the humanitarian justification of military interventions in nationalist conflicts is open to a number of objections of which I shall consider only two.

Let us start with an objection which rejects the three above (or any other) conditions as necessary for any humanitarian justification of military intervention in nationalist conflicts, including that in Kosovo. The objection could start with the observation that NATO's military action, by removing the Yugoslav administration and the military from Kosovo, stopped the mass killing of Albanians which had been taking place. In this way NATO's military action saved many innocent lives which would have been lost. The saving of these lives is, by itself, sufficient to justify its military action. No other consideration such as the number of deaths caused by this operation, what other options there were to stop the killing and so on, is in this case of any relevance to that simple justification. A lot of lives had been saved and that justifies the action taken to save them. Any attempt to make other considerations look relevant to this justification is a lot of ungrateful nitpicking. Theirs was an operation of saving lives *tout court*.

This objection, as it stands, is ambiguous in its implications. Are other considerations, apart from the over-all number ('a lot') of lives saved, irrelevant to all such justifications or only to this one? Had NATO used active nuclear weapons (instead of only enriched uranium shells) and caused tens of thousands of (immediate as opposed to delayed) civilian deaths, would this consideration of the deaths caused be irrelevant? Would the fact that many lives were saved in such circumstances be an adequate justification of military operations with such consequences? If this is not the case, and other considerations are irrelevant only in this particular case, one would need to know why they are so.

One reason for their irrelevance may lie in the simple *assumption* that the number of innocent deaths caused by NATO's military intervention was *not* larger than the number of innocent lives saved. In the preceding section I have argued, rather too briefly, that so far there is no evidence that this indeed was the case. Regardless of my or any other argument, this assumption is (so far) unsubstantiated; if the objection rests on this assumption, it is itself unsubstantiated.

However, if the objection makes no such assumption, then one needs to show why NATO's action of saving those lives justifies killing a lot of other innocent people in order to do so. In other words, one would need to show why the number of people killed by NATO's action (or inaction) is irrelevant to this particular justification of their killing. I think that the principle of equal value of human lives – which I have endorsed in the beginning of the essay – would make it quite difficult to show this. The principle implies that the value of each individual life saved by NATO's operation is equivalent in value to each individual life it terminated. For the purposes of the argument, we can restrict this to the lives of innocent people. If the number of innocent lives terminated is here irrelevant for the justification of the intervention, this suggests that these lives are not of equal value to the lives which were saved. I do not know how this suggestion can be resisted, and, therefore, I do not know how one could show that the number of innocent people killed is irrelevant without abandoning the principle of the equal value of human lives.

The second objection to be examined here is based on the distinction between wilful and inexcusable murder and unintentional and excusable killing. The innocent people killed in NATO's military operation were not intentionally killed: these people were not targeted and every effort was made (short of exposing the lives of NATO's personnel to risk) to avoid killing them. If they were killed, they were, the objection assumes, killed by accident. In contrast, the innocent Albanians in Kosovo were targeted to be killed, on the sole grounds of belonging to a national group, and therefore they were either murdered or in danger of being murdered. They were to be (or were) killed intentionally, premeditatedly, and not by accident. Killing by accident is, by definition, excusable. NATO's killing of innocent civilians, committed by accident, is thus excusable and is not, in any way, to be compared with the murder and planned murder of innocent Albanians. Therefore, saving innocent Albanians from murder is justified, regardless of the number of accidentally killed innocents.[13]

This distinction implies that those who kill by accident are not to be condemned in the same way as those who murder. If NATO killed the innocents only by accident, one cannot condemn it in the same way as one can condemn Milosevic's regime for its mass murder of Albanian innocents. This essay presents no grounds whatsoever to question this conclusion.

Yet this distinction does not absolve those who kill by accident of the blame nor of the responsibility for taking someone else's life: the killer in such a case is not freed from blame nor responsibility. NATO's command was responsible for conducting the bombing in a way which risked killing innocents. They were capable of predicting that some civilians would be killed: their killing was not an unpredictable or unexpected accident. Moreover, the killing of innocents did not result from sheer negligence to take appropriate precautions against killing civilians. While some precautions against this were indeed taken, many bombing raids were conducted with full knowledge of the risk to the lives of civilians. To put it rather crudely, NATO command knew that their bombing campaign would lead to the death of innocent civilians and that knowledge did not stop it from conducting the campaign in the way that they did. If so, their killing of innocents was not an accident which they were not in position to prevent. In short, NATO's killing of innocents cannot be excused or justified on the ground that it was an unpreventable or unpredictable accident.

But, if NATO's killing of civilians is not excusable solely on the grounds that it was done by accident, how can one justify it? Let us try this argument: the murder of innocents for self-interested reasons (such as any government's mass murder of its subjects) is incomparably worse than any killing of innocents by accident. In order to prevent or stop the murder, one is justified in committing acts which are not equally bad. Therefore, one is justified in killing, by accident, innocents in the course of an action aiming at prevention of murder. To put it in a much simpler if not too precise manner. Since murder is evil while killing by accident is not, from this follows a simple principle of justification: for the sake of the prevention of evil, one is allowed to use any means that are not equally evil. From this simple principle, it should follow that accidental killing of innocents, regardless of the number of innocents killed, is justified if done for the sake of saving other innocents from evil, that is, from murder.

To challenge this argument one does not need to disagree with the starting premise that murder and accidental killing differ in terms of their moral wrongness. One needs only to point out that sometimes they do not differ in terms of the specific harm they cause. From the point of view of the harm done to the families and, of course, to the victims themselves, it is of little if any consequence whether the action leading to their death was wilful but preventable murder by enemy forces or unintentional killing by these forces or their allies which the latter could have prevented. From the point of view of the nationalist ideologies and their mass following, any mass killing of unarmed civilians, in such a conflict, harms, in various ways, the national group to which these civilians belong. In view of this, it is possible to regard mass killings of innocents performed as unintentional killing on the same scale of harm (but not of moral wrong) as premeditated mass murder. If this is possible, then it is possible to ask how the prevention of harm caused by murder justifies the inflicting of harm by unintentional killing. The above argument and simple principle on which it is based offers no answer to this question.

The above argument implies that even if the number of innocents killed in this preventable but unintentional way is far greater than the number of innocents saved from murder, still the two acts – the latter act of (attempted) murder and the former act of preventable but unintentional killing – are not to be measured on the same scale of moral wrongness. In some cases, however, these two acts can be compared on the same scale of wrongness. Suppose in an operation to rescue a few kidnapped white tourists, a white rescue force killed indiscriminately a large number of coloured natives; they did not target the coloured natives specifically but fired indiscriminately in the crowds of coloured natives in which the kidnappers were hiding. Had the kidnappers been hiding among the white crowd of the same nationality as the rescue force, the latter would not have fired indiscriminately into the crowd. Their action, one can argue, exhibits their unspoken belief that the lives of the coloured natives are worth less than those of the white people. But killing people of a certain nationality or race, in the belief that their lives are worth less than the lives of people of other nationalities or races, one may argue, is on the same scale of wrongdoing as murder: as the latter, the former assumes that the lives of certain people are expendable. Indiscriminate killing of this kind may indicate a disregard for, or a breach of, the principle of equality of human lives.

The above two considerations – of the harm caused and of the breach of the principle of equality of human lives – indicate that the simple principle above does not, on its own, justify unintentional killing of (any number of) innocents for the sake of prevention of murder. As in the previous objection from the saving of lives *tout court*, further argument is required to show why either the principle of equality of human lives should be breached or that the principle is not, in fact, breached, in cases in which the number of 'excusably' killed innocents is allegedly irrelevant to the justification of actions saving (other) innocents from murder.

6. WHY DO WE JUSTIFY KILLING OF INNOCENTS BY REFERENCE TO THE LIVES SAVED?

There are many circumstances under which killing innocent bystanders can be justified by the attempt to stop a murderer or murderers commit murders or escape from justice. The simplest case is the one in which a lawful arrest is resisted by an armed murderer: as he fires at police officers, they return the fire in self-defence and unintentionally and by accident kill an innocent bystander who found herself at the scene. The bystander in this case was not in the line of fire but was killed by a bullet which ricocheted from the wall. The officers could not have predicted this and consequently could not have prevented this event (short of not defending themselves).

But suppose now that the armed murderer hid in a crowd of innocent people and fired from that crowd. In returning his fire, the police officers, using automatic weapons, sprayed the whole crowd with bullets, killing several people. They could have easily predicted and prevented this killing but believed that there was no other way to stop the murderer from continuing on with his murders and that, therefore, the sacrifice of a few innocent lives, randomly terminated, was justified.

Suppose that all of us agree with them that the indiscriminate use of automatic weapons was in this case the only way to stop the murderer getting away. In spite of this, many of us would disagree with them that their killing innocent bystanders was justified: many of us would argue that preventing (further) murder by sacrificing innocent lives in this case is not justified. The extent to which one would accept that their killing innocents was justified would depend, among other things, on the degree of danger that the murderer, hidden in the crowd, presented. If the murderer had access to weapons of mass destruction – for example, to nuclear devices – and the police officers knew that, many more people would share their belief that the sacrifice of a few randomly chosen lives is preferable than a much larger number of potentially lost lives. While this does not demonstrate that, under some circumstances, the sacrifice of innocent lives is justified, it does indicate that the ratio of innocents killed to the lives saved is of relevance in a justification of the killing of innocents in the course of prevention of murder.

In this paper, I have attempted to point out the difficulties which this kind of calculation of comparative harm encounters in cases of outside military intervention in a nationalist conflict. First, since the participants in the conflict do not believe that there are any innocents in this conflict, any mass killing of innocents will be perceived as a harm to one warring party, that one to which these innocents belong. However politically neutral the outside intervention may be, if it involves mass killing of any civilians, its effects are going to be perceived to be far from politically neutral. Second, by attempting, rightly, to minimize deaths among the interventionist personnel, the risk of deaths among innocents will be further increased, and may threaten to exceed the number of lives saved. Third, in protecting members of one warring party from the other, the interventionist force may enable the protected warring party to kill the innocents from their enemy group, thereby further increasing the total number of innocents killed. Fourth, in cases in which the interventionists are a dominant global or regional power supporting one warring party over the other(s), there will be some room for doubt that the interventionist power had no other option ('no other way') to prevent mass murder of innocents, except by going to war and thus killing other innocent people. Finally, I suggested that these difficulties arise both from the features of the nationalist conflict and from the conflicting obligations which the interventionist government has to its own citizens (the partial death minimization strategy) and to the non-citizens whose lives are endangered in a nationalist conflict.

While these difficulties may not be insuperable, they suggest that the consequences of humanitarian military interventions in nationalist conflicts may turn out to be much less humanitarian then their honorific title 'humanitarian' would lead us to expect.[14]

NOTES

[1] I would like to thank Robert Young of La Trobe University, Melbourne, for very useful suggestions and comments on an earlier version of the essay.

[2] For a further discussion of the murder/accidental killing distinction see section 5 below.

[3] The estimates of the number of victims of this policy vary from a half to two and a half million. In addition, from 90,000 to 150,000 people – mostly government or party employees and professionals – were executed in the 'interrogation' centres. For a survey of the evidence and of the number of victims see Gary Klintworth, *Vietnam's intervention in Cambodia in international law*, Canberra, AGPS Press publication, 1989, pp. 59-85.

[4] Klintworth points out that the Vietnamese did not justify their invasion by references to humanitarian considerations (Klintworth, op. cit. p. 11) and that their intervention was prompted 'by fundamental reasons of security and self-defence' (ibid, p. 60).

[5] See William Drozdiak, 'B-52 Strike Devastates Field Force In Kosovo...' *The Washington Post*, 9 June 1999, p. 19.
[6] For an account of killing and kidnapping of non-Albanians, see Human Rights Watch Report 'Federal Republic Of Yugoslavia Abuses against Serbs and Roma in the new Kosovo' August 1999, Volume 11, No. 10D, accessed at http://www.hrw.org/reports/1999/kosov2/, on 20 April 2002. Also, Letter to the President of the UN Security Council from the Deputy Prime Minister of Serbia, Mr Nebojsa Covic, of 24 April 2002. For an account of the organised killing of Serbs see 'KLA Units Specialized In Hunting Down Serbs,' *Agence France Press*, Pristina, 19 September 1999. Also 'Kosovo Resurgent,' *Economist*, 23 September 1999 and 'Reconstructing Kosovo,' *Economist*, 18 March 2000.
[7] The debate on the number of Albanians killed by the Serbian forces, prior to NATO's attack on Yugoslavia, is still carried out without any attempt to substantiate the claims that the bodies recovered by the teams of the Hague International Tribunal or other international forensics teams in Kosovo had been buried before the attack. For an example of this kind of polemic see Michael Ignatieff, 'Counting Bodies in Kosovo,' *The New York Times*, 21 November 21, 1999, section 4, page 15. For an early report outlining the problems of establishing the number of people massacred see Chris Bird 'Graves put Kosovo death toll in doubt: killings and forensics do not tally,' The Guardian, 11 November 1999. p. 2.
[8] The village of Racak, , the site of an alleged massacre of Albanian civilians, was a site of intense fighting a day before the bodies of around 40 Albanians (all allegedly civilians) were shown to the OSCE observers as evidence of the alleged massacre. No evidence of this kind – that is, bodies of Albanian civilians allegedly massacred by Serb forces – was presented to international observers or media prior to the NATO attack in March 1999. For a good survey of evidence, including the Serb government sources and the French reports from the village of Racak, see *Slucaj Racak: Zlocin i Kazna* (the Racak case: the crime and punishment), *NIN*, special supplement, Belgrade, 17. January 2002.
[9] In an interview on the US Public Broadcasting Service (PBS), General Wesley Clark told the interviewer, Jim Lehrer: 'Jim, we never thought that through air power we could stop these killings on the ground; it's not possible. You can't stop paramilitaries going house to house with supersonic aircraft flying overhead and dropping bombs; we all knew this....' A NewsHour with Jim Lehrer, interview with General Wesley Clark, on 29 March 1999, accessed at http://www.pbs.org/newshour/bb/europe/jan-june99/clark_3-29.html on 3 April 2002.
[10] The last in the series was held in February-March 1999 in Rambuillet, in France, under the chairmanship of British and French foreign ministers. The accords presented at this negotiation were then further negotiated separately with the Albanian delegates and the Serbian leader Milosevic.
[11] For the text see *Le Monde*, 23 April 1999, Appendix B, Article 8. Quoted in A. Pavkovic, *The Fragmentation of Yugoslavia: Nationalism and War in the Balkans*, London, Macmillan, 2000, note 26, p. 237.

[12] In an later interview, General Wesley Clark described the reasons for waging war against Yugoslavia as follows: 'Because what Milosevic never really understood was this wasn't a conflict strictly about Kosovo. It wasn't even a conflict, ultimately, about ethnic cleansing. It was a battle about the future of NATO, about the credibility of the United States as a force in world affairs. And the longer it went on, the more clearly the nations of the West would see those issues.' CBS News Interview of General Wesley Clark by David Martin, Tuesday, May 15, 2000, http://cbsnews.com/htdocs/pdf/clark.pdf, page 122, accessed on 2 April 2002.

[13] This is the argument David Runciman attributes to the British Prime Minister Toni Blair. See his 'The Politics of Good Intentions,' *London Review of Books*, Vol. 25, No. 9, 8 May 2003, pp. 3-11, at p. 8.

[14] An earlier version of this essay was published in *Lessons of Kosovo: The Dangers of Humanitarian Intervention*, edited by Aleksandar Jokic (Peterborough, Canada: Broadview Press, 2003). I am greatful to the publisher for allowing me to use the material from my earlier version.

MIROSLAV PROKOPIJEVIC

Humanitarian Intervention

A number of books and other publications suggest that genocide has culminated in the 20th century.[1] Some authors even feel it was invented in that century. However, this impression does not fit to the facts. The extermination of alien populations, including genocide, probably occurred more frequently in nearly any century other than the 20th. What makes the last century so different with regard to genocide and humanitarian crises is a feeling of the increasing unacceptability of such practices. Before the electronic age it was difficult to communicate disgusting pictures of mass starvation, ethnic cleansing or genocide. Modern media facilitated the decision to outlaw such practices in public international law, but at the same time their role became controversial because of apparent opportunity for manipulation. Anyway, contrary to the previous centuries when mass extermination of alien population was just a collateral of conquest, the 20th century has created some devices and provided incentives to reduce, if not to stop such practices. Public disapproval in conjunction with the creation of some rules governing the conduct of war and the readiness of some countries to intervene contributed to a dramatic decline in the incidence of genocide. HIs and similar actions probably have also contributed to the decline. This positive development does not make irrelevant the question of eventual constraints for HIs, with regard to either the lower or the upper limit. The lower constraint represents a possible duty to intervene if a larger humanitarian crisis emerges, while the upper one is related to conditions to be met in order for HI to be considered justified.

A) IS THERE A DUTY TO INTERVENE?

One can imagine several different reactions to humanitarian crises, reaching from one extreme, which is no intervention of any kind, to the other one – broad and massive military action followed by the reestablishment of a tolerable political order. It is difficult to generalize and say what would be the most appropriate reaction to a crisis.

Traditional thinking was centered around "just war" theories, and it was strongly against of what we now call HI, with the notable exception of John St. Mill (Mill, 1962). He held that intervention by one state against another was permissible – to help the people of a state throw off a foreign yoke. Mill was careful to avoid advocating interference in the absence of foreign conquest, because it could lead to wars among the powers of the day. Mill's concerns were alive during the Cold War era, since both superpowers tried to avoid interventions where larger troubles and a direct confrontation among them might have arisen. After the Cold War ended with American supremacy, the world became plagued by HIs during the 1990s.

Humanitarian interventions are used as a mechanism to raise the price of mass atrocities committed in a country, and as a device to stop such actions. Other mechanisms include diplomacy, sanctions and classical war.

By mentioning humanitarian intervention one immediately conjures images of Iraq, Bosnia, Somalia or Kosovo. All of these interventions were of the UN-type, but not all humanitarian interventions resemble the UN model. UN interventions are rather a small fraction among all humanitarian interventions, making them the exception rather than the rule. The majority of humanitarian interventions were in fact unilateral[2] and in this sense they share the unenviable destiny of unilateral sanctions.

Is there any obligation to intervene if something dramatic happens in an obscure corner of the world, say, if some group or nation is threatened with extermination by another group or nation? Some hasten to say "yes" to HI in any CNN-type crisis. According to them, all human beings are to be treated in equal terms, and so all human beings deserve equal protection. Others prefer to see that some abstract conditions must be met before intervention begins. Still others look for interests in order to justify any intervention. Finally, some say "no", since interventions either violate sovereignty or require additional deaths. The sovereignty, this thinking goes, is ranked higher than individual and group rights, while new killings are not allowed in any case. The UN Charter on the one hand respects sovereignty, but on the other hand allows intervention into the internal affairs of a state if developments there represent a threat to "international peace and security", as it is pointed out in Chapter 7. This ambiguity subject to arbitrary interpretation is of little help to our question.

It is not easy to escape this intellectual confusion, especially because humanitarian interventions are immensely complex and diverse phenomena. They are complex due to the large number of specific questions they need to address, sometimes even before they have started. Situations without clear cut-off criteria are very suitable for manipulation. Furthermore, our perceptions of what constitutes a "humanitarian crisis" requiring intervention change over time.

Let us start by asking why humanitarian crises are not always accompanied by humanitarian assistance. Apparently, HI carries significant costs, and those who were not involved in the emergence and development of the crisis should not be forced to pay for them. Without responsibility for emerging crisis, there should be no duty to intervene. Let us examine this point in some detail.

It seems that there is no *per se* obligation to intervene in the case of humanitarian disaster, like an obligation of country's police to act in the case of murder is. It does not mean that murder is a more serious crime than mass extermination of war prisoners or civilians. Extermination is clearly a much larger crime, and those responsible should be captured by local police and prosecuted by courts. However, this rarely happens, since the local police either do not exist, or they do but side with the party that has committed the crimes, and the crimes might be considered highly desirable in pursuit of some common end. If offenders are to be caught and prosecuted, some outside police or army should intervene. HI is not a job for soldiers but only soldiers can do it. However, it is not easy to gather a police force to perform HI. The point is not in the severity of the crime: it is rather in the absence of obligation for the outside world to create some external police force (1), and in the high costs accompanied with such a venture (2). Let us examine the second point first.

Ad 2) Regular police have a duty to try to catch criminals, since it is established to keep the order and to capture offenders. Two points are important. First, people enter police forces voluntarily, as they enter any other profession. Second, it is very costly to form a police force. Police need to be supplied with necessary equipment, buildings are needed for stations and headquarters, salaries need to be paid to the police staff including administrative aid, and some policemen may even lose their lives on duty. An equivalent police force does not exist at the world level. It may naturally be drafted *ad hoc*, provided that somebody is ready to cover material costs, and provided that there are those who are ready to enlist. But what if there is no such willingness? In that case any possibility of intervention is excluded. Nobody can be forced against his or her will either to contribute material means or to join the intervening force. Both contributions could be considered as a specific tax. But why should countries be entitled to draft an army even against the will of those in question, while the UN or other international organizations are not? In order to establish its army, the state needs to pass legislation. That specific piece of legislation providing for conscription in general governs the community by posing constraints to what individuals, agencies, firms or groups may do. It also provides for a national defense. Analogous legislation is missing on the world scene, at least for now. True, there is some public international law that covers certain areas, either there where bilateral arrangements cross national borders or where some larger spillovers occur. This law emerged since it is perceived to be in the interest of nearly all countries of the world. Adherence to law reduces transaction costs to all parties. That would not be the case with eventual HI-regulation, since troubled countries and the rest of the world would profit at the expense of those who intervene to stop a humanitarian disaster to continue. Disequilibria between costs and benefits explain merely why incentives for a passing HI laws are absent, but no why a basis for such a regulation is missing.

Even the officials and authors from the U.S., a country insisting on a more expansive concept of HI, declare a number of restrictions for HIs. For example, Caspar Weinberger, ex U.S. defense minister, asks for 6 conditions to be met in order for HI to happen: 1) vital interests of the U.S. should be at stake; 2) a reasonable assurance of congressional and popular support for action must exist; 3) the U.S. combat must be as a last resort; 4) there must be certain victory; 5) the objectives need to be clearly defined; 6) the size, composition and disposition of forces should be permanently reassured. Sure, the costs – including a death toll – are decisive factor behind restrictions. "America must be selective in its actions. It cannot take on all the world's troubles. The public will soon grow weary if this country takes on the role of world policeman, or world army, or an international Don Quixote".[3]

Ad 1) A telling reason for avoiding HI legislation might be a lack of the basis for it. All citizens of a state are assumed to be in a specific association, from which their obligations flow.[4] More generally, just by being in an arrangement one might be obliged to do something – to have a duty or responsibility.[5] So, for example, parents have some obligations to their children, neighbours to their fellow-neighbours, sellers to customers, etc. They all have different obligations, and the nature of the obligations depends on given arrangement. To make it clear, each individual has a number of bilateral or multilateral contracts (with a girlfriend, husband, kids, neighbors, school teachers, relatives, colleagues), and all obligations stem from these arrangements / contracts which may be but need not to be written. Countries emerged in a contingent way to put under unitary rule those who operate frequently on the basis of such obligations.

Similar does not exist at the world level, although some other arrangements do exist. Norwegians probably trade with Rwandans, or they occasionally travel there, and they are obliged (stay under duty) to pay for what they buy. But Norwegians or Australians do not stay in obligation to Rwandans or Macedonians to cover the costs of a humanitarian disaster or to join forces that are going to intervene there. Nor do they have a duty to Rwandans or Macedonians. Norwegians incur costs for goods or travel, and they have to bear them, while Norwegians do not cause costs created through the humanitarian disaster in Rwanda, so they have no obligation to cover them. Australians may do something about Macedonians if they freely and voluntarily decide to do so. That is, if they decide to help them, it would be purely supererogatory act, rather than an act of duty. To put it in a different way, Norwegians and Australians may be 'good Samaritans', and to be a 'good Samaritan' makes sense only if his actions are supererogatory. His readiness to help makes sense if it is a voluntary act and if he is not under legal obligation, i.e. under duty, to help. By becoming legal, one act *per definitionem* cannot be the Samaritan.

One may agree about the definition of the 'good Samaritan', but still object by saying that the large majority of states prescribe sanctions for citizens who refuse to help victims of traffic and other accidents, if giving assistance does not pose a serious threat to those assisting. Passive standers-by or passers-by cannot escape sanctions for non-action, although they have not contributed to the accident in question.[6]

The objection sounds strong at first sight, but actually there is no analogy. The assumption in the case of traffic and other accidents is that people have to assist if the life of victims is threatened, and if those assisting are not exposed to larger risk or other costs. (Even under such restriction the law is wrong, since there is no point to punish anybody for something he has not committed.)[7] The real point, however, is that an HI carries high costs, even in the case of a military non-combat operation.[8] Individuals must be drafted into an army; army must be built up and sent to a strange environment (humanitarian crises frequently occur where a strange climate prevails or epidemic rules) inhabited by a (likely) hostile population, for a long period, etc. These conditions carry high pecuniary and non-pecuniary costs, and they are to be borne by intervening countries. Having all that in mind, there is no duty of third countries to help a country in trouble by giving humanitarian assistance. Similarly to help for victims of an earthquake, where other countries provide help on a voluntarily basis and according to their capacities to assist, humanitarian interventions are highly desirable in cases where conditions for them are met, but there cannot be obligation to undertake HI in any form. This conviction provides the lower constraint for interventions.

B) HUMANITARIAN INTERVENTION IS NOT IN AN OPTIMAL SUPPLY

Deliberations above induce two following questions. If there is no duty to help people in trouble (having larger disasters in mind), isn't that good news for all potential offenders and criminals in charge, who might like killing people on the large scale without fear of punishment? Secondly, if there is a possibility (but no obligation) to intervene, isn't that an open invitation for conquerors and adventurers to intervene throughout the world? The answer to both questions is negative, and the reasons are listed bellow.

a) Fear of punishment

Despite the fact that there is no obligation to intervene in case of humanitarian disaster, adventures and conquerors will not get free rein for ethnic cleansing or even genocide, because of the mere chance the crime may be punished. Although there is no obligation for outsiders to capture, prosecute and punish the offender, there is at least a possibility that it may happen. This raises the price for committing crime, since criminals are forced to take into account that there is a possibility they may have to pay for what they have done. This may happen at random and a highly contingent way. Available evidence confirms such an assessment. Nevertheless, let us shed more light on this issue, before continuing the debate.

Since the beginning of the 1990s, there have been several cases where the humanitarian disaster has reached the level of either more than 50,000 violent deaths or more than 1 million refugees, but where neither the U.S. nor the UN have used any military intervention to prevent or to stop these disasters. The best known among these infamous cases was Rwanda in 1994, followed by Sudan, Angola, Congo, Burundi, Afghanistan (until 2001), Colombia, Chechnya or Sierra Leone.[9] This would indicate that those acting on the international scene may do something to assist troubled populations, but there is no obligation to intervene as such.

But even if conditions for a humanitarian intervention are met (and they will be reviewed later on), in the sense that some country or a group of countries are ready to make the necessary effort, there is no certainty that the intervention will happen, since a number of contingencies could prevent an HI. For example, sometimes human rights groups and press lobby for an intervention, but governments of relevant states are simply not interested in such an undertaking. Sometimes governments have an interest, but they do not see a reasonable exit strategy, or they consider such an action too costly. In some cases the situation in targeted country is so diffuse that the operation would be on a large scale against many fighting groups in a situation of complete anarchy. Also, it happens that, even if the disaster continues, the attention of HI's protagonists fades away and goes to some new, fresher story of humanitarian disaster elsewhere. The HIs address only some humanitarian disasters.

One may remark that this highly inconsistent punishment policy is far away from being optimal. That is true. It is not because all offenders are not going to be caught and punished. Perfect police and judiciary systems – if this would mean that all offenders are caught and punished properly – are not possible, except perhaps in a population of angels. These actions are costly and even if some nation was to invest its entire GDP for police purposes, some criminals are not going to be detected and punished. Optimal punishment policy should balance costs and benefits: what is a reasonable level of expenditures for fighting crime in order to keep it at a tolerable level. A decisive question is whether it pays off to invest additional resources in police activity in the light of a probable outcome. If so, just the possibility of humanitarian intervention will deter some offenders. Probably not too many and for sure not all, but at least some of them.

By being costly and risky, humanitarian interventions would be in short supply. This makes them not different from other goods and services. Due to a difference between policing a state and policing the world, it is likely that we will see much less intervention than needed. On the one hand, what is even more disturbing, there will be some interventions even when conditions for them are not met; and on the other hand, there will be no intervention in cases when conditions are met. The latter is to be explained by the costly nature of interventions and by the absence of a willingness among relevant countries to intervene, while the former may be explained by vested interests in some country to intervene. As the cases of Tanzania's intervention in Uganda and Vietnam's intervention in Cambodia show, the vested interests may be found also in smaller, not just larger countries. But regardless, a right of states to intervene, however framed, would weaken the general prohibition on intervention while not curbing either the power or willingness of states to act unilaterally in other spheres.

b) Open hands to intervene

Now about the second question posed above: if there is a possibility (but no obligation) to intervene, isn't that an open invitation for conquerors and adventurers to intervene throughout the world? As suggested earlier, the answer to this question is negative, too. Here is the reason. Any intervention is costly, and this is one limiting factor. But it will not stop those hoping to gain more through intervention than they pay for it. Another limiting factor is the possibility of counter-intervention. Any state which intervenes to relieve an allegedly humanitarian disaster may be aware that some other states may intervene to stop its intervention. One could object that such a development is beyond the point, since humanitarian intervention excludes such manipulation. To some degree this may be true, since in order to be an HI, the intervention might not be an apparent conquering or counter-massacre. However, the criteria to restrain manipulation are not so clear in order to allow drawing the demarcation line between an HI and classical act of war. This is even more complicated by the fact that intervening states always have their own interests, and that it is impossible to keep the interests (motives) and public justification for intervention completely separate.

Another complication is that a mere possibility of HI creates typical moral hazard problems. If HI is in principle available, some groups throughout the world will try to manipulate larger world powers, while those powers that have interests in that region may try to use the groups there for their own purposes. If a larger power finds some motive to intervene, its media will launch a huge campaign, including extensive reports on the suffering population, biased analyses, exaggerated incidents, selective reports and even open lies. Having seen these biased reports, the public will never get a real picture. Otherwise, the voters would refuse to support intervention. The same facts will be presented completely differently if there is no ulterior motive for intervention. Even worse, if disaster pictures are anticipated to be too disturbing, hundreds of thousands could be swallowed up in bloodshed without being reported beyond short, rare and distant news in leading media of larger powers.

There are also other possible hazards during HI. Local gangs may allow access to an endangered population, making humanitarian deliveries possible until humanitarian workers arrive and start to operate, and they may raise the price for continuing the humanitarian delivery by asking to get a percentage of the delivered goods or a lump sum fee. The intervening power may threaten local allies by the possibility of its withdrawal in order to extract more concessions. Combat missions may face much larger collateral damage if local warlords cause more casualties, and they can do it in different ways: for example, by targeting missiles launched by intervening forces and by changing their path (provided they end in urban areas), by using domestic civilians for shields around their positions, by using urban areas, schools and hospitals for military positions, etc. Intervening countries may smuggle their interests under a veil of humanitarian rhetoric while a potentially threatened population may try to embellish their suffering in order to induce intervention, and the HI may happen at the expense of some third party. Even without such complications created by moral hazard-situations it is not easy to establish whether there is any upper constraint for intervention, and if so, where it might be.

C) CONDITION(S) FOR HUMANITARIAN INTERVENTIONS

Humanitarian impulses of intervening states frequently coincide with more self-interested reasoning, let alone naked interests. For that reason humanitarian actions should be reasonably constrained.

Looking from a moral point of view, not all historical interventions were humanitarian, and not all interventions were justified humanitarian interventions (JHI). In order to be a JHI, the intervention should necessary satisfy the basic condition (BC), and meet some other conditions as much as possible. The BC is related to a massive and deep violation of vital human rights of larger rather than smaller groups, over a longer period of time (or explosive violation in a short period of time), which results in irrevocable harm for these groups. Let me explain the meaning of main components of the definition above.

"Massive" means that the violation of basic human rights is related to a larger number of cases, rather than to rare individual cases. What should the exact number of violations be? This is not easy to say, since any answer cannot avoid being arbitrary. Let us say that it includes tens of thousands of deaths, or several hundred thousand of severely mutilated, or 1 million expelled (ethnically cleansed) individuals. "Massive" may be used to cover developments where any of the three mentioned issues occurs either alone or in combination.

"Vital" means that crucial rather than peripheral rights are violated, which include, death, expulsion, and severe mutilation. "Deep" means that rights are heavily violated. Death cannot be partial, but mutilation can be graded. Minor offences are not a concern of humanitarian intervention.

"Longer period" means years rather than decades. Low intensity conflicts may cause a significant death toll over decades or centuries, but this is not a case for HI. Some conflicts are very explosive, and its death toll may exceed thousands per day. Finally, "irrevocable harm" refers to losses and damages which cannot be repaired or cured.

No HI is allowed if the BC is not fulfilled. All other conditions mentioned need not to be fulfilled completely,[10] but it would be better if they could to a significant degree, the more, the better. Among the other conditions are:

A Other means than HI (like diplomacy, sanctions) should be tried and found insufficient to solve the problem.
B The HI should be legal in terms of public international law.
C The HI should be efficient.
D The HI should reduce to the minimum possible the unnecessary harm to intervening troops, targeted troops and civilians.
E The HI excludes conquering the land, population and resources.
F The costs of the HI should include larger negative externalities of the HI itself.

Although the above conditions sound clear, let me add a few words of explanation.

Condition A should provide that other means (implying lower costs) have been tried, and that they were unable to get results. This condition actually guards against excessive means to be employed first.

Condition B is to exclude illegal acts in terms of public international law. Legalization is partly dependent on written rules (Chapter 7 of the UN

Charter), and partly on the assessment of the UN Security Council and eventually other international organizations. On the one hand, Chapter 7 is restrictive in the sense of prohibiting violation of sovereignty, and on the other hand it is permissive, since intervention is allowed if international peace and security are at stake. The UN Security Council decides whether or not some conditions are met. It actually may justify any move of the UN: an intervention – provided there is willingness to do so; non-action, if such an attitude prevails among the relevant countries. Since 5 countries in the SC of the UN have a veto power, any of them can block an action. This veto power should exclude acts that are in the interest of just one country (or one group of countries), and actions that would violate the interests of any among the five countries. Since countries with veto power have interests in nearly any corner of the world, a veto-decision is a likely outcome of casting votes in the Security Council. The five veto-powers back up the actions of many other, smaller states, and HI is likely to happen just when irrelevant countries are targeted. But even in such cases there are some incentives for its use. As is well known from game theory, because of such a form, this rule is very suitable for strategic bargaining.[11]

Condition C is to exclude inefficient action, which emerges when the intervening power has not engaged enough resources for intervention, or when interventionists pursue objectives other than humanitarian, which put the whole mission in question. For example, one can imagine an intervention that does not aim to reach its proper target, but rather to protect the offender from another, real HI. Inefficient interventions are not desirable since they can worsen the humanitarian crises.

Condition D is to exclude the excessive use of force and the employment of banned weapons and methods. It should contribute to reduction of intervention's costs to all parties involved in the intervention.

Condition E is to exclude conquest and other similar, non-HI wars and acts, which use HI just as an excuse for classical aggression and occupation of another country. It is not always easy to draw a demarcation line, since some types of HI are not possible without temporary occupation of another country, like interventions in Haiti or in Afghanistan.

Condition F is also to restrain the operations to their necessary degree, to make the intervening party responsible for collateral damage in the targeted country and elsewhere. In practice, this means that an HI should be followed by delivery of food, medicine and other goods for daily needs, by rebuilding the country, and, if necessary, by rebuilding the institutions in the targeted country. The international community and intervening allies should cover the larger negative externalities of the intervention in the region. This means a repair of the environment to a pre-war level, compensation of neighboring countries for large losses, compensation of families of intervening soldiers who lost their lives during the intervention, and compensation of families of civilians killed in the targeted country. To cover the larger externalities sometimes is more expensive than HI itself.

If only the BC is to be satisfied necessarily, does it mean that other conditions may be violated? It seems that the answer should be affirmative. Without satisfying the BC, no intervention can be justified. The moral profile of an intervention improves by satisfying more conditions, or by satisfying the same number of conditions to a higher degree. A clear, ethically correct HI should satisfy all mentioned conditions in their literal meaning.

By having moral criteria for humanitarian intervention, one cannot decisively change the prevailing rules of international traffic in crisis-like situations. There will always be interventions that resemble aggression more than a humanitarian mission, and there will still be classical wars. Ethics is able to define some standards that will be more or less reliable, depending on the morality and ethics in question; but it is not able to change the course of history, putting aside some exceptional cases. Beyond moral, there are legal, political, military and other objectives, all strongly influenced by interests. The most important result of having a moral standard for HI consists of the ability to assess situations of humanitarian crisis and intervention. But we need to keep in mind that there are different moralities and other different standards.

Some humanitarian interventions carried on during past decade failed not just to satisfy other conditions to a significant degree, but the BC as well (Somalia, Haiti), and in some cases the international community failed to intervene even when the BC was met (Rwanda) and in other formerly mentioned cases. The intervention in Kosovo was basically justified.

D) TYPES OF HUMANITARIAN INTERVENTIONS

Not all humanitarian interventions are of the same type, since HI is a splendidly diversified and fuzzy term. It includes all sorts of actions from suppressing air flights and creating "safe havens", via enforcing cease-fires and disarming insurgents, to restoring government and infrastructure. Among the different types of humanitarian intervention, one may distinguish the following ones:

a) relief of crisis pain without military intervention and without entering into the political or economic causes of crisis;
b) relief of the disaster, military non-combat intervention and partial assistance to obtain a political solution;
c) military combat intervention, and broad economic support for some period of time;
d) military combat intervention, broad economic support and the imposition and enforcement of a political solution.

All four types of intervention allow a number of modifications and subtypes, which enhances the variety of HIs. Also, one humanitarian undertaking can appear as several different types of intervention. For example, the U.S administration started to supply Somalis food, medical and other daily necessities in 1992, the UN extended that mission into a military non-combat operation in 1993, and the whole operation ceased to exist a few weeks after it became a combat operation, and once domestic warlords demonstrated an ability to inflict serious harm to the intervening troops. The operation in Bosnia also was undertaken relieve a humanitarian disaster in food and medicine, then was transformed into non-classical HI-combat operation (air strikes on Bosnian Serbs), and became stabilized as a non-combat military HI that includes the imposition of a political solution. Examples of HI, types a) and b) indicate that solutions contained in them are not based on stable equilibria, as is the case in c). Actually, both abstention and total combat involvement are more stable options, but that does not mean that they are the most reasonable options under given circumstances.

What is done in the case of a humanitarian crisis, if anything, often depends on the interests of intervening forces. If one or more relevant countries have an interest in controlling a territory for any reason, it is very likely that they would say that humanitarian aid cannot be supplied without establishing some political order, since gangs prevent deliveries or ask for high fees in order to allow deliveries. If accepted, this would justify a move from a) to either b), c) or d). Model b) is apparently less costly, since it does not require a combat action: if intervening forces successfully establish a friendly regime, which is supportive of the delivery of humanitarian aid, intervening forces will be able to go home sooner rather than later. It happens frequently that a so-established regime is not less oppressive than the previous one, or that a so-established regime loses control after some time, and a new humanitarian disaster emerges. Another HI is possible, but less likely to happen, in the light of means and costs for the former operation, which are to be considered squandered (wasted). After the UN and the U.S. operation in Somalia in 1992-3 failed, this country would hardly be considered for another operation, even if there were an urgent motive to do so. On the other hand, the U.S. have intervened several times in Haiti between 1815 and 2001, and sometimes the American troops spent decades there and nevertheless have failed to establish a workable market democracy and multicultural society.[12] It seems that the ability of intervening forces to establish market democracy under the rule of law decisively depends on:

1) whether such a regime ever existed in targeted country,
2) whether the formal rules to be introduced are consistent with the prevailing informal rules, and if yes, to what degree.[13]

So, for example, the U.S. led forces succeeded in re-establishing market democracy in Western Europe and Japan after the IIWW, since this type of regime existed there before, but they failed to achieve this result in Haiti, Somalia, Cambodia, Bosnia and Kosovo (at least up to now), since this type of regime never existed there. The same or similar legal rules may have quite different consequences on economic and political performance in different countries. "Many Latin American countries adopted the U.S. Constitution (with some modifications) in the nineteenth century, and many of the property rights laws of successful Western countries have been adopted by Third World countries. The results, however, are not similar to those in either the United States or other successful Western countries. Although the rules are the same, the enforcement mechanism, the way enforcement occurs, the norms of behavior, and the subjective models are not /the same/".[14] Building institutions by fiat seems a bad recommendation where prior developments constrain future change in that direction. However well meaning our intentions were, humanitarian intervention, like war, must be viewed as a failure of policy. For that reason, chance may be the best hope of re-introducing proper policy by HI.

NOTES

[1] This paper or its parts were used for several conferences and lectures in Serbia, Germany and Italy during 2000-2002. The paper would not be completed without generous support of the Alexander von Humboldt Foundation from Bonn in 2002-2003. Too numerous to be mentioned here are colleagues who helped me to stage the final version, but to skip one name would be simply unjust. I talked frequently with Georg Meggle about interventions at different occasions during several years and these talks helped me very much. However, responsibility is only mine, and usual caveat applies.
[2] The intervening states defend their actions as self defense under Article 51 of the UN Charter rather than His, as it has happened in the three credible cases – India/Bangladesh 1971, Vietnam/Cambodia 1978 and Tanzania/Uganda 1979.
[3] Schlesinger, 1991-1992, p. 23f.
[4] Studying some problems of colonial law in the then British colony of India, Lord Macaulay was probably one of the first historically important authors who argued along these lines.
[5] More about this, although related to quite another issue, in: Prokopijevic 1992.
[6] Among others, J. St. Mill (1987, p. 165) advocated this position too.
[7] Sanctions for violation of assistance-duty are very rare, although violations are not so rare, which also indicates that courts in practice relax this rule because of its weak plausibility. Joel Feinberg shares with Mill the position that passive standers-by should be punished. However, he feels that this stance is too demanding, and tries to weaken this position by adding 'no risk and no inconvenience' provisos. So, he is looking "...to extend liability very cautiously only to those Samaritans who could warn, assist, report or rescue without any peril, and without any (...) cost and even, what is more, without any inconvenience". (1984, p. 155) By adding 'no risk' proviso the position is just relaxed; by adding 'no inconvenience' proviso the position is nearly reduced to what I advocate here, since it is easy to provide justification based on inconvenience.
[8] Delivery of necessities (food, medicine, etc.) is more alike to foreign aid in goods and services. Donations and aid to underdeveloped nations is subject to a voluntary consent of donators.
[9] Nevertheless, losses in war, genocide and repression have sharply declined from 4.1 deaths on 100.000 population in the period 1925-50, to less than 0.3 deaths on 100.000 in 1975-2000. Cf. White, 2001.
[10] Conditions for HI resemble more or less throughout the literature; they are sometimes more implicit, or the number and articulation of conditions is different. Meggle (2000) and some other authors, for example, require all conditions to be fulfilled.
[11] For example, the U.S. have not gone for approval to the SC of the UN for the NATO intervention on Kosovo, anticipating that Russia will condition its consent by asking for a similar permission for its own action in Chechnya and that in addition, it will ask for some significant funds, while China would trade its vote for the U.S. support of China's membership in the WTO. None of these reasons has anything to do with the humanitarian situation on Kosovo, but the whole case illustrates how broad the field for strategic bargaining emerges around any intervention.

[12] If the disadvantage of options a) and b) consists in inherent instability of these options, the apparent disadvantage of c) is that it merely remains short of promise.
[13] Latin American countries have adopted provisions of the U.S. Constitution during XIX century, but the outcome of the rules in the USA and Latin America was different. The same formal norms produced different outcomes, since prevailing informal rules in two Americas and enforcement mechanisms were different.
[14] North 1990, p. 101.

REFERENCES

Arend, A. & Beck, R. (1993). *International law and the use of force: Beyond the UN Charter paradigm.* London: Routledge.

Ellis, A. (2002). *War, revolution and intervention.* Paper at the Conference "Humanitarian interventions / Ethics", Bielefeld, January 09-12, 2002.

Feinberg, J. (1984). *The moral limits of the criminal law.* Vol. I *Harm to others.* Oxford: Oxford UP.

Meggle, G. "Ist dieser Krieg gut? Ein ethischer Kommentar." In: Merkel (ed.) (2000), pp. 138-159.

Merkel, R. (ed.) (2000). *Der Kosovo Krieg und das Völkerrecht.* Frankfurt/M.: Suhrkamp.

Mill, J. St. (1962) "A few words on non-intervention." In: *Essays on politics and culture.* N. York: Doubleday, pp. 396-413.

Mill, J. St. (1987).*On liberty. Representative government.* London a.o.: Dent.

Mueller, J. (1989). *Retreat from doomsday: The obsolescence of major war.* N. York: Basic Books.

North, D. C. (1990). *Institutions, institutional change and economic performance.* Cambridge, MA: Cambridge UP.

Pogge, T. (2002). *Preempting humanitarian intervention.* Paper at the Conference "Humanitarian interventions / Ethics", Bielefeld, January 09-12, 2002.

Prokopijevic, M. (1992). "Some moral and legal aspects of AIDS." *Archives for philosophy of law and social philosophy.* vol. 78, 2, pp. 516-539.

Schlesinger, J. (1991-1992). "New instabilities, new priorities." *Foreign policy*, vol. 85.

White, M. (2001). *Historical atlas of the 20th century.* Available at: www.users.erols.com/mwhite28/20century.htm

II

International Ethics and Law

RÜDIGER BITTNER

Humanitarian Interventions are Wrong

Here is a story. Once Bill Clinton living in Washington D.C. asks Jay Norman from Cincinatti, Ohio, to go and kill Marta Petrovic from Nis. His reason for this request is that Mr. Milosevic from Belgrad has had Mr. Derkian from Kirnin killed and is going to kill Mr. Pernat from Kirnin as well unless he is resisted. Things are in fact as Clinton takes them to be: Milosevic did have Derkian killed, and he is going to get somebody to kill Pernat too unless Norman kills Petrovic. Question then: is it right for Clinton to ask Norman to kill Petrovic? More abstractly: may we kill others, or indeed ought we to kill others, if that prevents somebody's being killed?

We may not, and Clinton does wrong.

The reason is not that killing a human being is always wrong. This is not so. To kill oneself, or to kill somebody following his request, is sometimes not wrong. The mere fact, then, that Petrovic is going to die from Norman's attack does not show that Clinton does wrong.

Nor is the reason that Norman can only fulfill Clinton's request by entering a foreign country or flying over it without permission of its authorities. Entering a foreign country or flying over it without permission is morally irrelevant or nearly irrelevant. Frontiers of countries and of governmental jurisdictions are morally insignificant.

The reason is that it is wrong to kill a human being for a purpose that isn't his purpose. One may sometimes kill a human being, but one may not sacrifice human beings for alien purposes. Petrovic would be sacrificed: Pernat's life would be bought with hers. That must not be done to her.

It doesn't make a difference here whether it is her death itself that prevents Milosevic from killing others or whether her death is only an effect, not intended, but foreseen and accepted, of something else that makes Milosevic halt, for example the effect of bombing the important bridge in the neighbourhood. She is going to be sacrificed in either case.

Admittedly, this is the decisive difference for those who support their argument for humanitarian interventions with the doctrine of double effect. They do think that it is wrong to kill Petrovic in order to stop Milosevic. Yet to bomb a bridge in order to stop Milosevic is not wrong in their view, even if it is known beforehand that Petrovic is going to be killed in the bombing, provided only that it is not her death that is being intended, but Milosevic's being stopped.[1] However, the doctrine of double effect was traditionally, and rightly, countered with the argument that it draws a distinction unsupported by our ordinary moral consciousness; that in this sense double effect is an empty subtlety. We normally consider ourselves responsable not only for intended, but also for foreseen effects of what we did.

That Clinton does wrong in asking Norman to kill Petrovic is entailed by Kant's principle that humans must not ever be treated as mere means.[2] (This is a historical remark, not an argument. Kant's principle has met with serious objections.[3]) For when Clinton asks that Petrovic be killed he does use her life as a mere means to save Pernat's. Petrovic herself with her aims doesn't come into account here. Utilitarians, by contrast, do not think it generally wrong to sacrifice people. They recommend it if sufficient good can be expected to arise from doing so. Here, however, our ordinary moral convictions take Kant' side. The well-known example of the healthy person who is killed to give his organs to five others who badly need them, is generally considered an objection against utilitarianism, not an example of its fertility in moral insight.

Clinton in the story does wrong, this is the first premise of my argument. The second premise says: the story displays the basic form of humanitarian interventions and doesn't differ from these in a morally significant way. Which entails that humanitarian interventions are wrong.

What, then, is going to be objected to the second premise; what could be considered a significant difference between the story and a humanitarian intervention? To keep things simple, I shall restrict myself to humanitarian interventions whose aim it is to stop the killing of humans, and not to stop their oppression or deprivation of political freedom etc.

A salient difference lies in the fact that for humanitarian interventions a very complex institutional and technical apparatus needs to be set going, with the effect that such and such people are killed by such and such others. In the story, by contrast, the procedure is very simple. There is just one person asking another to go and kill a third one, and then the second person does go and kill the third one. This difference is surely irrelevant. Whether the procedure that gets Norman to kill Petrovic is simple or complicated is of no account for the question whether it is right that he is sent to kill her.

There is, furthermore, the difference that in the story we know the victim by name, whereas humanitarian interventions bring death to we do not know whom. That difference as well is irrelevant. Throwing a bomb into the crowd is no better, morally speaking, than sending out death squads.

Or you may point to the numbers. In the story there is just one life exchanged for another, and that's not a great bargain. Humanitarian interventions by contrast might save the life of thousands and pay for it with relatively few deaths. That difference again, though, does not seem to make a moral difference. If you must not buy with people's lives other advantages, then you must not do so even if the prices offered are attractive.

"But if you can save from one island ten people, from the other only one in the remaining time, aren't you going to take your boat to the island with the ten people?" – Yes, I am. Yet I do not thereby sacrifice the one who is alone on his island. It is just that I don't find the time to save him, because I happen to have something different to do, i.e. to save the ten. The case is different when the tyrant proposes: kill one, and I let you ten free, whom I shall kill if you do not kill the one. This deal I shall not accept. This would mean to sacrifice a human being.

"If the brakes fail in the trolley you drive, and there are five people on the tracks ahead whom you are going to kill unless you turn the trolley onto another track where there is only one, aren't you going to turn the trolley and to kill the one rather than the five? And didn't you then buy the life of the five with the life of the one?"[4] – Yes, I turn the trolley on the side track and kill rather one than five people. No, this is not to buy the life of the five with the life of the one. In this case I am not the origin of the misfortune that befalls the one person. The misfortune is already on its way, I just give it a different direction.[5] Not so Clinton in the story. He does not turn the same misfortune from Pernat to Petrovic. He sends a new one against Petrovic. This is why we can say that he buys Pernat's life with Petrovic's. Just as you put down something that is your property, a coin, say, and in exchange receive something that so far is not yours, an orange, so Clinton sends Norman to kill Petrovic, and in exchange Milosevic refrains from killing Pernat. This is a deal. Sure enough, it is a deal metaphorically speaking: Clinton and Milosevic have not reached an agreement on this way of proceeding. But it is a deal in the sense that Clinton puts in one life, Petrovic's, and receives another one, Pernat's, in exchange. It is a deal the way it is, metaphorically again, a deal when in the big stores you put a coin into that device and receive a cart in which you collect your groceries. Petrovic, and not something of her or about her, but she herself, is Clinton's coin, yet one that is used up in the process. This is why Clinton does her wrong.

"What about applying quantitative differences on the other side instead? If it is indeed unacceptable to buy the many people saved from Milosevic with the one life of Petrovic, what if we sacrifice instead only a small part of Petrovic, namely, accept a small probability of her coming to grief, and receive in exchange a full human life, do you reject that deal as well?" – No, there is nothing wrong with exposing someone, for the sake of an alien advantage, to a situation which will bring him, with a very small probability, serious harm. We do it all the time. To be sure, I do not know where to draw the line between an acceptable and an unacceptable risk imposed on a person. However, in the present context this is not a relevant worry. Humanitarian interventions do not merely impose a small risk of serious harm on people, a risk regarding which it may be doubted whether it is above or below the threshold of acceptability. Humanitarian interventions predictably kill people.

"And what if we adopt a strategy of small risks? For example, we may allow ambulances to drive faster than the speed limit. Any particular trip of an ambulance will only impose acceptably small risks on people, but the strategy as a whole predictably takes a certain toll of human life."[6] – Then we do wrong to adopt that strategy. We pay people's reaching faster the hospital with someone's life, even though we do not know as yet whose life that is, and thereby we do the person wrong who eventually is going to suffer. It is different with the individual driver of an ambulance who decides this time, and perhaps next time again, and next time again, to drive faster than permitted. He may each time impose only an acceptable risk on others.

However, the most significant difference between the story and humanitarian interventions may seem to be this: the story does not mention the fact that the individuals in question are members of a state, whereas this membership of individuals is the decisive point with respect to humanitarian interventions. Milosevic in the story is a private murderer, or a private employer of murderers, Milosevic in a humanitarian intervention is killing people in his official capacity. Similarly for Petrovic: in the story she is merely a third party, a passer-by, whereas in a humanitarian intervention she is very probably a citizen of just that state in the name of which Derkian and Pernat are killed. So perhaps it is wrong to kill an unconcerned third party in order to stop a private murderer. Once people are killed by the state of which they are members, however, it is justified to use violence against the state if such violence is a suitable and perhaps the only means to stop the killing; and the violence against that state will be, naturally and justifiably, violence against its citizens, for example against Petrovic. To stop Milosevic it is permitted to kill Petrovic, because Petrovic and Milosevic are only different aspects of the same thing, i.e. the people in question; and that people is in the last resort the agent of the killings ordered by Milosevic. To oppose with violence the one who uses violence is not unjust. That Milosevic starts the killing, but Petrovic is the victim of the counter-attack is for her only bad luck, not something she could justly complain about. As a member of that people she is liable for its deeds, liable in the sense that she may without injustice be harmed by counter-measures appropriate to these deeds.

Yet why should Petrovic be liable in this sense for what Milosevic as a political ruler does against Derkian and Pernat? She would be liable if she had authorized these deeds. This is the construction that Hobbes proposed in chapter 16 of the *Leviathan*. But in fact she has not authorized him, neither expressly nor, if there is such a thing, tacitly.[7] She would also be liable if Milosevic and she herself were indeed only different sides or parts of the same thing. The left hand cannot complain if it suffers from punishment inflicted for what the right hand did. But there is no such unity comprising the different inividuals. There is no common spirit, and while there may be to some extent a common history, a common descent or a common territory, all these yield only similarities between the individuals, not a unity comprising them. No reason can be seen, then, for considering Petrovic liable for Milosevic's killings. She is really only a third party to them.

It may be objected that in this case Clinton would be doing right if he asked Norman to kill, not Petrovic, but rather Milosevic, for then he would catch the one who had Derkian killed. Yet such attacks on foreign rulers are in fact considered inacceptable. So the argument justifies a proposition which is false and must be mistaken.

Distinguish between killing somebody to prevent him from killing others, and killing somebody to punish him for killing others. The first of these is under certain conditions permitted to anyone, the latter is permitted, if at all, then only to judges and their staff. Clinton, I supposed, is not Milosevic's legal judge. Hence Clinton is not permitted to send Norman against Milosevic in order to punish him for Derkian's death. Those who fight, and those who command the fighters, do not punish: military tribunals are square circles. If the point, however, is not to punish Milosevic, but to prevent him from killing Pernat, and if it is the case that killing Milosevic is the only suitable means, (and a means is suitable only if it does not just lead to further misery, for example to the replacement of one murderer by the next one) then we do think that Clinton does not wrong to ask Norman to kill Milosevic. So the argument does not entail a proposition which is false.

Thus it is wrong to kill Petrovic in order to stop Milosevic's killings, but it may be right to kill Milosevic to prevent him from going on killing. This raises the question where to draw the line between the two things. Petrovic, I have been supposing, is merely a citizen of the state ruled by Milosevic. She is living there, the country is close to her heart – none of this makes her liable, in the sense described before, for what Milosevic does. On the other hand there is Milosevic's army and Milosevic's staff. They appear to be as liable as he himself. But what about Milosevic's driver and Milosevic's cook? A sensible criterion might be: all those and only those are liable who contribute, directly or indirectly, to the killing. The people working in the ministry of finance will not be liable, but those working in the military administration will. The cleaning women will not be liable, but the transport units in the army will. That is to say, I recommend a criterion broader than the traditional one of combatant status.[8] The secretary in the army administration is not a combatant, but I should think that she contributes to the killing. Hence she is liable for it – again, this means that she has no just cause for complaint if she is harmed in an attempt to stop Milosevic's killing.

Humanitarian interventions are justified only to the extent that they try directly to halt the killers and their helpers. They are not justified if they sacrifice third parties in order to stop the killing. As a matter of fact, all humanitarian interventions sacrifice third parties to stop the killing. As a matter of fact, all humanitarian interventions are wrong.[9]

NOTES

[1] The classical formulation of the doctrine of double effect is Thomas von Aquin, *Summa Theologiae* II-II, qu. 64, art. 7. Applied to acts of war it appears in Elizabeth Anscombe, "War and Murder" (1961), in: Richard Wasserstrom (ed.), *War and Morality*, Belmont: Wadsworth 1970, and Richard Regan, *Just War*, Washington: Catholic University of America Press 1996, pp. 95 – 97.

[2] Immanuel Kant, *Grundlegung zur Metaphysik der Sitten* (1785), Academy-Edition IV, 428.

[3] See Nobert Hoerster, Zur Bedeutung des Prinzips der Menschenwürde, *Juristische Schulung* (1983), pp. 93-96, 647.
[4] The example is Philippa Foot's, "The Problem of Abortion and the Doctrine of Double Effect", *Oxford Review* 5, 1967.
[5] If I understand her correctly, I am following here Judith Thomson's line in: "he Trolley Problem" (1985), in: Thomson, *Rights, Restitution, and Risk*. Cambridge, Mass., Harvard University Press 1986, section 6.
[6] I owe the objection and the example to Thomas Pogge.
[7] For the difficulties in Locke's notion of tacit consent see John Simmons, *On the edge of anarchy*, Princeton: Princeton University Press, 1993, p. 80ff.
[8] Similarly Richard Wasserstrom, "On the Morality of War", in: Wasserstrom (ed.), *War and Morality*, Belmont: Wadsworth 1970, p. 95.
[9] I am grateful to the participants of the Bielefeld conference on humanitarian interventions and to Thomas Schmidt (Göttingen) for helpful discussions and criticisms. In the literature I found especially illuminating and encouraging the book by Robert Holmes, *On War and Morality*, Princeton: Princeton University Press 1989.

THOMAS MERTENS

Humanitarian Intervention: Legal and Moral Arguments

1. INTRODUCTION

Until recently, more precisely before the end of the Cold War, little attention was paid to the issue of humanitarian intervention. This was not because there was none, nor because there weren't any wars, but because international politics was dominated by two antagonistic blocs, that assumed the liberty, up until a certain point, to do whatever they wanted internally. Moreover, ideologically, the doctrine of political self-determination was supported, and legal and political thinking was still dominated by the Westphalian peace. Thus, it focussed on the meaning of the nation-state and treated the world between states as a by-product. For example, in his *Philosophy of Right*, Hegel considers the nation-state as the alpha and the omega of thinking about law and justice, and the issue of international justice is discussed in a very brief manner.[1] Although Hart's approach – more than two centuries later – is entirely different, *The Concept of Law* does not pay much attention to the problem of the validity of international law either. In his famous *A Theory of Justice*, Rawls deals with the problem of distributive justice within a closed society and hardly mentions the problem of justice in interstate relations. And when this works does pay attention to that problem, in paragraph 58, this attention is motivated by a domestic need. Rawls brings in principles of international justice in order to answer the then important question of when a society based on 'justice as fairness' has to respect incidents of conscientious refusal and when not. Fortunately, Rawls recently provided us with his *The Law of Peoples*, to which I will pay attention later.

Ever since the fall of the Berlin Wall, one cannot concentrate on the nation-state only. A number of different reasons must be mentioned in this regard. Firstly, the concept of the nation-state contrasts sharply with recent economic developments. Multinationals have become much more important. Their budgets amply exceed the economies of quite a number of states.[2] Secondly, influential forms of interstate and supra-state cooperation have emerged, of which the European Union is probably the best example.[3] Because of processes of integration, important international institutions have developed, ranging from traditional international organizations like the United Nations and, related to them, the Human Rights Commission, the UNHCR, the International Court of Justice to institutions like the World bank, the IMF, the World Trade Organization, and the International Criminal Court in establishment. Thirdly, there is the importance of human rights. After all, those are rights that everybody has, irrespective of time, space and nationality or citizenship. The idea of human rights is in itself oriented towards an international legal order.[4]

A nice indication of this development is the remarkably diminished attention for Hegel's *Philosophy of Right*, whereas Kant's treatment in *Perpetual Peace* has received increased attention.[5] In connection herewith the following subjects are frequently discussed: should an international legal order be more like an association of peoples or like a world republic?; should economic relations between first and third world countries be seen in the light of (re)distributive (economic) justice or not?; and relating to the issue of migration, the question is raised whether the importance of the integrity of national communities should prevail or the duty to give shelter to those who involuntarily seek asylum in other countries? The problem of the justification of humanitarian intervention is also received much attention, both in the field of public international law and in that of legal philosophy, partly in relation to the Gulf War and Kosovo War, but partly also because of its possibility being neglected during genocides in Rwanda and in Srebrenica.

With this paper, I want to contribute to the debate on humanitarian intervention. I will first briefly discuss public international law as it has developed within the setting of the Charter of the United Nations. After that, I will examine the current state of affairs within political philosophy and pay attention to a number of leading theories by opposing the rejection of humanitarian intervention by Kant and Stuart Mill and the acceptance of a limited right of intervention. Subsequently, assuming that such a right exists, I will ask what the corresponding duty should be. Here I will briefly discuss Hegel's critique on Kant and Habermas'hesitations regarding the Kosovo intervention. Finally, I will argue that a correct assessment of humanitarian intervention requires a new approach, and I suggest that Rawls' *The Law of Peoples* constitutes such an approach.

2. WHAT DOES THE LAW SAY?

Positive law alone can, of course, not solve the question of the legitimacy of humanitarian intervention. This, however, does not make the question "what does the law say?" redundant. It has often been stated that the existence of positive law itself is a value that is linked up with justice because of legal certainty.[6] Let me define humanitarian intervention as the use of foreign military force within the sovereign territory of a state against that state's will in an attempt to protect the fundamental interests of (a section of) the population of that state. With this definition, we find ourselves, legally speaking, within the domain of public international law, in which the United Nations and its charter play an important role. Because of the use of military force, a number of paragraphs in the Charter of the United Nations are relevant, like its paragraph 2, section 4: "All Members shall refrain in their international relations from the threat or use of force against the territorial integrity or political independence of any state ...".[7] This general ban on the use of force, however, has a number of provisos, especially those laid down in paragraph 2, section 7, and paragraph 51. The latter paragraph, which constitutes the right to individual and collective self-defence, is not relevant for humanitarian intervention. Paragraph 2, section 7, however, is: "Nothing contained in the present Charter shall authorize the United Nations to intervene in matters which are essentially within the domestic jurisdiction of any state or shall require the Member to submit such matters to settlement under the present Charter; but this principle shall not prejudice the application of enforcement measures under Chapter VII". This formulation seems to indicate that the Charter makes a clear choice in favor of bilateral unconditional respect between states, except for the provisions in Chapter VII. In this Chapter, paragraph 39 states the following: "The Security Council shall determine the existence of any threat to the peace, breach of peace, or act of aggression and shall make recommendations, or decide what measures shall be taken in accordance with Articles 41 and 42, to maintain or restore international peace and security." The reference to paragraph 41 amounts to measures not involving the use of armed force that can be taken against a state or states that, according to the Security Council, threatens or threaten international peace. Paragraph 42 then determines that, if the Security Council considers the actions taken under paragraph 41 insufficient, "... it may take such action by air, sea, or land forces as may be necessary to maintain or restore international peace and security".[8] Based on the Charter, the Security Council can decide to start a humanitarian intervention, if it deems it necessary to do so.

Do these provisions imply that according to positive law humanitarian intervention is only justified if it is based on a resolution of the Security Council? This problem became particularly urgent when NATO-countries decided to attack Serbia in order to prevent a humanitarian catastrophe from happening in Kosovo.[9] The answer to this question is: not necessarily. As the Security Council can be paralysed by its political composition, other justifications for intervention might be available. After all, the Charter commits itself explicitly to human rights as can be read in the Preamble: "faith in fundamental human rights"; in paragraph 1, section 3: "... promoting and encouraging respect for human rights ..."; in paragraph 55: "universal respect for, ..., human rights". This means that the Charter itself recognizes the boundaries to (the sovereignty of) domestic jurisdiction of a state, as mentioned in paragraph 2, section 7. Generally, human rights are not seen as a subject exclusive to the state's jurisdiction. They belong to the concern of the global human community. Moreover, states are bound to respect human rights not on the basis of the Charter, the Universal Declaration (1948) and the two important international treaties on human rights (1966) alone. The International Court of Justice, in its case law, has developed the concept of "obligationes erga omnes", which are obligations all states are bound to respect (regardless of the question whether they have consented or not), because they concern issues in which all states have an interest. The Court considers as part of these obligations the respect for human rights and the ban on genocide. Accordingly, the Court has opened the possibility of interpreting a state's behaviour towards its citizens as a violation of that state's obligations to other states.[10] Thus, *prima facie*, there seems to be no valid objections when one state tries to influence the way in which another state takes care, or the lack thereof, of the fate of the citizens of another state. Why should the Security Council be granted the prerogative to decide whether a state sufficiently obeys its internationally binding duties regarding human rights? However, the unilateral use of military force by one state or group of states within the national jurisdiction of another state, like in the Kosovo-case, remains very problematic because of its violation of the ban on the use of force under the Charter's paragraph 2 section 4. For this reason, many have argued that in cases like Kosovo, approval by the Security Council has at least to be aimed for. If "obligationes erga omnes" are not based on positive law, but merely on principles of natural law, one has to keep in mind Kelsen's splendid phrase that one who raises the veil (of natural law) without closing his eyes will confront the gaping stare of the Gorgon's naked power.[11] Natural law can be used to justify many issues. States that want to refer to it must be most careful in so doing.[12]

3. RIGHT TO HUMANITARIAN INTERVENTION CONTESTED: MILL, KANT AND WALZER

Humanitarian intervention is not only controversial within positive law, but also in legal philosophy. For some, there is only one exception to the ban on the use of state-to-state force: retaliation for aggression. Since only self-defence can justify acts of war, it is the unconditional duty of states to respect each other's political sovereignty and territorial integrity.[13] If humanitarian intervention would be acceptable, it would amount to an acceptance of an exception to the ban on aggression, and inter-state respect would no longer be necessary in all circumstances. Those who accept humanitarian intervention do not consider the ban on aggression as a categorical imperative.

This position has some important spokesmen. John Stuart Mill does not accept humanitarian intervention. Even if a state treats its citizens in a condemnable fashion, other states are obliged to refrain from intervention. After all, a people should free itself. It cannot be forced from the outside to have a free form of government, no more than that an individual should not be forced to lead a virtuous lifestyle. Self-determination means that peoples have the right to realize freedom by its their efforts.[14] Immanuel Kant would agree. An international community of states can only reach the condition of peace if these states accept the principle of non-intervention. Therefore, one of the so-called preliminary articles[15] of this treatise on peace reads: 'no state shall forcibly interfere in the constitution and government of another state'. This principle reflects Kant's notion that a state is not a piece of property, but rather a society of men whom no one else has any right to command or to dispose except the state itself. A state should be considered a moral person, which follows from the concept of the original treaty. It is true that Kant believes that only a republican state, characterized by a separation of powers and respect for human rights, can satisfy this idea. Whether a state fulfills its internal requirements, however, should not, according to Kant, be decisive for the manner in which states treat each other. Even if a state as a moral person treats itself badly, there is still no justification for other states to limit the former state's freedom of acting. No more than morally improper behaviour of an individual does not trigger the correcting effects of national criminal law, as long as that person does not infringe on the rights of others, does the bad example that a state gives to another state constitute an injury to the latter.[16] The recognition of even the smallest right to intervene based on morally objectionable acts would mean the introduction of the right to resort to war. States should, therefore, only be allowed to correct each other by force if their acts endanger the coming into existence of an international legal order, i.e. if they violate each other's right to political sovereignty and territorial integrity.[17]

This call upon the moral value of self-determination as a ground for rejecting the right to humanitarian intervention is not entirely convincing. After all, there is only a limited analogy between the individual harming herself without harming others and thus not violating their rights, and the damage a state does to itself, i.e. its citizens, without infringing on the rights of other states. To define a state as a moral person may mean that it is autonomous with respect to other states, but that does not make it an organic whole. The analogy is driven too far when a state that violates human rights on a large scale, is compared with a drunkard, who violates his duty to live a virtuous life, but does not hamper other's rights. It would be cynical to think that a state just gives shape to its right to self-determination in a bad way, when the government oppresses the population.

Today, therefore, only few defend an unrestricted right to self-determination. This right's meaning cannot include the authorization of a state to do whatever it wants with its citizens. Self-determination should, at least partially, mean that a government derives its authority to rule from the consent of its population. According to some, the legitimacy of humanitarian intervention resides in the notion that a collective right of the state fully depends on the possibility it offers its citizens to exercise their individual rights of freedom. Tesón takes the opposite position from Mill and Kant. He only recognizes the right of a state to self-determination if its citizens shape their own political, economics and cultural institutions. From such a viewpoint, not only a war in self-defence is justified, but also a war to defend 'socially basic (security and subsistence) rights,' provided that conditions of proportionality are met. Violations of human rights can function as a casus belli. Those who do not want to go that far, should show, how the sovereignty of a state could prevail over the rights of citizens of that state.[18] Therefore, the question in the literature is no longer whether, but to what extent, intervention is justified?

In his famous *Just and Unjust Wars*, Walzer tries to strike the balance and takes the just war doctrine as the starting position when discussing the question of the legitimacy of humanitarian intervention. As is well known, the core of this classical doctrine consists of the distinction between ius ad bellum and ius in bello. Based on these two clusters of rights, answers are given to the questions concerning against whom a war may be fought and with what legitimate means. The core idea of ius in bello is the distinction between combatants and non-combatants and non-combatant immunity. The core idea of ius ad bellum is the theory of aggression. Here, Walzer rejects Mill's argument for strict non-intervention. According to him, situations may occur in which a state is no longer required to respect the political sovereignty and territorial integrity of another state. Such situations occur if a state contains several political communities and one of these strives for secession, if there has been an intervention during civil war in favor of one party (counterintervention), and if human rights are grossly violated within a state.[19] In these situations of necessity or distress, states may legitimately neglect the prohibition on intervention. With this position, Walzer tries to combine two views, one of them emphasizing the value of self-determination and the plurality of sovereign states, and the other respecting the international legal position of the rights of individuals.

Some hold that Walzer with this position still underestimates the values of individuals by giving priority to the value of existing states.[20] In answering this reproach, Walzer emphasizes that the principle of non-intervention indeed intends to respect the distinctive character of political communities. It is a matter of fact that people live in historically and culturally determined communities that differ from each other, also with regard to how they answer the question of legitimacy. Therefore, these communities have to respect each other's autonomy in principle. Basically, communities have to assume that the governments of other communities reflect the will of those communities and that foreign governments are legitimate. In principle, it is not within the competence of outsiders to evaluate the extent to which government and community fit each other. This basic assumption of mutual respect can only be overruled if the discrepancy between government and community is obvious. Thus, humanitarian intervention is justified in the case of violations of human rights on a large scale, since the government that commits them obviously no longer fits the community, and, therefore, loses its legitimacy.

There are a few good reasons to follow Walzer. First, the recognition of such a limited right to intervention does not preclude efforts for a world-wide respect for human rights to be made. He only defends that the right to self-determination is not removed by limited violations of human rights. In such cases, other states have no right to use military force.[21] Other ways to express criticism, of course, remain. Second, Walzer rightly stresses the fact that ultimately only the members of political community can answer the question of the legitimacy of its government. According to democratic standards, legitimacy means that a people can exercise its rights of freedom and political participation. In history up until our day, however, many regimes of an authoritarian nature have existed, and continue to exist, that have nevertheless been accepted, or are accepted, as legitimate. Internationally, the fact that there is a plurality of values should be recognized. Legitimacy takes different forms in different communities, and members of political communities should for themselves decide whether the government "fits" the community to a satisfying degree. If a government is not or is no longer legitimate, its population should exercise its moral right to revolution. The existence of such a right does not imply a right of other states to intervene. Third, with the right to self-determination, a clear duty for all other political communities corresponds, namely that of non-intervention unless "the stakes are too high, the suffering already too great".[22] This is, perhaps, the only sensible way to conceive of a duty to humanitarian intervention, because the right to intervention raises the question as to the corresponding duty. Are states always obliged to intervene if the conditions are met?

4. DUTY TO HUMANITARIAN INTERVENTION: HEGEL AND HABERMAS

Many hold the view that a right to intervention in a broad sense should be rejected because such a right cannot sensibly be connected to a broad duty to intervene. This results from a reflection on the nature of a state. Some argue that the primary focus of a state should the well-being of its member and the interests of the political community as a whole. Therefore, it has no permission to put the lives of its soldiers at risk for non-state related aims, like the interests of citizens of another state. In the context of his rejection of Kant's proposal for a perpetual peace, Hegel argues in this direction. According to Hegel, the state should not be understood as resulting from a social contract between future citizens with an eye to protecting their life, liberty and estate. Conceiving of the state as resulting from such a rational calculus would leave unexplained citizens' willingness to eventually give up their lives and possessions in order to protect their political community. If the state were a means to protect individual interests, a willingness to make such a sacrifice in order to save that means would be contradictory.[23] Social contract theory is unable to understand the ties of solidarity[24] presupposed within a particular community. Like Walzer, Hegel holds that questions of legitimacy can only be answered from within, not from without. Since the state is not an arbitrary, but an ethical, community in which citizens can develop and maintain their freedom and identity only in loyalty with others, war even has an ethical meaning. The willingness of a citizen to protect his state, if necessary with his life, is not an inefficient way to secure his individual interests; rather, it is the way in which he defends the identity of the communal life he shares with his co-nationals. During war, citizens experience and accept that there are higher values, to which life, freedom and property are subordinate.[25] A state's foreign policy should, therefore, aim at serving the values of its particular community. Therefore, the state can only call upon civilians to endanger their lives as soldiers when their common interests are at stake. In Hegel's view, war is, therefore, not a conflict between a justified claim and an unjustified claim, but, rather, a conflict between two systems of values, in which one system has to make way for the other.[26]

Since the days when Hegel defended the value of particular political communities, much has changed. The fact that humanitarian intervention is no longer categorically rejected points out that ethical values to which states and citizens nowadays commit themselves are no longer merely particular ones. People tend to regard themselves not only as citizens of a particular political community, but as world citizens as well.[27] A plea for intervention on strictly humanitarian grounds demands that the intervening state puts aside its national loyalty for cosmopolitan solidarity. This, however, leaves the problem Hegel raises not completely answered, since war still entails a high price. Is a state allowed to risk the lives of its soldiers for the interests of the world community? Moreover, is it not justified to fear that a so-called willingness by states to interfere on humanitarian grounds is nevertheless fuelled by state interests? Does not 'humanity' function as a means to conceal particular interests?

These questions have recently been raised in relation to the NATO intervention in Kosovo. A clear example is Habermas' ambivalent judgment of the event. This ambivalence showed itself already in Habermas' earlier discussion of Kant's treatise on perpetual peace. Habermas here criticizes Kant's categorical affirmation of self-determination and his rejection of any intervention, since this implies a rather poor situation concerning the global protection of human rights. This protection would, rather, ask for a strong international executive power.[28] Kant's heritage can only be taken seriously today by arguing in favor of a reform of international law's structure and of strengthening the legitimacy of the organization of the United Nations and extending its legislative, executive and juridical competencies. Yet, Habermas takes also seriously Kant's warning against confusing perpetual peace by means of a free federation of states with an amalgamation of nations in a situation of universal despotism which would bring all freedom to an end. Since every state desires to dominate the world,[29] efforts to institutionalise world government must be met with suspicion. In his comment on the Kosovo intervention, Habermas admits that this lesson can be learned not only from Kant, but from Schmitt as well. Even if one rejects Schmitt's definition of 'the political' as the ultimate decision concerning friend and foe, it has to be acknowledged that the politics of human rights and humanitarian intervention might consist of concealed efforts to reach hegemony, by using quasi-moral justifications where clear juridical justifications are lacking.[30]

Habermas' cautiously formulated comment on the Kosovo-intervention in 'Bestiality and Humanity: A War on the Border between Legality and Morality' is marked by this ambivalence.[31] On the one hand, he sympathizes with the pacifist's view that every war, including humanitarian intervention, originates in the will to power and inevitably inflicts human suffering. On the other hand, he admits that peace between nations can only be based on truly binding rules. Law between states cannot be based on consent and "pacta sunt servanda" only. The cosmopolitan condition in which human rights play an important role implies the establishment of enforceable laws. For that reason, the Kosovo-conflict can be approached from different angles. Under the premises of the traditional law of states, the Kosovo-conflict should be seen as a violation of the principle of non-intervention. Yet, under the premises of human rights, it could perhaps be seen as a leap forward to a cosmopolitan world community. After all, the intervention aimed at protecting the human rights of an endangered minority, and such an intervention would follow from a duty "erga omnes" that does not require a Security Council mandate. Human rights definitively has more weight than state sovereignty.

Yet, what might be true in theory is not easily applicable in practice. Habermas is correct in being hesitant here, since Kosovo not evidently meant a shift in emphasis from a traditional international law of states to a cosmopolitan defence of human rights. Much depends here on the relevant facts and on the intentions of the intervening forces. Do references to "humanity" not resemble the rhetoric of the "just war"?[32] Is not there sufficient reason for concern with regard to the negotiations at Rambouillet, to the combatant party of the KLA, to the military means of high altitude bombing, and, especially, to the different conceptions of human rights? Some argued that human rights are of the supra-national nature and, therefore, require an effective system of cosmopolitan law, while others argued that human rights need not be embedded in such law, since they derive their legitimacy primarily from moral resources only.[33] In the former view, humanitarian intervention anticipates a true international law of peoples, while in the latter intervention derives its legitimacy from the principle that anyone who can help should help.[34] Habermas' hesitations relate to the lack of juridical legitimacy and unilateralism. The acceptance of unilateral humanitarian intervention could pave the way for expansionism, and the distinction between aggression and intervention could get blurred. Humanitarian intervention can only become part of international law when an independent judicial body has the authority to determine when it is justified and when it is not.

5. A FRESH APPROACH: RAWLS AND A DECENCY CONCEPT OF SOVEREIGNTY

If the issue concerning humanitarian intervention is confused both legally and conceptually, perhaps a fresh, constructive approach like in Rawls' *The Law of Peoples* might help. In this recent monograph, Rawls fills the gap left open in his earlier *A Theory of Justice*. In 'Theory', he constructs an account of justice acceptable in a domestic, yet pluralist, society whose foundation cannot be found in an all-embracing, comprehensive philosophy. In *The Law of People*, Rawls wants to do something similar, namely constructing principles of justice for the (international) society of societies. In order to do so, Rawls duplicates his original method to determine principles of justice for a domestic society and asks what would result from a deliberation by an assembly of representatives of liberal-democratic peoples within an initial position. For this purpose, the participants of this deliberation are placed behind the veil of ignorance and, thus, deprived of any knowledge on the condition of the nations that they represent. According to Rawls, these representatives of liberal-democratic peoples would opt for the principles that are already widely recognized and accepted in international law: the principle of legal equality of peoples; the principle of self-determination, so that every people has the right to its own affairs without outside interference; the right of self-defence; and the principle that treaties should be served. They would, however, add two principles, namely that peoples are to honor human rights and that they have a duty to assist other peoples living under unfavorable conditions that prevent them from having a just or decent political and social regime.[35]

Subsequently, Rawls wonders what the scope of these principles would be. It is obvious that liberal societies, which are internally characterized by respect for equality, will be inclined to accept that same in their relations to other peoples. Far from all societies, however, recognize equality as the fundamental principle for their internal political order. Would they all then reject the law agreed upon between liberal peoples? The answer is no. According to Rawls, a category of non-liberal peoples exists which does indeed not internally accept the notion of legal equality, but which will nevertheless accept the principle of equality for the law of peoples. Although these peoples are composed internally of different groups with different legal statuses, they can easily understand that an international principle of equality serves their rational interests. Rawls labels the societies of these peoples as decent hierarchical societies since they meet a number of criteria. Firstly, they recognize a judicial system which guarantees those human rights that are regarded as fundamental within the law of peoples to all members of society, independent of the way in which they are categorized in groups of unequal legal standing. This means that the following rights are respected: the right to life (to the means of subsistence and security); the right to liberty, which means that slavery and serfdom are outlawed and that a sufficient degree of freedom of conscience, religion and thought is respected; the right of personal property; and the right of formal equality. Secondly, those peoples recognize the fact that all members of the different groups within the political community are responsible and cooperative members of society as a whole. Therefore, all these groups of the population are consulted about decisions regarding important interests of society. Third, the judicial system should be lead by the sincere conviction of justices and other officials of that system that the law is guided by a common good idea of justice. With these virtues, peoples other than liberal ones meet the 'internal' criteria necessary for acceptance on their part and admission on the part of the liberal peoples to the society of societies based on the law of peoples.[36]

Clearly, human rights plays an important role here. They constitute the most important criterion to determine which peoples can agree with the law of peoples. Hierarchical, non-egalitarian peoples can have international standing because they comply with human rights standards. In this way, Rawls tries to find a balance between the very different manners in which peoples organize their political lives on the one hand, and the need for international cooperation that is nevertheless needed. After all, as Kant says, the earth is a "globe, in which peoples cannot disperse over an infinite area, but necessarily must tolerate each other's company".[37] For Rawls, human rights determine the boundaries of international tolerance, as they enable the distinction between well-ordered peoples led by the common principles of the law of peoples and not well-ordered peoples.[38] In order to do so, however, human rights have to be understood restrictively. Only the before mentioned, not politically parochial and urgent rights form part of the law of peoples.[39] Rawls thus introduces a distinction between these urgent rights on the one hand and the rights citizens have as free and equal citizens in liberal democratic states on the other. No society can be legitimate if it does not meet the requirements of these rights.

This overlapping consensus on legitimacy makes a Law of Peoples between liberal and hierarchical societies possible, which together form the international community of well-ordered societies. Opposite this community is the category of not well-ordered societies that consists of states that do not respect those human rights internally and rules of reciprocity externally and peoples that are burdened by unfavourable circumstances. With these peoples, only a 'modus vivendi' can be reached not a consensus. How should the society of peoples ruled by the law of peoples deal with peoples that do not? Rawls provides the following answer. Regarding societies that are burdened by unfavourable circumstances, the well-ordered societies have a duty to assist, in order to enable them to develop a well-ordered society. For this purpose, contributions have to be made to enable the change in the political culture of these societies and the development of decent public institutions. Internationally, there is, according to Rawls, no need or justification for an equivalent of the so-called difference principle, which he deemed necessary only in a society based on 'justice as fairness'. It is not among the goals of the law of peoples to redistribute prosperity internationally,[40] because not all peoples endorse egalitarian conceptions of justice. Furthermore, the acceptance of an international difference principle would entail fundamental global institutional reform and thus change the character of the law of peoples by drastically reducing the autonomy of its composing units. According to Rawls, these changes are not desirable.

The second group of not well-ordered societies consists of 'outlaw' states that refuse to recognize any principle of law or justice or the integrity of other peoples, since they are fully convinced of the supremacy of their culture or religion. The fact that these societies will not consent to the law of peoples does not, however, give the well-ordered societies the right to use military means to force compliance. Well-ordered societies only have the right to resist aggression by outlaw states and to strive peacefully for the situation in which all societies in the world respect the law of peoples. The establishment of international legal institutions and a federal centre, within which critical opinions can be formed and economic pressure can be bundled, fits those means. Those criticisms will be the more effective as they are based on a reasonable law of peoples that cannot easily be dismissed as typically liberal or typically Western. Resorting to military force is only justified, according to Rawls, if those outlaw states commit acts of aggression or grossly and massively violate minimal human rights that form part of the law of peoples.[41] Rawls, thus, accepts the legitimacy of humanitarian intervention an ultimate remedy, "if the offenses against human rights are egregious and the society does not respond to the imposition of sanctions"[42] and if the well being of a population under a terrorist regime cannot be defended in any other way.

One might have the impression that Rawls' position does not differ much from Walzer's *Just and Unjust Wars*, to which he often refers.[43] It seems as if Rawls agrees with Walzer that the decision on humanitarian intervention calls for political wisdom and that its success depends on luck, to which political philosophy has not much to add.[44] I think this first impression is false. *The Law of Peoples* makes some important intellectual progress. Rawls, after all, suggests that decisions concerning intervention should be taken in the context of new institutions that bring together the well-ordered peoples, either within or beyond the present United Nations scheme. Interventions should, then, not be a matter of unilateral decision-making, but should result from a deliberative process within the confederative center of the society of well-ordered peoples. With these remarks, Rawls distances himself from Walzer's view that the only global community is pluralist in character, a community of nations, not of humanity.[45] Rawls, however, intends to formulate a 'realistic utopia' of a reasonably just Society of Peoples, in which the measure of independence of political communities is based on reasonable consent[46] and the decision whether or not to militarily intervene is based on principles. This design of how the law for an international society of societies should look determines how its constituent parts should deal with societies burdened by unfavorable conditions and with outlaw states. Rawls aims at providing principles with "a target and a cutoff point". The duty to assistance aims at helping societies to manage their own affairs reasonably and rationally and this duty ceases when the poor are able to establish a well-ordered society. Mainly, this must be done by helping these societies to establish a decent political and social culture.[47] Pressure on outlaw states and, eventually, intervention has such a target and cutoff point too, namely preventing basic human rights from being violated on a mass scale. If these goals can be reached, the hope for a law of peoples acceptable for all societies is reasonable.

Correctly, I think, Rawls argues that the great evils of human history follow from political injustice and that these evils will disappear once the gravest forms of political injustice are eliminated by means of establishing just basic institutions, both domestic and international. The question of the legitimacy of humanitarian intervention cannot be separated from this utopian goal. Rawls is following Kant's lead: the duty to contribute to the realization of that goal follows from "cosmopolitan right, in so far as individuals and states may be regarded as citizens of a universal state of mankind".[48] The roots of the cosmopolitan values underlying both Rawls' *The Law of Peoples* and Kant's *Towards Perpetual Peace* must be found in the Stoic emphasis on the fact that we all belong both to our domestic community of birth and to the global community. Rawls locates the issue of humanitarian intervention at the intersection of those two communities. Answering the question of its legitimacy boils down to finding the delicate balance, 'reflexive equilibrium', between respect for local autonomy and concern for global values. If international actors refuse to aim at striking this balance, humanitarian intervention, if approved, is nothing less but a concealed effort to establish global hegemony and, if denied, a sign of moral indifference.

NOTES

[1] See e.g.: Th. Mertens, Hegel's Homage to Kant's *Perpetual Peace*. An Analysis of Hegel's *Philosophy of Right* §§ 321-340, in: *The Review of Politics* 57 (1995), p. 665-691.

[2] G. Robertson, *Crimes against Humanity. The Struggle for Global Justice*, Harmondsworth 2000, 441-2.

[3] J.H.H. Weiler, The Transformation of Europe, in: Idem, *The Constitution of Europe. Does the New Clothes have an Emperor*, Cambridge 1999, 10-101.

[4] See e.g. T.W. Pogge, The International Significance of Human Rights, in: *The Journal of Ethics* 4 (2000), 45-69.

[5] See e.g.: G. Cavallar, Annäherung an den ewigen Frieden. Neuere Publikationen über Immanuel Kants Friedensschrift, in: *Deutsche Zeitschrift für Philosophie* (46) 1998, 137-143; G. Cavallar, *Kant and the Theory and Practice of International Right*, Cardiff 1999; C. Clovell, *Kant and the Law of Peace*, Houndsmill etc. 1998; M. Kaufmann, Kein ewiger Friede für Kant. Ein Rückblick auf einige Literatur zu 200 Jahren Zum ewigen Frieden, in: *Allgemeine Zeitschrift für Philosophie* (25) 2000, 271-280.

[6] See e.g. G. Radbruch, *Rechtsphilosophie*, seventh edition (ed. E. Wolf), Stuttgart 1970 (orig. 1932), 172-3.

[7] This emphasis on sovereignty was underlined in 1970, in the General Assembly Declaration on Principles of International Law Concerning Friendly Relations and Coopreation among States in Accordance with the Charter of the United Nations: "No state or group of states has the right to intervene, directly or indirectly, for any reason whatever, in the internal or external affairs of any other state. Consequently, armed intervention and all other forms of interference or attempted threats against the personality of the state or against its political, economic and cultural elements, are in violation of international law", General Assembly Resolution 2625 (XXV).

[8] This formulation was used in the Security Council's authorisation of the Gulf War.

[9] See e.g.: B. Simma, Nato, the UN and the Use of Force: Legal Aspects, In: *European Journal of International Law* 10 (1999), 1-23.

[10] Barcelona Traction Case 1970, *ICJ Reports* 3, 32.

[11] Quoted in: A. Carrino, Reflections on Legal Science, Law and Power, in: St.L. Paulson, B.L. Paulson (eds.), *Normativity and Norms. Critical Perspectives on Kelsenian Themes*, Oxford 1998, 509.

[12] N. Krish, Review Essay: Legality, Morality and the Dilemma of Humanitarian Intervention after Kosovo, In: *European Journal of International Law* 13 (2002), 323-337, at 324: "Yet the history of humanitarian intervention is one of abuse".

[13] This is the core of so-called legalist paradigm, see: M. Walzer, *Just and Unjust Wars*, New York 1977, 61 et seq.

[14] J. S. Mill, A Few Words on Non-intervention (1867) in: *Collected Works*, Vol. XXI, p. 111 et seq.; M. Walzer, *Just and Unjust Wars*, 87-8.

[15] The first part of *Zum ewigen Frieden* contains preliminary and final articles. The former describes negative prohibitions and the latter positive recommandations.

[16] I. Kant, *Zum ewigen Frieden*, Akademie Ausgabe (=AA) VIII, Berlin 1902 et seq., 346.
[17] I. Kant, *Die Metaphysik der Sitten, Rechtslehre*, AA VI, 349; See Th. Mertens, War and International Order in Kant's Legal Thought, in: *Ratio Juris* 8 (1995), 296-314.
[18] F. Tesón, *Humanitarian Intervention: an inquiry into law and morality*, New York 1988, 31; In the same line: D. Luban, Just War and Human Right, in: *Philosophy and Public Affairs* (9) 1980, 161- 81.
[19] M. Walzer, *Just and Unjust Wars*, 90; Idem, The Moral Standing of States, in: *Philosophy and Public Affairs* (9) 1980, 216-7.
[20] E.g. G. Doppelt, Walzer's Theory of Morality in International Relations, in: *Philosophy and Public Affairs* (8) 1978, 3-26.
[21] M. Walzer, The Moral Standing of States, 214, 229.
[22] M. Walzer, The Argument about Humanitarian Intervention, see this volume.
[23] G.W.F. Hegel, *Grundlinien der Philosophie des Rechts*, Theorie Werkausgabe Bd.7, Frankfurt am Main 1973, § 324 + Anm.
[24] Mill refers here to common sympathies, see: J. Rawls, *The Law of Peoples; with 'The Idea of Public Reason Revisited'*, Cambridge, London 1999, 23n.
[25] Not only Hegel says so: *Grundlinien der Philosophie des Rechts*, § 324 Anm, but also Kant admits of this: Kritik *der Urteilskraft*, AA V, 263.
[26] S. Avineri, *Hegel's Theory of the Modern State*, Cambridge 1972, 202-3.
[27] This awareness might be the contemporary cosmopolitan translation of what Hegel considered to be the common customs and habits of the European states on the basis on which these states would be able to seek justice not any longer by means of violence, but on the basis of these communalities, G.W.F. Hegel, *Grundlinien der Philosophie des Rechts*, § 339 Z.
[28] J. Habermas, Kant's Idea of Perpetual Peace, with the Benefit of Two Hundred Years' Hindsight, in: J. Bohman, M. Lutz-Bachmann (eds.), *Perpetual Peace. Essays on Kant's Cosmopolitan Ideal*, Cambridge, London 1997, 130. See also: Th. Mertens, From 'Perpetual Peace' to 'The Law of Peoples'. Kant, Habermas and Rawls on International Relations, to appear in: *Kantian Review* 6 (2002).
[29] I. Kant, *Zum ewigen Frieden*, Akademie Ausgabe VIII, 367.
[30] J. Habermas, Kant's Idea of Perpetual Peace, with the Benefit of Two Hundred Years' Hindsight, 147-8.
[31] In: *Constellations* 6 (1999), 263-27. Originally in: *Die Zeit*, 29 April 1999.
[32] Habermas quotes Schmitt's saying 'whoever says humanity wants to deceive', in: Bestiality and Humanity, *Constellations* 6 (1999), 266-7; C. Schmitt, *The Concept of the Political*, New Brunswick 1976.
[33] The general turn to ethics in the Kosovo War: M. Koskenniemi, 'The Lady Doth Protest Too Much'. Kosovo, and the Turn to Ethics in International Law, in: *Modern Law Review*, 65 (2002), 159-175.
[34] M. Walzer, The Argument about Humanitarian Intervention; see this volume.
[35] J. Rawls, *The Law of Peoples*, 37.
[36] J. Rawls, *The Law of Peoples*, 64.
[37] I. Kant, *Zum ewigen Frieden*, AA VIII, 358.

[38] Rawls uses this concept of well-orderedness already in: *A Theory of Justice*, Oxford 1971,4-5.
[39] J. Rawls, *The Law of Peoples*, 65, 68.
[40] The absence of such a principle of redistribution has received fierce opposition, see: T.W. Pogge, An Egalitarian Law of Peoples, in: *Philosophy and Public Affairs* 23 (1994), 195-224.
[41] LP: 81, 94 n: if the offenses against human right are egregious and the society does not respond to the imposition of sanctions, such interventions in the defense of human right would be acceptable and would be called for. See also: J. Rawls, *The Law of Peoples*, 8, 81.
[42] J. Rawls, *The Law of Peoples*, 94 n.
[43] J. Rawls, *The Law of Peoples*, 95 n.; For Walzer, too, the concept of decency is central, in: The Argument about Humanitarian Intervention, see this volume.
[44] J. Rawls, *The Law of Peoples*, 94.
[45] M. Walzer, The Moral Standing of States, 226.
[46] J. Rawls, *The Law of Peoples*, 27: ' … peoples' rights and duties in regard to their so-called sovereignty derive from the Law of Peoples itself, …'
[47] J. Rawls, *The Law of Peoples*, 109.
[48] I. Kant, *Zum ewigen Frieden*, 349 n.

RUDOLF SCHÜSSLER

Principles of non-UN Humanitarian Intervention

Not long ago, the assent of the UN or the UN security council was considered necessary for the legitimation of Humanitarian Interventions.[1] NATO broke with this rule, claiming an exceptional right to defend human rights in the Serbian province of Kosovo. NATO's claim presupposes that some evils can be huge enough to justify deviations from UN intervention governance. Today, this view is widely accepted. But accepting non-UN Humanitarian Interventions[2] implies considerable risks. How can we guarantee that power will not erode international law, if the legitimacy of exceptions from UN rule is judged by those who have the power to intervene? How can war be restrained, if rules of restraint are abandoned and not replaced? I will argue here that confidence in the wisdom of governments is a misguided answer to these questions. Without criteria of legitimacy (or legality) for interventions we are likely to lose track in the turmoil of moral rhetoric and ethical reasoning that accompanies all wars.

Of course, this is no new insight. Criteria of legitimacy for interventions have been postulated in the literature on international law ever since the 17th century. And even medieval theories of just war contain legitimacy criteria for interventions, because the practice of interventionism is older than the term. It is interesting to note that some core criteria of legitimacy have hardly changed over the centuries. This is especially important because these core criteria are supposed to restrict military power even in the absence of international governance – such governance simply did not exist when the criteria were designed.

The present paper accepts most traditional criteria for legitimate interventions. It regards them as good, but not as good enough. Recent developments in international law, like the imminent prospect of an international criminal court, and the role of the UN as a possible judge of interventions should lead to modifications and extensions of the traditional set of intervention criteria. Additionally, an old and seemingly forgotten rule against wars of doubtful legitimacy should be revived, because moral uncertainty is a constant companion to war. The present paper develops these points and it thereby hopes to contribute to a clearer moral picture of contemporary interventionism.

1. HISTORICAL REMARKS

Controling Humanitarian Interventions through checks and balances against the abuse of military power is no new idea, and it seems worthwhile to begin an inquiry into this subject with some historical remarks. The term "Humanitarian Intervention" seems to be a product of the late 19th century.[3] The idea, however, is considerably older. Some Roman wars can be reckoned among the earliest examples of military interventions allegedly in favor of suppressed people.[4] Interventions with such an aim satisfied Cicero's definition of a just war. Cicero maintained that a just war would help to avenge injuries (*ulcisci injurias*) or repell enemies.[5]

In the High Middle Ages, the situation became far more complex. By then, a well developed theory of just war had evolved.[6] As part of it, military inventions resembling todays Humanitarian Interventions appeared legitimate in theory. The medieval theory of just war approved wars for the defense of innocents against atrocities.[7] In practice, however, the defense of innocents was restricted to the "defense" of fellow Christians. The crusades were advertised in this spirit as defense of Christians in Asia Minor against the expansive Turks.[8] The practical application of just war theory to the alleged defense of nonchristian innocents seems to be a post-medieval development. It first became prominent in the context of the Spanish conquests in America. The spokesmen of the Spanish conquerors justified the wars against the Indians – among other things – as interventions against the horrors of human sacrifice and cannibalism.[9] This sounds cynical, but it is no more cynical than Jean Bodin's praise of the Mongol raider Tamerlane as champion of Humanitarian Intervention.[10] Sometimes, it seems, the rhetorics of Humanitarian Intervention can become quite hypocritical.

Despite the bleak practice of military intervention in the Middle Ages, it should not be forgotten that medieval just war theories aimed at a humanization of warfare. Above all, the theory of just war contained a system of checks and balances against the abuse of power. This included regulations for the practice of warfare (*ius in bello*) as well as standards for the legitimate entry into war (*ius ad bellum*). Princes could not declare just war at will. They had to apply a catalogue of criteria with regard to a just cause for fighting, the legitimate authority of the prince and his good intentions.[11] Furthermore, there was a rule of proportionality in order to prevent excessive warfare. And princes could not apply the criteria of just war theory simply according to their best judgement. They had to take counsel from expert jurists and theologians. If the counsellors reached a consensus against war, a prince who nevertheless declared war sinned mortally. And mortal sinners faced not only punishment after death but risked the loss of political compliance in this world.

It is disappointing that the elaborate system of checks and balances in the medieval theory of just war did not work better in practice. But at least the necessity of checks and balances was acknowledged in the allegedly "dark" Middle Ages. Modern international law did not much to improve this state of affairs. Eighteenth and nineteenth century ideas of legitimate warfare were often anti-interventionist with regard to European powers (lately including America) and interventionist concerning colonies or non-christian countries. It is important to recognize that the Post-Thirty-Years-War era in international law did not abandon interventionism completely – interventionism retained a foothold in the affairs of Europe and reigned supreme in European relations with non-christian powers.[12] For these reasons, wars against "less civilized" people became the prototype of Humanitarian Interventions.[13] Even the term Humanitarian Intervention was largely coined in connection with such wars.[14] The possible application of interventionism in European conflicts, however, ensured that legitimacy criteria for interventions were considered necessary by most specialists in international law throughout the 18th and 19th century.

2. TRADITIONAL CRITERIA OF LEGITIMACY FOR HUMANITARIAN INTERVENTIONS

It is within the jurisprudence of the 19th century that we first find legitimacy criteria for interventions which were explicitly labelled humanitarian. Fonteyne's survey of Humanitarian Interventionsm in this period shows that there was an overlapping consensus of jurists concerning such criteria. Fonteyne mentions four general conditions for legitimate (or legal) interventions on humanitarian grounds that can be found in most treatises on this subject:[15]

(a) disinterestedness of the intervening power(s): the intervenor(s) should not seek profit from the intervention;
(b) restriction of interventions to cases of extreme atrocities or breakdown of order;
(c) atrocities are commited by or with consent of the sovereign of the country at which an intervention aims;
(d) interventions should be conducted by groups of states, not by single states.

The first three criteria are taken from traditional just war theories. Criterion (a) obviously derives from the medieval criterion of good intention. Criterion (b) embodies the old iusta-causa-condition. The atrocities in question are not precisely delineated, but killing, torture, unlawful imprisonment and slavery are standard examples. Criterion (d) seems to be new. It reflects the post-medieval, "Hobbesian" assumption that there is no universally acknowledged moral authority which could judge the conduct of sovereign powers. The self-interest of powers, therefore, can only be restrained by the self-interest of other powers in a coalition.

If we now turn to a recent reconsideration of criteria for Humanitarian Interventions, we find important similarities with Fonteyne's account. Ankenbrand insists on massive crimes against humanity as sole causes of just interventions and stresses that collective intervention may serve as a check against the abuse of interventionism.[16] This is important, because Ankenbrand's position reflects the Kosovo experience and its impact on international law. [17] Under the normative control of the UN it does not matter whether one or more powers carry out an intervention. The condition of group action regains relevance only because the non-UN intervention in Kosovo has lead us back to a Hobbesian conception of international affairs.

Ankenbrand states that an up-to-date catalogue of extreme atrocities, which would justify military intervention, can be derived from the international catalogue of crimes against humanity. Thus, killings, harm to the body of persons, torture, slavery and massive social or political discrimination will count as just causes of war. Intervention becomes legitimate if these crimes outweigh the expected evils of war. Note that the criterion of disinterestedness is lacking in Ankenbrand's account. Today, many experts regard this criterion as futile. It is mainly required that an intervenor does a good job in terminating massive atrocities without curbing the territorial integrity and post-intervention sovereignty of a country.

But there is more to the traditional criterion of good intention than mere disinterestedness. One should be aware that good intention originally was measured by the compatibility of an individual's will with a good world order. We may translate this demand into the claim that Humanitarian Intervenors should act in accordance with today's most widely accepted ideas of a good world order. We can derive a legitimacy criterion for interventions from this claim. This will be my first step toward an extended and revised set of intervention criteria.

3. THE CRITERION OF THE GOOD WORLD ORDER: ACCEPTANCE OF INTERNATIONAL JURISDICTION

What is a good world order? In the Middle Ages a good world order was defined by theology. Today we usually strive for a secular world order governed by democratic and juridical principles. Respect for Human Rights is an important aspect of such a world order. But respect for law and for democractic procedures in international affairs seem equally important if a stable good world order is to be achieved. We may express this assertion in a principle:

Conjunction Principle

Humanitarian Interventions should have a double aim. They should prevent crimes against humanity and follow the priciples of a free, law-based and democratic world order. Fulfilling one aim at a cost to the other may be approved only in exceptional cases.

The Conjunction Principle will probably appear obvious to many. Furthermore, it already seems to be embodied in existing UN-regulations and in international law. According to UN-statutes, military interventions can only be legitimate under specific conditions and if approved by the UN security council. This council, however, does not represent the democratic will of the community of nations. Neither is it an apt interpreter of international law. Nevertheless, its control over Humanitarian Interventions may count as a step in the right direction. It may be considered as the best existing approximation to a law-based and democratic control of military power.

The insight that some progress towards a good world order has already been made supports the following interpretation of the Conjunction Principle. A Humanitarian Intervention contributes to a good world order if it:

(a) prevents or stops large-scale crime,
(b) fosters the establishment of a law-based, democratic world order,
(c) or at least does not lead to a fall-back behind an already achieved stage of the development of a law-based, democratic world order.

Under ideal conditions, claims (a)-(c) seem uncontroversial. But unfortunately, the conditions can conflict in reality. In the Kosovo case, NATO claimed that criterion (a) legitimized military action which was not approved by the UN security council. This may be seen as a violation of criterion (b) or (c). Similar conflicts may arise if it seems obvious to potential intervenors that massive crimes against humanity occur in a country, while the UN security council takes no steps to stop these crimes or even to call them by their names. May not countries or coalitions of countries intervene and circumvent the UN security council in such cases? Will not the moral weight of (a) sometimes justify a violation of the merely formal requirements (b) and (c)?

Let us first observe what is at stake, before discussing an answer. The obvious risk of a self-imputed right to intervene without UN approval is that right gives way to force. If we accept that a country or coalition of countries assumes both, the role of judge and intervenor, a decisive rupture with established democratic practices will be the consequence. The traditional criterion of group action does not suffice as a remedy here. We should never forget that this criterion emerged in the 18th century, when a concert of powers existed in Europe. The idea of a European "concert of powers" was based on the fact that no power was absolutely dominant. Group action guaranteed some balance of interests under this premise. But group action did never function as bulwark against the exploitation and oppression of non-European people. And group action is not likely to function as restriction against war under present conditions. Today, the USA is wastly predominant in the international sphere. The present situation resembles hegemonial Rome and its auxiliaries more than Europe's former concert of powers. The need to form coalitions, therefore, does not effectively curb the means of the USA to serve its own interests as it thinks fit. In consequence, the criterion of group action becomes void.

So we are back in square one. Only the existing UN regulations ensure that no single country can be arbiter as well as executor of military actions against other nations. Therefore, UN control arguably represents at least some advance towards a law-based, democratic world order. Any unilateral usurpation of the role of judge as well as that of executor undermines this achievement and causes a serious de-democratization of the existing world order.

But let us give this assertion a second thought. One may argue that a democratic separation of powers can only function if practiced by the right institutions. This means that the moral or judicial legitimacy of interventions, e.g., should only be assessed by court-like institutions. Under this premise, the UN security council would be a complete misfit as judge of military interventions. A separation of powers reached with its help would constitute no democratic achievement whatsoever. Perhaps, this is a defensible point of view. Note, however, that it entails a complete normative devaluation of the security council. The Kosovo war could then not be regarded as exceptional. Moreover, it would be nonsensical to ask for the approval of the UN security council for future interventions, since this would mean approval by an institution whose judgement has been normatively nullified.

Let us assume now for the sake of the argument that security council control creates no defenseworthy separation of powers in the international sphere. Even this assumption would be no reason to abandon the criterion of good world order completely. Democratic powers would still have a moral duty to foster a true separation of powers in the international sphere, and they should still act so as to minimize the distance between such an ideal and the present day situation. Contribution to a law-based, democratic world order would then be a test for what was called "good intention" of an intervening power according to traditional just war theory. Without such a test of good intention there exists a considerable danger that the legitimation of interventions becomes the high water mark of hypocrisy in power politics.

But how can a test of good intention be operationalized? The considerations of the last section have at least shown that it is prima facie bad to put the role of judge and intervenor into the same hand. Such a concentration of power facilitates its abuse. Correspondingly, the juridical control of unilateral intervenors becomes a primary objective. The imminent creation of an international criminal court, especially for the persecution of crimes against humanity, brings such control within realistic reach.[18] It is obvious that a good world order should include the prosecution of persons who commit crimes against humanity. It also follows from the ethical core of western enlightenment that such prosecution should be controlled by a court which is independent and neutral relative to political interests. In sum, support for an international criminal court may serve as a test for the intention to create a law-based, democratic world order. Powers who plan military interventions in other countries must therefore be willing to accept that their military conduct is screened by an international criminal court. Hence we arrive at a first criterion:

Criterion 1

(a) *Those who want to serve international law and justice by Humanitarian Intervention must accept the jurisdiction of an international criminal court.*
(b) *Those who do not accept such a court cannot legitimately intervene in other countries.*
(c) *Military interventions by powers who do not accept the jurisdiction of an international criminal court are illegitimate and should be regarded as violation of international law.*

An international criminal court could come into existence in the near future, but it has not yet been established. Therefore, Criterion 1 cannot be applied as it stands. But there are some straightforward extensions of Criterion 1, which could be applied already. Countries who obviously impede the establishment of an international criminal court, or even threaten others who want to establish it, are to be treated as if they do not accept this court. Criterion 1 thus has some obvious normative bite in present international affairs, since the USA is openly hostile to the international criminal court *in statu nascendi.*[19] Because of this hostility a controversy about the international criminal court has arisen. We shall now look at some arguments, which can be directed against a duty to accept the planned court's jurisdiction.

Cannot a country pledge allegiance to the idea of an international court and legitimately reject the specific statute of the planned court? It should first be noted that the suggested statute has been accepted by most countries with a long-standing democratic tradition. The court statute can therefore be seen as a suitable implementation of democratic juridical principles. Furthermore, Criterion 1 does not demand that a country accepts the jurisdiction of the international criminal court in general or even with regard to all wars. Criterion 1 speaks about Humanitarian Interventions. In principle, a country could state that it accepts the international court's jurisdiction just for such cases. Non-acceptance would thus impede offensive military actions for alledgedly humanitarian purposes. It would not ipso facto delegitimize defensive wars of a country attacked from outside.

But wouldn't we have welcomed a US-intervention in Ruanda, where hundreds of thousands of Tutsi were butchered, despite US-hostility against the international criminal court? Firstly, it should be remembered that Criterion 1 is meant for non-UN Humanitarian Interventions. If the UN approves of an intervention, even powers who do not accept the international criminal court may intervene – but I would add: in especially bad cases and in the absence of more suitable intervenors. The problem with Ruanda was, however, that it was not classified as genocide by the UN in time. This was partly the result of US pressure not to classify the systematic murdering of Tutsi as genocide in order to avoid a moral duty to intervene.[20] The case of a possible non-UN intervention by the USA in Ruanda is therefore quite academic. Nevertheless, it has to be taken serious as an academic ethical question (or question of future international legislation). It will now be treated as such.

Imagine that you need a partner to stop a truly horrible crime. The only available partner is willing to commit some minor crime on the way. You cannot prevent the crime of your partner. Still, you prefer that a violation of law occurs if only the really horrible crime is stopped. This does not mean that you approve of the minor crime. You may wish (and maybe plead to no avail) that your partner desists from crime. If he nevertheless commits a crime that is in no way necessary to stop the larger crime, he is reprehensible and not you. This shows by analogy that one can legitimately call a power in – and possibly have a moral duty to call a power in – which will predictably violate moral rules or international law, as long as the result will clearly count as lesser evil. Still, according to Criterion 1, this helpful power can be held responsible for illegitimate warfare at some later time. However, the accusation will not be "offensive war" or "intervention" but "intervention without acknowledging the international criminal court". In practice that may count as basis for claims by the international criminal court to hand over war criminals of the intervening power (if there are any) or to put them to trial in national courts which are acceptable according to international legal standards.

What about the political leaders of an illegitimate intervenor: should they also face persecution in the international criminal court? The international criminal court will mainly deal with crimes against humanity. Non-compliance with Criterion 1 is no such crime, although it could at some time become a formal violation of international law. Violations of international law may justify reprehensions in international affairs, but I will not discuss here what kind of reprehensions should follow.

Finally: would not Criterion 1 render it practically impossible to find a Humanitarian Intervenor under present international circumstances, even in cases of genocide? The real problem seems to be that powers intervene only if their interests are at stake. Therefore, there was no intervention in Cambodia or in Ruanda. Ethical considerations can change this state of affairs only slowly and if they align themselves with national interest (through international reputation and, maybe, consumer pressure). Under the premise of sufficient public pressure towards an intervention e.g. in Ruanda, other powers besides the USA, like France and probably even Belgium, could have handled the military task. Thus, there was no need to invoke a power that showed no inclination to accept the international criminal court. In Kosovo, on the other hand, US military strength was much needed. But the case for a Humanitarian Intervention in Kosovo was at best doubtful and obviously much less pressing than in Ruanda. This shows that in practice one should not hasten to sacrifice high ranking principles of good world order just in order to increase the numbers of protential intervenors.

4. THE CRITERION OF CRIME IRREVERSIBILITY

The modern just-cause-condition for Humanitarian Interventions is based on the concept of a massive crime against humanity. Massive crimes against humanity are commonly regarded as justifying intervention, but do they also justify the additional fusion of judicial and executive roles in the hands of an intervenor? Since non-UN interventions imply a greater risk of power abuse than UN-mandated interventions it seems plausible to plead for stronger restraint. This means that the set of just causes for non-UN interventions should be smaller than the set of just causes for UN-controled interventions.

A first idea how this claim can be implemented could be that the crimes against humanity which justify even non-UN interventions should be greater evils than those which justify UN mandated interventions. But can be distinguish between larger and smaller crimes against humanity? Of course we can, and we usually do. Holocaust is worse than apartheid, and death is worse than expulsion. Correspondingly, there is a class of cases, which are commonly regarded as proof that non-UN interventions can become a moral duty. This class can be labelled the "megamurder category". I take it to include all cases of genocidal mass murder with more than one million victims. The number seems arbitrary but it roughly suffices to form a class that includes e.g. the Holocaust, Stalin's genocidal programmes, Cambodian mass killing and perhaps the recent genocide in Ruanda. Given the feasibility of an intervention, these are clearcut cases of possibly legitimate non-UN-intervention, at least for those observers who accept deviations from UN statutes at all.

But what about less clearcut cases? How bad must a crime be, to count as a greater evil than war combined with a fusion of powers? This question can lead to considerable differences of opinion even among equally well informed and rational persons. Public discussions about human rights violations often proceed as if no differences between various kinds of human rights violations exist. Some defenders of human rights even regard it as dangerous to distinguish between lesser and more important human rights. Political criminals could exploit this distinction to violate rights which are not staunchly defended. On the other hand, the leveling of human rights can be exploited by governments who seek political profit from war. If a concept as vague as that of a "serious human rights violation" serves as a just cause for war, restraint of war becomes almost impossible. According to the human rights standards of, say, Amnesty International, any nation could legitimately attack any other nation. Therefore it is necessary to restrict interventions to cases of massive crimes against humanity. But this category seems still too wide. Political and social discrimination are often regarded as crimes against humanity, but should we resort to war in order to abolish all kinds of discrimination? Unfortunately, there is no hope for universal agreement how human rights or crimes against humanity are to be weighed. In consequence, there will be no universal standards for a comparative weighing of evils of war and crimes against humanity.

That does not mean, however, that the search for standards of evaluation has to be abandoned. Instead, we probably should pay less attention to the measuring of crime repugnancy and more to the temporal structure of legitimacy. The quest for a law-based, democratic world order implies that a fusion of judicial and executive power can only be temporarily legitimate. Any such step must count as interim, i.e. as a provisional remedy against evil. In the long run it must be superseded by a better democratic solution. This assumption can be used as a basis for the assessment of non-UN Humanitarian Interventions.

Given the interim character of the legitimacy of interventions with conjoined judicial and executive roles, we should restrict such interventions to cases which by their nature cannot wait. In particular, these are cases where irreversible harm is done to a large number of persons. In some sense, of course, every harmful action leaves an ineradicable trace in its victims. But there are also crimes which are irreversible by nature or irreversible in a strong sense. Stolen goods, e.g., can be restituted, but murder is strongly irreversible. Taking this into account, we get a second criterion:

Criterion 2

The interim character of interventions which do not respect the separation of judicial and executive power calls for a restriction to strongly irreversible crimes against humanity.

Among strongly irreversible crimes I reckon murder, serious mutilation, torture and rape. For torture and rape it is recognized that they lead irrversibly to serious life-long psychic harm. Of course, the justification of military interventions presupposes a high number of such crimes. The harm caused by irreversible crimes against humanity should clearly be larger than the unaviodable collateral harm of even the most carefully planned military intervention. Since the collateral damage of war easily adds up to hundreds of casualties, the respective crimes should at least rank in the thousands before war is considered a "humanitarian" remedy.

By now we have a workable standard for the evaluation of intervention proposals. Note that ethnic cleansing (or political discrimination), which figured so strongly in NATO's justification for the war in Kosovo, is not by nature irreversible.[21] Ethnic cleansing, of course, can go hand in hand with mass murder, mass torture or mass rape. In these cases, intervention is justified by mass murder, mass torture or mass rape. But ethnic cleansing can also mean the forced expulsion of ethnic groups from their home-land. Despite the damage done to the expulsed, expulsions are in principle reversible. Ethnic groups can return to their former home-land. Therefore, there is no need to deviate from a separation of powers in cases of expulsion. Those who ask for intervention against expulsion should help to create good international institutions as bulwarks against human rights violations. In the meantime and in the absence of such institutions, other means except war (economic blockade, international proscription of perpetrators etc.) can be employed against the crime of forced expulsion.

5. THE CRITERION OF NO-WAR-IN-DOUBT

Many of the arguments in this inquiry center around the problem that the judicial and the executive role in Humanitarian Interventions are held by the same power or coalition of powers. It is important to discuss this problem because the practice of non-UN intervention shows that a fusion of roles in fact occurs. Moreover, this fusion seems almost inevitable if the UN security council is bypassed. A reconsideration of the history of just war theory shows, however, that these first impressions are deceptive. There are intermediate points between an institutionalized separation of judicial and executive roles and the straightforward self-empowerment of intervening nations. In the absence of judicial institutions, the voice of experts on international law and perhaps of experts on the ethics of international affairs could guide the normative assessment of interventions.

But can the legitimacy of interventions be judged on a basis as inhomogenous and shifting as expert opinion in law? We should recognize first that not only expert consensus but also expert dissensus about the legitimacy of a military intervention is informative. As long as no authoritative institution for the normative assessment of interventions exists, expert opinion remains the best available indicator. A deep-going expert dissensus tells us that the legitimacy of an intervention is not obvious enough to quench reasonable doubts. In this case, war should not be waged. War is always a horrible evil, and therefore at best an ultima ratio of politics. To wage doubtfully legitimate wars means to use ultima ratio precociously. Of course, one should take into account that some expert opinions may simply be ill-guided. But if a considerable quantity of reputable experts speaks out on either side of a question, one should, in the absence of better normative information, assume that the question remains doubtful.

From a historical point of view, this is no news to just war theory. Medieval moralists emphasized again and again that nobody can legitimately begin a doubtfully legitimate war. As indicator of doubt an even split of expert opinions for and against the legitimacy of a war was widely accepted in the Middle Ages. Today, this old guide-line seems almost forgotten. I think, however, that we need such a safety catch in cases, where no authorized judicial gremium for assessing the legitimacy of Humanitarian Interventions exists. This leads to criterion 3:

Criterion 3

Wars of dubious legitimacy should not occur. It follows that military interventions, which are not approved by an authorized international gremium, are illegitimate if they are considered illegal and illegitimate by a large quantity of experts in law and ethics.

At first sight, Criterion 3 seems too vague for practice. But its application in traditional just war theory as well as its possible use in the Kosovo case show that it has some bite, shadowy areas notwithstanding. In some early modern cases there was enough consensus about expert dissensus that the justness of wars could not convincingly be defended.[22] In the Kosovo case many experts in international law, and perhaps even a majority of such experts, assumed that the intervention was illegal and not warranted by a moral state of emergency. Thus, the legitimacy of the Kosovo war was at best doubtful and this should have led to the renunciation of war.

6. FINAL REMARKS

This investigation emphasized the role of legitimacy criteria for non-UN Humanitarian Interventions. There are other roads towards an ethics of intervention, but the criterial approach is classic. It originated in traditional just war theory and was revived in the modern literature on international law. I mention this, because I regard the longstanding acceptance of the criterial approach as no mere coincidence. Clear criteria help to focus our moral attention. This is important because political and military campaigners show great skill at blurring the moral vision of the public. The exploitation of moral dissensus and moral camouflage is no less a basic feature of informational warfare than the manipulation of facts. Only a common public focus for moral discussion can block the success of such strategies.

Several modernizations of criteria that figure central in traditional just war theory have been suggested here. This reflects the belief that war largely remains subject to the same ethical questions at all times although weaponry and the immediate motives for war may change. Therefore, criteria which have stood the test of time should not be abandoned rashly.

For a final overview it seems helpful to compare the criteria I suggest with more traditional criteria (see section 2). Let us first look at the three core criteria of just war theory:

1. just cause:

(a) kind of crime
this criterion is modified. Usually crimes against humanity done by or tolerated by a regime in its own country count as just causes of war. I argue for a restriction of non-UN interventions to the prevention of irreversible crimes against humanity.

(b) order of magnitude
no modification. A weighing of the good of intervention against the evils of war has to occur.

2. good intention:

this criterion is revived. Humanitarian Interventions should follow the principles of a law-based, democratic world order and prevent crimes against humanity at the same time. Exceptions from this double requirement are possible, but all countries which participate in legitimate Humanitarian Interventions should acknowledge the jurisdiction of an international criminal court.

3. right authority:

normally the UN is the right authority. In the case of non-UN interventions this criterion is abandoned. In contrast to most of the literature, group action is not seen as viable substitute for UN control.

4. Some further standard criteria of intervention control are accepted (most often silently):

no change of borders,
no permanent loss of sovereignty,
traditional *ius in bello* criteria, like e.g. proportionality of warfare.

5. One traditional domain of consideration that is missing in most modern accounts is revived:

ius ad bellum under uncertainty. Doubtfully legitimate or legal interventions should be avoided.

NOTES

[1] A military operation is a Humanitarian Intervention if it is legitimate, conducted by powers foreign to a country, aiming at the prevention of massive human rights violations, and if it proceeds without the consent of the country's government. For similar definitions see Parekh (1997), p. 144; Malanczuk (1993), p. 3.
[2] I use the term non-UN Humanitarian Intervention for all allegedly Humanitarian Interventions which are not approved by the UN or the UN security council. Furthermore, it is assumed that such interventions are not approved by some other gremium which has been authorized by the UN to judge the legitimacy of Humanitarian Interventions.
[3] See Tomuschat (2000), p. 31. Grewe (1984), p. 575 cites a source from 1910 which speaks of "L'intervention d'humanité" looking back to 19th century interventions.
[4] Abiew (1999), p. 21f., p. 44f., mentions examples of allegedly Humanitarian Interventions from antiquity and the early modern era.
[5] Cicero (1993), II, 23, 35: "Illa iniusta bella sunt, quae sunt sine causa suscepta. Nam extra ulciscendi aut propulsandorum hostium causam bellam geri nullum potest".
[6] See Russell (1977).
[7] See Schüßler (2001).
[8] See Riley-Smith (1986).
[9] See Höffner (1972); Pagden (1982); Justenhoven (1991); Ramos et al. (1984); Pietschmann (1991).
[10] Bodin (1981), Buch II, Kap. 5, p. 363.
[11] See Aquin, Summa Theologica II-II, q. 40.
[12] See Grewe (1984) on the "Spanish" and "French" era of international law.
[13] See Muldoon (1994), p.176: "The call for the return to European colonial control of Africa, the demand for American and western European intervention in the crises afflicting eastern Europe at the moment strongly echo the arguments made by sixteenth- and seventeenth-century Europeans as they came to know the new worlds that were opening up to them."
[14] See Grewe (1984), p. 577ff.
[15] Fonteyne (1973: 235), cf. also Stowell (1921).
[16] cf. Ankenbrand (2001).
[17] See the very similar conditions in Delbrück (2000), p. 24. Delbrück demands that exceptions from UN-rule satisfy the following conditions. They should: 1. be directed against heaviest violations of fundamental rights (especially genocide); 2. be collective

interventions, preferably by regional organizations which are recognized by the UN; 3. aim at humanitarian rescue and not include changes of territorial borders; 4. be proportional to the crime; and 5. come under UN control as soon as the UN security council is willing to step in.

[18] See Bruer-Schäfer (2001); Schabas (2001).

[19] Note that the US-led war in Afghanistan is not conceived as Humanitarian Intervention. Instead, it can be conceived as defensive war against large scale terrorist attacks originating from a foreign country.

[20] Cf. Power (2001).

[21] The same can be assumed for slavery, which is often explicitly mentioned as crime against humanity (see Bruer-Schäfer 2001, p. 156).

[22] Spanish theologians did not regard the Conquista as straightforwardly just (see Baciero 1984). It was legitimized by rules of conduct under moral uncertainty. Of course, this included a claim of legitimacy, but only a restricted one, which called for a quite far-reaching acknowledgement of the Indians' rights.

REFERENCES

Abiew, Francis: The Evolution of the Doctrine and Practice of Humanitarian Intervention,The Hague 1999.

Ankenbrand, Birthe: "Humanitäre Interventionen. Anwendungsvoraussetzungen für ein politisches Konzept," Vierteljahresschrift für Sicherheit und Frieden 19, 2001, 132-137.

Baciero, C.: "Conclusiones Definitivas de la Segunda Generacion," in: Ramos (1984), 413-456.

Bodin, Jean: Sechs Bücher über den Staat, Bd. I, München 1981.

Bruer-Schäfer, Aline: Der Internationale Strafgerichtshof, Frankfurt/M. 2001.

Cicero: De Re Publica/Der Staat, München 1993.

Delbrück, Jost: "Effektivität des UN-Gewaltverbotes," in: Lutz (2000), 11-29.

Fonteyne, Jean-Pierre: "The Customary International Law Doctrine of Humanitarian Intervention," California Western International Law Journal 4, 1973, 203-270.

Grewe, Wilhelm: Epochen der Völkerrechtsgeschichte, Baden-Baden 1984.

Höffner, Joseph: Kolonialismus und Evangelium, Trier 1972.

Justenhoven, Heinz-Gerhard: Francisco de Vitoria zu Krieg und Frieden, Köln 1991.

Lutz, Dieter (ed.): Der Kosovo-Krieg, Baden-Baden 2000.

Malanczuk, Peter: Humanitarian Intervention and the Legitimacy of the Use of Force, Amsterdam 1993.

Muldoon, James: The Americas in the Spanish World Order, Philadelphia 1994.

Pagden, Anthony: The Fall of Natural Man, Cambridge 1982.

Parekh, Bikkhu: The Dilemmas of Humanitarian Intervention, London 1997.

Pietschmann, Horst: "Die Conquista Amerikas," in: Karl Kohut (ed.), Der eroberte Kontinent, Frankfurt/M. 1991.

Power, Samantha: "Bystanders to Genocide," Atlantic Monthly, September 2001, 84-108.
Ramos et al., Demetrio: La Etica en la Conquista de America, Madrid 1984.
Riley-Smith, Jonathan: The first Crusade and the Idea of Crusading, London 1986.
Russell, Frederick: The Just War in the Middle Ages, Cambridge 1977.
Schabas, William A.: An Introduction to the International Criminal Court, Cambridge 2001.
Schüßler, Rudolf: "Humanitäre Intervention und gerechter Krieg," Vierteljahresschrift für Sicherheit und Frieden 19, 2001, 138-145.
Stowell, Ellery: Intervention in International Law, Washington D.C. 1921.
Thomas von Aquin: Summa Theologica II-II, Salzburg 1966.
Tomuschat, Christian: "Völkerrechtliche Aspekte des Kosovo-Konflikts," in: Lutz (2000), 31-35.

REINER STEINWEG

Early non-Military External Interventions. A Plea for a United Nations Intervention Council (UNIC)

The history of the Kosovo war is not the only case of missed opportunities for preventive action, but it is certainly one of the most dramatic. As early as 1991, or at the latest in 1992 with the publication of the book by Christine von Kohl and Wolfgang Libal with the telling title “Kosovo: The Gordian Knot of the Balkans”, it was clear to anyone studying the situation that there would one day be an attempt to adopt Alexander the Great’s approach to unfastening the knot. This attempt was made seven years later, costing thousands of lives and resulting in the apparently permanent expulsion of 231,000 people, as well as massive destruction, large-scale and long-term environmental damage, fresh hostilities (e.g. between the Kosovo Albanians and Roma), and continuing acts of “ethnic cleansing”. (The only factor which could not be predicted in 1992 was that one of the potential parties to the conflict would eventually succeed in drawing an international organisation such as NATO into the conflict, thereby deciding the outcome in its own favour.)

There is no doubt that under different circumstances, given the likely escalation of tensions, external civilian intervention would have been possible in the years from 1992 to 1994. This could have paved the way for civilian approaches to resolving the protracted ethnic/national conflict between the Serbs and Albanians in Kosovo and the Belgrade government. To this end, it would have been essential to establish an efficient, internationally controlled Supreme Court for Kosovo, possibly with several subordinate administrative courts, set up on a non-ethnic basis, whose jurisprudence would have complied with international human rights laws. In addition, an international police force and stronger OSCE intervention would have been required. The latter was eventually attempted in late 1998, six months after the war began, but only partially realised.

“But the Serbian leadership in Belgrade would have never allowed this type of intervention!” This is the most likely objection to this concept. Certainly, the Serbian leadership would have resisted such a move. Yet assuming that this temporary measure would not have been decided by NATO (which would not have been the body responsible anyway), or declared opponents of Yugoslav socialism, but by an UN body which was already recognised by Yugoslavia and held a legitimate mandate, and also assuming that acceptance of the measure would have brought clear economic and political advantages for Serbia and the Kosovo Serbs, then this intervention, in my opinion, would have had realistic chances of being implemented, even under Milosevic.

The costs of this intervention would have been merely a fraction of the actual expense of the Kosovo war and the year-on-year costs of deploying KFOR troops now and in the foreseeable future. In other words, the money was – and is – available, or would have been available if the "international community" had been aware of the immense financial – and, indeed, political – burdens that they would incur just a few years later once military intervention came to be regarded as the only solution.

Obviously, since we are dealing with "virtual" developments, the effectiveness of such measures cannot be proven today. However, assuming it could be proven, NATO's military intervention was doubly unethical. Alongside all the arguments put forward in this present volume against NATO's justification of its attack on Serbia on ethical grounds – i.e. the need to defend the human rights of the Kosovo Albanians (which indeed had to be defended!) – one more argument can be added: It is ethically unjustifiable to *wait* for a development which is highly likely to result in expulsions on ethnic grounds under the threat of massive collective violence, and only to intervene once the first massacres have taken place in order to "stop the killing!"

Why was no conclusion drawn from this simple insight in the case of Kosovo, as in almost every other comparable case so far, namely that prevention is imperative on ethical and economic grounds when violent conflict is clearly foreseeable? (Only a few sections of western European *civil* society tried to influence the Belgrade government and/or support the nonviolent resistance of the Kosovo Albanians.[1]) There are three answers to this question: one is socio-psychological, one is pragmatic and one concerns international law.

The *socio-psychological answer* is as follows: preventive action by governments is likely only when there is a clear, precise and timely *public recognition* of the acute danger of escalation. In the years between 1992 and 1996, when there was still a good chance of transforming the conflict constructively without military involvement, there was a failure to convey this recognition – which was widespread among the committed parts of Western civil society and, at least, among OSCE diplomats[2] – through the media in a way which would force the European governments to take action.

The *pragmatic answer* is as follows: There are currently an estimated 1000 crisis regions worldwide. There were probably no fewer in 1992/93. Due to the sheer abundance of cases, the UN Security Council generally reacts only when the flames of conflict are already burning – by which time, of course, it is too late for preventive action.

The *answer in international law* is as follows: In line with Chapter VII, Article 39 of the UN Charter, the UN Security Council could have legitimately assumed that the threat of genocide or other crimes against humanity posed an *impending* "threat to world peace", and thus taken action. However, in spite of the current tendency to expand the scope of application of this Article, the Security Council could not bring itself to arrive at such a far-reaching interpretation in relation to the recognisable but not yet acute threat in Kosovo in 1992. The international legal mandate to take preventive measures that restrict the sovereignty of states was thus absent during the decisive years of the Kosovo conflict (1992-1996).

As far as the socio-psychological and the pragmatic levels are concerned, some initial steps are becoming visible: The United Nations Secretary-General has set up a special Early Warning Unit which guarantees much earlier recognition of probable dramatic developments and alerts the highest levels of power.[3] Another example is the European Union's Crisis Prevention Programme.[4] As a consequence of the crisis in late 1998, when it became impossible to provide the required number of 5000 OSCE workers in Kosovo within the given time limits, the OSCE budget was substantially increased at the Istanbul Summit in November 1999.[5] However, at the level of *international law*, nothing has been done so far.

It is of course understandable from a human point of view that some experts in international law were deeply disillusioned by its violation on 24 March 1999, the day when the former Yugoslavia was attacked[6], and by the upheavals in international law during the aftermath of 11 September 2001[7], as well as by Israel's continued and unpunished breach of the Geneva Convention.[8] *Firstly*, however, even today, there is still consistent recourse to international law,[9] e.g. the securing of a Security Council mandate for the attacks on Afghanistan by the USA and the UK. *Secondly*, international law has been effective in the past as a means of at least mitigating violence, even during the terror of the National Socialist regime[10].

Thirdly, it is better to have an only partially enforceable body of international law than none at all while there is still no democratically legitimate international monopoly on the use of force: for if the "major" powers act on the basis that "might is right", the "minor" powers cannot be expected to follow the law. In this sense, there is certainly an indirect connection between NATO's actions in 1999 and the events of 11 September 2001. This top-down effect applies to all levels of society. So if international law did not exist, it would have to be invented.

What could and should happen on the level of international law, then, in order to create a legal framework for preventive, non-military measures which nonetheless restrict the sovereignty of states? Is the Security Council mandate laid down in the UN Charter not sufficient for such measures?

Firstly, as mentioned above, the UN Security Council reacts almost exclusively ex post facto, i.e. when a conflict has already developed into a tangible threat to world peace. Secondly, this body is defined by *political interests* which are not necessarily driven by rule of law imperatives or general principles of non-violence.[11] If the Security Council is unable to react for political reasons, yet individual states or international alliances want to and are capable of intervening, they should not – indeed, they must not – take it upon themselves to do so, as in Kosovo, even if the violation of basic human rights is very dramatic and obvious (which was certainly not the case in Kosovo in the months before the NATO operation started[12]). Any action should be taken only after careful consideration by a legitimate international body. The establishment of a *United Nations Intervention Council (*UNIC) or a World Intervention Court, as has been suggested by others, is therefore urgently called for.[13]

Candidates for appointment to this Council could be nominated by the national parliaments or supreme courts; the UN General Assembly could then elect members based on these nominations.[14] The UNIC would require close institutional interlinking with existing Early Warning Systems[15], making it *obligatory* for it to react according to clear rules and within a fixed timeframe, in the case of foreseeable traumatic events, if at least three of these systems indicate the danger of genocides or crimes against humanity. International NGOs should also be given the right to press charges. Furthermore, its mandate should not be restricted to guaranteeing the *legitimacy* of an external intervention, i.e. measures restricting the sovereignty of a state; it should also be able to decide the *means* by which any intervention can and should be lawfully conducted, such as conflict training with a broad outreach, mediation, human rights monitoring, international police and internationally controlled courts.

RESPONSES TO POSSIBLE OBJECTIONS

1. One might ask: What is the "added value" of a new UN body, when the ultimate power to decide whether the decisions of this body are implemented lies with the Security Council and/or with national governments? *Response*: Merely the fact that oppressed minorities or NGOs which are familiar with and monitor their problems would be able to approach a formally established international agency would be a significant improvement on the present situation. It would enable the actors to refer to decisions and recommendations by this body in their involvement in the political process. Such decisions would at least disqualify the *excuse* that action is "unfortunately" impossible due to the lack of a mandate and the restrictions of international law (as was repeatedly claimed in response to Rugova's futile appeals for international support to the Kosovo Albanians' non-violent resistance). Finally, as long as international law were respected, it would be possible to prohibit unlawful actions which have devastating consequences, such as the NATO intervention in 1999, when the pretext of having to act in an emergency situation in abeyance of the law was used.

2. A further possible objection is that the vast number of acute conflicts worldwide could block the UNIC or overburden its capacities just as much as they do presently in the Security Council. *Response*: The procedures and the actual capacities would need to be tested first. If there is too much for the UNIC to handle, the UN's regional organisations, such as the OSCE, could be given a mandate to set up their own intervention councils. In this case, the UNIC would function as an appeal body.

3. "Considering the political interests of the permanent Security Council members, it is improbable that the Security Council would voluntarily surrender any of its de facto pre-democratic, absolutist powers to such a body." *Response*: This is probably true; however, the same could be said of almost all the proposals put forward in the recent democratisation debate in the UN. Nonetheless, the debate remains essential and is a *precondition* for the necessary changes in the desired direction at some point in future, probably in the wake of political failures or even crises.

4. "If there is no military pressure behind measures that restrict the sovereignty of states, the Milosevics of this world will never allow other governments to intervene in their affairs. Since no government in the world would welcome external intervention, except in the interests of their own survival, the other governments will not be keen to react, so finally everything will remain on paper." *Response*: With the International Criminal Court (Rome Statute), a milestone has already been reached. There is no doubt that the minimum number of ratifications required for the ICC to be established will be achieved. Similarly, the establishment of a body such as the UNIC would also have a positive impact so that in future, even the most hardened power-hungry politicians and world powers would recognise that it is not in their interests to stay on the sidelines. Even if the only governments initially supporting the establishment of an international intervention council, within the framework of international agreements (such as the International Criminal Court), were those which are highly unlikely to face any threat of intervention in response to massive human rights violation thanks to their long-term stability, a great deal would be still achieved. There are no guarantees that the situation in any country will remain stable. (Even in the EU Member States, recurrences of quasi-Fascist conditions are still conceivable in the long term.) In such a case, a voluntary commitment by the nation states greatly facilitates the prevention of violence in future domestic conflicts – with the cooperative involvement of external powers. The European Union is an example of how sanctions reached on the basis of consensus are effective, purely because they *could potentially* lead to the loss of reputation and further domestic or national disadvantages. It is therefore not necessary to use military pressure in the event of violations at all. Once the *advantages* of joining such a community of states who are prepared to forego temporarily certain stakes in their sovereignty under clearly defined circumstances are evident, even states which are currently more likely to face a situation in which these approved rules could be applied will ultimately join the organisation.

As it is hardly ethical for academics to put forward what they regard as plausible suggestions without any tangible action to follow them up, we have already embarked on the first practical steps. The "Linz Appeal for a Peace Politics" contains, as its central innovative recommendation, the concept of setting up a United Nations Intervention Council (see annex). It has been signed by peace researchers, scientists, philosophers, political analysts, psychologists and international legal experts, as well as by prominent representatives from public life and Austrian parliamentarians. Other recommendations which promote similar aims are also worth considering in this context.[16]

The first step towards the implementation of these recommendations is to initiate a *broad public debate*. It is also necessary to discuss all the recommendations and ideas with the appropriate staff at the UN and the OSCE and refine and strengthen the proposals, feeding the outcomes of this dialogue back into the public debate. This process has already begun. Only persistent work including test runs before the establishment of the Council can enable what currently may appear to be an utopian idea to become political reality at the appropriate historical moment in the future. No one can predict how long this process will take: perhaps one, two or even three decades. Yet that is precisely why we must embark on this task immediately.

ANNEX

Linz Appeal for Peace Politics[17]

It is clear that after the massive human rights violations in Kosovo, East Timor and Chechnya, new ways must be found to prevent war, mass murder and ethnic cleansing in the future.

We appeal to all governments, particularly those of neutral or non-aligned countries, totake the lead with the following initiatives for peace:

- To agree a ten-fold increase in the resources available to the OSCE and the international peace services.

- To create an "UN International Intervention Council" composed of independent experts (Nobel Peace Prize laureates, human rights activists and renowned experts in international law, economists, psychologists, political scientists, andpeace and ethnic studies researchers) who have been endorsed by their respective parliaments for a period of 8-10 years. These experts can decide, by secret ballot, whether massive human rights violations that occur or are committed by a country require action from the international community, above all through non-military means.

We need tangible steps in order to develop an international legal system which guarantees peace and human rights and prevents interventions that violate international law.

- To form a task force of conflict mediators for ethnic and national conflicts.

- To build a system for the early recognition of conflicts which may escalate into war; this system should promptly deploy increased civilian personnel and financial resources for conflict resolution.

These initiatives will cost only a fraction of the expense resulting from Kosovo and its aftermath.

Peace and compassion are worth it!

The Linz Appeal for Peace Politics is supported so far by

Bishop Dr. h.c. Maximilian *Aichern*, Diocese of Linz; Prof. Dr. Ulrich *Albrecht*, Free University of Berlin (FU) and President of the German Society for Peace Research (AFK); Prof. Dr. Rudolf *Ardelt*, Principal of Johannes Kepler University, Linz; PD Dr. Thea *Bauriedl*, Institute for Political Psychoanalysis, Munich; Prof. Dr. Hanne M. *Birckenbach*, University of Giessen and Schleswig-Holstein Institute for Peace Sciences (SCHIFF), Kiel; Prof. Dr. Lothar *Brock*, University of Frankfurt/M. and Peace Research Institute, Frankfurt (PRIF); Dr. John *Bunzl*, Austrian Institute for International Politics; Dr. Andreas *Buro*, Emeritus Professor, Grävenwiesbach/Ts. bei Frankfurt/M.; Dr. Ernst Otto *Czempiel*, Emeritus Professor. Peace Research Institute, Frankfurt (PRIF);. Dr. Franz *Dobusch*, Mayor of the City of Linz; Mag. Hansjörg *Eichmeyer*, Superintendent of the Protestant Church of Upper Austria; PD Dr. Tilman *Evers*, Forum for Civilian Peace Service, Kassel; Prof. Dr. Horst *Fischer*, Institute for International Law (Institut für Friedenssicherungsrecht und Humanitäres Völkerrecht), University of Bochum; Dr. Leo *Gabriel*, Ludwig Boltzmann Institute for Research on Latin America, Vienna,; Dr. Klaus Jürgen *Gantzel*, Emeritus Professor, Hamburg; Dr. Franz *Gmainer-Pranzl*, Theological University, Linz; Dr. Hildegard *Goss-Mayr*, Vienna, Honorary President of the International Fellowship for Reconciliation (IFOR), Dr. Erich *Gumplmaier*, Secretary of the Unions of Upper Austria; Prof. Dr. Josef *Gunz*, Johannes Kepler University, Linz; Father Karl *Helmreich*, OSB, refugee support worker, Stift Melk; Prof. Dr. Otmar *Höll*, Director of the Austrian Institute for International Politics (ÖIIP), Vienna; Mag. Hans *Holzinger*, Robert Jungk

Library, Salzburg; Prof. Dr. Egbert *Jahn,* University of Mannheim; Prof. Dr. Gert *Krell*, University of Frankfurt/M.; Dr. Ekkehart *Krippendorff*, Emeritus Professor, Berlin; Franz *Küberl*, President of Austrian Caritas, Graz; Dr. Franz *Leidenmühler*, Institute for International Law, University of Linz; Dr. Gerald *Mader*, President of the Austrian Institute for Peace and Conflict Resolution, Stadtschlaining (ÖSFK); Prof. Dr. Georg *Meggle*, Institute for Philosophy,University of Leipzig; Dr. Barbara *Müller*, Institute for Peace and Constructive Conflict Management, Wahlenau; Dr. Heinrich *Noller*, Emeritus Professor, Vienna; Prof. Dr. Franz *Nuscheler*, University of Duisburg; Helmolt *Rademacher*, Conflict Consultant for schools in the federal state of Hesse; Dr. Norbert *Ropers*, Director of the Berghof Research Center for Constructive Conflict Management, Berlin; Dr. Severin *Renoldner*, Catholic Action and Pax Christi, Upper Austria; Prof. Dr. Manfred *Rotter,* Institute for International Law, University of Linz; Prof. Dr. Hajo *Schmidt*, Hagen Open University; Prof. Dr. Dr. Rolf *Schwendter*, University of Kassel; Prof. Dr. Dr. h.c. Dieter *Senghaas*, University of Bremen; Prof. Dr. Eva *Senghaas-Knobloch,* University of Bremen; Prof. Dr. Dorothee *Sölle*, Publisher, Hamburg; Toni *Steinmetz*, Secretary of Metals and Textiles Union, Upper Austria; Dr. Reiner *Steinweg*, Acting Director of the Berghof Research Center for Conflict Management and Director of the Linz Institute for Peace Research; Helga *Tempel* (Ahrensburg/Hamburg), Forum for Civilian Peace Service; Konrad *Tempel* (Ahrensburg b. Hamburg), Society for Social Defence (Bund für Soziale Verteidigung), Berlin; Dr. Christian *Wellmann*, Vice-Director of the Schleswig-Holstein Institute for Peace Sciences (SCHIFF), Kiel; Dr. Erika *Weinzierl*, Emeritus Professor, University of Vienna; Hubert *Wipplinger*, President of the Chamber for Workers and Employees, Upper Austria (AK) and of the Unions of Upper Austria; Dr. Veronique *Zanetti*, University of Tübingen; Prof. Dr. Valentin *Zsifkovits*, University of Graz; Dr. Georg *Zundel*, Emeritus Professor, Salzburg/Munich.

The Appeal has also been signed by almost every Member of Linz City Council, as well as – among others – the following Members of the Parliament of Upper Austria:

Deputy Prime Minister Erich *Haider* (SPÖ), the two Presidents of the Parliament, Angela *Ortner* (ÖVP) and Gerda *Weichsler* (SPÖ), and the chairmen of three parliamentary groups: Rudi *Anschober* (Greens), Dr. Karl *Frais* (SPÖ), and Dr. Josef *Stockinger* (ÖVP).

NOTES

[1] Cf. R. Steinweg, "Über die Bedeutung der kleinsten Schritte und was man dabei falsch machen kann. Vorbeugendes Friedenshandeln am Beispiel des Kosovo-Konflikts," in: Thomas Dominikowski/Regine Mehl (eds.), *Dem Humanismus verpflichtet. Zur Aktualität pazifistischen Engagements. Festschrift für Karlheinz Koppe, Münster* (Agenda) 1994: 155-166.

[2] Author's conversation about the "Linz Appeal for Peace Politics" with the Finnish OSCE Ambassador in Vienna, 12 March 2002.
[3] Information provided by Jehangir Khan (Policy Planning Unit, Department of Political Affairs, United Nations) at the Conference "*Towards Better Peace Building Practice*" held by the European Platform for Conflict Resolution and Transformation, 24-26 October 2001 in Soesterberg/NL.
[4] Cf., for example, Communication from the [European] Commission on Conflict Prevention of 11 April 2001 [COM (2001) 211 final]. The Swedish OSCE Ambassador speaks of a "clear breakthrough" of the idea of conflict prevention within the EU over the last eighteen months (conversation with the author on 12 March 2002).
[5] Cf. the European Security Charter agreed at this meeting.
[6] While the great majority of experts in international law viewed this as a violation of the UNCharter, a minority argued that other rules of international law legitimised the NATO intervention; cf. the references in: Franz Leidenmühler, "Interventionismus oder Kollektive Sicherheit," in: F Leidenmühler/R. Steinweg, *Kosovo und die Folgen. Völkerrecht und Friedenspolitik im Zeichen des Kosovo-Konflikts,* Idstein/Ts. (Meinhardt) 2000: 17-50.
[7] Horst Fischer, "Globale Rechtskultur: Das heimliche Terroropfer?" in: *Humanitäres Völkerrecht*, no. 4, 2001: 215.
[8] This is at least the position of a number of Israeli military and experts in international law, expressed at a conference "*Israel on its way to The Hague. Six voices from Israel on war crimes and Israel's security, plenary discussion on 9 January 2002 in the Tzavta Hall, Tel Aviv*" (speeches by Yigal Schochat, Eyal Gross, Adi Ophir, Dov Tamari, Michael Tarazi, Schulamit Aloni, translated into German by Catharina Herbst, Ernst Herbst, Hermann Kopp und Ellen Rohlfs), e-mailed by Adalbert Kuhn (adalbert_kuhn_es@nikocity.de), Spring 2002. cf. also http://www.gush-shalom.org
[9] Cf. the discussion on international regimes, e.g. Andreas Hasenclever, Peter Mayer, Volker Rittberger, *Theories of International Regimes*, Cambridge 1997 (Cambridge University Press); here: *Regimes as Links between States. Three Theoretical Perspectives*, Tübinger Arbeitspapiere zur Internationalen Politik und Friedensforschung, no. 29 (University of Tübingen), Tübingen 1997.
[10] For instance, Helmuth James Graf Moltke, the founder of the Kreisau Circle (a prominent resistance group against Nazism in the Second World War), who worked as an expert in international law for the German High Command, was able to save the life of thousands of POWs and hostages until he was arrested and later killed by the Nazis; cf. Marion Gräfin Dönhoff, "*Um der Ehre willen*". *Erinnerungen an die Freunde vom 20. Juli,* Berlin 1994 (Siedler), p. 107-109; cf. also Ger van Roon, (ed.): *Helmuth James Graf von Moltke – Völkerrecht im Dienste der Menschen. Dokumente*, Berlin 1986 (Siedler).
[11] Cf. Franz Leidenmühler: "Demokratisierung des UN-Sicherheitsrats," in: H. F. Köck / M. Hintersteininger, *Europa als Sicherheits- und Wertegemeinschaft*, Vienna (Verlag Österreich) 2000: 132f.
[12] See article by Dieter S. Lutz in this volume, *The Example of Kosovo: Didactics against Humanitarian Interventionism.*

[13] Michael Zürn/Bernhard Zangl, "Weltpolizei oder Weltinterventionsgericht? Zur Zivilisierung der Konfliktbearbeitung," in: *Internationale Politik* 8/1999, p.17 ff. The main difference between the two concepts is that UNIC should:

1. not only decide on the legitimacy of military intervention, but also on the need-for non-military intervention in the early stages of a conflict;
2. also have the power to decide on the legitimate means of intervention and therefore
3. not only consist of experts of international law.

[14] At a study workshop on 8 June 2002 at the Berghof Research Center for Constructive Conflict Management in Berlin, the "Platform for Civilian Conflict Management", led by the author, developed recommendations on possible procedures for elections and other aspects of UNIC; details available from reiner.steinweg@berghof-center.org.

[15] On existing early warning systems and their problems, cf. article by Alexander Austin, "Early Warning and Early Response," in: *Berghof Handbook for Conflict Transformation*, www.berghof-center.org/handbook

[16] Cf. the proposal to establish a UN Conflict Council, made by the German delegation (Heide Schütz, Ingrid Lottenburger-Bazin) at the Fourth UN World Conference on Women in Beijing in 1995, as well as the idea of a Civil Peace Council at the UN discussed by Mohssen Massarrat, a former spokesperson of the independent German peace movement; cf. R. Steinweg, "Friedensbewegung am Anfang des 21. Jahrhunderts. Zur Dialektik der Ohnmacht "oben" und "unten" oder von der Kooperation wider Willen zur gemeinsamen Entwicklung friedenspolitisch tragfähiger Strukturen," in: Astrid Sahm/ Manfred Sapper / Volker Weichsel (eds.), *Die Zukunft des Friedens. Eine Bilanz der Friedens- und Konfliktforschung* (Festschrift Jahn), Wiesbaden (Westdeutscher Verlag) 2002: 193-212.

In the meantime the protagonists of all three proposals have developed together a statute for an extension organ of the UN, called UNCOPAC, which is strictly limited to non-military measures of prevention. The draft takes up the proposal of the Secretary General of the UN from June 2001 and plans? that the *civil society* is enabled to take influence in clearly settled manner onto the composition and the agenda of this committee. UNCOPAC stands for United Nations Commission on Peace and Crisis Prevention. This proposal is being discussed momentarily. For example take a look at the homepage Pro UNCOPAC, the homepage of the Platform Civile Konflict Prevention, "Plattform Zivile Konfliktbearbeitung", and the hompage of the city of Linz, headword "Friedensstadt". The "Initiative Pro UNCOPAC" is coordinated by Ute Hegener: e-mail: utehegener@t-online.de

[17] This text was written at the end of the war in May 1999 with a few amendments in Spring 2000. A more comprehensive argument is put forward in: Franz Leidenmühler/ Reiner Steinweg (eds.), *Kosovo und die Folgen. Völkerrecht und Friedenspolitik im Zeichen des Kosovo-Konflikts*, Idstein/Ts. (Meinhardt) 2000: 113-138.

VÉRONIQUE ZANETTI

Humanitarian Intervention: An Individual Right or a State Right?

THE PROBLEM

It is a well-known fact that international law is torn between two frequently incompatible imperatives. Its function is to watch over or maintain peace and security, which entails the obligation to defend state interests. Simultaneously, it must permit people all over the world to exercise their fundamental rights, which entails the obligation to take the side of individuals and even guarantee their rights over those of the state, when this latter does not respect them. Customary law well illustrates this tension. On the one hand, the evolution of norms clearly indicates we are witnessing the emergence of an international right that accords the individual the statute of legal subject alongside that of states and non-governmental organizations. On the other, it remains true that the content of international law is modeled on state interest.

Contrary to what some would desire, it is not therefore certain that international law can continue to adapt without necessarily altering its fundamental categories or structure. The idea of a right to humanitarian intervention perfectly illustrates the tension in question. Its hybrid nature is evident in its terminology. As the term in part indicates, it is a question of intervention in the internal affairs of a sovereign state whose actions have been recognized as reprehensible; in this case, we are led to ask the reasons which legitimize violating the principle of the sovereignty of nations. Yet this intervention is also termed humanitarian, thus stressing that its legitimacy is intimately connected to fundamental human rights. The question of justification therefore passes from the legal to the ethical register. Finally, it is a question of rights. However, independent of knowing whether the right to humanitarian intervention truly consists of a right, as long as it remains uncodified, international law remains vague as to the subject of the right in question. Are we talking about the right of states to intervene, or about the right of individuals to have someone – and just who this may be has yet to be defined – intervene in their favor in cases where they are exposed to massive violations by their own governments? In other terms, are we talking about the right to intervene, or the right to intervention?

In cases where we accentuate intervention and conceive of this as a right of the state, the concept remains within the framework of the theory of 'just war' and the idea that, in certain extreme cases, a state – either unilaterally or by common assent – can legitimately bear arms against a third state which persecutes certain of its citizens. Interference is most often seen as punishment: it is because a government's official behavior toward its citizens is reprehensible, and because it represents a threat to peace that the interdiction on aggression can be unilaterally suspended. This can only occur, however, in cases of capital offense. Moreover, the punishment must be proportionate to the wrong. To justify foreign intervention, there must therefore be a threat to the maintenance of peace, or violation on a massive scale: massacres, forced displacement of a large part of the population, ethnic cleansing, or persecution of minorities.

On the other side, parallel to this interpretation, as mentioned above, certain documents in international law, following a more liberal policy of individual rights, clearly open the door to interpretations favoring the right of individuals to humanitarian intervention. Such understanding is nevertheless difficult to reconcile with both the principle of proportionality in the doctrine of just war and the idea of collective punishment. What, in effect, happens to individual rights when the violation is weighed solely in terms of its magnitude? What happens to these rights when an entire population is punished for a wrong it did not commit? Such questions reveal the distinctly hybrid nature of the right to humanitarian intervention as linked to two distinct normative sources, the right of the state and the right of the individual.

TOWARDS AN INDIVIDUAL RIGHT TO INTERVENTION?

As it gradually emerged in documents in international law toward the end of the 1980s, the right to humanitarian assistance helped broaden the concept of intervention to include the idea that individuals have a right to intervention in their favor when they are subject to wide-scale violations. Through the right to humanitarian assistance, humanitarian organizations or states unilaterally call for free passage within a third state to deliver emergency aid to victims of natural catastrophe or massive human rights violations. The resolution adopted by the first Conference on Law and Humanitarian Moral Doctrine affirmed, for example, that based on a single international document, every member state of the international community must recognize both the right of victims to humanitarian assistance, and the obligation of the state to contribute to this assistance.[1]

In spite of this, official documents remain standoffish regarding the idea of a right to assistance which would be incumbent on the international community. As a result, the obligation falls first on the country ruling the victims, while the engagement of other states is subsidiary. Even on this point, the distribution of obligations remains unclear. On the one hand, the majority of documents recognize the existence of individual rights which can be asserted towards a state; on the other, third states, intergovernmental organizations and non-governmental organizations are under no obligation if the victim state does not assist its own citizens.[2]

The right to humanitarian assistance must certainly not be confused with the right to humanitarian intervention. Humanitarian assistance most often requires the right of free passage for victims, personnel, and material aid; which is to say, the creation of humanitarian corridors. Moreover, the reform it introduces – the principle of free access to victims – remains strongly subjected to the principle of nonintervention, since it requires the consent of the recipient state, on the one hand and, on the other, numerous guarantees concerning the respect of this stateís sovereignty. Humanitarian corridors, for example, are limited in time (they give only the right of transit for the necessary duration of the aid); in space (they are limited to access routes alone); and in objective (their sole function is to deliver food, medical care and/or related assistance).[3]

That said, the codification of the right to humanitarian assistance has undeniably broken a barrier, moving towards the actualization of individual rights and the recognition in the international community of at least a moral obligation to step in and perform the duty of the state when this latter is unable or unwilling to assume its function. The key question – the use of force when the country concerned opposes the deliverance of aid – nevertheless remains unresolved. It must be noted, however, that certain jurists point to a change in attitude over the last few years in the international community as indicative of a modification of customary law. The United Nations operation in Somalia in 1992, for example, in which humanitarian convoys were accompanied by military escort, constituted the first instance of the imposition of humanitarian assistance.

Even if customary law only very hesitatingly indicates a change toward the global implementation of individual rights, this shift nevertheless represents a revolution. It is the philosopher's task to analyze in detail what, from an ethical and political point of view, it means, based on the recognition of fundamental rights in international documents, for all individuals in the world to be entitled to have the international community intervene in their favor if their governments commit massive violations against them. How should the duty of the world community be actualized in order to insure impartial assistance? What kind of international structure do we need to be certain that the executive world power will neither become a threat to the world's citizens nor in fact take possession of power through a coalition of countries? What becomes of individual rights if we only measure human rights violations quantitatively?

What is remarkable about this evolution is that by accentuating the right of assistance for individuals in distress and the duty of the international community to perform the duty of states when these latter are incapable of assuming it or refuse to do so, documents in international law have opened the way, no matter how timidly, towards an interpretation whereby individuals have the right to humanitarian intervention. To speak of the individual's right to humanitarian intervention signifies, theoretically at least, that by virtue of various international documents consecrated to fundamental rights, all individuals possess the right to have their lives and possessions protected by an authority which is obligated to them to do so, even if pragmatic and ethical considerations inevitably introduce a quantitative factor reducing the number of legitimate interventions. The obligation is first the responsibility of the government to which the individual is subject. When the government itself is at the origin of rights violations, or if it is incapable of offering a sufficient guarantee to its inhabitants, the obligation devolves to a supranational authority to whose competence it has been relegated. Humanitarian intervention therefore does not constitute a tolerated exception to the rule of non-intervention, but follows a logic inherent to fundamental rights. This is the position that I myself defend.

Undeniably, the argument that individuals have more than a moral claim to the establishment of institutions to protect and adequately guarantee their fundamental rights leads to a concept of world order, the relationships between states, the responsibility of the international community towards world citizens, and – consequently – the principle of intervention which all differ from the concepts which the theory of international relations still defends. In an article proposing intervention as a duty, I explored the question of which minimum institutional and procedural conditions which would be necessary to permit the codification of the individual right to humanitarian intervention.[4]

As the article further demonstrated, it is part of contractual logic that individuals be motivated to conclude a social contract which moreover leads them to seek maximum protection of their fundamental good. After having signed, as it were, a primary insurance policy with their government, individuals seek complementary protection from a supranational organization for cases where a government does not keep or contravenes its promises. The initial contract precisely establishes how tasks will be divided between the first 'insurance agency' and the second, just as it also precisely establishes the cases in which the latter is authorized to intervene, or rather, when it must do so.

This model does not conceive of intervention as a punishment inflicted by the international community on a guilty state, but as a judicial instrument designed to reinforce the guarantee of rights individuals enjoy. The right to humanitarian intervention would thus be analogous to the right of individual citizens to have their lives protected by their government. Parallel to the national police, which should guarantee the protection of citizens' lives and security, we would have a world police whose duty to intervene would be subsidiary to that of the national police. The world police would only intervene if a government were incapable or refused to guarantee a minimal level of security for its citizens.

I do not mean to repeat myself here, but rather to examine an important consequence tied to the position I am now defending, a position strongly in favor of the individual right to intervention: the inevitable gap between the expectations of the victims and the practice of the state. Indeed, even if we agree to recognize that individuals have a right for the international community to intervene on their behalf when genocide or large-scale massacre occurs, we must admit that this right can only be actualized under the conditions which define it as legitimate.

However, from the point of view of customary law, intervention is considered legitimate whenever a government officially practices the politics of apartheid, ethnic cleansing, or genocide, or when a government's fall from power results in a large portion of its population being menaced by death. In each of these cases, what matters is the number of threatened or actual victims, to which we must add, in cases of ethnic cleansing or genocide, the aim to eradicate a group of people either in part or in whole. Individual interests are considered in terms of the number of people who have a claim to them, and weighed against the dimensions of the commitment needed to insure their rights. In other words, the right is only actualized after measuring the consequences of doing so by pondering individual claims in terms of their cost to society, and evaluating the victims' right to intervention in light of the right of intervening forces not to endanger their own lives.

The problem I here refer to is well known in the theory of rights. Rights are founded on individual interests in the measure that there is no reasonable objection to their codification. In turn, rights create obligations only if the interest of those who are entitled to them constitutes a sufficient reason for another person or collectivity to have an obligation to protect or promote the interest of the titleholder. When a set of considerations – for example, a conflict between individual rights – weakens the claims on which the right is based, the right does not necessarily lose its validity, but it can be suspended under the circumstances in question. Remembering that the attribution of rights serves as the base for the corresponding attribution of obligations, it is necessary to ask if the realization of the right to intervention and its corresponding obligations are not too heavy to bear in order to be morally required. The desire of the oppressed to receive foreign assistance as rapidly as possible is indeed difficult to reconcile with the equally understandable desire of solders in the intervening forces not to endanger their lives. Inevitably, a position based on principle, which measures the legitimacy of intervention by the nature of the violation of individual rights (and I will come back to this) must be weighed against a position which considers the consequences, taking into account the human, political and economic cost of military intervention.

As long as humanitarian intervention is conceived as a military enterprise carried out by allied forces under the aegis of the United Nations against a country in which fundamental rights have been systematically and massively held in contempt, it is perfectly understandable and desirable that intervention be an ultimate measure taken after careful reflection on the costs and hoped-for benefits. The pertinent criteria then relate to the scale of the violations, their significance to the peace of the region, and the likelihood of whether the forces of intervention will succeed and the violations will stop. All the same, we must not neglect to ask whether the means exist to intervene preventively before the situation in the country degenerates, and how much responsibility states which fail to act preventively bear for the deterioration of human rights. In other words, rather than acting as a fire brigade, we must determine who set the fire and examine the conditions which allowed the flame to erupt.

I will come back to the question of preventative intervention, but first it is necessary to clarify what I mean when I speak of the violation of rights. This is all the more important in that the concept of the individual's right to intervention leads, as I've already said, to the necessity of justifying the inaction of international organizations when they judge the number of victims to be insufficient to warrant intervention.

WHEN CAN WE SPEAK OF A VIOLATION OF RIGHTS?

It is important to clarify that a violation of rights does not necessarily amount to the unjust deprivation of a freedom or a fundamental right. When a person is the victim of aggression, whether the person be killed, raped or beaten, he or she is the victim of an isolated criminal act. In this case, we cannot qualify the act as a violation, even if the attack on the integrity of the victim is identical to that carried out against victims of a massacre, collective rape or torture. The difference is neither in the number nor the gravity of the wrong committed. It is in the underlying structure of the crime.[5]

An attack on fundamental rights becomes a violation when the official authorities of a country command or tolerate it. It indeed makes an important difference if an individual knows whether a criminal attack is an isolated act, or the result of an act which is institutionally encouraged or tolerated. In the first case, the institution can be held responsible only up to a certain limit which is recognized as tolerable. In the second, when the violence is institutionalized, it is the very idea of rights and justice which is violated under cover of legality. It is morally scandalous for authorities who represent the law and on whom we depend to violate rights. In such a case, the quality of the lives of those who are ruled by unjust institutions is lessened, even if it turns out that qualitatively speaking, individuals are not exposed to more serious cruelty than they would have been by criminal acts which a just state cannot entirely prevent.

This determination assumes a large importance for the question of intervention, for it permits us to identify the types of structures which divest individuals of their rights, without placing the primary accent on the quantitative dimension of the violation. It is not for the international community to interfere in the internal affairs of a country whose laxism concerning the rules of the road and automobile security or laws authorizing the carrying of weapons cause tens of thousands of innocent deaths each year. By contrast, we would expect this same community to take measures against a country that systematically makes use of torture in its prisons, and this would be so even if many fewer victims in this instance were definitely deprived of their rights than in the first example.

It is, however, possible to find a way out of the thorny question of the legitimacy of intervention as soon as we agree that to define an act as a violation, it is neither sufficient that there be a breach of fundamental rights, nor necessary that this breach be massive (in the qualitative sense of the term). Even taking into consideration the human, political, and social consequences of an intervention, the position that foregrounds the nature of the violation to justify humanitarian intervention is above all a position based on principle. It maintains that the violation of fundamental individual rights, when officially carried out, encouraged or tolerated, represents an attack on the very essence of humanity – its dignity – by publicly denying the dignity of the people who are victim to official discrimination. When the use of power is perverted and made into an instrument of hate, domination and racial discrimination, not only individual people but humanity as a whole suffers, and humanity itself is menaced and violated. As Johann Benjamin Erhard impressively puts it in his essay on the right to revolution, when the fundamental laws of a state hold the rights of man up to ridicule, the rights of an entire people are potentially scorned. In this case, he says:

> "not me alone, but mankind in my own person simultaneously suffers from injustice. My tolerance is therefore not necessarily to be prized as moral, because it contains the possibility that many thousands after me will suffer from injustice."[6]

I thus retain the following characteristics as criteria justifying measures of intervention: a) the official character of the violation, i.e., the fact that it is not the product of individual acts but fostered by a state institution; b) its racist or ideological motivation; c) its systematic nature, i.e., that it consists of repeated violations of such proportions that we are lead to conclude that the discrimination taking place has been planned.

To mobilize the international community, we thus should consider not only the quantitative aspect of a wrong, but also its nature. Discriminatory treatment of a political, ethnic or religious minority, when practiced deliberately and systematically as part of official state policy, may very well justify humanitarian intervention, and not because most or a large part of the population is threatened, but because the discrimination or violation has been institutionalized. In taking this stance, I base my position on the principle that, since fundamental rights are universal rights belonging to all human beings by virtue of their membership in the human race, all people should be able to claim these rights from the society or state in which they live, independent of the existing Constitution.

Is it morally reasonable, or even politically defensible, to give the priority to principle in some cases over consequentialist considerations? For it still remains a profound, inalterable contradiction to cause the death of innocent victims in the attempt to establish a regime respectful of rights in a country which officially violates them. It is an unbearable contradiction, and it is right to emphasize it. Yet discussion of the ethics of humanitarian intervention is much too centered on questions concerning the number of victims, the legitimacy of goals, and the means of war, all of which neglect the capital importance of prevention.

PREVENTIVE INTERVENTION

"It is evidently better to prevent conflicts though early warning, quiet diplomacy and, in some cases, preventive deployment than to have to undertake major politico-military efforts to resolve them after they have broken out."[7] Even while giving diplomatic efforts at prevention a new and promising political dimension, the Secretary General of the United Nations, Boutros Boutros-Ghali, concedes that paralysis is programmed in:

> "Experience has shown that the greatest obstacle to success in these endeavors is not, as is widely supposed, lack of information, analytical capacity or ideas for United Nations initiatives. Success is often blocked at the outset by the reluctance of one or the other parties to accept United Nations help. [...] Clearly the United Nations cannot impose its preventive and peacemaking services on member States who do not want them."[8]

Thus, if the principle violator refuses to allow the Secretary General of the United Nations to intercede in search of a peaceful solution to an international or internal conflict, if the violator refuses an envoy of observers or the deployment of intervening forces, this refusal paralyses the preventative action of the United Nations, which then must wait for the violations to attain intolerable dimensions in order to legitimize the use of sanctions or means of imposing peace.

This situation is doubly paradoxical: on the one hand, the United Nations uses strong measures when the situation has degenerated to the point of threatening international stability and has become dangerous and costly, while it refuses to do so when the use of preventive means would permit it to spare lives at relatively small human and material cost. On the other hand, it creates an incentive for cynical heads of state well versed in the strategy of war (such as Saddam Hussein, Milosevic or Sharon) to reject the mediation of the United Nations and continue to poison the conflict on the bet that the international community will fail to react. If, as Boutros-Ghali states, the means to detect hotbeds of conflict exist – if the principle obstacle is neither an inability to identify nor the lack of information and analytical capacity, but the lack of authorization to deploy the forces of assistance – we must conclude, as Bettati puts it, that "to maintain we are putting in place a network of alert is, at best, an illusion, perhaps an equivocation, and, at worst, an imposture."[9]

The notion of preventative intervention is problematical, for it implies interference in the internal affairs of a country before a major crisis erupts, and even before the scope of the violations legitimizes the international community to take action on victims' behalf. On the other hand, with the experience of ex-Yugoslavia, Rwanda, Somalia, and Kosovo, humanity has paid the price for ignoring numerous warnings by non-governmental organizations, commissions of inquiry, and diplomats based in these countries.

The cynicism of repressive governments is thus not the only reason the politics of prevention fails; this failure is equally attributable to the indifference or passivity of the international community. For, if victims have a right to assistance, there must be a corresponding duty for those who are authorized to assist them, especially if the measures that are taken to do so are preventive and non-military, and do not necessarily endanger the lives of the intervening forces. Further, preventative intervention is the only acceptable response to the selectiveness inherent in decisions concerning humanitarian military intervention. It is indeed materially impossible to require the international community to intervene militarily in every zone of internal conflict where innocent civilians lose their lives, are mutilated, or forced to flee their homes. There are just too many conflicts. It is thus inevitable that a certain selectiveness take place in deciding the locus of military engagements. It would be possible to avoid this selectiveness at least in part if we could more rapidly clarify the stakes at hand, and especially if we could lower the threshold legitimizing (non military) intervention. The existence of a larger and larger network devoted to detecting nascent conflict is not enough. We must further gather this information; those responsible for analyzing the material at the United Nations must do so rapidly and submit their findings to the Secretary General; and this latter, in turn, must be able to mandate the Security Council to take concrete measures.

A vast catalogue of available measures that can stop the breakout of conflict already exists, measures which necessarily vary in function of the trouble we seek to prevent. Limitations of space here constrain me to giving a partial inventory: freezing the capital which members of governments guilty of violations have placed abroad; deploying forces of intervention or police forces with a view to protecting a wobbling democracy or threatened minority; sending observers on missions to establish and monitor disarmament programs all are measures which become interventions the moment they are imposed in response to pressure in the international community and take place against the will of the states concerned.

THE INTERNATIONAL CRIMINAL COURT

One aspect of the international community's politics of prevention remains to be systematized: its judicial arm. By according itself the means to put an effective and permanent criminal court in place, the international community would opt for a tool of judicial intervention which unquestionably would act as a deterrent to the authors of war crimes or crimes against humanity.[10] It is necessary, in effect, that all who participate in officially recognized violations of fundamental rights – whether they furnish arms to militias or to those who perpetrate violations, or use the media to spread racist messages and incite violence, or be titled heads of government – know that they are subject to punishment by the International Criminal Court. The international community must manifest the common will to show its solidarity towards victims of violations by punishing their torturers. We should not underestimate the dissuasive effect of such a Court on authoritarian governments as well as on individuals who, in the name of such governments, participate in genocide, crimes against humanity, or war crimes (art. 6 to 8 of the statute).

Nevertheless, the International Criminal Court can only become an instrument of prevention against organized violence if the Court works quickly and efficiently. Neither the example of trials held too late, as in the Eichmann, Barbie and Touvier cases, nor that of thousands of Rwandans still crouched in tiny cells awaiting judgment can serve as a guide. It is indispensable that the Court have at its disposal all financial means necessary to its proper functioning. To the deterrent effect of the Court we must add its psychological effect on the victims. If the condemnation of at least some of the criminals does not render the victims the loved ones and possessions they have lost, it does testify to the support of the international community. They henceforth will know that they are not double victims: of the abuse of power or hate, and of the indifference of other nations.

CONCLUSION

I wish to make perfectly clear that I am no advocate of unbridled interventionism which, used as a watchword in the name of the rights of man, would unleash a new contemporary crusade. I am perfectly conscious that, whenever it requires the use of force, intervention endangers the lives of the innocent, be they civilians or soldiers. It is thus an extremely dangerous instrument whose use is always subject to dramatic turns. I am equally conscious that interventionism can become an instrument of power in the hands of a group of nations seeking to interpret international law in their own favor. It is nevertheless deplorable that, for political reasons, situations of conflict are so often allowed to degenerate: that is, they are not worsened by arms shipments or the erection of puppet governments anxious to serve the interests of multinational corporations. In such cases, the decision to intervene far too often comes only when the situation in the area has become morally unbearable and then requires the use of drastic means.

And then there is the risk of an abuse of power in connection with the introduction of the right to humanitarian intervention. This risk is inherent to the unequal division of power among states, and it is certainly not lessened by confiding the responsibility of deciding the legitimacy of intervention on a case-to-case basis to the Security Council, under the domination of the five most powerful nations. On the contrary, I believe we can only arrive at an equitable and morally defensible formula once we have codified the right to intervention.

For in its current state, the five largest powers not only posses the right of veto in the Security Counsel, which permits them to block any initiative the majority of states may take, but the articles of the Charter – in particular those related to the use of force in cases of legitimate defense or a threat to peace – remain so vague that large and middle-sized powers can impose any interpretation which suits them. Thus the codification of humanitarian intervention should not only allow us to avoid the arbitrary treatment of individual cases; it should also formulate rights in such a way as to reduce to a minimum the extant uncertainties in areas determining the application of the law. Parallelly, it is indispensable to decide the global institutional structure we need to put in place. Only then can we make certain that humanitarian intervention not be codified in ways that prohibit the most powerful nations from taking carte blanche to impose a new world order best suited to their own convenience.

NOTES

[1] Résolution de Copenhague, 31.8.1986.
[2] See Dietrich Schindler (1996): "Le droit à l'assistance humanitaire: droit et/ou obligation?" In: *Le Droit à l'assistance humanitaire.* Proceedings of the international conference organised by UNESCO, Paris, January 23-27 1995, Paris: 34-38.
[3] Mario Bettati (2000): "Les États et l'ingérence humanitaire", *Les Temps Mordernes*, Nr. 610, Paris : 243-256.
[4] Véronique Zanetti (2000): "Menschenrechte und humanitäre Interventionspflicht". In: Gustav Gustenau (ed.): *Humanitäre militärische Intervention zwischen Legalität und Legitimität.* Tagungsband des Instituts für Internationale Friedenssicherung, Wien: 83-108.
[5] See Thomas Pogge (1995): "How Should Human Rights be Conceived?". In: B. Sharon Byrd et al. (eds.): *Annual Review of Law and Ethics/Jahrbuch für Recht und Ethik*, Vol. 3: 103-120.
[6] Johann Benjamin Erhard (1976): *Über das Recht des Volks zu einer Revolution und andere Schriften*, ed. by Hellmut G. Haasis, Frankfurt/Main: 50.
[7] Boutros-Boutros Ghali, "Supplement to an agenda for peace", 3. January 1995 paragraph 26. Http://www.un.org/Docs/SG/agsupp.html#SANCTION.
[8] Ibid., paragraphs 27 and 28.
[9] Mario Bettati (1996): *Le droit d'ingérence. Mutation de l'ordre international,* Paris: 252.
[10] Mario Bettati, op. cit.: 245.

III

Kosova / Kosovo
The Moral Combat

ULRICH STEINVORTH*

On the Legitimacy of NATO's Kosovo Intervention

1. MY THESIS AND MY AIMS

My thesis is that NATO's Kosovo intervention has been legitimate. I base my thesis on the following argument.

(1) We can conceive of crimes the prevention of which justifies military intervention,
(2) There have been such crimes in human history, even in recent history,
(3) The Serbian attack on the Albanian Kosovars is such a crime,
(4) In spite of grave mistakes and violations of the rules of just war, NATO intervention in Serbia was justified.

I will not discuss steps (1) and (2) of my argument. I presuppose without argument the truth of the normative premiss that there may be just wars. Moreover, I presuppose the truth of the descriptive premiss that there have in fact been in history crimes and crimes in preparations that justify and even morally require military intervention to prevent their continuation or execution. For instance, I think the defensive war of the Poles against Germany in 1939 and the non-defensive war that Britain and France declared on Germany on September 3, 1939, have been just.

It is steps (3) and (4) which I am interested in discussing. The problem for both defenders and critics of (3) and (4) is that the knowledge of the reasons by which we decide who is right is empirical and depends on what sources of information we trust. But the legitimacy of the NATO intervention does not only depend on which facts we presuppose or on which values we recognize but also on which facts and which values we think pertain to the question of the legitimacy of the intervention. At least some commentators have judged its legitimacy by their conjectures about the *in-*

tentions and *interests*, in particular the secret interests the U.S. and its allies had when they intervened. My first aim is to show that my argument is sound. My second aim is to show that an intervention may (sometimes, not always) be justified because of its welcome consequences in spite of the interveners' dubious intentions.

That is one reason I hope that my thesis on the legitimacy of the intervention will not depend primarily on questions of fact. I even dare hope that I do not presuppose facts that you will not accept as well. The sources I rely on are the information that you can read both in Michael Ignatieff's book on the Kosovo war[1] who says the intervention was legitimate and in Noam Chomsky's book on the same subject[2] who says it was a moral desaster.

2. WHAT HAPPENED BEFORE THE WAR?

Let us turn to step (3) and ask whether there has been a Serbian attack on the Albanian Kosovars and whether it belongs to the crimes whose prevention justify a war. I presume the following facts are generally considered more or less established.

In 1989, Milosevic abolished Kosovar autonomy, re-asserted Serbian direct rule and purged Kosovo Albanians from jobs in government and education. The Kosovo Albanians rallied to the non-violent Ibrahim Rugova and demanded equal rights with the Serbs. The Serbs responded to the non-violent resistance with arrests, detention and harassment. After the Dayton accord of 1995, that gave Bosnia peace but failed to make any mention of grievances in Kosovo, young Kosovo Albanians began to plan for an uprising and to terrorize and kill (and now I quote the description given by Michael Ignatieff) "Serb policemen, postmen and government officials. The Serb military police … counter-attacked with reprisals directed at villages which gave shelter to the KLA guerillas. In late February 1998, one such reprisal killed 80 civilians, in the Drenica region of central Kosovo. This massacre sent shock-waves throughout Kosovo: it marked the end of the campaign of non-violent resistance and the onset of mass armed struggle. Hoping to exploit this tide of local support, the KLA launched an offensive which by July had seized up to one third of the country. But in the late July they over-reached themselves, taking Orahovac, a town too large for them to hold. Milosevic launched a counter-attack, and in the Serbian offensive which followed, villages were rocketed, two hundred thousand civilians were driven from their homes into the mountains, and the KLA were driven back to the areas bordering Albania. Throughout the summer of 1998, the international community issued condemnations of the Milosevic counter-offensive, but it became clear that many Western governments were quietly doing nothing...."[3]

In September, after threatening the bombing of Yugoslav installations the United States, through its special envoy Richard Holbrooke, pressed Milosevic to relent and allow the deployment in Kosovo of a Verification Mission of unarmed monitors constituted by members of the OSCE. Its purpose was to ensure that the Yugoslav army stayed in barracks and the Kosovar guerillas stayed up in the mountains. Simultaneously, Milosevic committed himself to negotiate with the Kosovars about the future of the province. He insisted that it remain part of Yugoslavia while the Kosovars insisted that it be independent.[4] In December, the guerillas controlled the mountains, the Serbs the asphalt roads and the capital Pristina. Everyone expected the fighting to begin again in the spring.[5] But still in the winter, the killings went on. Yugoslav forces killed 31 guerillas, masked gunmen killed more than twenty Serbs in a bar in Pec in Western Kosovo, including teenagers,[6] Yugoslav army tanks left their barracks and engaged in fierce firefights with guerilla units and in Pec and other towns, Serb police beat up Kosovo Albanians and dragged them off to prison.[7] In January 15, Serb paramilitary and police units murdered 45 civilians in the village of Racak. On January 31, NATO authorized air-strikes against Serbia if it did not agree to talks with Kosovar leaders. Serbs and Kosovo Albanians met in Rambouillet. Since they failed to produce agreement, the Americans proposed autonomy for Kosovo, accompanied by NATO troop deployments. The Kosovars agreed, the Serb did not. The Americans set the Serbs an ultimatum for agreement, after which they would start bombing the Serbs. The Serbs refused the ultimatum, and the war started on March 24, 1999.[8]

3. WAS IT LEGITIMATE TO INTERVENE?

If this story is true, I think two points are evident. First, the Kosovo Albanians were not innocent of the predicament they were in. They took to violent resistance after the Dayton accord, and the Serbs responded. On the other hand, though this is no longer evident, the Albanians were harassed and their rights were violated. According to the moral standards most people believe in, they had a moral right to resist and even to take up arms.

Moreover, the Serbs responded brutally and disproportionately. They "passed the point of legitimate self-defence".[9] In the view of most observers in 1998 and early 1999, the Albanians had to fear extinction and genocide from the Serbs.

The second evident point is, that if the Dayton accord had taken account of the explosive situation in Kosovo and given securities to the Kosovo Albanians instead of punishing their non-violent resistance by neglecting them, then much misery would have been prevented, and that the U.S. bears responsibility for failing to prevent the misery. But does that mean it had lost its right to intervene? More generally, were the Western governments permitted to look at what happened under their eyes in an area some hundred miles east and south of Italy and Austria without intervening?

I think if they were not under the moral *duty* and obligation to intervene they had at least the *right* and were morally permitted to intervene. This judgment depends on the premiss that the Albanians had to fear extinction and genocide. *Did* they have to fear extinction? There is evidence that some of the destruction in Kosovo attributed to the Serbs has in fact been committed by Muslims. For example, as the former director of the Counterterrorist Center at the CIA, Yossef Bodansky, reports,[10] the village of Meja and surrounding villages had been destroyed and emptied of its population, and that had been attributed to "Serbian ethnic cleansing" by a NATO spokesman. In fact, it was the UCK that destroyed them. But they did so, as Bodansky explains, in order "to alienate and radicalize the population so that they would fight the Serbs and to coerce the civilians to escape into exile so that there can be no normalization and [no] Kosovo Albanian population under the control of the Serbs. This is a classic 'revolutionary' strategy that has been implemented in several previous Islamic Liberation struggles such as those in Afghanistan, the Philippines, and Bosnia."

Such evidence does free the Serbs from responsibility for some of the crimes attributed to them but it does not seem to free them from responsibility for the attempt to commit genocide against the Kosovo Albanians. Milosevic won his power in Serbia after a speech he held in 1989 at Kosovo Polje, the famous plain in Kosovo where the Turks defeated the Serbs six centuries before in 1389. In this speech Milosevic launched his campaign for a Greater Serbia, proclaiming that Kosovo was the heartland of the Serbian nation that must again come together in a great nation, by force of arms if need be.[11] The Kosovo Albanians therefore had good reasons to expect the realization of this proclamation after the Serbs had withdrawn their troops from Croatia and Bosnia and were ready to tackle what they took for their most important problem, the re-Serbization of Kosovo.

But did this make it necessary to present the Serbs with an ultimatum and press them to accept NATO supervision of Kosovo? Why not supervision by UNO? And why did NATO insist, in Appendix B of the Rambouillet Agreement which Milosevic rejected, on its right to "unrestricted passage and unimpeded access throughout the Federal Republic of Yugoslavia" and not only Kosovo?[12]

UNO military supervision needed the agreement of Russia and China, and it was well known that China would not agree.[13] But it was known as well that the war between the Serbs and the Albanians would escalate, and it was predictable that that war would end in the defeat of the Albanians and the expulsion of the survivors. Hence, their expulsion could only be prevented by the intervention of an effective military force, and NATO was the only international one available. As to NATO's insistence on free access throughout Yugoslavia, I do not know whether it was *necessary* in order to bring peace to Kosovo. But I think NATO had a right to insist on it because such access would make it better able to keep the peace in Kosovo.

Now immediately after NATO began bombing, as Noam Chomsky states, the Serbian terror of Kosovo Albanians "reached the capital city of Pristina, mostly spared before, and ... large-scale destruction of villages, brutal atrocities, and a radical increase in generation of refugees" were credibly reported.[14] Therefore, Chomsky says, "Clinton and Blair decided in favor of a war that led to a radical escalation of ethnic cleansing along with other deleterious effects",[15] and such a war, as he suggests, must be illegitimate since if Clinton and Blair had not decided in favor of the war, the Kosovo Albanians would have been spared the atrocities.

Chomsky would be right if it was the war that caused the atrocities. But if it is true, as most observers in spring 1999 believed, that the Serbs had long planned to "cleanse" Kosovo of its Albanians and used the beginning of the war as the occasion to execute what they had planned before, then it was not the war that caused the atrocities but the Serbs. Since we have strong reasons to stick to the judgment of 1999, we must recognize that the war prevented still worse atrocities, probably even genocide, and the success of the expulsion.

One of the reasons for denying the legitimacy of NATO's intervention is the argument that the Albanian rebels, as was judged already 1998 by Western envoys, were a terrorist organisation[16] hardly less brutal than the

Serbs. I do not think this is a sound argument. If the UCK was a terrorist organisation and was as brutal as the Serbs, the Albanian population, neither identical with the UCK nor in its majority sympathising with it, had still strong reasons to fear the fate that the Croats and Bosnians had suffered at the hands of Serbs some years before. True, there are credible reports from observers who stayed in Kosovo in March, 1999, describing the behaviour of the Yugoslav army as rather moderate.[17] But even if the Serbs did not intend to execute genocide in spring 1999, their moderation may well be explained by their fear of NATO bombing. In judging the situation in March 1999, we ought not to abstract from what had happened before. It is worth remembering that in 1998 the Serbian methods were described by the saying "A village a day keeps the NATO away".[18] What led to this saying were not false impressions but hard facts.

Therefore I still think, though not without doubts and less confidently than I did two years before, that both the Albanians and neutral observers had to fear that the Serbs would attempt to cleanse Kosovo of Albanians, which in effect meant an attempt at genocide. Therefore I still judge it was legitimate for the West to intervene militarily. The West would have become guilty of permitting genocide in spite of its ability to prevent it if it had not chosen to realize its threat of intervention after its ultimatum had expired.

4. SOME REMARKS ABOUT THE AMERICAN INTENTIONS

In principle these considerations should be enough to prove step (3) of my argument above. Yet there is a widepread inclination to argue against (3) by turning to the *intentions* of the Americans and its allies in intervening in Yugoslavia and attributing to them economic, military or other self-interested intentions, from the badness of which the illegitimacy of the intervention is inferred. There are many examples of this form of argument in Europe, the U.S. and all over the world, and its perhaps most prominent advocate is Noam Chomsky. Yet it cannot prove what it wants to prove, the illegitimacy of the intervention. For even if the Western states had bad intentions in intervening, the intervention was still legitimate if it prevented the Serbs from committing a crime the prevention of which justifies a war.

Let me give a comparison. Let us suppose the British and French governments, when they declared war on Germany on September 3, 1939, after Hitler had not responded to a short-termed ultimatum that demanded that his invasion into Poland stop, did not really care about justice in Europe, that they only wanted to avoid losing face by not realizing the threat connected to their ultimatum. Let us presume moreover, since Britain had concluded a mutual aid pact with Poland only some days before, that the British government had an interest in finding an occasion for a war against Germany. And let us suppose that Hitler would have agreed to some proposal after some more negotiations and conferences. We may even assume that some people in the British or French governments looked forward to a war as an occasion to use and test some new military technology. Nevertheless, their choice to realize their threat was the only morally acceptable one. It was right to put Hitler an ultimatum at the time Britain and France did so, and it was right not to renounce the threat of war but to put it into effectit when Hitler neglected the ultimatum. What Britain and France intended in doing so is absolutely irrelevant.

In the same way, we may well suppose that the United States and its allies did not give an damn about whether human rights were violated in Kosovo, that their only interest was not to be duped once more by Milosevic and not to be ridiculed as paper tigers. We may even grant that we cannot know for sure whether after some more time of negotiations and conferences Milosevic would not have agreed to some proposal. What is more, we may grant there were people in the U.S. government who looked forward to a war as an occasion to use and test some new military technology. Still their choice was right, because it was right at the time they did so to present Milosevic with an ultimatum demanding that he consent to a foreign control and supervision of Kosovo to protect both Serbs and Albanians from human rights violations. It was in the interest of the people who must be afraid of such violations to be protected by reliable foreign forces after both Serbs and even UN forces had proved unable to do so in Bosnia.

Let us even take one more step in our comparison. Let us assume, contrary to historical facts, that Britain and France had tolerated and even silently, though not officially, helped an allied nation to invade a neighbour nation at the very same time when they demanded of Hitler to put his hands off Poland. Would it then have been unjust for them to declare war on Germany? I think, not at all. On the contrary, it would have been one more injustice, in addition to that of tolerating the allied nation's invasion, to tolerate Germany's invasion of Poland.

In the same way, the fact that the U.S. and NATO tolerated the Turks' suppression and violation of rights of the Kurds at the same time when they did not tolerate the Serbs' suppression and violation of rights of the Kosovo Albanians is no reason at all to judge the intervention in Serbia unjust. On the contrary, if they had tolerated the crimes in Kosovo, that would have been one more injustice in addition to that of tolerating the Turkish crimes. Therefore, Chomsky, who makes much of the NATO's toleration of the Turks' suppression of the Kurds in his criticism of the NATO intervention in Serbia, falls victim to a fallacy.[19]

Allow me a third and last time to try your moral imagination. Let us assume, again more or less contrary to historical facts, that historians had to attribute to Britain and France a horrible list of political failures, crimes and atrocities committed before and after their declaration of war on Germany. Would that imply that their war on Germany was illegitimate or immoral? Again, I do not think so. On the contrary, that would be the one deed that would make their historical record a tiny bit better. In the same way, let us grant that the horrible record of political failures, crimes and atrocities that Chomsky cites against the U.S. is true. Does it follow that the NATO intervention in Yugoslavia was immoral? Not at all. We must judge that intervention by its own virtues and vices. And as I have already tried to show, it had the virtue of preventing the expulsion of the Albanians from Kosovo and the murder of some hundred thousands more of them.

I do not argue that intentions are never pertinent. Very often they are. But not if we are to judge the legitimacy of preventing a crime. The prevention of a crime is always justified, whatever the intentions behind it. I do presuppose that what NATO prevented by its intervention, just as what Britain and France prevented by their declaration of war on Hitler, was a crime, genocide of the Kosovo Albanians in the one case, subjection of the Poles in the other.

Now you may consider my comparisons of 1999 and 1939 a failure. Hitler, you may say, invaded another sovereign state while Milosevic did not; he stayed within the boundaries of his own sovereign state, and international law grants sovereign states the sovereign right to enforce order over their territories howsoever they think fit. I do not think that this difference is relevant here. If, again contrary to the facts, Hitler had started on September 1, 1939, not the invasion of Poland but the ethnical cleansing of all German Jews from their places of residence, and if then Britain and France, after a short-termed ultimatum, had declared war on Germany on September 3, 1939, they would have been justified in doing so, even though they transgressed international law or the sovereignty of states.

Or you may object against my comparison of Hitler and Milosevic. Hitler's crimes are just of another dimension than those of Milosevic, you may say. I agree. But you did not know that 1939. With the knowledge of 1939, it was right to declare war on Germany.[20] Or you my say that Milosevic did not endanger the security of the free world while Hitler did, and that therefore there was sufficient justification for waging war on Hitler but insufficient justification for waging war on Milosevic. I answer that defending one's own security is no better justification for waging war than defending the human rights of a people that has to fear genocide.

6. DID THE WAR RESPECT THE RULES *IN BELLO*?

So far I have only defended (3). How about (4)? I shall presuppose in my short discussion of (3) that there are not only legitimacy conditions for beginning a just war, rules *ad bellum*, but also rules for fighting a just war, rules *in bello*. There are still a lot of philosophers who think that every war is unjust and that therefore there can be neither rules *ad bellum* nor rules *in bello*. I shall not try to convince them nor to defend my theses against them here.[21]

The rules *in bello* and even the rules *ad bellum* can be summarized in the principle or idea of proportionality or fit of the means of a war to the ends of the war. For justifying the beginning of a war, it is never enough that the cause of a war is just. Rather, the injustice the war is to prevent must be very grave. What means of war are allowed depends on the gravity of the crimes the war is fought to prevent. We cannot radically distinguish between the rules *ad bellum* and the rules *in bello*. The atrocities a war is fought to prevent must be extreme if they are to justify the use of nuclear weapons. If the atrocities are less extreme and still justify the use of war to prevent them, only the use of less destructive weapons is justified.[22]

In order to explicate the idea of fit between the means and ends of a war, let us be more concrete. The atrocities the *Gulf war* was fought to prevent were less extreme than the atrocities *World War II* was fought to prevent. The Gulf war was fought to prevent Iraq from annexing Kuwait, which is less atrocious than what the Poles had to expect from the Germans when the Germans invaded Poland in 1939. The Kuwaitis did not have to expect from Saddam Hussein to be treated worse than the Iraqis were treated whereas the Poles did have to expect from Hitler to be treated much worse than the Germans were. Therefore, to prevent atrocities, the use of more atrocious weapons was justified in the war against Germany than in the war against Iraq. Therefore, if the Gulf war was just at all, which I doubt, the use of only moderately atrocious weapons was justified. It does not seem to me that the use of the weapons that were used in the Gulf war was justified.

There is another consequence of the principle of fit of means and ends of war that pertains to something the NATO spokespersons made notorious, namely *collateral damages*. The more extreme the atrocities are that a war is fought to prevent, the graver the collateral damages may be. If you think the crimes that Milosevic was about to perform and the war was to prevent were no extreme atrocities, you will easily find many NATO actions that offend the rules *in bello*. The more atrocious you consider the actions the war is used to prevent, the less easily you will find offences of the rules *in bello*.

It is a macabre logic that in an explication of the idea of the fit between means and ends of war shows up. Still, we must follow it when we want to judge whether the NATO violated the norms *in bello*. Now we can only follow it after we have judged about the grade of atrocity the Kosovo war was used to prevent. I think its atrocity was graver than the atrocity the Gulf war was fought to prevent and less grave than the atrocity World War II was fought against. And I dare say that the collateral damages of the Kosovo war are justifiable.

As Michael Ignatieff reports in his book on the Kosovo war, there were some means that the American legal advisors judged legitimate and the French and British advisors judged illegitimate. Among them were the bombing of the Serbian TV and power grid and the Belgrade bridges that the French and British governments, following their legal advisors, rejected.[23] I encline to the French and British advisors' judgment.

It seems probable, moreover, that NATO bombed parts of Serbia without reasons to do so. Thus, as Chomsky has pointed out, the bombing of the province of Vojvodina, the home of the Hungarian minority, seems to have been just arbitrary and stupid.[24] This act, as probably many others, must be deplored and condemned. But I do not think they are enough to judge the war unjust. I would rather count them to the part of human weakness and stupidity that can be nowhere avoided.

May be still more information about arbitrary and stupid acts will show up that will force me in the end to concede that the war did violate the rules *in bello*. Up to now, I don't think so. The NATO did try, not without success, to keep collateral damages down. Belgrade was heavily bombed, but the bombs brought by missiles were targeted and the loss of civil population was relatively small. Every victim is to be deplored, yet we should recognize that the collateral damages, though they became Germany's word of the year in 1999, were much less than those in World War II.

7. HAS THE WAR BEEN PRUDENT?

I have argued that the Kosovo war did not transgress the rules *ad bellum* nor *in bello* and that therefore the war was just. But that does not mean, as I have argued at another place, that it was morally necessary. As most of our actions, also wars can be just or morally permitted but not morally necessary nor prudent.[25] Therefore we can still ask, even if we concede that they are just or morally permitted, whether they are prudent. They are so only if they do not contradict long term interests of the party that wages a just war. Now we can doubt whether the Kosovo war did not contradict long term interests of the West.

The reason for such doubt is that the war may be misunderstood as a model for problem solving that one cannot approve of. One might see in it the proclamation, not by words but by deed, of the rule: If you cannot enforce what you consider justice, bomb! This rule generates another one: If you want to escape U.S. bombing, get nuclear weapons! Such consequences cannot be in the West's interest. This is why a respected Israeli commentator spoke of "the foolish initiatives of NATO and the U.S. to establish new rules of the game".[26] Samuel Huntington, who is not in danger of being considered a radical critic, even suggested in 1999 that in the eyes of much of the world the U.S. is "becoming the rogue superpower" and "the single greatest external threat to their societies", and pleaded for a reconsideration of the politics started with the Kosovo war.[27]

It would indeed be a moral disaster if what has been in 1999 a right to wage a war would become an easily available means for every state or group considering itself strong enough to have its way. But though this is possible, it is certainly not necessary. It depends on the ways the NATO states and particularly the U.S. act in the future. The more unilateralist their politics becomes, the greater the danger that the Kosovo war will be a paradigm of politics that the West cannot be interested in.

NOTES

* I thank James Allen for correcting my English and Oliver Krug for discussing a former version of the paper.

[1] Michael Ignatieff, Virtual war. Kosovo and beyond, London (Chatto) 2000.

[2] Noam Chomsky, The new military humanism. Lessons from Kosovo, London (Pluto) 1999.

[3] Cf. Ignatieff 13f.

[4] Ignatieff 14.

[5] Ignatieff 15.

[6] Ignatieff 18.

[7] Ignatieff 34.

[8] Ignatieff 35f.

[9] Ignatieff 21. Chomsky 38ff judges similarly. It is only because similar violations of human rights were committed in Turkey against the Kurds and elsewhere in the world against other minorities that Chomsky rejects Western nations' claim that the war against Serbia was humanitarian and hence justified. I think Chomsky is right in rejecting this claim but wrong in concluding the war can therefore not be justified.

[10] Yossef Bodansky, bin Laden. The man who declared war on America, Rocklin (Forum), 1999, 399.

[11] Ignatieff 24.

[12] Quoted from Chomsky 107.

[13] In 1998 the UN Security Council agreed only on Resolution 1199 that does not threaten military intervention. Even the weapon emborgo imposed by the UN Security Council at the end of March 1998 on Yugoslavia was never written into a UN Security Council resolution because China, among others, refused its approval: cf. General Report of the NATO Parliamentary Assembly § 33.

[14] Noam Chomsky, The new military humanism. Lessons from Kosovo, London (Pluto) 1999, 20.

[15] Chomsky 16.

[16] Cf. the General Report: Kosovo Aftermath and its Implications for Conflict Prevention and Crisis Management, edited by the Political Committee of the NATO Parliamentary Assembly November 2000 (http://www.naa.be/index.html) § 27.

[17] I thank Dieter S. Lutz for giving me insight into a letter he received from a German diplomat who stayed in Kosovo in spring 1999 and wanted to remain anonymous. According to this letter, the Serbs did not intend genocide.

[18] Cf. the General Report of the NATO Parliamentary Assembly § 64.

[19] Noam Chomsky, 12f. Though Chomsky says himself ibid. 15: "It is easy to find historical examples in which actions undertaken on cynical grounds, or worse, had beneficial consequences that were plausibly anticipated, so it might have been appropriate to support such actions whatever the motives and goals".

[20] The comparisons of Hitler and Milosevic have not been rare in the 90s in the media. Even Timothy Garton Ash compared them in New York Review of Books June 24, 1999. Chomsky ibid. 60 and 94 is scandalized about the comparisons. In fact, the chal-

lenge Hitler posed to Western nations in the 30s differed from the challenge Milosevic posed to them in the 90s only by its immediate imperilling of their security interests.

[21] For a discussion of the rules of just war, see Reinold Schmücker, Gibt es einen gerechten Krieg? Deutsche Zeitschrift für Philosophie 48, 2000, 319-40. I do not think the rules Schmücker lists are final but I consider his discussion excellent.

[22] I presuppose here that collateral damage to non-combatants can never be justified by some mistake the non-combatants are guilty of. They cannot be justified at all. But it is not always the military power causing the damages that is responsible or guilty of the damages. Rather, it is the power that is responsible of the crime that the war is waged to prevent or minimize.

[23] Michael Ignatieff, Virtual war. Kosovo and beyond, London (Chatto) 2000, 207 and 199, cf. 100.

[24] Chomsky 34.

[25] That implies that even a just war must not always be *ultima ratio*. The war the British and French declared on Germany on September 3, 1939, was in fact not *ultima ratio*, for there was still the alternative of negotiations. Still, it was just.

[26] Amos Gilboa, "NATO is a Danger to the World", *Ma'ariv*, May 9, 1999, quoted after Chomsky 141.

[27] In Foreign Affairs March/April 1999, quoted after Chomsky 143.

GEORG MEGGLE

NATO-Morality and the Kosovo-War An Ethical Commentary – ex post

0 All it took for the 37000 or so NATO air raids against Serbia/Yugoslavia in 1999 to receive such broad public blessing in most NATO-countries was the goal (genuine or alleged) expressed in the term used to describe the entire operation: it wasn't war, it was a "Humanitarian Intervention". The only fly in the ointment was the lack of a mandate from the UN. Yet this snag was actually relished by the strongest proponents of intervention, who interpreted NATO's action as a victory for morality over mere law, a victory for human rights over international law. At least, that's one side of the story.

Others – and they above all include the addressees of this Humanitarian Intervention – regard this, NATO's first war, as something else: as a relapse into the barbarism which the so-called civilised states have at least tried to avoid since the Peace of Westphalia, albeit not completely successfully (and certainly not in the 20th century).

Morality is the most effective means of justification for wars, which doubtless makes it one of the most important instruments of warfare. There can be no military morality without 'proper' morality as the rearguard.

But what's this got to do with ethics?

There are only few cases where the practical relevance of ethics (a philosophical discipline which is equally interested in theoretical principles and critical application) can be shown more clearly. Morality is the most important part of all our military decisions and propagations; morality is the software deciding for or against war. Cruise missiles can be stopped. But once the morality program has gathered steam, halting it is almost impossible.

We, too, are concerned by the questions raised by this war and the justification propagated – as philosophers, but perhaps also otherwise. The questions include the following: What makes an intervention humanitarian? What are the moral assessment criteria for such an intervention? What strength do these criteria have compared to the pertinent regulations and considerations of international law? What are the specific moral problems of humanitarian intervention compared to the common problems of fighting between different states? And what moral lessons do we learn today from that war? (Please don't raise your hopes too much; I won't be able to answer all these questions now!)

The following thoughts carry on from my paper "Is this war good?" from the last few weeks of the 1999's war. The first section sums up the essence of that paper.

PART I

1. *Self-defence and emergency assistance*

1.1 Let's start by taking the customary tack of self-defence and assistance in an emergency. If someone makes an attempt on my life and I can't ward off his attack in any other way, I may defend myself by killing him before he kills me. Note the use of 'may' – I am under no compulsion to do so. I might not value my life so much that I'm even prepared to kill in order to save it. Self-defence is a right, not an obligation.

By contrast, whenever emergency assistance is concerned, it's not my life which is at stake but that of at least one other person. Say a murderer wants to kill a defenceless child. If there's no other way of saving the child's life, may I try and kill the murderer? Of course I may. Indeed, it's probably my duty to do so. Although I may choose to relinquish my own life, I might not be able to morally refrain from saving the child's. In other words, we have a right to self-defence in an emergency, and we may even be obliged to provide emergency assistance. Of course, the scope of actions obligatory for or expected of me when providing emergency aid is not unlimited. It depends on my own personal risk, as well as on whether I am duty-bound to take certain action (e.g. if I am a policeman or lifeguard). Moreover, not all possible actions are permitted in either self-defence or emergency assistance. We'll return shortly to the limits of what is allowed.

1.2 This approach via self-defence and emergency assistance is almost always taken when weighing up the moral justification of a licence or even a duty to kill. It is also used if war is involved. After all, the general assumption goes, states are individuals, too. And any individual, be it a single person or a collective of people organised in the form of a state, may defend its existence – even if this might mean the end of the attacker. Wars of defence are nothing more than cases of a state's self-defence, and wars of assistance (regardless of whether they are fought within the framework of a defence pact) are nothing more than cases of emergency aid. Hence, according to the main argument, they are morally justified. And consequently, as far as the right to enter wars (the *jus ad bellum*) is concerned, these wars are described as "just wars". So far, so good – perhaps.

1.3 But at this point a problem crops up. States themselves consist of individuals and thus of groups of individuals. Although the chief aim of a state is supposed to be to protect its citizens, not every state actually serves this purpose. What about cases in which the state apparatus turns against its own citizens, or usually of course against individual groups? Do they, too, have a right to self-defence if their very existence is threatened? Of course they do. This is the famous right of resistance – a moral right which the threatened group has vis-à-vis its own state, even if such a right is not enshrined in the state's laws or is even explicitly ruled out. Consequently, external parties have the right to provide emergency assistance in such cases, too, if the group under threat is unable to help itself.

1.4 However, groups – such as political parties, ethnic or religious groups etc. – may be threatened not only by states but also by other groups. The respective state is responsible for countering such threats in line with its main aim, its role of protector. Yet this role still leaves much to be desired in some cases; moreover, the repression, expulsion or destruction of one group by at least one other group sometimes suits those in power, and as well as concealing it they might even encourage or initiate it. In this case, too, if the state ignores its responsibility, outsiders may come to the aid of those not sufficiently able to defend themselves.

1.5 Let me ask you a question: Have you accepted the justification of self-defence and emergency assistance so far without any qualms? If so, you have already crossed a critical frontier; that of the state concerned. Those who concur with the principle that we may also come to the aid of a population under threat on another state's territory evidently believe that the provision of assistance itself is more important – more important than the source of this help, be it domestic or foreign.

And rightly so. If Hitler had not embarked upon foreign conquest and had limited his concentration camps to Germany, ought the rest of the world to have stood idly by because his policy of extermination was kept local? Well, the world might have done so. But under no circumstances would this have been acceptable. (And now comes the sentence which in my 1999 speech deeply affected some people:) This is the point where pacifism becomes a crime. The entreaty "No more Auschwitz!" may well outweigh "No more war". If a second Auschwitz *can* be prevented, it *must* be prevented, regardless of its location. Put more generally, violations of human rights are not domestic affairs. Compared to the violation of human rights, violating national borders is the lesser evil, and in fact no evil at all given violations on the scale of Auschwitz. State sovereignty is not the highest good.

1.6 The quintessence is that even interventions by external states can be justified – as long as they are genuine interventions for the purpose of emergency assistance. Such interventions are always described by those carrying them out as "Humanitarian Interventions". If we adopt this linguistic use, the quintessence of this study of emergency assistance is nothing more than:

✥ *Central Humanitarian Interventions can be morally justified.*

This is the central axiom of all interventionists. This is hardly surprising, for "Interventionists" is the term given to those who subscribe to this axiom. I am one of them, for despite all the ifs and buts – for which there is no room here – I believe the entire process of justification outlined so far to be basically correct.

An interventionist philosophy is also advocated by the USA and – under its leadership – NATO. It is also subscribed to by other states and organisations, including the United Nations.

1.7 The differences between the USA and NATO etc. on the one hand and the UN on the other concern at most the question of whether the two following intervention axioms – which together characterise strong interventionism axioms – should apply:

✥ HR Human rights can count more than states' rights of sovereignty.

✦ NoUN Humanitarian Interventions may if necessary also be launched without the approval of the Secrurity Council or any other UN mandate.

As my crash course on the justification of emergency assistance showed, I too am a strong interventionist.

1.8 As already mentioned, these axioms belong to the very core of NATO's moral software. This software was also deployed during NATO's intervention in Serbia and Yugoslavia during the 1999 Kosovo-war. Does that mean that this war was and is morally legitimised?

No. These axioms are not a blank cheque. Even Humanitarian Interventions are subject to the same restrictions which apply to emergency assistance. Any moral assessment of Humanitarian Interventions largely depends on whether at least these conditions of emergency assistance are met. In order for a Humanitarian Intervention to be justified, not only the criterion of *ius ad bellum* must be met (i.e. in this type of war there must exist a corresponding emergency situation justifying intervention), but also the criteria for the justifiability of the particular way in which this emergency assistance is carried out. Put classically, the relevant criteria of *ius ad bellum* must also be met for this type of war. Exactly what they are and how last year's NATO intervention appears in the light of these criteria are the questions we will now address.

2. *The concept of Humanitarian Interventions*

2.1 The range of actions which can be described as interventions is extremely broad. In the most common usage, interventions are nothing more than actions in which the actor intervenes in a process in order to modify or prevent it. In a nutshell, interventions are hence instrumental actions – actions with which the actor aims to achieve certain goals. "Intervention" is thus not an expression of success. In order to be interventions, such actions need not necessarily achieve their aim. They are defined via the existence of corresponding intentions.

2.2 Humanitarian Interventions, in the broadest possible sense again, are actions with humanitarian aims. A multitude of things can be interpreted as humanitarian aims. And the means more or less suitable for such aims are equally diverse, ranging from displays of affection, nursing, a minimum of social assistance, and humanitarian aid missions by the army to a total ban on cars – at least potentially, of course. And just as diverse are the groups of Humanitarian Intervention addressees, i.e. those whom actions of Humanitarian Intervention are designed to benefit.

2.3 The Humanitarian Interventions involved here concern assistance for people who are in an emergency – in situations in which they are no longer able to help themselves. And not just individuals in emergencies, such as a mountaineer who has fallen into a glacial crevice and can't get out by himself. No, what we're talking about is the emergency of many, very many people, and what is at stake is the survival of entire sections of the population – for example when the population of a village is cut off from the rest of the world by flooding and would starve without external assistance. Such interventions are the paradigms of Humanitarian Interventions. How lucky we are if in such cases there are enough military helicopters stationed nearby to carry out rescue missions.

2.4 Let's now be a little more specific. We're not talking simply about people in need, but about self-defence. People are threatened and are unable to defend themselves against this threat. Moreover, this threat is not targeted against individuals, but against an entire group. Furthermore, the type and extent of this threat are extreme. The characteristic aim of the interventions discussed today is this: the protection of groups whose members are already the victims of massive and systematic crimes against humanity, and who will remain so without outside help.

2.5 In the context of NATO and other military organisations, the term humanitarian intervention applies to something much narrower. Humanitarian Interventions are characterised by the following conditions:

✥ 1: The aim of an intervening X is to prevent, end or at least reduce massive systematic violations of human rights inflicted on members of the group Z on the territory of the state of Y.

✥ 2: Actor X: a state or a group of states (e.g. NATO)

✥ 3: Action: military deployment including combat mission

✠ 4: Foreign-state proviso: intervened state Y ≠ X

Human interventions as defined by NATO are hence not only defined by their aim or the group of intervention addressees envisaged in this aim, but rather by considerable restrictions to the scope of the potential actor (the intervention subject) and the method of intervention (the action) plus an additional proviso. Humanitarian Interventions are thus now limited to military combat missions by one or more states on the territory of another state.

2.6 It should be obvious what this means: from now on, we're talking war. Those who are in favour of Humanitarian Interventions defined in this way are in favour of war. (This is just to clarify the issue; it shouldn't be seen as condemnation!) What distinguishes Human Interventions from other wars is the wars' particular aim.

Such humanitarian wars, even if only states are foreseen as the intervening party, are still wars in the two conventionally different forms: wars in which at least two states are involved (interstate wars) and civil wars – albeit only those taking place in another state due to the foreign-state proviso. In the latter case, the intervened state Y (the state where intervention is taking place) need not also be the intervention enemy (i.e. the targets of military deployment). The intervening party may have been formally invited to take action by Y – for instance if the group Z is threatened with destruction not by a state but by another group, and both the threatened group itself and the state Y responsible for defending Z are powerless to ward off this threat. Alternatively, the intervention may at least be tolerated by the intervened state in such a case.

2.7 If a state starts Humanitarian Interventions, it wages war. Merely for analytical reasons, such interventions concern issues of life and death; this is part and parcel of the reason for intervention in the first place. Of course, assuming we are the intervening party, it is other people who are being threatened. But this asymmetry vanishes as soon as for analytical reasons other conditions turn our intervention into war. At this point our lives, or at least those of our soldiers, are at risk. [2] At least, this has always been the case so far.

2.8 So much for semantics. Humanitarian Interventions in the above-defined sense (cf. 2.5) are now dubbed Humanitarian Military Interventions, or to be clearer, Humanitarian Intervention Wars [3], just to emphasise that we're dealing with more than just humanitarian military missions to supply earthquake victims or other Red Cross military operations.

3. *Humanitarian Military Interventions – the moral restrictions*

The list of the criteria which need to be met to legitimise Humanitarian Interventions is as follows. [4]

A HMI is only allowed/justified if:

(i)
- (a) The aim is to end etc. massive crimes against humanity (≥ "Kosovo Dimension";
- (b) this cannot be achieved in any other way

(ii) The manner of intervention:

- (a) serves the purpose of intervention;
- (b) minimises harm to third parties;
- (c) minimises the harm or risk to the intervening agents themselves;
- (d) enables the aim of intervention to be achieved with the lowest possible harm to the intervention precipitator

(iii) The intervention itself does not involve massive crimes against humanity

(?-iv-?) The intervention is sanctioned by (a) international law and (b) in particular a resolution by the UN Security Council

Criterion (iii) is only included by way clarification; it ought to follow automatically from the other criteria, especially (ii) (b) and (d). The question marks in criterion (?-iv-?) are justified, since this criterion contradicts the "No UN" axiom of strong interventionism.

PART II

4. *General things first*

4.1 Moral assessment of emergency assistance or intervention only arises when the above list of criteria is considered as a whole. Just what the 'minimal damage' classified in (ii) into three types (harm to third parties, harm to the intervention subject, and harm to the intervention precipitator) actually means can only be defined more closely by taking other aspects into account. In particular, we will be unable to evade morally weighting these different groups. Morally speaking, does minimising harm to third parties take priority over minimising harm to the those precipitating intervention? And also priority over minimising harm to the intervention subject? It certainly cannot be said for example that the less harm suffered by the intervening party itself (at the cost of third parties), the morally better it is. (This is especially important in our concrete case of intervention.)

4.2 Humanitarian military interventions are terribly complex actions or activities. 'Intervention' covers a multitude of things. It can be used to describe the start of an intervention, the manner of an intervention (e.g. air raids as opposed to ground troops), the same thing but in more detail (e.g. aerial bombing from a greater height), and the manner of intervention used in the various phases of intervention, etc. These are all very different kettles of fish. Consequently, moral judgment of these different things may also be different. Judgments of an intervention as such, i.e. judgments of NATO's Kosovo-intervention as a whole, encompass something terribly complex. It is inevitable that different judgments will attribute very different importance to the different aspects involved.

4.3 The number of subjects/actors is also terribly high in a Humanitarian Military Intervention. In NATO's intervention they included for instance NATO itself, the member states of NATO involved (i.e. the USA, the United Kingdom, France, in particular Germany), the North Atlantic Council, NATO's Secretary General (who ultimately gave the order to attack), the various war ministries, some national parliaments, the population of western Germany (which at the beginning of the war was 90 per cent in favour of it), the population of Greece (which was 90 per cent against it), etc. This is hence a thorny model for all those interested in the topic of Collective Intentionality & Agency.

4.4 Moreover, for each of these levels (of both actions and actors) we must distinguish as strictly as possible between the three classical evaluation viewpoints *ex ante*, *in actu* and *ex post*. Simultaneously exactly what is being evaluated must also be clearly stated: are we talking about an actor, their contribution to the intervention, a certain action aspect, the consequences of a certain action or those of the entire strategy? You can see what I'm driving at. These last few remarks might sound exactly like the start of what in our circles is referred to as the outline of an entire research programme – a programme which in this case would equate to at least three SFB's funded by the German Research Council (DFG). Hence your expectations regarding the rest of my reflections should be correspondingly 'large'. Like everyone else who dares to speak out on this topic, I will endeavour to achieve a terribly reduced degree of simplicity.

4.5 My first reduction is as follows: of the legitimacy conditions in (ii) – the *ius in bello* criteria – I shall hardly deal with criterion (c), i. e., minimisation of harm to the intervening agent. There's not much to be said about this, since during NATO's intervention this was the criterion which was best fulfilled; NATO suffered no losses whatsoever. (An attacker suffering zero loss was unprecedented in military history anywhere in the world.) If this was the only criterion which mattered, the NATO intervention would be the perfect example of a legtimised Humanitarian Military Intervention *par excellence*. And perhaps that's just what it is for some people.

By the way, note that this assessment only works if harm or damage to the intervening agent solely means the loss of human life.

4.6 Criterion (ii) (d), according to which those against whom emergency assistance and in particular intervention for this purpose are directed must not suffer more harm than necessary also requires little explanation at this point. It, too, was largely met by NATO's intervention – at least as far as what according to official NATO declarations were the two main precipitators of intervention: the Milosevic regime and his military apparatus (including the paramilitary and various volunteers' groups). The military apparatus, emerged from the whole action relatively intact; the regime itself was actually strengthened by the intervention. (Seen *ex ante*, wasn't this inevitable? Every group gathers around its leader in times of attack. There are even said to be leaders who know how to take this into account in their calculations.)

4.7 Before going into the other conditions in (ii), let us first look at (i), which could be termed the Intervention Presupposition. This really does deserve though examination.

5. *Criterion (i)*

5.1 A Humanitarian Military Intervention is only allowed/justified if:

(i) (a) The aim is to end etc. massive crimes against humanity ($\geq$ "Kosovo Dimension");

(b) this cannot be achieved in any other way

5.2 This criterion specifies the very much more general requirement that in order for an action of emergency assistance to be allowed, it must involve a genuine case of emergency assistance, i.e. that the presupposition of such assistance is fulfilled. This means firstly that a situation of emergency assistance must exist, and secondly that the actor must perceive the situation as such (i.e. as a situation of emergency assistance). This difference is important. If the actor perceives – incorrectly – the situation as one of emergency assistance, the 'aid' provided, whatever it is, will not in fact be emergency assistance, but at best supposed emergency assistance. Supposed assistance may be excusable (albeit only under very strict conditions, e.g. concerning the agent's information obligations); it's certainly not legitimate.

5.3 This dual aspect – the intention of emergency assistance on the one hand and the facts of emergency assistance on the other – are shared by all interventions, including humanitarian and military ones. But only regarding their evaluation, not in conceptual terms. (Perhaps this, too, is something which makes interventionist self-justification so natural.)

Let us take for example 'deterrence interventions'. These are simply actions with which the deterrence subject intends to deter somebody – period. The mere existence of such an intention is enough to make an action one of deterrence. In other words, deterrence actions in this broad sense are nothing more than attempts at deterrence – without any presupposition of facts. Such types of deterrence interventions hence have a thoroughly subjective touch. They become such interventions simply when they are perceived as such by the intervention subjects. We know of many deterrence actions in which there was no reason justifying deterrence in the first place.

This is exactly the same in conceptual terms for Humanitarian Interventions. An intervention is humanitarian if it is associated with a humanitarian intention. Whether the state of emergency assistance supposed by the subject actually exists is a different matter. Humanitarian Interventions being launched without the elements of emergency assistance existing is not a conceptual impossibility. It may occasionally not even be a real one.

But let us return from this little conceptual digression to ethics.

5.4 In order to be morally justified, Humanitarian Interventions – now in parallel again to the general emergency assistance analogy – also have to correspond in practical terms to their self-imposed image of emergency assistance. In other words, the group on whose behalf the intervention has been undertaken must actually be in a situation of emergency.

But exactly what sort of emergency? The criteria specified in the relevant literature vary enormously. This is partly due to the fact that what I call Humanitarian Intervention Wars are rarely sharply defined and are hardly ever called as such by name. It is generally believed that the relevant reasons for emergency intervention should be violations of human rights. As globalisation proceeds, Humanitarian Interventions should (according to common opinion) be developed into an increasingly accurate instrument of universal human rights policy.

However, it is usually acknowledged that not every violation of human rights is an acceptable reason for intervention – not even those carried out systematically by a country. Otherwise, a war of humanitarian intervention would even have to be carried out against the USA, for according to Amnesty International, capital punishment (which is practised in the USA) is a violation of human rights. We, too, would be at risk: after all, many people outside the Western world fail to understand why in our society hundreds of thousands of people to whom we owe the most are kept in isolation in 'special isolation centres' as soon as they have reached the age of 80 and require nursing care. Hence the oft-used definition of a reason for definition as a "reason for people's abhorrence" might not be so good after all – not even for us. And I am assuming that the definition sought cannot be a culturally related one.

The definition of a reason for intervention put forward by one of the most commonly quoted writers on Humanitarian Intervention theory as a situation inviting "transboundary [forcible] ... help, provided by governments to individuals in another state who are being denied basic human rights and who themselves would be rationally willing to revolt against their oppressive governments" (Fernando R. Tesón: *Humanitarian Intervention: An Inquiry into Law and Morality*, p. 5) is probably also unusable since it declares the overwhelming majority of states in the world to be precipitators of intervention.

The question is, how serious must violations of human rights be in order to justify intervention?

5.5 In my 1999 paper on the Kosovo-war, I simply ignored this question. The "Kosovo Dimension" was sufficient, ran my answer. By this I meant the scale of those crimes against humanity "which we were made to believe caused NATO to intervene in the Kosovo crisis", i.e. all the massacres, organized rape, mass expulsions etc. listed by the USA and other states as the reasons for their intervention. Let us refer to the scale of these reported crimes in the following as the Kosovo Dimension (which is already referred to in criterion (i) (a)).

A HMI is only allowed/justified if:

(i) (a) The aim is to end etc. massive crimes against humanity ($\geq$ "Kosovo Dimension")

5.6 I believe that last in 1999 many other interventionists used the same "Kosovo Dimension is sufficient" solution to circumvent the issue. That this is no longer possible, as a number of questions of general importance and on the actual facts have since cropped up. Let us start off with the general questions, or at least with some questions which are more general.

The question is not whether the thus defined Kosovo Dimension corresponded to the facts. I shall simply continue to assume this. The two most important questions of general intervention assessment relevance are then:

(α) Is criterion (i) (a) perhaps *too strong*? Must massive crimes really assume this Kosovo Dimension before intervention can take place?

And vice versa:

(β) Was the willingness of NATO (and many of us) to intervene somewhat premature? Was the "Kosovo Dimension" really enough to cross the critical threshold necessary for Humanitarian Military Intervention to be be obligatory / permissible? In other words, is criterion (i) (a) perhaps *too weak*?

Even if formulated clearly, these questions are ticklish. This is why they are almost never asked. Nevertheless, they have to be asked, since the lives of thousands of people on all sides involved depend on the answer (unless of course NATO's high-tech is used). Can we simply skirt around clarifying these questions?

At exactly what point do violations of human rights become so bad that intervention is obligatory? And if you're not keen on the word 'exact' here and would rather avoid precisely determining this grey area, at what point is intervention unquestionably required? (At this point you will, as some of you will already have realised, have simply repeated the initial question, but this only serves to make the two questions appear all the more urgent.)

5.7 At this point we should mention something which perhaps should already have been said a while ago. Regardless of where the intervention threshold is to be drawn, the scale of the crimes addressed by these considerations is such that our question appears inappropriate. At what point are crimes against human life and human dignity so bad that action may be taken against the criminals responsible? This sounds as if whether the opposite might also be allowed were a moot question. But this is not and must not be allowed to be the case.

Hence the following should now apply to Humanitarian Intervention Wars: they are only allowed if they are also obligatory; in a nutshell, if being allowed and being obligatory coincide.

(A=O) HMIs are allowed iff they are morally obligatory

5.8 Note that no formal problems result from this (A=O) postulate. After all, the equivalence:

(A=O)* Allowed (p) = Obligatory (p)

can always be made true by means of interpretation structures in which there is exactly one deontically perfect world. In such a structure, the following holds: If X holds in least one deontically perfect world (X is allowed), X holds in all deontically perfect worlds (X is thus obligatory) – and vice versa.

5.9 By contrast, the (A=O) postulate may prove problematic in terms of content. One objection could run as follows: Assume two exclusive alternatives X1 and X2 are equally good. Since they cannot both be implemented, both X1 and X2 cannot be obligatoy. However, owing to (A=O) neither of them would be allowed. But this (runs the objection) is plainly counter-intuitive. There is doubtless something in this general objection geared towards the structure of the principle. However, it fails to take into account that if a Humanitarian Intervention War has two equally good alternatives, this war is not the last possible means (hence violating (i) (b)) – and is thus neither obligatory nor 'merely' allowed. The "possibly two equally good alternatives" premise of this objection is not fulfilled for allowed/obligatory Humanitarian Intervention Wars.

5.10 Although the (A=O) postulate doesn't help particularise the intervention threshold, it still delivers something important: namely, a metacriterion for the adequacy of each such particularisation. One conclusion of the postulate is namely:

> HMIs are only allowed if the violations of human rights to be ended are so appalling that a military intervention as response to them is obligatory.

Note, however, that this doesn't rescind the other intervention presupposition (i) (b), according to which such an intervention may only be the *ultima ratio*. It thus continues to hold that a Humanitarian Military Intervention is not allowed if other permissible alternatives exist.

5.11 However, let's not avoid even tortuous problems (even if analytica philosophers are especially inclined to do so). How awful do crimes have to be for war to be obligatory as the *ultima ratio*?

This is a question which has been avoided by more than just analytical and other good philosophers. It has also been sidestepped by those who decide over whether to fight or not to fight, or (to take into account the German contribution in 1999, and also possibly the year before) those who share responsibility for such decisions.

Everyone knows the easiest way of rhetorically concealing such evasions. Instead of answering the difficult question, you answer a much simpler one with the strongest possible answer imaginable. Let me repeat the question it all boils down to: How bad must crimes be for war to be obligatory as the last possible means? The ultimate answer in 1999 was "Auschwitz". As a paradigm for a humanitarian worst case in which the question of war is anyway only hypothetical, this answer would have been correct. (This is precisely how I myself argued in my first quick attempt at justification; see § 1.5 above.) Yet as threshold justification for NATO attack? In this case, the attack should definitely never have taken place. However, this example of Auschwitz instrumentalisation wasn't meant quite like that.

Claude Lanzmann, the French director of the film *Shoah*, put this very aptly in an interview: "These ... references to the Holocaust are a way of muzzling all discussion. Talking forbidden! Argument over!" (Tariq Ali (ed.), *Masters of the Universe?* London/New York, 2000, p. xviii.)

5.12 Paradigms for justified humanitarian intervention include India's 1971 intervention in what was then East Pakistan (to put an end to the genocide of the Bengalis) and Tanzania's intervention in Uganda in 1979, which ended the massacres carried out by Idi Amin. However, with respect to the scales of the massacres which preceded them, both these interventions exceed the maximum of the "Kosovo Dimension" victims 100 times over. Moreover, India's intervention in East Pakistan is also the paradigm of justified humanitarian intervention without a mandate from the UN. By the way, the state which protested most sharply in this case against the lack of a UN mandate was the USA.

5.13 We will have to carry on tormenting ourselves for some considerable time before we can find answers to our moot questions which go beyond *ad hoc* responses. What the aforementioned research project would have to achieve is obvious: it amounts to nothing less than drawing up a scale classifying types of human rights violations by varying severity: the nightmare of the Holocaust, the genocide of the Armenians, expulsions, rape camps, torture, Srebrenica, children's transports, mutilations, etc. etc. – the almost endless list of all the dreadful things mankind is capable of doing.

5.14 However, even drawing up a scale of *Homo sapiens'* negative potential of species still fails to address a classification scale for the intervention obligation. What factors need to be taken into account when weighting the intervention obligation borne by outsiders? Other things being equal (for example assuming the same military potential), is it those who are closest who are most obliged to intervene? But does 'closest' mean geographically closest, or members of the same culture or religion? A nation who speaks the same language? Or should all intervention armies be mixed to prevent further escalation? And should the members of such campaigns be restricted to volunteers, or may conscripts also be sent? Or alternatively, are only the very best fighters, usually mercenaries, good enough for these humanitarian purposes?

5.15 The most important question of all is who should decide all this? When it comes to asserting universal questions of human rights by means of military force, what sort of decision-making procedures are permissible? Should all these questions only be left up to Washington, Moscow and Beijing? Or perhaps the organisations of states of the continent concerned, e.g. the OSCE?

5.16 And what needs to be done to prevent something which totally contradicts the basic universalistic idea of the moral/intellectual software thus conceived for these 'human rights wars' being built into them in the first place, namely the chip which sets off the great mutual Humanitarian Intervention War, the 'clash of cultures'?

5.17 These and similar questions will keep philosophers busy over the coming decades if humanitarian human rights wars become the strategy of the future. They arc at any rate the Pentagon's future strategy. The recent attempts at restructuring of NATO and the German Armed Forces follow the same concept. Now that NATO and the German Armed Forces have officially abandoned their strict defence character without even a hint of public discussion, another semantic correction would soon be in order: ministries of defence would have to be renamed ministries of intervention. I mean ministries of humanitarian intervention, of course.

If this is to be the future, you don't need to be a prophet to predict that the need for humanitarian intervention experts will spawn a growth sector in practical philosophy. In fact this need already exists; this is one of my core sentences today.

5.18 But let us return to the present. Was NATO's Kovosov-intervention okay? As far as this question is concerned, we are still dealing with the first step, with criterion (i) (a) – the humanitarian intervention presupposition. And to be honest, we're not making much headway.

So let's ask again. Assuming there really had been no alternative, given the Kosovo Dimension, was NATO's intervention really obligatory/permissible?

6. *The "Kosovo Dimension" vs. the Kosovo Dimension*

6.1 To be able to tackle this question, we need to know one thing right from the start: how big was the "Kosovo Dimension"? What exactly does it comprise? Assuming it really was this factor which tipped the scales, what prompted former Spanish anti-NATO activist Javier Solana on 24 March 1999 in the role of NATO's Secretary General to order the attack on Yugoslavia?

This may not be an easy question to answer. Nevertheless, it's still the easiest of my long list of questions. As we have already seen, not everything counts which may have been decisive: only the humanitarian aspect is relevant for determining the "Kosovo Dimension" at the time – in other words the essence of the reports which then (and now) filled us with such revulsion. This dimension is easy to verify, since the reports still exist.

6.2 Assuming these reports were correct, were we really obliged to attack? The attitude "We cannot simply stand by and watch" is a matter of course in reaction to such humanitarian disasters. But this by no means justifies war – not by a long chalk. However, we'll not change the subject like everyone else seems to, but repeat the question: With the benefit of hindsight, was the "Kosovo Dimension" on a scale justifying Humanitarian Interventions? In other words, applying the universilisability postulate and allowed-iff-obligatory postulate, something which – other things being equal – would need to be done in other cases on the same scale?

Let's assume it was. This would then have had consequences – including (to name just one of the weakest ones) this: Supposing in all cases in which a) the "Kosovo Dimension" was also reached and possibly greatly exceeded, b) we were in no lesser a position to intervene, c) this intervention did not require a Humanitarian Intervention War or any other type of military campaign whatsoever, and d) all other emergency assistance legitimacy conditions (with the exception of (ii) (d)) would easily be met anyway – where would we be in such a case? At the very least forced to provide some justification. You all know that such cases are far from just hypothetical. Just think of Turkish Kurdistan. What are the arguments here? And do these arguments stand up to closer analysis?

The question is not one of possible explanations. A number are already emerging. It boils down to justifying why certain differences between these two cases are morally relevant. But how can they be justified?

6.3 One of the many explanations is trivial: for NATO to launch a war of Humanitarian Intervention against Turkey would be conceptually impossible – this follows from the interventionist foreign-state proviso. But wouldn't this be another argument for initiating pro-Kurdish Human Interventions? Interventions which, as we have already said, are a) (for a number of years) at least relevant and necessary compared to the Kosovo Dimension, b) are incomparably easier to carry out, c) would not involve any military action whatsoever on our part, and d) would optimally meet all claims of legitimacy required for emergency aid.

There are plenty of other similar cases. The US president could have relaxed the economic boycott against Iraq at a stroke – and the lives of some 300,000 children would have been saved.

6.4 This inconsistency argument does not argue *per se* against the legitimacy of NATO's Kosovo intervention. If intervention is really obligatory at three different places, it is always better to carry out intervention at one place at least rather than none at all. But this raises a new problem of justification. What factors argued *ex ante* for intervening at the place where intervention was the most risky? How does this disappear *ex post*? What rule justifies these differences? Are interventions more moral the riskier they are – riskier for everyone up to the point of jeopardising world peace? Do military interventions really always take priority?

We're not stupid. We know that international politics involves a wealth of other factors alongside morality. There are economic interests, superpower ambitions and forces, exactly timed diversions of attention, and thousands of other factors. The only crucial question is whether all these things together are allowed to make a difference? The moral difference between a stroke of the pen and 37,000 air raids?

6.5 How bad was the "Kosovo Dimension"? The cause of military intervention, does it still stand up to our moral analysis? After all, the "Kosovo

Dimension" always meant the dimension we were made to believe by the media to be genuine.

But was it? This is certainly not irrelevant for the *ex post* assessment of the NATO intervention. How can it be verified? What channels can be used to find out – CNN, ZDF, TV Belgrade, UCK pirate broadcasters, Zet-Net, Human Rights Watch? It quickly emerges that our entire philosophical problems with verification and falsification, testing hypotheses, coherence presumptions and whatever geared towards the scientific community are a piece of cake compared to those encountered when we try to find out the 'truth' about the actual dimensions of our real world. These are thus problems which at the moment are even too big for me.

But there is one area in which nearly all the serious sources agree. As far as the number of dead is concerned, the actual Kosovo Dimension was about a tenth of the "Kosovo Dimension" portrayed in the media. This indicates that when we are considering Humanitarian Intervention War, we should be at least three times more sceptical than we were in 1999. But as we know from experience, this advice has never yet been followed.

Are there any more questions regarding criterion (i) (a)? Of the above-mentioned three major DFG-research programmes, this criterion would occupy a whole programme by itself. The main question "Was the Kosovo Dimension a reason for an Intervention War?" will doubtless continue to dog us for a while yet.

What about the other criteria? Re: (i) (b): Alternatives? Permissible alternatives to do what? To carry out air raids? Certainly. To carry out any form of military intervention? I don't know.

7. *Criterion (ii) (a)*

A HMI is only allowed/justified if:

(ii) the manner of intervention (a) serves the purpose of intervention

7.1 The purpose of intervention? Well, any action can have many different aims. And the action concerned may help achieve some of these aims but not the others. This also holds for interventions, irrespective of whether they are humanitarian. *The* aim of an action usually doesn't exist, unless one means either the overall goal of the action, i.e. the sum of all the aims, or the primary goal, i.e. the reason for which the actor performs the action in the first place, with the other aims for their part only being means to reach this primary aim.

7.2 Criterion (ii) (a) focuses exclusively on the aim which makes the Intervention War a Humanitarian Intervention – the prevention of those massive violations of human rights whose problems of scale we have just tackled. And this goal need not be the same as the overall aim of the intervention – for why should not such a huge action (with so many actors involved) also be combined with other aims? And this aim needs not even to be the primary one.

7.3 In a Humanitarian Intervention War, must the humanitarian aim also be the primary one in order for such an intervention to be morally okay? No, it need not. This is not even required of simpler aid actions – at least when we are assessing the action, not the actor. Suppose a child is locked in a burning house. If a somebody rescues the child, even though their sole aim is to become a hero, such supplementary aims do not worry us as long as the child is rescued, even if they were primary aims for the rescuer. Rescue, whatever the motives, is still better than no rescue.

With respect to the NATO intervention, contrary to the popular game of speculation about all the possible aims and motives possibly associated with it, I will simply have to leave them aside. Moreover, speculation simply diverts attention away from the central questions.

7.4 And they include, even though it still belongs to the preliminary clarification, this: Supposing an intervention had certain positive effects which had not originally been intended? The response is clear: although these consequences cannot be attributed to the actor, they remain associated with the action, which in this respect was also positive. Hence, even if it is difficult to imagine, suppose (rather counterfactually) that NATO had bombed bridges in the Vojvodina, i.e. far in the north of the rest of Yugoslavia, and that these bombardments in the north had actually stopped (in some way or other) the expulsions in Kosovo right in the south of the country, yet NATO's aim was not the latter, but rather – well, it doesn't matter what it was. How should the intervention then be assessed with respect to these humanitarian consequences (and for the time being simply ignoring all the others)? This is no different from the case of a child trapped in a burning house who is only saved because a burglar who just broken in had managed to crack the electronic locks preventing the child from escaping.

7.5 Was NATO's humanitarian aerial warfare against Yugoslavia useful to its (at least thus declared) humanitarian aims? Did the bombardment of Yugoslavia day and night for 78 days minimise the "Kosovo Dimension"?

No. As far as the humanitarian aim of the intervention is concerned, the humanitarian bombs were solely counterproductive. They couldn't have been anything else. This must have been clear to all the experts right from the very start. And it was clear to the military experts. This type of intervention was counter-productive for two reasons.

Firstly, without the bombardment, the floods of refugees would not have occurred on the scale which we came to read about as the Kosovo Dimension reaching over a million people once the bombing was over. For hundreds of thousands of people in Kosovo, it was the start of bombing itself which caused them to flee their villages and across borders, and it was only when bombardment started (or to be more accurate when the OSCE observers began to be withdrawn and bombardment was announced) that the Serbian attacks escalated. This had been predictable; this escalation was for example forecast by top 'experts' such as Wesley Clark, NATO's Supreme Allied Commander Europe with a master's degree in Philosophy, Politics and Economics from Oxford University. By bombing Yugoslavia, NATO was pouring oil on the fire in Kosovo which had by no means been stirred up by the Serbs alone.

7.6 Secondly, the bombardments did not just directly contribute to the escalation of the cleansing directed against the Albanian population and hence increase rather than reduce the number of expulsions; they also helped to bring about what the intervention was allegedly supposed to prevent, namely further ethnic cleansing. Nowadays, thanks to the bombardments and the victory of the UCK they brought about, ethnic cleansing in Kosovo is largely complete – albeit the other way round. Therefore the opinion that bombardment prevented further violations of human rights is incorrect.

7.7 Nowadays, the then strategists proudly report that most of the Albanian refugees driven out of Kosovo could since have returned home. This, thank goodness, is true. But it is not an argument justifying (by way of necessity or usefulness to the aim) the bombardment. The refugees and expellees have not been 'bombed back' to their homes; it was only the cessation of bombardments and not the bombardments themselves which enabled them to return.

The air raids were not just the worst conceivable means of protection against murder and expulsion; they were totally unsuitable for bringing about this protection.

7.8 This assessment contains many premises I cannot vouch for. Too much depends on the uncertainties regarding the factual Kosovo Dimension, rather than that presented in the media. And at least as much again depends on something which previously has not been mentioned at all – on the reasons and the historical, religious and social background to the whole affair. Consider on account of all these premises my assessment to be merely something like my personal opinion. But do let me know if you have good reasons for a different assessment.

My assessment still leads me to a clear conclusion. The NATO war violated criterion (ii) (a) – it was neither permissible *ex ante* nor justifiable *ex post* given the deterioration of the situation thus caused.

7.9 NATO's air raids affected not only Kosovo but also the rest of Yugoslavia. They were not restricted to the military infrastructure. In fact this was affected least of all; the attacks were primarily aimed at destroying the country's infrastructure. And this aim was largely achieved. To what purpose? If I intend to reduce somebody's willingness to commit violence, can I achieve this aim by destroying his basis of life? Let me ask again: To what purpose? To what purpose, mark you, which could be comprehensibly associated with the allegedly primary Humanitarian Intervention aim? And to what purpose, whose necessary attainment was accompanied by the unavoidable side-effect of "collateral damage" amounting to over 500 dead, including about 80 children, into the bargain? Try as I might, I cannot find such a purpose. But perhaps someone can tell me otherwise?

8. *Re: Criterion (ii) (b)*

A HMI is only allowed/justified if:

(ii) (b) the manner of intervention minimises harm to third parties

8.1 Humanitarian Interventions are cases of emergency assistance. This was the beginning which, assuming you followed me, made us interventionists. [5] Following this start, assuming it is strictly orientated towards our starting-point (self-defence and emergency assistance), we wouldn't have to spend too much time on criterion (ii) (b). After all, the relevant section of criminal law states quite clearly who must not be harmed in the case of normal self-defence or emergency assistance: self-defence and emergency assistance may only be directed against the attacker, not third parties or their property. The well-aimed sniper's bullet against the terrorist holding hostages, if this really is the last chance of saving them, may be okay under criminal law, yet ceases to be so as soon as another innocent person is jeopardised by this bullet.

8.2 Although thoroughly acceptable under criminal law, within moral consideration (our activity here) it will be impossible to maintain this prohibition under all circumstances. At this point we ought to embark upon a process of weighing-up similar to that acted out for or against utilitarianism in any introductory seminar course. To borrow one of the most common exercises, let us assume that a terrorist has taken 20 hostages, and let us assume we are all absolutely certain that as his demands have not been met, he will blow himself up together with all the hostages in the next few seconds. Shouldn't the SAS marksman who already has his sights trained on the terrorist be allowed to fire, even if he can't completely rule out the chance of hitting an innocent passer-by who suddenly appears and strays into his line of fire? And if you hesitate, would you do the same if the terrorist had taken 50 hostages? Or what about 200? Or 1,000? These reflection games are terrible. Then again, ethics isn't supposed to be a barrel of laughs.

8.3 The Kosovo Dimension easily outweighs all bank-robber scenarios. Those who in view of this scale of difference accept a Humanitarian Intervention War as I have defined it as a prima-facie option have already made up their minds. For moral reasons they are willing to overstep the bounds of what (in related contexts) is permissible under criminal law. We are thus entering a field where what is forbidden by criminal law is morally allowed. Intervention Wars which do not jeopardise external parties simply do not exist. Even Intervention Wars with the highest of humanitarian intentions are no exception. It's impossible to approve of Humanitarian Interventions and at the same time to rule out others being put at risk.

8.4 This certainly doesn't mean that the greater the horror the Humanitarian Intervention is supposed to combat, the less careful we need to be about putting innocent parties at risk. Students of intervention ethics will have to tackle tortuous questions such as the degree to which a link nevertheless exists between the necessary struggle against the intervention precipitator and the risk to outsiders. Human shields tied to attacking tanks, workers at factories important to the war effort – these are the sorts of cases which need to be examined more closely in connection with this question.

8.5 However, we don't need this discussion for the first NATO war. At least not if you share the view that the air raids were not a means which served the humanitarian purpose – for there was no need for the "collateral damage".

9. *Closing remarks*

9.1 Even if the actual Kosovo Dimension matched the "Kosovo Dimension" in the media which was accepted by us (at least accepted in spring 1999) as a good reason for intervention – i.e. the *causa iusta* actually existed, this *causa* actually corresponded to the intention of the intervening agents, and that in addition there was no genuine alternative – even given all these assumptions, in my view the manner of the intervention contravened the central rules of the *ius in bello* and must therefore be condemned.

9.2 I hardly paid any attention to questions of international law in my paper. This isn't because these questions are unimportant for intervention ethics. The reason is quite simply that if something is already forbidden for moral reasons, this prohibition is not rescinded by legal legitimisation. Clarifications from the angle of international law are of course highly relevant, but this would sidestep the essence of whether this war was morally justifiable.

9.3 The discussion in Germany about the NATO war was doubtless not analytical. The actual question over whether this war is really morally permissible, i.e. really morally obligatory, has been largely ignored; in order not to ignore it, plenty of other questions (as I have tried to show) should have prompted. These questions have not been shelved. Humanitarian Interventions are still on the agenda of the USA, NATO and other states. We must ask ourselves these questions, even if they hurt. We need to tackle them with the best instruments at our minds' disposal, including analytical philosophy.

HAJO SCHMIDT

"Humanitarian Intervention": Media, Ethics and Law in the Kosovo War

1. ON THE QUESTION

Like most of the "humanitarian intervention" wars of the 1990s, NATO's war in Kosovo is also distinguished by a war-favourable extreme power asymmetry of the parties involved and the determined reversion of the western governments to morals. As effectively as both facts of the matter also knew how to ensure the loyalty of the populations of the intervening states, questions still remain: how convincing are the normative (legal ethical) justifications for the war? And how sure can we be that the super strength of the interventionists didn't come to fruition in such a way and means which violates the declared noble intention (the protection of human rights?).

During the course of the war, the second question, the quaestio facti, was extended: has indeed the conflict situation been appropriately described, is "our" involvement principally comprehensible and undisputed? The basic reason, the derived objectives and the designated means available, control at least of the basic correspondence between the declaration of principles and the actions of the interventionists – are they all medially guaranteed (so that, if necessary, the democratic sovereign can delegitimize the action of war)? Is there a serious investigation being carried out to examine the relationship between the objectives and results after the war? It is clear that the reasoning and judging publics of western democracies expect an appropriate reappraisal of both questions. I would like to justify at least the approaches for my opinions in the following,

a) why and to what extent the treatment by the media of the quaestio facti (before, during and after the war) is regarded as unsatisfactory and, directly related,
b) that and to what extent the rational reference of quaestio facti and quaestio iuris, essential to the formation of the opinions of the public and politicians, were subject to major questioning, and rebus sic stantibus seems basically neglected and, finally,
c) that and to what extent the most wide-spread lethical legal justifications of the Kosovo war seemed – and still seems – unacceptable to me.

2. MEDIA IN CONFLICT AND WAR[1]

I do not consider it an inadmissible simplification to claim that the pro-interventionist reasoning of the scientists, the political journalists and ideologists as well as the population were generally led by anything but conviction: that the violation by the NATO states against applicable international law was morally motivated, that the terrorisation of the Serbian population wasn't due to any sinister intellectual considerations. This opinion should have been energetically dealt with when the ethically highly motivating objectives were replaced and increasingly profaned – at the latest. Arresting the Serbian killing machine – implementation of "Rambouillet" – return of the expelled population – NATO credibility – punishment of Milosevic and the Serbs. This, however, is how the relinquishment of an interest-conscious and past-conscious contextualisation of the actions of the participants of the primarily moral qualification for the war increasingly granted all features of naivety (citizens, intellectuals), if not indeed culpable ignorance, unprofessionalism and hypocrisy (politicians, media system, journalists).

The suspicion expressed at an early stage that NATO's resort to war served the anticipatory confirmation of the new NATO doctrine and the associated interested debasement of UNO and OSCE was confirmed by the Washington declarations of April 1999. The obligations of reluctant partners to participate in massive military actions against the statutes of the UN enhanced the US claim for world hegemony, increased the NATO's expansions in the East, and created new opportunities of political and military control of the Eurasian continent by the West.[2]

Not only political and military reasons were behind making Kosovo into "the largest US base since Vietnam" (Jan Øberg), as this development was as useful for the continual flow of oil from the Caspian basin to the Adriatic Sea as for the control of natural resources[3] in Kosovo.[4] As economic motives for the war, the hope of lucrative reconstruction contracts, the competition between the Euro and the dollar and the fear of new (and expensive) waves of refugees were quoted. A cultural aspect also worth thinking about: for centuries, the catholic and protestant Christian regime in Serbia and Kosovo had been fighting against the undesired Slavic-orthodox variety of Christianity, in this case in the favour of an Islamic population (which could not have gone unnoticed by their Arabic oil-producing co-religionists).

That the Kosovo war could, and should, serve very different interests and interested parties within the international "community" should have been obvious; it was already conspicuous at the EU summit held in Cologne, Germany, in June 1999, which pushed qualitative arming and re-arming, i.e. the strengthening of the EU's military autonomy. For the Federal Republic of Germany, however, the Kosovo war meant a "push towards normality" from the point of view of foreign policy and military policy, yet its strengthening certainly meant economic as well as political and military hegemony power in the EU.

In his important study on the past history of the war, the former Army General, OSCE observer and historian Heinz Loquai observed "a completely uncritical take over of official government positions by the parliament and the media", with disastrous consequences for all concerned. Not only did the government act more or less without parliamentary control, "Even that non-parliamentary organ so important to democracy, the media, was largely absent. They formed a mirror-image of the parliament..., as a large coalition with all the negative consequences for the proper and objective informing of the public".[5]

Loquai sees as exemplary for the failure of the media system the treatment and acceptance of the dubious "Hufeisenplan", whose alleged disclosure of Serbian expulsion, annihilation and destruction plans functioned as a central means of official government war propaganda, although the official government presentation was characterised by considerable contradictions right from the start.[6]

The presentation and effect of this plan also give me cause to point out dubious political and secret service propaganda activities on the effect of now well-known (usually Anglo-American) concerns specialised in war

PR who gave their all to sell to the media the idea that their clients' activities were impeccable, and that those of the other side were unacceptable or even criminal.

It is thus that the PR agency Ruder Finn, paid by Croatia, Bosnia and Herzegovina and the "Republic of Kosovo", enjoyed its "greatest success... in that terms such as ethnic cleansing and concentration camps, automatically associated with Nazi terror and Auschwitz by the public, were basically linked with the Serbs"[7]. Finn's massive campaign condemned the relevant Serbian PR agencies to widespread failure, in so far as "a deep-rooted negative image had to be changed into a positive one, which makes the research into national image demonstrably more unequally evaluated than vice versa".[8]

Even without the aspect of current war propaganda well known to a larger audience since the second Gulf War and MacArthur's book "*The Battle of Lies*" things didn't look good for Serbia concerning western war dialogue. A media system associated with the economy and ideology of the NATO states, i.e. of a warring party, managed, at international level and almost without any opposition, to carry through a conflict scenario which, as a struggle of the Milosevic totalitarian regime against the human rights democracies of NATO, was concise and rousing, yet anything but fair to the reality of the situation. Not only did the public, exposed to a continuous barrage of medial pressure, easily forget that a civil war had been going on in Kosovo since the emergence of the armed UCK; the media also forgot the fact that, in increasing accordance with Rambouillet, three and not two parties were pursuing a "warring" solution in the former Yugoslavia: alongside the long-since morally discredited Milosevic regime and the (US/UK-led) NATO, there was the armed faction of the Kosovon Albanians – the UCK – promoted from the status of a terror organisation to a freedom-fighting organisation by the West in mid-1998.

The resurgence of the UCK into the (pre) war events by official documents or documents only made accessible later, for example by the current general report by the parliamentary assembly of NATO (!) – "The Serbian repressions diminished under the influence of the KVM (i.e. the Kosovo Verification Mission of the OSCE – HS) between October and December 1998. However, there were no effective measures for containing the UCK. Attacks on Serbian security forces and civilians increased significantly from December 1998. The conflict escalated further to create a humanitarian crisis which would cause NATO to intervene"[9] – came late, yet in retrospect it confirms the war-favourable and artistic character of the official /

semi-official portrayal. Politics and the media changed a three-way constellation of the Serbian government, UCK and NATO suitable to deal with the conflict in a friendly way, into a dualism / antagonism of Serbs / human rights violators and NATO states / human rights advocates prepared to use force. The medial representation of the aforementioned double narrowing of views by a targeted shortage of information on the one hand, and by a one-sided selection of images of Kosovo Albanians whose human rights obviously were fundamentally hurt. on the other, produced a reliable, compassionate morally founded and stabilised anti-Serbian feeling in large sections of the population that made even formerly pacifist circles desire the beginning of the war.

Undoubtedly, the moral basis – due to Serbian actions no less than to medial constructions and political insinuations – of this parti pris of the German population did not remain unaffected by the manner of the NATO war and its consequences. However, that neither individual catastrophes nor the extent of the so-called collateral damage definitely eroded this basis is not least due to the fact that the – characteristic of military interventions – power asymmetry mutated to a moral one by the media system. "Dès le depart", according to the important dossier by Serge Halimi and Dominique Vidal, "l'asymétrie avait été théorisée: les démocraties ne pouvaient faire le mal qu'innocemment, les Serbes, collectivement coupables et collectivement sanctionnés ... le perpétraient délibérément".[10] Undoubtedly, the justifications of war criticised in the next chapter play an important role in this!

Many investigations refer to the particular problems and the precarious consequences of a concentration of the television as the main form of media in the forming of opinions by liberal democratic societies which urgently require further clarification should the fundamentals of each form of critically controlled publicity not be divulged. To name but a few themes and outcomes: the functioning of the self referring 'truth sense' eye necessarily conceals the essential contextualisation and observation directions supplied to the observer in the form of speech and writing; the limited access to television information compared to print media for analytical and reflexive political purposes are further reduced by the priority of speed ascribed to the medium; the the explosion and fragmentation of information caused by the technological development oppose the citizen's desire for knowledge and justified judgement no less than the demands for truth of the journalist profession (independent research: information check up using sources independent of each other).

Apparently, in times of continuous declarations of autonomy and authorisation of democratic sovereignty, not only knowledge and faculty for judgement but also the citizen's capacity to act are at issue. Half a century ago, the Austrian philosopher Günther Anders analysed the social consequences (as yet not generally taken as a central theme) of the introduction of new information and communication technologies and also showed that the TV system has a depoliticising individualisation effect and therefore creates the species of "mass hermits"[11] incapable of political involvement due to the isolating arrangement of the television. Paul Virilio's "dromological" studies criticised the "technical fundamentalism" of the West,[12] not least due to its "tyranny of the real time"[13] which expects too much of human processing of the news and tends towards annulling democracy. Hans Saner's criticism of the "totalitarian", non-reciprocal communication structure of the audiovisual media[14] makes one ask whether the liberal democratic publics' demand for political assessment and structuring for reasons of technological development hasn't already become obsolete.

The necessary concretisation of the above explanations with reference to the Kosovo conflict is obvious. Its fundamental / generalised aspects should have made it clear that and to what extent media-technological development processes break the ties between civic determination and judgement of the facts, which threaten to make impossible the critical and control function of a debating public. With regard to the level of individual, international and supranational democracy, contemplating counter guiding will become a decisive task both in theory and in practice if the particular potential for peace of developed democracies is to be seriously maintained.[15]

3. INTERVENTION APOLOGIA IN THE LEGAL ETHICS CRITICISM

The explanations in the above chapter allow a conclusion transcending the Kosovo war. The dangers of a systematically distorted perception of reality by the media users built in the man/media system became manifest on the one hand; a targeted shortage and selection of information in favour of a controlled construction of reality by the media on the other hand. Both tendencies threaten the political-moral formation of judgement of members and groups of liberal publics. Furthermore, doubt arises not about the principle justification, but rather about the concrete foundation of sympathetic ethical votes for war and force.

This discovery must, at least in rule of law democracies, weigh much heavier in so far as far-reaching lack of media in this position prevents the "normal citizen" from checking the analytical and normative demands of elaborate justifications for the use of force favoured in crises and times of crises by politicians and spokespeople.

A thorough public investigation would have been urgently required for reasons pertaining to international law should the NATO war against Serbia and Montenegro have unambiguously violated the ban on the use of force expressed in article no. 2(4) of the UN Charter without there having been a justifiable mandate from the Security Council for the application of legitimate sanctions or the exercise of the collective defence law according to article no. 51 of the Charter. Moreover, Germany was in danger of violating article no. 2 of the "Two plus four" agreement from 12 September 1990, whereby the "unified Germany may never use its weapons, except in accordance with its constitution and the Charter of the United Nations".[16]

The substance of the pro-interventionist international law justifications appears less than convincing to me. The cited Knut Ipsen quoted several assertions which may legitimise NATO and Germany's entry into war from the standpoint of international law, and two of them were widely supported. Namely, one of them would decisively and basically reject the emphasised interpretation of the violation of article no. 2(4) of the UN Charter regarding the equal status of peace keeping, protection of international security and respect of human rights as the objectives of the UN Charter. On the other hand, the war could be justified by the character of emergency assistance /state of emergency, transcending the law. Both assertions provoke massive protests.

Relating to that which affects the alleged equal status of human rights in the catalogue of UN objectives and the latest developments of new interpretations taken into account from article no. 2(4) of the UN Charter, Michael Bothe and Bernd Martenczuk have reminded us – convincingly in my opinion – that the formulation of article no. 2(4) of the UN Charter reinforces the ban on the use of force, yet not any loopholes – and that an appeal to the increasing esteem of human rights in international law should not open up the use of military force.[17] Furthermore, it seems to me that neither the text in article no. 1 of the UN Charter – with the sequence "World Peace" (no. 1) before "Human Rights" (no. 3) – nor the discussion about "humanitarian intervention" in the UN Security Council of the 1990s, which militarily sanctioned the massive violations of human rights as (threatening) attacks on peace and international security, convincingly supported Ipsen's claims on a current equal status of human rights with the two other quoted legal properties.

The stance of the federal government of Germany, amongst others, was based on Ipsen's second position. Generally, one refers to the case that a legally "protected top quality commodity can only be protected from violation or destruction by the violation of another legal provision". That violations of human rights on a massive scale qua "ethnic cleansing" represent such a violation of a top quality commodity ensure that it is generally agreed that military acts of force, concludes Ipsen, could "then be at least justified against the perpetrators of this said ethnic cleansing, violating the ban on the use of force as self-defence, should ethnic cleansing not have been avoidable using a means underneath this threshold".[18]

It is one of the weaknesses of this and comparable arguments to leave it unclear as to how such proof should be obtained. At least such an ultima-ratio argumentation must deal with the accusations that the NATO states neither carried out the disputes in the Security Council nor were capable of putting into place the number of OSCE observers negotiated with Milosevic intended for peace-keeping missions in the region and also, related to this, the affirmed accusation that the intervening states were either not wiling or not in the position to stop the activities of the UCK.[19]

Yet, to acknowledge the mainstay of the argument, whom was the emergency aid to help, whose threats were to be repulsed – if those in danger in Kosovo were afraid for their lives, yet the bombs landed in Serbia? If these bombs evidently only made the majority of those frightened for their lives, whose life was it that NATO's military actions were supposed to be saving?

Let's leave it at that. The public in the Federal Republic of Germany appears to have been less interested in the precise legal foundations of the Kosovo war than one appeared to have had the sufficient "moral" in order to secure or substitute disputable legal titles (e.g. "humanitarian intervention", self-defence).

In Germany, the comparison with Auschwitz played a special role – an (as it soon emerged) ethical overkill whose influence, however, could not fail to affect even a critical public. For, on the one hand, and not only due to media reports, it helped to stabilize the extremely understandable anger directed at the Serbian "dictator" and to maintain a low level of sympathy for the Serbian population. On the other hand, it legitimised a military campaign which promised the reunified Germany an unexpected military and foreign policy flexibility ("normality") and its population a (partial) pardon for its national socialist past: a moral driving force with promise for the future which serves political reasoning and the subconscious of the public equally. As the factual intolerability of these accusations must have been obvious to many of those responsible before and at the beginning of the attacks[20], it would appear crucial of the alleged particular peace potential of democratic systems from an ethical point of view to prevent such a manipulation of the public by their leaders by way of improved institutions for clarification and energetic sanctions.

Mutatis mutandis also affects the accusation of genocide. The accusation – apparently confirmed by the shocking images of Kosovon Albanian refuges and those expelled along with political and medial permanent rumours – increased the inclination of even the non-German public and politicians to speak of a "justified war", with the emphasis on "justified grounds" (genocide, at least gravest violations of human rights by the Serbs) pushing to the background the weakness of a further central war legitimisation item, that is of the legitimate leadership (legitima potestas).

However, since the doctrine of the legitimate war, should one take it seriously as an ethical theory, always has at the ready a (historically variable) number of criteria to legitimise war, whose cumulative fulfilment makes a war "justified", it could not fail to happen that, with reference to the non-fulfilment of individual or several criteria, the war in Kosovo was disqualified in the name of the same ethical teachings.

Not only the almost impossible to solve problem of the determination of a sufficient number as well as – even more importantly – the convincing operability of the legitimisation criteria, make the rejection of this political ethics – claiming to identify certain wars as "just" ones – seem advised (not, however, on the ethical judgement criteria of war and warring measures worked out in this tradition). The Kosovo war showed that the technological development above all makes the "just war" talk referring to "humanitarian interventions" ideological. The same technological superiority encouraging the alliance to the war with its noble objectives led to the mass violation of the ius in bello[21], including its central principle of immunity, which strictly forbids the deliberate killing of innocent people. There may therefore be no doubt that the morally justified war encouraging material and logistical considerations of the NATO states are due to technical developments which progressively exhaust the principles of the ethics they claimed to abide by as well as the applicable humanitarian international law.

Western supporters of war must fall back neither on the motive of preventable genocide nor on the theorem of the justified war if the character of NATO as a community defending values seems to them to indicate the need for moral action. That a stock of joint convictions of value, worthy of being unconditionally defended, connects the constitutions of most of the member states of NATO, i.e. the protection of the dignity of each and every individual as well as democratic and lawful responsible governing – will also be acknowledged by those who reject the wide-reaching reconstruction of NATO from a territory defence alliance to one of an alliance which defends interests. In the smouldering dispute about publicly reputable values and public-shy interests, there is always the danger of the splitting of the highly-esteemed values of their supporters. Therefore, if NATO spends weeks flying missions to the existential disadvantage of those it is supposed to be urgently helping, then such a conduct may find its explanation in the fact that it is defending the values of the military alliance without offering any concrete help to human beings in need!

"In defending values", the conservative philosopher Robert Spaemann gets to the heart of the argumentative deficiency of a value ethics in support of war, "human beings can drop by the wayside. In order to fight against the "unworthiness" of expulsion, it is not a matter of who is being helped in the long run".[22] No less disturbing: as the value of values, i.e. their worth, endures independently of concrete actions, then, vice versa, these actions can not be subject to any of the limits which have arisen from this value: "The struggle for values can be… continued as long as it continues to please you". Obviously, this (pseudo) ethical outlook on values guarantees only a small degree of comfort and hope to those who are the recipients and victims of military defence measures.

That the "ideology-critical suspicion" also discernible in Spaemann, that the universal war justification means of NATO states conceals particular interests in case the Kosovo war amounts to nothing, is one of the insinuations worthy of investigation in the well-known pro-interventionist comment of Jürgen Habermas'[23], Habermas' plea to judge the Kosovo war as a legitimate peace project of "legal pacifism" (!) in the sense of the implementation of a cosmopolitan condition of generally assured law, astonishingly rejects a discourse ethical stance. It would have been systematically interesting how a discourse ethics which elevates the symmetry conditions and expectations of reciprocity of communicative actions to the valid foundations of moral discourses and practices deals with a situation in which one party refuses discourse or in which this party's access to discourse is denied. However, the "Serbs" – i.e. government, opposition, population, perpetrators and victims alike – do not even come up as the subjects of moral discourse in the text! Instead of discourse ethical elements, elements of the philosophy of history characterise Habermas' main argument.

According to Habermas, the cosmopolitan condition which the NATO states were allegedly striving to attain, demands neither a global government nor a true global monopoly on force. "Yet at least a functioning Security Council is needed, the binding legal practice of an international court of justice and the completion of the general assembly of governmental representatives by the "second level" of a representation of the citizens of the world".[24] As the institutional design of the cosmopolitan condition complained about here is only frail, and as the human rights / cosmopolitan rights are still as yet "under-institutionalised", NATO could only morally legitimise its military legal anticipation, i.e. its emergency assistance measures in Kosovo; however, with the intention of converting this human rights moral into substantive law and prescribed procedure as soon as possible in order to principally prevent a moral-violent charging of future disputes about human rights.

The philosophy of history elevation of the NATO aerial war could provoke double criticism. Of course, it is possible to see an up-dating of the best explanatory traditions in Habermas' high expectations of an institutional framework for a cosmopolitan society worthy of defending, in which the Kantian vision of globally assured human rights become reality. These trains of thought have, through developments in international law, doubtlessly maintained institutional foundations which are open to a further development in the direction indicated by Habermas. However, making the NATO states which are severing their ties with this development to guarantors and motors of this development, and making this insinuation to an ethical-legal justification of their intervention, is a pure petitio principii!

At the same time, however, it appears that the philosophy of history dimensioning of the outlined argument tempts one towards an underestimation of the primary and essential function for assuring peace – and the appropriate ability for assuring peace! – of existing international law. This defence also affects the usual criticism aimed towards the – certainly highly problematic and requiring improvement – right of veto as part of the UN system if it means that it only serves selfish, often ethically unacceptable interests of the privileged veto powers. This criticism underestimates – and this must be an important lesson of the Kosovo conflict – that the states exercising their veto can have extremely justified doubts in the motives of the states and alliances affected by vetoes. In case of doubt, this dubious instrument may also prevent a world war: which responsible German politician could have ruled out the use of atomic weapons by an internally destabilised Russia humiliated in her foreign policy should the Russian special envoy have been the victim of NATO rockets instead of three Chinese embassy staff?!

4 SUMMARY / OUTLOOK

The aforementioned ethical-legal criticism surely does not remove all possibilities of an ethical justification of war of war. An ethics of peace working with Kantian trains of thought and the tradition of the just war may continue to represent the protection of nations from massive violations of human rights as a matter of priority, without deteriorating into the shimmering double ideology which achieves validity in the term "humanitarian intervention". It could continue to use the irreplaceable inspection catalogue of the bellum-iustum doctrine in order to clearly present its peaceful intention inter-subjectively in a manner that could be inspected, without making a new claim on "just war", (yet occasionally on a justified use of military force).

The presented ethical-legal considerations, associated with a critical end result of the success of the Kosovo war – which can be summed up in the conclusion that in the Spring of 2002 around the same number of Serbs, Jews and Romanies were prevented (by violence if necessary) from returning to their homes in Kosovo, as the Kosovon Albanians before the war – formulate a massive objection against the opinion on the Kosovo war held by the governments of the alliance as one of a model case of successfully solved crisis, future-looking for the strategy and arming of the NATO and EU military. They can also be used as a normative foil for a resolution of conflicts by using less force and whose institutional requirements: expansion of the UN system in a democratic-rule of law meaning, a transfer of significant financial and personal resources for the good of the institutions and ways of solving conflicts which do not include military measures; eventually, the promotion of a democratic media system more inclined towards peace.

NOTES

[1] The following criticism of the media, which in my opinion is indispensable as part of an ethical reflexion of war, corresponds widely to my statements in: Gerhard Beestermöller (ed.): Die humanitäre Intervention – Imperativ der Menschenrechtsidee? Rechtsethische Reflexionen am Beispiel des Kosovo-Krieges, Stuttgart, chapter 2.3 (not yet published).

[2] Cf. the study by Johan Galtung: "Die NATO-Osterweiterung oder: Der Beginn des Zweiten Kalten Krieges", in his book: Die andere Globalisierung, Münster 1998, pp. 68-80, but as well the geostrategic specifications by the "realist" and former national security adviser of US-President Carter, Zbgniew Brzezinski ("The continuing of America's hegemony depends on how long and how effectively it can master itself in Eurasia"), in his book: Die einzige Weltmacht, 1997.

[3] In the context of Mitrovica, which has been taken on by international missions, Jan Øberg speaks of "allegedly Europe's biggest concentration of mineral resources" ("Post-Milosevic dilemmas – and an imagined way out". Pressinfo # 103, p. 3: www.transnational.org/pressinf/2000/pf 103).

[4] Øberg places this interest within a larger framework of power interest: "Kosovo could be used within a much larger policy framework related to the Balkan's strategic role, containment of Russia, access to and control of oil pipelines from the Caucasus and the expansion of NATO and of German influence in the East and South East of Europe." (op. cit, p. 2).

[5] Loquai, H.: Der Kosovo-Konflikt – Wege in einen vermeidbaren Krieg. Die Zeit von Ende November 1997 bis März 1999, Baden-Baden 2000, p. 157. The analysis of 190 editorials of leading German daily papers (Die Welt, Frankfurter Allgemeine Zeitung, Süddeutsche Zeitung, Frankfurter Rundschau und Tageszeitung) done by researchers of the Wissenschaftszentrum Berlin confirms this statement impressively. Some of the summaries: "Neither a redefinition of Germany's role and the one of NATO nor the official explanation for the intervention and the profile of the political problem generate intensive discussions... The discourse short-circuited ... questions concerning the vital expediency and legitimacy of the war. The problem of the mission's coverage by international law remained largely excluded. To the extent in which the media concentrate on the strategic aspects of the war, they fail as speakers for the question of legitimacy and negative consequences of the operation, which played only a marginal role in the parliamentary discourse." (WZB-Mitteilungen, Heft 89/September 2000, p. 4f.)

[6] Loquai's sober analysis provides a stock-taking ot the contradictions and inconsistencies of the plan (op. cit, pp. 138-144. His concluding statement combines the criticism of politicians and that of the media: "There is a connection between the massacre of Racak and the 'Hufeisenplan'. The Head of the KVM, Walker, sparked the fuse with his unproven version of Racak which led to war against Yugoslavia. The German Minister of Defense, Scharping, extinguished the criticism against the war by means of this plan. Both accusations were regarded as true, though doubts would have been advisable and thus could fulfill their purpose". (p. 144) Loquai himself regards the plan as fiction, but on no account as a real plan of operation by the military and political

leadership of Yugoslavia. (158) The up-to-dateness of this assessment was supported by a TV-documentary (Monitor, Feb. 8, 2001: "It started with a lie"), by Jo Angerer and Matthias Werth. The manuscript of the transmission is available on the Internet: www.wdr.de/online/news/kosovoluege. Regarding the 'Hufeisenplan', cf. op.cit, p. 11ff.)

[7] Statement by Karl Unger in an informative radio review from November 10th, 1999 ("Das Gerücht als Waffe – Die Rolle der Medien im Kosovo-Krieg", Sendemanuskript des Hörfunk WDR 3, p. 3), which alleges to the publication: La NATO nei Balcani, Rome 1999, p. 74.

[8] Mira Beham: "Der Informationskrieg um das Kosovo", in: Sicherheit und Frieden 3/2000, p. 221.

[9] Quoted after Lutz: "Krieg nach Gefühl", in: Freitag 51/2000; manuscript available under: www.Freitag.de/2000/51/00510701.htm

[10] "Médias et désinformation. Lecons d'une guerre", in: Le Monde diplomatique, Mars 2000, p. 13f, here p. 14.

[11] Die Antiquiertheit des Menschen, vol. 2: Über die Zerstörung des Lebens im Zeitalter der dritten industriellen Revolution, München, 3rd edition, 1984, p. 90.

[12] Paul Virilio: Revolutionen der Geschwindigkeit, Berlin 1993, p. 15f.

[13] Paul Virilio: Krieg und Fernsehen, München/Wien 1993, p. 142, cfr. 48f, 63.

[14] "Die Symbolokratie als neue Herrschaftsform", in: Saner, Hans: Macht und Ohnmacht der Symbole, Basel 1993, here p. 255.

[15] According to Johan Galtung's convincing criticism of continual bellicism within democracies, one should adhere to their (self-) pacifying potential. Galtung's criticism does not consider itself as a denial to the peaceful possibilities of democracies, but as a warning against their disdainfulness which can be attributed to their historical success.

[16] Quoted after Knut Ipsen: "Der Kosovo-Einsatz – Illegal? Gerechtfertigt? Entschuldbar?" in: Die Friedenswarte 74/1999, no. 1-2, p. 19), who, in addition, refers to the fact that Germany in the present case would be part of a war of aggression according to Art. 26, para.1 of the Constitution. According to para. 80 of the penal code the preparation of an act of aggression constitutes a crime.

[17] "Die NATO und die Vereinten Nationen nach dem Kosovo-Konflikt. Eine völkerrechtliche Standortbestimmung", in: Vereinte Nationen 47/1999, no. 4, p. 129, footnote 29.

[18] Op. cit. (footnote 16), p. 22f.

[19] Cf. the report of NATO's parliamentary assembly, quoted above, as well as the position report by intelligence officers of the Department of Defense: "The KLA on it's part will probably continue to try to provoke the massive reactions of Serbian forces by hit-and-run-actions, hoping that these in their results will assume a level of destruction and refugees which will immediately bring about NATO airstrikes." This assumption was to prove itself right.

[20] Cfr. the documents quoted by Lutz (footnote 9). An analysis by the Department of Foreign Affairs announces on March 19th, 1999 that the different population groups in Kosovo are equally affected by expulsion, eviction and destruction. "Only a few hours before the outbreak of the attack, an analysis by Department of Defense intelligence

officers declares: 'The start of a coordinated offensive by Serbian forces against the KLA in Kosovo cannot be confirmed so far.'"

[21] Not only weapons ethically hardly justifiable before the humanitarian international law are mentioned here (cluster bombs, bombs containing uranium ecc.); this is also about the character of the war as a war against the environment, as a war using chemical gases against the Serbian population. Regarding these allegations, cfr. Knut Krusewitz: "Umweltkrieg – Ökologische und Humanitäre Folgen", in: Ulrich Albrecht/Paul Schäfer (eds.): "Der Kosovo-Krieg. Fakten – Hintergründe Alternativen", Köln 1999, pp. 142-147.

[22] Robert Spaemann: "Die Verteidigung der Werte", in: Friedens-Forum, Hefte zur Friedensarbeit 13/99, no. 2-3, p. 25.

[23] First published in: Die Zeit, April 29th, 1999, reprinted in: R. Merkel (ed.): "Der Kosovo-Krieg und das Völkerrecht", Frankfurt am Main 2000, p. 51-65, here p. 59.

[24] Op. cit, p. 52.

JOHAN GALTUNG

Bombing Yugoslavia: Several Readings
Text, Supertext, Subtext, Deep Text, Context – and a Pretext (with a Posttext)

1. THE ISSUE

We cannot stand by, watching a government committing serious crimes against humanity, even genocide, on its own population.

Certainly not. The doctrine of national sovereignty, "within recognized borders", like the doctrine of *patria potesta* giving the *pater familias* a carte blanche for terror regimes within the walls of a recognized home, are cultural crimes against humanity drawing artificial borders for human solidarity, delivering the subjects to the *dominio* of what may be tyrants. The Roman law construct relating owners to whatever can be owned paved the way for such institutionalized crimes against humanity as slavery and colonialism. The problem arises when "whatever can be owned" includes human beings, for almost any definition of "ownership".

Thus, humanitarian intervention, in all such cases, coming to the assistance of human beings in distress, is a human duty, flowing from norms of solidarity with human beings everywhere, respecting no artificial borders. If action under that heading is done for such selfish goals as access to raw materials or to establish military bases, it should be known as conquest. But even with no such elements of hypocrisy, there are problems:

[1] Could the crimes have causes that could be removed without intervention, like solving an underlying conflict?

[2] Are there nonviolent alternatives to military intervention?

[3] Is the military intervention adequate for humanitarian ends, or could the "side-effect" costs even outweigh benefits?

Real, and hard, issues that have to be confronted; not standing by, watching. Intervention has today high level legitimacy.[1]

2. HUMANITARIAN INTERVENTION = HUMANITARIANISM + INTERVENTION

We are dealing with a verbal molecule, "humanitarian intervention".[2] Following the cartesian dictum of subdividing entities we explore, and the chemistry dictum of having a look at the atoms constituting a compound to get more insight into the molecule, we start with "humanitarian" and "intervention". Of course, this has to be done mindful of the fact that a whole may be more than the sum of the parts. There may be something *sui generis* we lose by this approach. The approach is certainly not sufficient. But it is necessary, even indispensable.

There is a *tradition of humanitarianism* expressed in an article by Jon M. Ebersole who played a key role in the "Mohonk Criteria for humanitarian assistance in complex emergencies".[3] The criteria, adapted by a broadly based conference, are five:[4]

[1] *Humanity*: Human suffering should be addressed wherever it is found. The dignity and rights of all victims must be respected.

[2] *Impartiality*. Humanitarian assistance should be provided without discriminating as to ethnic origin, gender, nationality, political opinions, race or religion. Relief of the suffering of individuals must be guided solely by their needs, and priority must be given the most urgent cases of distress.

[3] *Neutrality*. Humanitarian assistance should be provided without engaging in hostilities or taking sides in controversies of a political, religious or ideological nature.

[4] *Independence*. The independence of action by humanitarian agencies should not be infringed on or unduly influenced by political, military or other interests.

[5] *Empowerment*. Humanitarian assistance should strive to revitalize local institutions, enabling them to provide for the needs of the affected community. Humanitarian assistance should provide a solid first step on the continuum of emergency relief, rehabilitation, reconstruction and development.

The criteria fit into a long lasting old tradition of humanitarianism, associated with NGOs such as the Red Cross,[5] but also with states, big and small, in nature-made and in man-made disasters. The Mohonk criteria mark a news phase, as does DMTP, the Disaster Management Training Programme of the United Nations Development Programme.

But we also sense a gendering of the issue: the Mohonk criteria address suffering "wherever it is found". The trigger for action is a basic human need insulted, the need for physical well-being. According to Karol Gilligan this compassion is more frequently found among women. Men tend to be steered by other and more abstract principles, more removed from basic needs. Thus, "one prominent American expert questioned some of the basic, time-honored principles which form the basis of humanitarian action", formulating what in that perspective is a very male view:[6]

> "Impartiality and neutrality, when applied in cases such as Bosnia, can be counterproductive. For example, while giving Serbs humanitarian aid under the principle of neutrality, the United Nations has essentially legitimized the Serbs' claim that they, not the Bosnians, are victims. Furthermore, by providing the humanitarian assistance, they have freed the Serbs' resources, such as fuel and food, to supply their troops in forward areas. In many cases there are clear examples of right and wrong in international conflicts and in those the questions of impartiality and neutrality need to be examined much harder."

The abstract principles in this text are certainly old, if not necessarily time-honored: "the Serbs" as a general category, lumping all together with no distinction between perpetrators (of suffering) and "innocent victims/civilians/by-standers", and then "right and wrong". From this position there is but a small step to a distinction between worthy and unworthy victims, internally displaced person (IDPs), refugees. No general human compassion.

There is a *tradition of interventionism* today, after the Second World War, particularly associated with the USA, and before that with colonial powers in general. The general idea is to intervene militarily across borders (there are also internal military interventions), with overwhelming force, to stop violence whether [1] committed by those in power, [2] is directed against those in power or [3] is among other groups.

Stopping violence has humanitarian aspects by ending suffering from more violence. The problem is how the suffering from violence already committed is handled, and more particularly whether there is a distinction between "worthy" and "unworthy". There is, if the interventionists take sides; by definition against the violent group if there is only one, often in favor of one against other(s) if there are two are more, and in favor of themselves. The "punishment expedition" makes a very clear distinction between "right" and "wrong"; at least clear in the eyes of the intervening beholder.

Grossman[7] lists 134 military interventions by the USA for the 111 years period 1890-2001. Blum[8] lists 67 from 1945 (Grossman has 56 as the criteria are a little different), with 25 cases of bombing, 35 of attempted or successful assassinations of political leaders, 23 of perverting elections abroad. The point of gravity for all these activities has moved, in the analysis of the present author[9], from East Asia (till the mid-1970s) via Latin America (till the late 1980s) to West Asia, and then on to Central Asia. The total amount of violence, overt and covert (CIA+) is also overwhelming. If we count at least ten bereaved – next of kin, near friends – for each person killed, most of them in need of assistance and add the number of wounded, then there is certainly a case for humanitarianism in connection with these interventions.

Humanitarian intervention is located at the crossroads between these two traditions; as cross-border intervention to protect people against gross human rights violations by its own government. The problem is how it is done in political and military reality, and more particularly, which tradition prevails, humanitarianism or interventionism.

Linda Ryan, in "Narcissus Empire"[10] explores the "theaters of humanitarian intervention", gives one perspective on that reality:

> "Iraq 1991: 180 000 killed by the "international community" in the Gulf war and 80% of the country's infrastructure destroyed, at an estimated cost of $ 150 billion.
> Somalia 1993: 4000 killed by UN troops over 12 months; 700 on one night, 5 September.
> [Humanitarian prose is interesting: 'We're not inflicting pain on these fuckers,' Clinton said – 'When people kill us they should be killed in greater numbers. I believe in killing people who try to hurt you. And I can't believe we are being pushed around by these two-bit prick' (from George Stephanopoulos, *All Too Human*).]
> Iraq 1992-9: Some 500 000 dead due to lack of basic foods and medicine under the regime of economic sanctions. Raids continue.
>
> Yugoslavia 1999: 2000 civilians and 600 military personnel in NATO bombings that destroyed 44% of the country's industry."

She then quotes an exchange between a pilot and AWACS (from the US journal of International Strategic Studies Association):

"Pilot: -- Under me columns of cars, some kind of tractors. What is it? Requesting instructions.
AWACS: Do you see tanks? Repeat, where are the tanks?
Pilot: I see tractors --
AWACS: What kind of strange convoy is this? Civilians? Damn, this is all the Serbs' doing. Destroy the target.
Pilot: What should I destroy? Tractors? Repeat, I do not see any tanks. Request additional instructions.
AWACS: This is a – completely legitimate military target. Destroy the target. Repeat… destroy the target.
Pilot: Okay, copy. Launching."

In this last lethal exchange the AWACS control officer has become a victim of the West's own propaganda about the Serbs, having dehumanized them so that there are no human Serbs left. The pilot, at 3000 feet having a closer view, but is overruled and does the killing.

And with that comment the problem has been formulated.

3. A FALSE DILEMMA

Too soft humanitarianism or too hard interventionism?

The dilemma is clear: between a *too soft humanitarianism* to stay the hand of an oppressor committing crimes of war, crimes against humanity and/or genocide, and a *too hard interventionism* "by all necessary means" (UN phrasing lifted from Clausewitz) committing these crimes or bordering on them. Doing nothing is as mentioned not even an option worth discussing, coming, as it usually does, out of a disconcern, a lack of empathy with human suffering often associated with considerable social (racial, national, class, gender) distance, and steep declines in human solidarity.

We are not talking about letting Auschwitz happen by not even bombing the railtracks. But this option, "standing by, watching", is used as a contrast to military intervention, legitimizing the latter in the light of the obvious immorality, illegitimacy, even illegality of the former. Not to mention the stupidity bordering on feeblemindedness of seeing only two options. There are more.

The basic position in this paper is the refusal to be caught on the horn of this false dilemma, with its implicit or even explicit *tertium non datur*, *quartum non datur*. There are some simple reasons why. Using the terms above two categories are missing: *hard humanitarianism* and *soft interventionism*. Humanitarian assistance protected by UN peacekeeping, or simply by observers capable of reporting, are concrete operationalizations of both of them, in concrete situations. That they may not work in all cases is as little reason to throw them out as to throw out a drug that is not a cure-all. More important is to have a very broad spectrum of action/reaction options when intolerable suffering is protected by "sovereign" borders. We shall argue later that this would probably have worked in Kosovo/a.

However, there is another important approach to the *tertium*. Violence is often a symptom of conflicts badly handled. Violence may be stopped, there may be a cease-fire. But untransformed conflicts tend to erupt as violence again. And again.

This is related to a very common pattern when governments and the UN intervene: first get a ceasefire, then bring the parties together, then solve the conflict. Generally this is a major error of the cart-before-the-horse variety. A ceasefire often means victory for the status quo party: nothing has been changed, only untold suffering; usually arms are hidden for the (likely) case that no solution emerges; meeting "at the table" becomes an empty ritual. The search for a solution should be everybody's task long before violence. Parties should meet if not at the governmental, at least at the nongovernmental level. And the arms, and with them the violence, may simply wither away.

But a two-point "humanitarian interventionism" or "do nothing" discourse hides an even worse danger than ruling out the search for a creative third option. There is also the possibility that one of the two may be chosen, not because it is superior to the other as a way of addressing "human suffering – wherever it can be found", but in order to promote some other goal or goals.

Hard intervention may be chosen over soft humanitarianism because it serves other goals held by the intervening power, whether it leads to decreasing or increasing suffering. The distinction between worthy and unworthy victims is important to produce a positive moral balance (unworthy victims are not counted). And humanitarian assistance may be chosen over hard intervention to facilitate the military victory of one of the parties, with the same comment as above.

4. TEXT, SUBTEXT, SUPERTEXT, CONTEXT, PRETEXT – AND POST-TEXT.

Nobody should take a *text* lightly. The text *may* simply mean what the text says. If the text proclaims "intervention to protect people against gross human rights violations by its own government" then that may be a goal promoted and a goal valued. At least as an hypothesis about the text-author relation. But to assume that this is the only goal promoted and valued presupposes a single-mindedness against the thesis that humans can have more than one motivation for any act (Avicenna).

The problem is not mixed motives, spoken or unspoken, but

[1] whether interventionism is adequate for humanitarian goals,
[2] whether interventionism serves extra-humanitarian goals,
[3] whether extra-humanitarian goals counteract humanitarianism,
[4] whether alternatives to interventionism have been considered and tried and with what results.

We then mean by

text: conscious/spoken statement of means and humanitarian goals

subtext: conscious/hidden/internalized extra-humanitarian goals

supertext: conscious/hidden/internalized-or-not Big Power demand

deep text: subconscious/hidden/collective goals, unreflected under the 3C conditions of *crisis*, *complexity* and (need for) *consensus*
context: all the conditions in time and space, history/future and structure/culture influencing the other four texts.

pretext: when the sum of sub-, super-, deep-, con-texts predict action better than the text, then the text is (partly) pretext.

Texts are available as speeches, press releases and propaganda. Sub- and super-texts have to be inferred from leaks, past behavior, archives. Deep texts from analysis of national and elite deep culture. Context from state interests analysis.

Pretext hypotheses have to be inferred from the balance.

Deep texts may include martyrdom/narcissism/paranoia for many Serbs, and megalomaniac, invincible God/Yahweh self-images for many Americans. The context would include ex-Yugoslavia and the Balkans for Serbs, and Eastern Europe/Central Asia/"World island" geopolitics for Americans. However, this is not the place for any details about that kind of background analysis.

Interventionism takes place using texts of humanitarianism; so-called humanitarian intervention. How do we analyze? First, with an open mind. We bridge the "gap" between intentionalism and consequentialism, and between state of mind/*Gesinnung* and state of action/*Handlung*, with "both-and". Military intervention opens for *ad bellum/in bello* classical analysis, with classical criteria for the former and Geneva conventions for the latter.

The problem with *ad bellum* analysis is that it is based on a lot of ad lib hypotheses, especially for the proportionality (of the means employed relative to the evil to be abolished) thesis, and particularly if some victims are considered unworthy so that their suffering can be disregarded. But a deeper problem is that this type of cost-benefit analysis, including the *in bello* consequences/effects also calls for an evaluation relative to a corresponding analysis for the alternative(s); usually missing.

But that is also insufficient. We also need an analysis of short and long term consequences of possible extra-humanitarian goals, spoken or not, conscious or not; in humanitarian terms.

To assess NATO's bombing of Yugoslavia we need a plausible range of motives, at least one plausible alternative course of action, and plausible consequences. The first two were prepared (by this author) before that war and cannot be accused of *l'ésprit d'éscalier*; the third immediately after. Comments follow.

5. PLAUSIBLE MOTIVES FOR THE US/UK-NATO BOMBING OF YUGOSLAVIA

When two countries with a track record of being among the most belligerent countries in the world, but also among the countries most able to legitimize their belligerence, launch one more war, then we are entitled to ask for motives in the subtexts and not only for the frequently published and broadcast texts. A list:

(0) *A sincere wish to stop Serbian violence against the Kosovars and to secure for the Kosovars a safe future* (the means include acceptance of the Rambouillet *diktat* after the pain limit has been reached, withdrawal of Serbian forces, a NATO protectorate in Kosovo, safe return of the refugees, and, possibly, independence. Problems: the Rambouillet *diktat*[11] does not give the Kosovars independence, the protectorate may last long given guerrilla warfare, the Kosovars may also terrorize the population and fight among themselves, Kosovo may be close to uninhabitable. Given that the means chosen may be neither efficacious, nor efficient. The goal may be laudable, the means stupid. Could there be some other, less honorable goals that would make the means chosen look more intelligent? How to judge NATO in general, the US/UK in particular and the USA even more in particular: is it honorable but stupid, or criminal but bright?

Political motives. We see four different motives:

- *punish the Serbs* for their past action, with the two goals of punishment: individual prevention (the Serbs will never try ethnic cleansing again) and general prevention (scare others). The Iraq treatment is a model: destroy military infrastructure, and then civilian infrastructure, as it can also be used by the military (a truism). Add to this economic sanctions, and Serbian children will soon die like Iraqi children do;
- *destroy Serbia*, by at least bombing it back to 1945 when Tito started reconstruction after the Second world war; detaching from Serbia Kosovo (mineral resources, cultural identity), Vojvodina (bread basket) and Montenegro (access to Adria), leaving a small country to eke out a mediocre existence;
- *secure the Western control post for the Eurasian continent*, the Eastern post being in Japan-Taiwan-South Korea;
- *the New World Military Order*, substituting NATO/AMPO/TIAP for the UN Security Council, securing automatic US leadership for bombing Russia, North Korea, Colombia with obedient "allies".

Economic Motives:

- *Corridor 8*, the idea of a Muslim/Russian-free oil pipeline, through Georgia, from Sukhumi/Sochi to Varna/Burgos by ship, then pipeline through Bulgaria-Macedonia-Kosovo/a-Albania to

Dürres/Flora; *from the Black Sea to Adria*; used to bribe and as pressure on the British (and the Norwegians?) as it competes with North Sea oil, appealing to their interest in flow control.
- *Reconstruction contracts*, presumably proportionate to the destruction wrought. Alternative model: USA destroys, Europe pays for the reconstruction, including to US companies.
- *The very rich mines in Kosovo/a, estimated at $ 5 billion*
- *Collection of Yugoslav debt that Yugoslavia is unable to pay*

Military motives:

- *testing old and new weapons,*
- *sales promotion for old and new weapons,*
- *testing the will and capacity of NATO allies*

Cultural motives:

- *The cosmic drama: our God against theirs, whose is stronger?*
- *humiliating the enemy into submission*

And yet: Serbian resilience may very well outlast the US empire.

6. THE ALTERNATIVE: A PEACEFUL OUTCOME, A PEACEFUL PROCESS

And yet peace could be near; guided by former UN General Secretary Pérez de Cuéllar's advice to Genscher December 1991: be sure that minorities accept, that the parts of Yugoslavia are dealt with symmetrically, that there is a policy for Yugoslavia as a whole. But first a condition for a peace beyond ceasefire:

[0] *Equal recognition of the suffering and rights of all*: They are all victims, most of them more innocent than others, of a situation most nations would have found impossible. They need compassion, help; not guns and bombs. Divide them into "worthy" and "unworthy" victims, and peace becomes unattainable. They have all the same right to recognition and self-determination.

[1] *Build on the symmetry Croatia-Bosnia/1995 and Serbia/1999:*

The 650,000 Serbian refugees in Serbia were in part driven out by the Croats/USA from Kraina/Slavonia August 1995.[12] Serbian ultra-reactions included total condemnation of the international community, and "we can do the same". The Western media found little or no space for their suffering. Hence, both must be recognized as basic problems, they must all be guaranteed their safe return. And then upgrade the status of Kraina/Slavonia in Croatia, and Kosovo/a in Serbia, possibly to republic status.

[2] *A possible quadrilateral deal*: A (Croats) gives return and status to B (Serbs), B gives return/status to C (Kosovars), C gives access to mineral resources/harbors to D (Slavic Muslims) and D inclusion of the Croat part of Bosnia/Herzegovina to A.

[3] *A Yugoslav confederation*: If some autonomy is given to all minorities in Yugoslavia we end up with close to 15 parts. "Jedinstvo", a unitary or federal state, is out. But "bratstvo" as confederation of human rights respecting countries, is not.

So much for a *peace outcome*. For that to happen there has to be a *peace process*. Here are elements of a *peace process*:

[4] *The killing on all sides stops, offensive NATO/Serbia/UCK forces are withdrawn*, NATO from the Balkans; Serbian and UCK from Kosova; UN forces with OSCE observers, with a composition acceptable to all parties, and in big numbers, take over.

[5] *The UN Secretary General appoints a board of mediators known for wisdom and autonomy*, like Jimmy Carter, Pérez de Cuéllar, Mikhail Gorbachev, Nelson Mandela, Julius Nyerere, Mary Robinson, Richard von Weizsäcker for one-on-one dialogues with all parties to identify acceptable and sustainable outcome.

[6] *The UN Secretary General convenes a Conference for the Security and Cooperation in South East Europe (CSCSEE)*, with all parts of Yugoslavia, and all SE European countries as members, with points like [1]-[3] on the agenda, pending the report from the team mentioned in [5] above.

[7] *The Presidents of Slovenia and Macedonia convene a civil society conference,* using expertise in all parts of Yugoslavia, to project images of

future relations within ex-Yugoslavia, and does the same for future relations within South East Europe (in cooperation with, say, Hungary and Greece).

[8] *The peoples of Yugoslavia are invited to participate in the peace process*, forming multi-national dialogue groups all over, coming forward with concrete ideas based on local dialogues.

[9] *Reconstruction is systematically used for reconciliation* by having belligerent groups cooperating, doing the task together, not giving that enormous task away to outside entrepreneurs.

[10] *If any border has to be drawn or redrawn the principles of the Danish-German 1920 Schleswig-Holstein partition are used.*

This is for Yugoslavia in general, and in line with UN Secretary General Pérez de Cuéllar's admonition to have a policy for Yugoslavia as a whole. But 1998/1999 the focus was on Kosovo/a, so an alternative course of action has to be specific to that issue. That alternative certainly existed, presented in countless speeches and on the TRANSCEND web-site, but rejected by mainstream media before the war started 24 March 1999. There were six points dealing with violence and with conflict resolution in and around Kosovo/a:

[1] Step up the OSCE Kosovo Verification Mission (KVM) from 1,200 5-10 times to 6,000-12,000. Handies and binoculars, living in the villages, bringing in volunteers. Create a dense network.

[2] See to it that they are genuine observers, not there to identify targets for a bombing campaign, with homing devices, including human contacts.

[3] Extend the UN mandate closing the Macedonian-Kosovo border to the Albanian-Kosovo border, as the US ambassador (Gelbard) had told Beograd that the USA was of the view that KLA were terrorists – certainly also the Beograd position.

[4] Guaranteed return of all refugees and IDP to Kosovo, doing the same for Serbian refugees to Kraina, West and East Slavonia.

[5] Put republic status for Kosovo/a inside Yugoslavia (like for Montenegro) on the agenda, with a deadline for negotiating the details; including the option of independence within X years if the arrangement is found unsatisfactory (X to be negotiated). Massive UN peacekeeping forces would be necessary both places.

[6] Call a major UN Conference on Security and Cooperation in South East Europe; including the possibility of close cooperation in the Serbia-Kosovo/a-Albania triangle.

Nothing like this six-point package (the basic point is the synergy effect of the six points) was tried. The observers were ordered out and the place was made ready for bombing (although most of the bombing was in Serbia). All the elements of a plan like this was very well known to the decision-makers, no great jump was needed to put them together as is attempted done here. Not true, even a lie, that there was no alternative. There was.

7. AND WHAT WAS THE OUTCOME, THE EFFECTS, THE CONSEQUENCES?

The "Consequences of NATO's War on Yugoslavia" conference in London already on 26 June 1999 highlighted the following:

- NATO state terrorism against Yugoslavia destroyed 300 factories and refineries, 190 educational establishments, 20 hospitals, 30 clinics, 60 bridges, 5 airports;
- to the estimated 2,000 deaths (600 military) and 6,000 wounded come those who die from destruction of health infrastructure;
- only 12-15 tanks (of 300 main battle tanks) were destroyed;
- almost all destruction was to public, not private enterprises;
- the US hatred of nonaligned/neutral countries may have been a factor in targeting Yugoslavia;
- some countries join NATO as an insurance against being bombed;
- November 1998-March 1999 no evidence of ethnic cleansing in Kosovo, Germany sent back 11,000 Kosovar refugees;
- the Spanish pilot Adolfo Luis Martin de la Hoz, in *Articulo 20*, 14 June 1999: "They are destroying the country, bombing it with novel weapons, toxic nervous gases, surface mines dropped with

> parachute bombs containing uranium, black napalm, sterilization chemicals, sprayings to poison the crops and weapons of which we even still do not know anything. The North Americans are committing one of the biggest barbarities that can be committed against humanity" – he refused to bomb, so did his superior, a colonel – both removed.

This was right after the war had ended, since that time more information has been made available on the consequences. But this one is quoted here to show how consequences were seen as they unfolded, not as an afterthought much *post facto*. What was not known in advance was the US/UK bombing strategy (to a large extent from the Italian Aviana base). The texts were about precise targeting with "smart bombs" of military targets, everything else was called "collateral damage". Either the bombs cannot have been smart at all, or the damage to the civilian sector was intended, as pointed out in a famous statement by a US general.[13]

This is further elaborated by Michael Parenti.[14] And for the German involvement, there is the book by Matthias Küntzel.[15]

Consequences beyond Yugoslavia were pointed out that time:

What does this remind us of? How many years have we been set back by this war by "19 democracies" (NATO)/"democratic totalitarianism" (Zinoviev)? Possible answer: 65 years.

The parallel that comes to mind, mentioned by Solzhenitsyn, is Hitler's use of the national conflict between Sudeten/Germans and Czechs, the pressure on Czechoslovakia (with the support of England). Japan's attack on Manchuria 1931-45 and Italy's attack on Ethiopia 1935-41 were also against the Kellogg-Briand Pact of 1928 (Briand got the Nobel Peace Prize in 1926, Kellogg in 1929): 62 states, among them all major powers, agreed to renounce war as political instrument and to settle all international disputes by peaceful means. The exceptions were wars of self-defense or miliary obligations from the League Covenant, the Monroe doctrine or alliance obligations – very similar to the UN Charter Article 2(4), with exceptions.

The three dictatorships were above the law and the League, brushing all resolutions aside, lifted by their visions of a New Order. Their propaganda was as massive as the NATO propaganda with is insulting "apologies" for "collateral damage" that so obviously was intended by those on top from the very beginning. Well, the world did not have Internet at the time, that helps. But the power was on the side of those "above the law" because of a criterion of their own choice (there was probably more popular will behind what those dictatorships did than for the sneaky action by the "democracies"). The dictatorships followed up what they started: the Second world war. The USA, using NATO-AMPO-TIAP may be tempted to do the same, starting with North Korea and Colombia, to implement the New World Order.[16] And elsewhere.

8. SOME REFLECTIONS

Future historians will have much to sort out. Each point in the preceding three section can be justified, but this is not the place for that exploration. The conclusion is certainly that

[1] Motives went far beyond protecting Kosovars against genocide
[2] There was an alternative course of action
[3] The short and long term consequences were/are very negative.

The hypothesis that the text to a large extent was a pretext is strengthened. But another hypothesis can also be entertained, in no way excluding the pretext hypothesis: incompetent, left-handed, simply bad politics from beginning to end, continuing up to our days with no basic problem solved at all, with the exception of Slovenia, never much of an issue in the first run anyhow.

Below the reader will find twelve points, all of them elementary. No great knowledge is needed to state these things, and they were said by many, in one form or the other. There is nothing blindly "pro-Serbian" in these points, but an effort to correct for some of the massive Serbo-phobia found in the Western media, maybe particularly in the countries that think they lost the First world war (Habsburg Austria) and the Second world war (Nazi Germany) due to Serbian machinations and resistance rather than due to their own imperialism and stupid failure to understand the counter-forces engendered (eg., by annexing B-i-H in 1908).

But the policy in, about, above Yugoslavia was not only in the hands of suspect Austrian/German circles with their own agendas, amply documented by, for instance, Matthias Küntzel in *Der Weg in den Krieg*[17]. History may have blinded rather than enlightened them. For others there is no such excuse.

[1] *The failure to take seriously the European macro-divides, Catholic-Orthodox and Christian-Muslim*, playing with fire inside Croatia, Serbia and B-i-H, playing with fire in the near context and in the remote context; EU, Russia, Ottoman/Muslim countries; and the USA that ultimately came down on the side of the latter. To get an "anchor" in Eurasia? An oil corridor? An Osman empire?

[2] *The failure to take seriously Yugoslav divides:* the Croat spring 1971, Serbian action 1987-89, minority autonomy demands in Kraina/Slavonia, B-i-H and Kosovo/a; the fascism of *ustashe* and *chetnik* para-military forces. Atrocities were predictable.

[3] *The failure to take seriously outside party histories,* like Austria and Germany wanting revenge for the First and Second world wars and their loss of empire, possibly also Italy.

[4] *The one-sided demonization of the Serbs*, as the center of Evil in Yugoslavia, oblivious of where the shooting started (in Slovenia), and the blatant ethnic discrimination (in Croatia).

[5] *The one-sided demonization of Milosevic*, as the center of the Center of Evil, oblivious of harder nationalists like Seselj and Arkan, also failing to understand Milosevic's appeal as a reaction to Titoist anti-Serbian policies, and his efforts to protect (like Saddam Hussein) some kind of welfare state.

[6] *The failure to take Pérez de Cuéllar's warnings to Genscher seriously: no undue haste in recognition, protect minorities, no one-sided policies, have a policy for Yugoslavia as a whole, take time*; indeed, the failure to make his views public at all.

[7] *The failure to call a general Conference on Security and Cooperation in Southeast Europe* as an alternative to a Contact Group of six heavily involved big powers with their own agendas.

[8] *The failure to grant the parties in Yugoslavia "equal rights to self-determination";* for Slovenes and Croats, but also for the Serbs in Kraina/Slavonia; for Bosniaks, but also for Serbs and Croats in B-i-H; for Serbs, retaining their UN and OSCE membership, but also for Hungarians in Vojvodina and Albanians in Kosovo/a; for Macedonians, but also for Albanians in Macedonia.

[9] *The failure to think in terms of a Yugoslav confederation.* With Montenegro as one entity, equal self-determination leads to 12+ entities as opposed to 8 in the 1974 Yugoslav constitution; not a dramatic change and a very preferable alternative.

[10] *The failure to take the religious dimension seriously*; the conflict is not over theology, but religion serves to identify the parties across state borders and produces true believers.

[11] *The failure to take the economic dimensions seriously*; there are debts to be collected, and oil pipe lines to be built.

[12] *The failure to take media manipulation seriously*, like by Hill&Knowlton and Ruder Finn; and by governments in ex-Yugoslavia.

Do failures serve as an excuse? Well, *errare humanum est*. But at that gigantic scale, with those gigantic consequences? The major Yugoslav parties did what they were programmed to do, very much of it dictated by their history, particularly by the Second world war. For Serbs to draw the conclusion that Serbs shall never again to be governed by Zagreb, Sarajevo or Pristina is not paranoid, it borders on the rational in spite Serb proclivity for the narcissistic/paranoid. Nor should it be confused with having Great(er) Serbia as a goal. To the contrary, it opens for a lot of possibilities for creative conflict transformation, some of it indicated above. The Serbian stupidity, crime, stupid crime was not to grant to Albanians who were even fighting nonviolently what Serbs demanded for themselves in other parts of what was once a proud, well administered, rapidly grown FSR of Yugoslavia. With a terrible past hidden under the carpet and a stifling inability to go beyond *R*econstruction to the other 2 R's after violence: *Reconciliation* and *Resolution*.

But nothing of this absolves US/UK-NATO from the crimes committed by, and in the NATO-Yugoslavia war. Interventionism it certainly was, leaving behind two protectorates (so far) with very uncertain futures and a host of other unsettled problems. Humanitarianism, focused on human suffering, impartial, neutral, independent it was not. There has been some empowerment of local institutions of affected communities; how sustainable remains to be seen. But there certainly has been an imposition of "clear examples of right and wrong in international conflicts", as seen by and partly provoked by outsiders. Instead of understanding and helping the Yugoslav peoples out of their predicaments; rather than laying the basis for future violence, for future wars.

APPENDIX. *A Note on the Military Culture of the USA*

"The Military" is a social institution, with a culture = standards for true-false, right-wrong, good-bad, sacred-profane, beautiful- ugly, etc. Given the enormous destructive power US military culture ranks among the more important cultures in the world.

Here are some recent excerpts from US military journals:

> "In essence, US forces are imbued with the spirit of the offensive, characterized by an indomitable will to win and an aggressive determination to carry the battle to the enemy. The aim is to inflict on the enemy an early and decisive defeat. This spirit, while likely to produce battlefield success, is often at odds with instincts of political leaders, who may prefer a more graduated force application concurrent with diplomatic and other pressures."
>
> "US forces preferably wage war as part of a multinational force, one having the widest possible international representation. The object is not simply to gain additional power, but to enhance legitimacy."
>
> "Peace monitoring, peacekeeping, disaster relief--nation assistance, counterdrug support, antiterrorism and noncombatant evacuation operations-while perhaps politically essential or morally desirable-often degrade combatant force readiness to perform their prime mission-warfighting and preparing for war."
> (Colonel Lloyd J. Matthews, "The Evolution of American Military Ideals", *Military Review*, January-February 1998, pp. 56-61)

The excerpt identifies a contradiction between warfighting and other activities undertaken by the military, developed further in:

> "What do I mean by the term 'warrior spirit'? Above all, it is a state of mind. A soldier with the warrior spirit thinks aggres-

sively, always seeking ways to close with and defeat the enemy. He is confident that he is tough enough to meet the enemy on any level. He is less concerned for his personal safety and more concerned with inflicting as much pain as possible on the enemy. – He draws his satisfaction from continually developing his fighting prowess. He takes it personally when he loses in training because he knows it is unacceptable to lose in combat. In sum the warrior spirit drives a solider to fight and, or die trying. –
In recent years – technological advances – have brought about a decline in the development of the warrior spirit. – Peacekeeping deployments-with the necessary emphasis on following strict rules of engagement and preventing the outbreak of hostilities-have further contributed to the weakening of the warrior spirit."

"Most of our potential adversaries know two things about the United states that they will try to use against us: We are very sensitive to casualties, and our strength is in open terrain, where our technological superiority is at a premium."
(From Captain William M. Connor, "Developing the Warrior Spirit in Ranger Training", *Infantry*, Vol. 89 No. 2 May-August 1999, pp. 45-47. The author recommends boxing and pugil stick training).

"– simple military operations, such as observation and traditional peacekeeping with a political influence dominant over token military forces and involvement-all predicated on the belligerents' acceptance of a UN presence-are the core competence of the UN. The more dynamic military operations should be undertaken only by rehearsed military alliances or coalitions leg by a major military power. The Gulf War comes quickly to mind. Most Americans, opposed to UN command and control of U.S. military forces, probably would agree with these conclusions of Mr Hillen." (Colonel George G. Eddy, reviewing John Hillen, *Blue Helmets: The Strategy of UN Operations*, in *Infantry*, Vol. 88 No. 3 Sep-Dec 1998, pp.49-50)

But this is then contradicted in the politically more correct:
A Force for Peace. US Commanders' Views of the Military's Role in Peace Operations, Peace Through Law Education Fund, 1999:

> "The senior officers interviewed *unanimously* agree that participation. in these operations is *in our interests* and strengthens U.S. leadership. This conclusion contradicts a suspicion in some Capitol Hill circles that the military is reluctant to engage in peace operations and would prefer to preserve all of its resources for warfighting."

That was 1999. Three years later we read:

A Force for Peace and Security: US and Allied Commanders' Views of the Military's Role in Peace Operations, Peace Through Law Education Fund, 2002:

The European Approach:

> "[Peace Operations] are operations *amongst the people*. If you're in your shirtsleeve and your weapon is down the side of your leg and you're no *looking* aggressive, then you have a calming effect ... The more you seek to isolate yourself from the people, be it in your helmet and flak jacket, be it in your large four man vehicle patrol, the less you will be able to find the person or people who matter to you, among those people."
> (General Rupert Smith)

The U.S. Approach:

> "It's pretty simple. When you're under arms, you wear your combat kit. We insist on helmets in HUMVEES and trucks because it saves lives when there's an accident. The U.S. Army's philosophy on this is, 'Look, if you want us to go to the field and do peace enforcement, under arms, you get an organization with military discipline that's ready to respond to any kind of lethal threat. If you don't like that, send for the U.N.'"
> (General Montgomery Meigs)

As an afterthought, about images, convictions:

> "The PSYOP /psychological operations/ teams helped convince the villagers that US troops were there as peacemakers, not foreign conquerors-a very important distinction in gaining public acceptance."

(Colonel C.H. Swannack and Lieutenant Colonel David R. Gray, "Peace Enforcement Operations", *Military Review*, vol. 77,No.6.)

Conclusion: US military, particularly younger officers, may see others as "sissies" and "wimps" and themselves a doing the real job. Others may agree, incidentally, and accept a division of labor.

Added to the warrior ethos "characterized by an indomitable will to win", comes the postmodern aspect of targeting civilian infrastructure and civilians. This seems to have been the US Air Force doctrine from February 1943, already practiced in the massive bombing of German and Japanese cities during the Second World War, and carried over in the major operations afterwards in Korea, Vietnam, Iraq, Yugoslavia and Afghanistan. Of course, any civilian target destroyed will have some indirect military impact. But the impact is not necessarily negative; it could also strengthen the moral by strengthening the hatred of a cruel enemy, in our times also breaking the laws of war. The basic US theory (not confirmed by the studies of the massive bombing of civilian targets in the Germany and Japan campaigns) is that civilian hatred will be deflected toward their own leaders as the cause of the suffering due to the war on civilians. The civilians may focus on the immediate cause, however, the US way of waging war, compatible with "we are very sensitive to casualties, and our strength is in open terrain, where our technological superiority is at a premium". Bombing civilian targets from high altitude meets the bill.

Added to this comes a third factor. Commanders-in-chief (CINCs) exercise a power on US foreign policy incompatible with the theory of civilian control of the military (*Washington Post, 27 Sep 2000*):

They travel non-stop, oversee multimillion dollar foreign study institutes and round-the clock intelligence centers – American generals and admirals – have long exercised independent influence abroad – jockeyed with diplomats and intelligence agencies to shape U.S. foreign policy. – The swelling institution of the CINC has shifted this balance during the 1990s. Sheer budgetary prowess is one reason. – Peacekeeping and nation-building has steadily pushed the uniformed CINCs into expanded diplomatic and political roles.

The CINCs control their own aircraft, can call up a fleet of helicopters, and often travel with an entourage approaching 35. The commanders are routinely received by heads of state who offer gifts, share secrets and seek advice.

ERGO: The USA today is a country unfit for "humanitarian intervention".

NOTES

[1] See, for instance, Mario Bettati, *Le droit d'ingérence. Mutation de l'ordre international*. Paris: Editions Odile Jacob, 1996, and Thomas Hoffnung, "Entretien avec Mario Bettati", *Politique Internationale*, No 87, spring 2000, pp. 447-461.

[2] For an excellent more US-oriented analysis see Noam Chomsky, *The New Military Humanism. Lessons from Kosovo*, Monroe, ME: Common Courage Press, 1999.

[3] *Human Rights Quarterly*, Vol. 4, No. 3 1995, pp. 14-24.

[4] The meeting at Mohonk, NY, was the fourth in a series organized autumn 1993 by the Task Force on Ethical and Legal Issues in Humanitarian Assistance formed by the Programme on Humanitarian Assistance at the World Conference on Religion and Peace, an NGO. Broadly based in participation the criteria have often served as a point of reference, as is also done here.

[5] That symbol, however, is ambiguous, associated with assistance to civilian victims, but also with military units assisting the perpetrators, the military themselves. To argue two different symbols in no way is to argue that military personnel should not also be relieved of their suffering.

[6] *ibid.*, p. 15. Whether the view is predominantly male or predominantly American is a moot point; the two categories obviously do not exclude each other (but may reinforce each other).

[7] "A Century of US Military Interventions from Wounded Knee to Afghanistan", based on *Congressional Records* and the Library of Congress Congressional Research Service.

[8] *Rogue State: A Guide to the World's Only Superpower*, Monroe MA: Common Courage Press, 2000.

[9] See "September 11 2001: Diagnosis, Prognosis and Therapy" www.transcend.org, published many places in many languages.

[10] *LM* (London) 126, December 1999.

[11] See Wilfried Graf, "Warum es keine Friedensverhandlungen gab", in Bilek, Graf, Kramer (eds.), *Welcher Friede? Lehren aus dem Krieg um Kosovo*, Münster: Agenda Verlag, 2000.

[12] The major ethnic cleansing, entirely intended, in Yugoslavia was Operation Storm 4-7 August 1995 on what under UN protection was called Sector North and South (Kraina), with the result that 200,000 Serbs left (of them at least 180,000 civilians), around 600 Serb civilians were killed, and at least 22,000 (Serb) houses were burnt and mined. "All Serb mobile property was looted, the whole cattle fund was destroyed, as well as public

utilities and infrastructure, and all memorials/monuments from WWII. Industrial plants and factories, all schools, cultural objects, libraries, were also destroyed". See Croatian Helsinki Committee for Human Rights, *Military Operation Storm and Is Aftermath: Report*, Zagreb: HHO, 2001, p. 135.

[13] There is a rich literature on the effect of the US/NATO bombing. to the warfare, see, for instance, Zvetan Todorov, in *Mémoire du mal. Tentation du bien* Paris: Laffont, 2000, quoting General of the Air Force, Michael Short and his famous "Hey Slobo-" statement, to the effect that Serbs will put pressure on Milosevic when their infra-structure (water and gasoline reserves, electric installations, transport, factories and hospitals, etc.) no longer works (Todorov, p. 280; from *Washington Post*, 24 May 1999). Also see Richter, Schmaling, Spoo; *Die Wahrheit über den NATO-Krieg gegen Jugoslawien*, Schkeuditz, 2000, Point 9 on pp. 24-5.

[14] See the chapter "NATO's War Crimes" (pp. 1214-129) in Michael Parenti, *To Kill a Nation: The attack on Yugoslavia*, London, New York: Verso, 2000. A reference to Captain (Martin) de la Hoz is found on pp. 122-123. Parenti alleges (p. 123) that "NATO had devised the devilish technique of bombing a site, then waiting fifteen minutes-just time enough for rescue teams to arrive and start working-to hit the target a second time, killing many of the would-be rescuers, and making it extremely dangerous for teams to dig for survivors". General Wesley Clark is quoted as saying that the aim of the air war was to "demolish, destroy, devastate, degrade, and ultimately eliminate the essential infrastructure of Yugoslavia". Parenti also summarizes the situation very well: "-the Albanian exodus from Kosovo began *after* the NATO bombings that trampled on human dignity and human rights. And at Rambouillet, it was the US that rejected "a perfectly peaceful" solution to the Kosovo conflict."

[15] Matthias Küntzel, *Der Weg in den Krieg*, Berlin: Elephantenverlag, 2000.

[16] I did not foresee 11 September 2001, or not in exactly that shape, nor that a war in Afghanistan (highly predictable) would be linked to 11 September. But the tacit warfare in Colombia has been going as "Plan Colombia" for some years, so has the tension with North Korea.

[17] Berlin: Elephanten-Verlag, 2000.

DIETER S. LUTZ

The Example of Kosovo: Didactics against Humanitarian Interventionism

1. A PLEA FOR WIDE-SPREAD SOCIETAL DISCUSSION

Many of our citizens – including myself – miss the fundamental discussion on peace and security policy issues, which has been promised for years in particular by politicians of the current coalition government. Meanwhile even the President of the Federal Republic of Germany has repeatedly called for resuming these discussions, long overdue:

> "I consider this discussion as very important because very few political courses set have had such an extensive influence on our whole society ... What we need is a broad societal discussion on these issues beyond the 'facts and figures' ... I would hope that this discussion will not only be limited to political parties and associations, the media, the German Army (Bundeswehr), those serving community service as an alternative to military service, those in peace research, but that as many citizens take part as possible. ... We have to be perfectly clear on how we want to maintain the external security of our country under the changing circumstances. We have to have a clear view of what contribution the Federal Republic of Germany can make and wants to make for peace, freedom and human rights within the framework of NATO, the EU, the WEU and on commissions from the United Nations. ... I am hoping for an intensive, serious and broadly discussed social debate, at the end of which not less than a new social basic consensus on the tasks of the German Army will be achieved and on how these tasks can be best fulfilled in the interests of our country.... We require a discussion between as many people from various disciplines and convictions who are ready and able to take on responsibility. We need discussions and impulses that flow against the trends and popular opinions. We need this discussion in view of the pressing issues, which touch and influence all our lives. Therefore I say ...: The ability to think and follow the arguments

> is not only allowed, it is desirable.... On the keyword: security policy, ... This is not just about a few facts and figures, this is about a society that was prepared for national defence by German Basic Law, by the party programme, and that is now experiencing national defence as alliance defence, that is undergoing a change in policies and policy-making, in security and foreign policy that is serious. I believe that because this is true a sophisticated discussion must take place that deals with the goals of defence and not only the instruments of defence, which must be discussed as well. ... I consider this discussion to be extremely important because the courses set have such far-reaching consequences for our entire society: This is about the security of our country and our role in the North Atlantic Alliance. This is about the most far-reaching societal understanding possible of the tasks, financial framework, equipment and personnel strength of our armed forces. This is about the question of how, under the changed circumstances, we can hold on to compulsory military service and whether we want to do this. ... We need wide-spread societal discussion on these questions beyond the 'facts and figures' ... I would wish that not only the parties and the associations, the media, the army, those doing community service and those in peace research would participate, but that as many citizens as possible also take part. ... It is our every right and our responsibility to pose the necessary questions, to discuss them publicly and to demand convincing answers."[1]

Why is the President so insistent and why have I quoted him in such detail? The reason is obviously that the discussion is long overdue. We have been promised this discussion at least three times during the past three years. Up to now it has not taken place at all:

(1) There was no fundamental discussion on a new peace and security-policy concept when the new government took office,
(2) neither did it take place on the army reform plan, allegedly a centennial reform,
(3) nor on the Kosovo War, the mistakes made there as well as the lessons learned, something that had been promised repeatedly during and after the war by leading politicians.

I am therefore extraordinarily grateful to the organizers of this congress for their initiative – especially my colleague Georg Meggle. This meeting is an outstanding opportunity to break the paralysis that has seized the peace and security debate since the Kosovo War.

2. INTERVENTIONS À LA KOSOVO MUST BE RESOLUTELY PREVENTED

I must add that personally I have learned a tremendous amount from the papers and lectures at this meeting. On the whole, the considerations discussed here have produced a framework not only for a theory of humanitarian intervention, but also in a nutshell the ethical and normative basic elements and principles for the realization of "good" practical courses of action. If I nevertheless, am against pursuing the idea of humanitarian intervention – beyond an academic discussion – and also against the fact that it may be anchored in customary international law and not least against its political instrumentalization – and this point-blank and decisively – this is because of two points that we have touched upon too little in our discussion up to now:

(1) one of these is the lack of success in humanitarian interventions,
(2) and the other – moreover this is the predominant issue – is the danger of misuse this instrument holds (after all its implementation is a matter of life and death for innocent people).

If – and I insist upon this – the case of Kosovo has been an ethical and moral lesson at all, then this is the fact that the humanitarian intervention á la Kosovo has not been a positive instrument whose use we should consider further. Rather, the lesson from the "case of Kosovo" is that this type of and similar types of intervention should in future and for all time be stopped completely.

In the following, I will try to justify this statement briefly taking into consideration the two points mentioned above.

3. WAS THE INTERVENTION IN KOSOVO A SUCCESS?

I will start with the question of whether the NATO Kosovo intervention achieved its goals. Or ethically speaking: Did it do more damage than good?

The NATO war in Kosovo began on 24 March 1999. In the 78 days of aerial warfare, NATO:

(1) conducted 38,000 aerial missions with military and civilian targets in the Serb province of Kosovo and in other parts of Yugoslavia,
(2) used 23,000 bombs and missiles, about a third of which were precision-guided weapons,
(3) in addition, dropped about 1,100 cluster bombs that can each carry up to 202 "bomblets" (a total of 200,000) which in turn can each hold 300 shards of steel,
(4) fired depleted-uranium ammunition and dropped modern graphite bombs,
(5) attacked and destroyed mostly civilian or were more likely to destroy civilian targets, for example streets, bridges, factories, power plants, oil refineries, communications establishments as well as schools, hospitals, cultural monuments etc.
(6) destroyed property worth many billions of US dollars – not to mention the civilian victims who lost their lives.[2]

NATO aerial warfare could not prevent the flight and expulsion of over 800,000 Albanian Kosovars. On the contrary: One cannot exclude that the bombing aggravated the humanitarian catastrophe or at least encouraged it.[3]

In contrast, military targets were hardly destroyed at all, at any rate on a much lower scale than was expected and also propagated. For example, not even 20 Yugoslav battle tanks were hit. In comparison, three years before, in June 1996, the regional arms control negotiations of the Dayton states were concluded. As a result of this agreement, which on the whole can be traced back to German initiative, the Yugoslav army were obliged to scrap 420 tanks: 20 times the number they lost in the Kosovo War.[4]

Civilian crisis prevention including negotiated and agreed disarmament can obviously lead to much more convincing results than a bomb war, as elaborate and costly as this type of war may be. The same was true for the question of whether to remove Milosevic from power through military or civilian means. It was not because he lost the war, that the former president was disempowered in the year 2000. The bomb war and its threat had – at least directly before and during the war and even for a period thereafter – strengthened rather than weakened his power. But rather, he was forced out office because the West in the electoral campaign in Autumn 2000 supported the Serb opposition with 80 million US dollars – 40 million donated by the US, as Thomas Carothers, the Vice President of Carnegie Endowment in Washington writes, and a similar sum from the EU states.[5]

One must agree unreservedly[6] with the OSCE High Commissioner on National Minorities, former Foreign Minister from the Netherlands, Max van der Stoel, when he emphasizes the advantages of conflict prevention including those financial:

> "It is my firm belief that capital invested in conflict prevention (and I say 'invested' intentionally and not simply 'spent') is capital invested sensibly and well. For conflict prevention is less expensive than peacekeeping measures which are in turn less expensive than war."[7]

Despite all the lip service paid to prevention and the lessons learned in its implementation in the past years, it has remained insubstantial and without consequence: Whether intentionally or not, Kosovo was, for example, forgotten at Dayton. Over the years, moreover, the Kosovo Albanians had gained little hearing from the European nations. First when passive defence of the Kosovo Albanians made a turn around, first when the freedom fighters became terrorists, first when the Serbs began to massacre Albanian civilians, first when the Albanian nationalists threatened to involve the entire Balkans in a war for the sake of a Greater Albania, first then did Europe awaken from its lethargy and force the Serbs and Kosovo Albanians to come to the negotiating table in Rambouillet. Too late! Prevention is no longer an option at five past twelve. And not at all, if the seriously necessary structures, mechanisms, financial resources and people are lacking or must first be found or created in order to carry out effective and successful prevention. Thus the Holbrooke-Milosevic agreement in October 1998 also failed *inter alia* because the OSCE verifiers in the European security order that had been promised were not available and also not found quickly enough. Thus, the "protectorate" set up by NATO after the war was unable to prevent expulsion, looting and murder, because the necessary (international) police force was simply lacking.

On the other hand it is also true – and we should keep this in mind in all of our considerations – that at the beginning of the conflict, there was a Serb policy of oppression. This involved terror, murder and expulsion. It is my firm hope that Slobodan Milosevic and others will have to answer for this before the International Court of Justice.

But it is only withdrawal into self-righteous contemplation that allows the community of states to overlook the current disaster. Without the excesses of expulsion committed against the Albanians in April 1999, and without the counter-terror of expulsion committed against the Serbs and other non-Albanians in June 1999, one could not explain the increase in hate and irreconcilability that has dashed any hopes for self-sustaining peace today and in the foreseeable future. Both displacement flows were concomitant events and/or consequences of the aerial warfare against Yugoslavia. The West has even to this day not come up with a concept for the political future of Kosovo. Success is already measured as an achievement when the administration of the protectorate manages to prevent the revival of the worst hostilities. The current situation in Kosovo has no more meaning than the suppression of violence.[8]

To put it more clearly: There is still no peace in Kosovo. What is more serious, there is also no situation emerging which would be worthy of being called "peace". The enemy ethnic groups enjoy merely a minimum standard of security because heavily armed international troops protect them from one another.

Against this backdrop, a return of the Serbs who fled or were forcefully displaced from Kosovo during the middle of 1999 is unthinkable currently or in the foreseeable future. In my opinion, nothing illustrates our share of the responsibility and our guilt more in the tragic events in the Balkans than the high number of refugees who have still not returned home. It was in particular the danger of expulsion, of ethnic cleansing – which politicians and the media presented with large gestures and sharp words – as the reasons why we were ready to make war to prevent these from happening. It is therefore no coincidence that the then politicians and the media suppress the problem today, as do all of us, not even knowing the exact number of displaced persons, a fact that should be nagging at our conscience daily. At this point – as an examination and a self-examination – a question to all of us: Who among us knows how high the number of refugees is – Serb and other non-Albanian minorities like the Roma etc. from Kosovo – at this very moment and where is the limit in the number of refugees at which

(1) first, we would consider the NATO war a failure because it had been overly excessive: At 10,000 people? At 50,000 people? At 100,000 people? Or 200,000 people, women, and children, old and young?

Too put it even more clearly: What is the limit at which

(2) second, we would demand that NATO, if it was not already acting in Kosovo, intervene for moral and ethical reasons so that the Serbs and other minorities who had fled and were displaced forcefully could return. At 10,000 people? 50,000 people? At 100,000 people? Or 200,000 people?

And if I am asking these questions, does not their logic – whether I like this logic or not – theoretically also demand

(3) third, that perhaps because of the outcome of the Kosovo War we may have to intervene against ourselves or allow others to intervene against us? For example, the world power China (who after the painful experience of having their embassy in Belgrade bombed during the Kosovo War) who in future will orientate itself to the power politics of the US? Or the potential world power India who would like to model itself on the US?

In any event, statistics on refugee and displaced persons reveal the following:[9]

(1) up until October 1998, there were 280,000 fleeing Kosovars,
(2) after the deployment of OSCE observers in Kosovo in October 1998, the number fell to 248,000 until 22 December 1998,
(3) after the beginning of the NATO bombings on 24 March 1999, the number rose rapidly from 800,000 to 900,000,
(4) the number of Serbs and members of other minorities who fled or were forcefully displaced from Kosovo after the return of the Kosovo Albanians today totals exactly 231,000 people.[10]

I will let you make your own interpretation of this last figure, which in my view is dreadful and intolerable two and a half years after the war started, and will now deal with the second point already mentioned: the misuse of the instrument of humanitarian intervention. In the following, I would like to elucidate this line of reasoning according to two points of view,

(1) the abuse of this instrument by the victims or better put: its strategic use by one or the other of the conflict parties and
(2) the abuse of this instrument by the interventionists.

4. HUMANITARIAN INTERVENTION AS A PART OF THE STRATEGY OF THE KOSOVO LIBERATION ARMY (UCK)

I will begin with the misuse of this instrument through a masterly strategic performance by the UCK: Relatively unnoticed by the media, the NATO Parliamentary Assembly issued a "General Report"[11] in autumn of 2000, which would have deserved broad societal discussion if not a public outcry of indignation.

In this report entitled "Kosovo Aftermath and its Implications for Conflict Prevention and Crisis Management", the failure of Western politicians in the Kosovo conflict was admitted officially for the first time. Under number 83 and 84 with an eye on the "liberation organization", the UCK of the Kosovo Albanians, it was admitted outright that: The NATO states were "interested in stability in the region". However, in Kosovo

> "...the UCK sought to worsen the situation in order to motivate the population to take part in an uprising for independence. The UCK used the Holbrooke-Milosevic agreement as a pause to regroup and to gather strength after the setbacks suffered during the summer. Under the influence of the Kosovo Verification Mission (KVM) the level of Serbian repression eased off in the period from October to December 1998. On the other hand, there was a lack of effective measures to curb the UCK, who continued to raise money from donations in the United States and Western Europe – particularly in Germany and Switzerland – to advertise for recruits, and to smuggle weapons across the Albanian border. As of December 1998 there was a strong increase in the number of UCK attacks on Serbian security forces and civilians. The conflict escalated again, creating a humanitarian crisis which motivated NATO to intervene."

In other words: According to the General Report of the NATO Parliamentary Assembly and in contrast to the official NATO presentations, especially before the war, it was not or not only the Serbs, but also and especially the UCK that were responsible for the escalation of the conflict and the creation of a humanitarian crisis in Kosovo.

This insight came late, too late! Critics who expressed this before and during the Kosovo War, were maligned as conspiracy theoreticians and friends of the Serbs. Critical peace researchers were punished also financially. The only – as far as one knows – German soldier who was upright about the situation, Brigadier General Loquai,[12] lost his job at the OSCE in Vienna after the intervention of the German Ministry of Defence – against the clear cut wishes of the OSCE incidentally. And what about all the innocent people who lost their lives due to so-called collateral damage?

If one takes the late admissions of the NATO Parliamentary Assembly seriously, then who will take responsibility, who will take personal blame for the death of the night guard in the tobacco factory bombed by NATO, and furthermore for the death of the Bulgarian retailers in the bus, the Montenegrins and the members of a Hungarian minority who were on foot, the mother of the two little girls in the car on the bridge, the fleeing Albanians on a tractor, the Serb deserters on a bicycle, the cancer patients in a hospital dependent on electricity, the journalist in the Chinese Embassy and all the others … ? Was it really that demon in Belgrade as Western democrats would have us believe? Or was it the democratically legitimised members of parliament, the state secretaries, the ministers, who decided to conduct an aerial war, most of them not even having the slightest idea of what the destructive the force of thousands of missions would be and for whom even the terms "cruise missiles" and "cassette bombs" had absolutely no meaning? Who would have thought that democrats – that is: *our* politicians – would have waged a war because of a "humanitarian catastrophe", but would not make any provisions in the run-up to military activities for the care of the victims of just this humanitarian catastrophe, who on the contrary either intentionally or unintentionally simply forgot to provide them with medical help, food, water treatment, tents etc.? And above all: Who would have dared to guess that German democrats would contribute to destroying human life without knowing all the facts and figures – and even win applause from journalists, philosophers, writers, lawyers and peace researchers for this?[13]

According to German Constitutional Law, the decision for war without knowledge of the facts and figures is unconstitutional. Article 26, paragraph 2 of German Basic Law, on the contrary, demands – as a lesson from the Second World War – absolute and unequivocal certainty.[14] The NATO decision, which included Germany, to bomb Yugoslavia was not only *not* based on unequivocal certainty, but rather on a vague "feeling", as the NATO Parliamentary Assembly today admits:

> "The alleged massacre of Racak, the circumstances of which have not been fully clarified to this day, created the feeling that there was a need to act and led to the NATO air strikes strongly desired by the UCK after the failure of the Rambouillet negotiations."[15] (Emphasis – DSL)

But even worse: Were the facts and figures really unknown before the beginning of the war? Was the Kosovo War inevitable simply because, from the beginning, the status reports of the authorities and the services did not allow conclusions to the contrary – or if you will – feelings to the contrary?

With this question I come to the point already mentioned on the misuse of humanitarian intervention by the interventionists.

5. THE MISUSE OF THE INSTRUMENT OF HUMANITARIAN INTERVENTION BY THE INTERVENTIONISTS

Let us simply leave aside the many "dirty secrets"[16] like the "massacre" at Racak or the alleged massacre at Rugovo or the alleged concentration camp at the football arena in Pristina or the self-drawn so-called "Operation Horseshoe" and many other similar subjects. Let us thus leave aside the conscious manipulation of the public by creating "feelings", in which not only NATO strategists, but also and especially German politicians were involved. What do the confidential situation analyses from the services – not made known to the general public – say *before* the beginning of the war? Do they correspond to or contradict the picture of the Kosovo conflict and its escalation, which was put in such plain terms two years after the war by the NATO Parliamentary Assembly?

If one follows the situation analyses of the Federal Foreign Office of 19 March 1999, it is clear that the political decision-makers knew (must have known) before the war. In the internal documents which were prepared a few days before the beginning of the NATO bombings on 24 March and distributed to the Foreign Minister as well as the Ministry of Defence, the authors were explicitly clear that the armistice was not only not being observed by the Serbs but that it was "no longer being observed by either side". Furthermore, genocide and expulsion were not the stated goals of the Yugoslav armed forces (VJ). More exactly, the goal was stated to be "the elimination of all possibilities for an UCK retreat by clearing targeted terrain". It was also stated that the civilian population was as a rule even "warned about the threat of an attack by the VJ". However, the "evacuation of the civilian population was prevented occasionally by local UCK commanders". After the withdrawal of Serb security forces, most of the population would return to the towns and villages. A mass exodus into the forests was not observed. Further it was stated that:

> "The refugee flows, expulsion and destruction in Kosovo have affected all ethnic groups there equally. Around 90 of the villages formerly inhabited by Serbs have in the meantime been abandoned. Of the once 14,000-strong group of Serb Croats, there are only 7,000 left in Kosovo. In contrast to the autumn/summer of 1998, there is no threat of a supply catastrophe."[17]

This situation analysis from the Federal Foreign Office was reinforced by a confidential situation report by the intelligence officers of the Ministry of Defence of "23 March at 3 P.M.". In this report written a half day before the beginning of the war, it is explicitly stated that: "The start of a co-ordinated large-scale offensive of the Serb-Yugoslav forces against the UCK in Kosovo can up to now not be confirmed". The Serb-Yugoslav forces would not be capable of a large-scale operation against the UCK. Further, the intelligence officers drafted a statement, which is also to be found in the General Report of the NATO parliamentarians:

> "The UCK on its part will probably continue to try through hit-and-run campaigns to provoke the Serb-Yugoslav forces to massive reactions, in the hopes that this would take on such proportions with regard to destruction and refugees that it would incite NATO to start air strikes immediately."[18]

Finally, let us take a look at the paper entitled "Briefing to the Parliament"[19] from the Federal Ministry of Defence drawn up by its "situation management". This paper for official use originates from 25 March, that is the day *after* the war began. In this situation paper, there are words and phrases like "provocations on the part of the UCK" or "recently discovered gun-running operation from Montenegro to Kosovo" or "Serb-Yugoslav army operation against the UCK" or "UCK attacks on police stations". In this 12-page paper, you will neither find the term "humanitarian disaster" – which all the same was the official reason for the NATO to make war – nor will you come across a similar term.

Those who read these reports for the first time are undoubtedly greatly astonished. For example, about the information that the Albanians were warned ahead of time and then were also able to return to their villages. This information does not fit with the picture of what was being said at the time. Furthermore, we are astonished that refugee flows, expulsion and destruction affected *all* of the ethnic groups in Kosovo *equally* – as we had always assumed that the Albanians and only Albanians had suffered the most and were the victims. We also read with great consternation that "local UCK commanders prevented the evacuation of the civilian population". Our next thought is: Why was this information withheld from the general public? And at the end of the day, we realize that what we have just read is a description of civil war or events similar to civil war – with all the cruelty and crime associated with war – but not a report that justifies speaking of genocide, Auschwitz, concentration camps, ethnic cleansing and systematic forced displacement.

Our picture of the Kosovo conflict has in particular been characterized by the Yugoslav policy of oppression *since* 1989, the manipulation by the West *before and during* the NATO war and through the crimes done to the Kosovo Albanians *after* the start of the NATO air strikes in March 1999. Because of the manipulation of public opinion before and during the NATO bombings, the developments seem to us like a continuous sequence of violence and criminal behaviour committed one-sidedly by the Yugoslavs which was inevitably destined to lead to NATO intervention to prevent something even worse from happening.[20] This picture is not valid in every case. There were repeatedly times in the past years in which peace had a chance and this chance was not taken. This was particularly true of the autumn 1998.

While considering this, one should on no account play down or pardon the crimes of the Serbs against the Kosovo Albanians during the period *before* the Holbrooke-Milosevic agreement, that is up until October 1998, and *after* the start of the NATO air strikes, that is after 24 March 1999. On the contrary! Prosecution of violent crimes is imperative, whether this occurs within the framework of the legal proceedings of a nation state, or of an international court of law.

When and as long as the international community, international organizations or individual states for the most diverse reasons are prepared to conclude treaties and agreements with alleged or actual lawbreakers – the Dayton Agreement or the Holbrooke-Milosevic agreement are just as much examples for this as similar agreements with Saddam Hussein – then all parties to the contract are obligated to honour the stipulations therein. Otherwise, what would be the sense of these agreements? One-sided partisanship at the cost of one of the treaty partners and/or its population by making a reference to an event that occurred before the conclusion of the treaty is in any case no longer an option – neither politically nor legally and least of all morally. A bias to the advantage of one party against better judgement and which is, as a result of war, a burden to innocent bystanders, is more than unacceptable. On the contrary: One must even expect and demand that the potential guaranteeing power – in this case the NATO – would with this kind of a breach of contract by the former "victims" intervene in favour of the former lawbreakers. NATO with full knowledge of the situation in Kosovo made itself the instrument of the UCK, at least it allowed itself to be made the instrument. From the perspective of the Charter of the United Nations, this was a breach of international law due to the alleged law of the strongest to the disadvantage of the strength of the law with immeasurable consequences for the future development of international order. In view of the Basic Law, this was an unconstitutional war of aggression with devastating effects on the credibility of politics. From the perspective of an UCK striving for power and independence, however, it was a strategically brilliant achievement, even though they tolerated numerous innocent victims.

Again: Who actually has taken personal responsibility for the death of these victims who through the decisions and actions of NATO politicians have been dehumanised as collateral damage.

One of the achievements of civilization is that war is acceptable only as the *ultima ratio*, the extreme exception. Decisions on war and peace doubtlessly demand certainty beyond all doubt. Offence and defence cannot be allowed to degenerate into victor's definitions. If there is uncertainty, one cannot and must not decide to make war.

It is therefore not enough under any circumstances when NATO parliamentarians self-critically admit in clause 91 of their General Report:

> "The international community cannot allow actions to be imposed on it by an extremist minority."[21]

The lessons of the illegal NATO Kosovo War must go much further, be more fundamental and simultaneously more conceptional. President Rau drew the following conclusions in one of his speeches:

> "For me, the most important lessons is the following: We must through preventive policy seek to avoid the wrong alternative, that is burdening ourselves with guilt by looking away or burdening ourselves with guilt by deploying military means that could affect totally innocent bystanders."[22]

Thus for Rau, war and peace are just as little natural alternatives as war is not really a normal continuation of policy by using other means. The most distinguished task in politics is rather to prevent not make war. Situations, which only allow the evils of burdening oneself with guilt or killing innocent people through military operations as alternatives should not be permitted to happen. If these occur, politics has failed. Thus it is not in war that politics must prove its worth, but in peace. With these considerations President Johannes Rau has remained firmly in the tradition of his predecessor Gustav Heinemann.[23] Not only the German public, but in particular and above all the politicians in the foreign and defence ministries should follow President Rau without any ifs and buts.

With a view to the title of my contribution, what does this mean, which brings us to the question of the alternatives? Namely in the areas

(1) of foreign, peace and security policy?
(2) within society and in democracy theory?

6. A PLEA FOR A SYSTEM OF COLLECTIVE SECURITY IN AND FOR EUROPE[24]

One of the paradoxes of the current security system is that in the years after 1989/90, there was, and even today there still remains, the chance of the century for creating a stable and long-lasting peace and security order in and for Europe in the form of a regional system of collective security as provided for in Chapter VIII of the UN Charter, as well as in Article 24 of the Basic Law of the Federal Republic of Germany. This chance has up to now not been taken.

Measured against the rupture of epochs in 1989/90 and the possibilities opened by this, merely betting on NATO is a missed opportunity, even a fundamental mistake. This ascertainment must correspondingly be valid for NATO's eastward enlargement. Military alliances like the North Atlantic Treaty Organization (NATO) or the West European Union (WEU) only include – with or without eastward enlargement – a part of the European continent. They lead to the continuing division of Europe into secure and insecure, stabile and instable zones. They cannot deal preventively with conflicts outside their borders as the example of the former Yugoslavia shows. In contrast to a system of collective security, they do not have the means or the mechanisms to do this. However, even the problems between the partners in the military alliances cannot be managed as the conflict between Turkey and Greece in the Aegean Sea or the unremitting decade-long Cyprus conflict illustrate. Military Alliances neither have the capacity to deal with nor are they designed for this purpose. In addition, they are even a latent factor in producing perceptions of isolation or threat to the states excluded from membership. Counter alliances, armament escalations and concepts on deterrence can result from this. And as reality shows repeatedly: war.

A system of collective defence cannot replace a system of collective security. It is not enough to simply redeclare NATO as collective security system, as the Federal Constitutional Court did in a paradoxical obiter dictum on 12 July 1994. Positively expressed, this critique means: Those of us who understand the obiter dictum of the Federal Constitutional Court as a call for action, who take the 1990 Paris Charter and the discussion following it seriously, who understand the rupture in the epochs in 1989 as a unique chance for Europe, have to want more for Europe than the form NATO Europe has taken up to now. This does not mean incidentally that NATO will have to give up or will lose its current role with respect to transatlantic relations.

How should a European peace and security order that, considering the points of criticism mentioned above, really deserves this name, be shaped? If the historical chance, resulting from the time of change, is not to be completely squandered, the security systems in and for Europe, in its present form, must be turned upside down. The NATO military alliance, whose members are only a tenth of the community of states in the world, lays out five eighths of world military expenditures. Nevertheless, it is unable to prevent genocide and war in Europe. What Europe urgently needs is a regional system of collective security, as anticipated in Article 24 GG of German Basic Law and as is also provided for in the UN Charter as a regional arrangement. The European security order would then be based upon a legal system which would not require further mandating, it would possess sufficient and efficient instruments for anticipatory crisis prevention as well as for peaceful and civil dispute settlement ("the aggressor in an armed conflict is the party that evades arbitration"), it would be able to prosecute aggressors and war criminals as well as take them to court and it would (in cooperation with NATO and W/EU)possess the means for military enforcement action, which as an *ultima ratio* would not open the gates of political arbitrariness, but would follow an integrated pan-European legal system and if necessary re-establish it ("legal system replaces intervention").

A system, which in this sense deserves the name "European security order", must still be created. Currently, it does not exist. All the more, currently there is no security order in Europe that is worthy of the name "*peace*" order. Paradoxically, the statement that there is no "European peace order" does not mean there is no peace order "*in*" Europe, to be more exact: that there is no "*West*"-European peace order. On the contrary, the European Community and the European Union have doubtlessly not only contributed decisively in the past decades to fundamentally changing Western Europe but in addition the EC and EU must be given the credit for a service that cannot be evaluated highly enough: They have developed the only multinational structure in Europe that not only represents a security order but also a peace order. It is almost certain that military conflict between EU members today would be structurally impossible. Along with economic prosperity, peace is the decisive result of the integration of Western Europe – namely through the most fruitful of all methods: conflict prevention by eliminating conflict causes. Experience has shown that EU Europe can introduce peace through integration into the pan-European future. This contribution, strategic for peace, that the European Union can make for all of Europe, and even must make, goes beyond the short-term aid for the economic and political consolidation of the "remainder" of Europe. It is directed towards the middle- and long-term opening and enlargement of the Union itself. To make this more clear: Those who desire a "European peace order" in the literal sense, must speak out resolutely in favour of opening the EU's doors and enlarging it.

Those of you who agree with this statement, must thus place two fundamental views alongside it: First, the time required for such an ambitious project as opening and enlarging the EU with the goal of creating a European peace order will be more like decades than years. Second, as comprehensive as this project for long-term economic integration is, it will be able to achieve nothing or little to put out the fires already smouldering in the crisis regions of Europe. Thus in the short and middle term, Europe needs something different and supplementary, namely a functional and efficient structure of collective security which in the sense already described aids in settling conflicts peacefully, and if violence should break out anyway to stop it at the earliest possible stage and the lowest level. A peace order must grow, a security order, however, like the "collective security system in and for Europe" can be created.

7. PLEA FOR THE CREATION OF A "COUNCIL FOR THE FUTURE"[25]

Those of us who make demands like that of a collective security system in and for Europe, must realize that its implementation will not just fall from the sky and that urgently necessary decisions and actions do not just take place in a vacuum. In fact, they are given, reached and realized within the framework of societal structures, state entities, political forms of power and government.

Those of you looking for the answers and solutions to questions and problems that recognizably affect the limits on the ability of a political class to take decisions, actions and in the end make peace in a time of rupture, will not be able to avoid criticizing the system itself. This holds true even for the democratic system the way we know it. In the face of increasing military violence, the growth of meanwhile excessive environmental problems, the fact that the problems of resource distribution in "one world" have yet to be overcome, the exponential increase in the technological risks, which the entire human race faces in an existential sense – must we not, and swiftly at that, discuss whether the present democracy is up-to-date and appropriate for the future? Can we imagine a democracy beyond the democracy that we know?

Even if this is close to a breaking a taboo: It is democracy that must become more modern and efficient. The only alternative would be to vehemently cut through the Gordian knot by using Alexander's sword.

Why is there no "parliament of experts", namely no "council of the future" in addition to the general parliament that we already have and presumably will also continue to require? A "council of the future" dealing exclusively with existential questions, on the one hand elected and thus legitimised democratically, and on the other composed of experts and thus furnished with the knowledge to look for and find alternative solutions, further they would only be voted into office for one term allowing them to be as free as possible from inappropriate influences and interests and finally they would have the right to veto and thus have the capacity if necessary to put a spoke in the wheels of politics, research, the media and big business?

Even today there is in Germany a division of sovereignty, a division of competencies, rights and obligations between the Federation and the *Länder* (German provinces), the *Länder* parliaments and the *Bundesrat* (upper house of parliament). Why should the responsibility for "existential questions" of human beings and humanity (war and peace, development, poverty, environment, climate, human dignity), not be assigned to a new third "chamber", a "Council of the Future"?

Even today in the Federal Republic, there are institutions, which independent of institutions that are in the traditional sense democratic due to the fact that they are elected, like the parliament and the government, make decisions which give direction, correct the mistakes of every-day politics and even initiate policies. I am referring to the (former) Federal Bank of Germany and in particular the Federal Constitutional Court. In this sense, particularly the latter has for a number of years also taken decisions on policy (including security-policy), to the extent that politics and policy-making have degenerated more and more to simple day-to-day policy-making. The fact that the decisions of the Federal Constitutional Court are accepted equally from – and are even approved by and searched for by – the electing public as well as the elected class of politicians, speaks well for the court, but less for representative democracy in its present form.

Thus why not then put both together? On the one hand, create an institution with the independence and the authority of the Federal Constitutional Court and on the other, furnish it with the sovereign right to act on the existential questions of humanity and with the legitimation of elections like a parliament. This kind of institutionalised unification would be much more than anything we have today. Nevertheless, it would not be sufficient to deal properly with existential problems, nor would it solve the Gordian knot without violence. Rather, a third element would be decisive in putting together this chamber: the nomination of independent experts with a good reputation.

Thus this council of the future would be made up of the academic elite of the country. Does this mean that this council of the future would – deliberately or inadvertently – open the gates and doors to an elitist democracy without any connections with the sovereign entity, i.e. the people? This question would be a justified reproach if the experts were to be limited exclusively to full-time representatives of the academic and research community. However, this is exactly the opposite case: Strategic competence can also be gained through voluntary involvement and specialized knowledge through having participated in the social movements and especially in NGOs. It is no coincidence that meanwhile even at high-ranking academic conferences, representatives from the "practical world" are sought as speakers and participants in discussions.

Moreover, the relationship with civil society, in particular the communications structures of the movements and the NGOs, could be promoted through the creation of – not just one central federal council of the future – but 16 *Länder* councils of the future. This kind of federalization would not change the border-crossing character of the tasks of this third chamber, but it would bring us even closer to the solution of several complicated questions. These include the problems of selecting candidates as well as the question of legitimation through elections. The elections to a third chamber could be linked to those of the *Länder* parliaments. It would not be the parties who drew up the list of candidates, but institutes, NGOs and different political movements (even those competing with one other). However, because of the complexity of the problems to be dealt with, the period in office should not be limited to four years, but rather eight. Re-election would be strictly out of the question for reasons of independence and protection from inappropriate influences and interests.

The future is always also the *post* present. And the present leads up to the future. Those of you who understand this as a chance and then implement this chance in policies will be able not only to master a future in democracy and peace, but also guide and structure it.

NOTES

[1] Quotes in: Rau, Johannes, *Friede als Ernstfall. Reden und Beiträge des Bundespräsidenten.* Edited by Dieter S. Lutz, Baden-Baden 2001, in particular. pp. 37, 73, 74, 78, 82, 118, 208, 212. (author's translation).

[2] Cf. *inter alia*: Neuneck, Götz/Scheffran, Jürgen, "Die Grenzen technischer Kriegführung." [The Limits of Technical Warfare.], in: *Spektrum der Wissenschaft.* Januar 2000; Lutz, Dieter S., "Der Preis der Krieges ist seine Legitimität. Zu den Kosten und Folgekosten des Kosovo-Krieges." [Loss of Legitimacy is the Price of War. On the Costs and Follow-up Costs of the Kosovo War.], in: Cremer, Ulrich/Lutz, Dieter S. (eds..), *Nach dem Krieg ist vor dem Krieg. Die Sicht der anderen zum Kosovo-Krieg und ihre alternativen Lehren und Konsequenzen.* [Succeeding War is Preceding War. The View of the Others on the Kosovo War and its Alternative Lessons and Consequences.], Hamburg 1999, pp. 129-146.

[3] Cf. Lutz, Dieter S. (ed.), *Der Kosovo-Krieg. Rechtliche und rechtsethische Aspekte.* [The Kosovo War, its Legal and Legal-Ethical Aspects.], Baden-Baden 1999/2000; Lutz, Dieter S. (ed.), *Der Krieg im Kosovo und das Versagen der Politik. Beiträge aus dem IFSH.* [The War in Kosovo and the Failure in Politics. Articles from IFSH], Baden-Baden 2000; Lutz, Dieter S./Christmann, Stefanie, *Die Zerstörung der Vernunft in*

Zeiten des Krieges. Zum Demokratieverlust nach 1989. [The Destruction of Rationale in Times of War. On the Loss of Democracy after 1989.], Berlin 2000.

[4] Mutz, Reinhard, "Der Graben wird tiefer." [The Rift is Getting Deeper.], in: Hermann Hagena/Reinhard Mutz, *Streitkräfte und Strategien.* [Armed Forces and Strategies.], Baden-Baden 2001, pp. 123-126, here: p. 126.

[5] Carothers, Thomas, *Ousting Foreign Strongmen: Lessons from Serbia, Carnegie Endowment for International Peace.* Volume 1/No. 5, May 2001, in particular pp. 3 and 5.

[6] However, one should not forget the basic problem that especially democracies have with expensive preventive measures: Paradoxically, the difficulty is that financial expenditures must be justified when the case has been successful. Were the financial resources really necessary to prevent or end the conflict? Would not lower expenditures also have been enough? Would the conflict have emerged at all or would it have reached violent levels? How should democratically elected members of parliament respond when they are reproached for squandering funds? How can they prove that something has not occurred for the very reason that it has been prevented successfully?

[7] Van der Stoel, Max, "Demokratie und Menschenrechte. Rede des Hohen Kommissars für Nationale Minderheiten der OSZE vor dem Institut für Friedensforschung und Sicherheitspolitik, Hamburg, am 17. März 1997." [Democracy and Human Rights. Speech of the OSCE High Commissioner on National Minorities to the Institute for Peace Research and Security Policy, Hamburg, 17 March 1997.], in: *Hamburger Vorträge am Institut für Friedensforschung und Sicherheitspolitik 3/1997,* p. 4. (author's translation).

[8] Cf.: Lutz, Dieter S. / Mutz, Reinhard, "Für die politische Zukunft des Kosovos hat der Westen kein Konzept. Vor Zwei Jahren begann die Nato mit dem Bombardement Jugoslawiens." [The West has no Concept for the Political Future of Kosovo. Two Years Ago, NATO Bombings Began in Yugoslavia.], in: Frankfurter Rundschau Nr. 71; 24 March 2001, p. 8.

[9] Cf. the work of: Schütz, Cathrin, "Die Lutz/Mutz-Erler Kontroverse." In: *Hamburger Beiträge zur Friedensforschung und Sicherheitspolitik*, i.e.

[10] This last figure I obtained recently from the UNHCR.

[11] NATO Parliamentary Assembly, Committee Reports, Political Committee, General Report: Kosovo Aftermath and its Implications for Conflict Prevention and Crisis Management, International Secretariat, November 2000 (Markus Meckel/Germany, General Rapporteur), At: http://www.nato-pa.int/publications/comrep/2000/at-261-e.html.

[12] Cf.: Loquai, Heinz, *Der Kosovo-Konflikt – Wege in einen vermeidbaren Krieg.* [The Kosovo Conflict – Paths to an Unnecessary War.], Baden-Baden 2000.

[13] Cf. already in : Lutz, Dieter S., "Die mächtigste Allianz der Welt – Ein Sündenfall." [The Most Powerful Alliance in the World – Its Fall from Grace.], in: Frankfurter Allgemeine Zeitung 113 of 18. May 1999, p. 53.

[14] Lutz, Dieter S., *Der Kosovo-Krieg. Rechtliche und rechtsethische Aspekte.* [The Kosovo War, its Legal and Legal-Ethical Aspects.], cited above (Note 3); Lutz, Dieter S., "Dieser Krieg war keineswegs unabwendbar." [This War is in no Terms Inevitable.].

Letter to Erhard Eppler, in: Dieter S. Lutz (ed.), *Der Krieg im Kosovo und das Versagen der Politik.* [The War in Kosovo and the Failure of Politics.], cited above (Note 3), pp. 445-455; Lutz, Dieter S., *Krieg und Frieden als Rechtsfrage im Parlamentarischen Rat 1948/49. Wertentscheidung, Auslegungsmethodik, Dokumentation.* [War and Peace as a Legal Issue in the German Parliamentary Council, Decisions on Values, Methods of Interpretation, Documentation.], Baden-Baden 1982.

[15] General Report, cited above (Note 11).

[16] Lutz, Dieter S., "'Dirty Secrets'" oder: War der Kosovo-Krieg wirklich unabwendbar?" ["'Dirty Secrets' or Was the Kosovo War really inevitable?"], in: *Vierteljahresschrift für Sicherheit und Frieden.* (S+F) 3/1999, pp.143-145.

[17] "Lageanalyse des Auswärtigen Amtes vom 19. März 1999 zur humanitären Situation im Kosovo." [Situation Analysis of the Federal Foreign Office.], in: *Vierteljahresschrift für Sicherheit und Frieden.* (S+F) 3/1999, p. 211 (author's translation).

[18] FüS II, *Zusammenfassung der Lageentwicklung im ehemaligen Jugoslawien. Politische und militärische Lage (Stand 23.03.1999, 15.00 Uhr)* [Summary of the Development of the Situation in the Former Yugoslavia. Political and Military Situation (Status on 23 March 1999, 3:00 P.M.)].

[19] This document is in the possession of the author.

[20] Loquai, cited above (Note 12), p. 11.

[21] General Report, cited above (Note 11).

[22] Cf: Rau, Johannes, "Antrittsrede nach der Vereidigung zum Bundespräsidenten bei der gemeinsamen Sitzung von Bundestag und Bundesrat, Bonn, 1. Juli 1999." In: Ders., *Friede als Ernstfall, Reden und Beiträge des Bundespräsidenten.* Edited by Dieter S. Lutz, Baden-Baden 2001, pp. 215-228, here: p. 220.: "'War is not the real proof of worth ...'. This sentence uttered by Heinemann contradicts European intellectual history. It contradicts Heraclit. It contradicts Schiller. 'War is not the real proof of worth, peace is the challenge and we must prove our worth in times of peace because beyond peace there is no existence.' Gustav Heinemann stated this in 1964 ... (Today) Gustav Heinemann's statement that 'peace is the real proof of worth' has a much more comprehensive meaning than it did 36 years ago: At the time when Heinemann expressed this, it was a negatively definable and defined task, it was regarded as preventing the Cold War from escalating into a hot war. Today the positively defined task of moulding the peace process is on the agenda in Europe. Today times of peace have become the real proof of worth." – Cf. Rau, Johannes, "Der Friede ist der Ernstfall. Der Beitrag der OSZE zu einer Friedens- und Sicherheitspolitik im 21. Jahrhundert." Ansprache anlässlich der Eröffnung des OSZE-Forschungszentrums am Institut für Friedensforschung und Sicherheitspolitik an der Universität Hamburg ["Times of Peace are Times in Which Worth is Proved". Opening Ceremony of the Centre for OSCE Research on 6 January 2000.], Hamburg, 6. Januar 2000, in: ibid., p. 229-234, here: pp. 229-231.

[23] Heinemann, who was a decided opponent of rearmament, did not regard himself as a pacifist. "Peace and its sustainability" were nevertheless "the primary task of 'proof of worth' in policy-making". Cf.: Rau, Johannes, "Zum 100. Geburtstag von Gustav

Heinemann, 23. Juli 1999." [Johannes Rau on Gustav Heinemann's 100th birthday, 23 July 1999.], in: ibid., pp. 41-43, here: p. 41.

[24] Cf. on the following: Institute for Peace Research and Security Policy at the University of Hamburg, *The European Security Community (ESC). The Security Model for the Twenty-First Century.* Baden-Baden 1996.

[25] Cf. on the following: Lutz, Dieter S., "Gibt es eine Demokratie jenseits der Demokratie, wie wir sie kennen? Plädoyer für die Schaffung eines 'Zukunftsrates'." [Is There a Democracy beyond the Democracy That We Know? Plea for the Creation of a "Council for the Future".], in: *Zur Lage der Nation. Leitgedanken für eine Politik der Berliner Republik.* [On the Situation of the Nation. Guiding Ideas for a Policy of the Berlin Republic] (Ed. Willy-Brandt-Kreis), Berlin 2001, pp. 253-262.

CONTRIBUTORS

RÜDIGER BITTNER, Institut für Philosophie, University of Bielefeld, Germany, rbittner@philosophie.uni-bielefeld.de, www.uni-bielefeld.de/philosophie/personen/bittner

UWE CZANIERA, Institut für Philosophie, University of Bayreuth, Germany uwe.czaniera@uni-bayreuth.de, http://www.uni-bayreuth.de/departments/philosophie/deutsch/people/Uwe/cv_d.htm

MARTIN FRANK, Institut für Interkulturelle und Internationale Studien (InIIS), University of Bremen, Germany, mkfrank@uni-bremen.de, www.institute.uni-bremen.de/~iniis/mitarb/mf.htm

JOHAN GALTUNG, Dr. hc mult, Professor of Peace Studies at numerous International Peace Universities; Director of TRANSCEND: A Peace and Development Network, galtung@transcend.org, http://www.transcend.org

DIETER S. LUTZ, Institut für Friedensforschung und Sicherheitspolitik, Hamburg, Germany; died in Jan 2003. *RIP*.

GEORG MEGGLE, Institut für Philosophie, University of Leipzig, Germany, meggle@uni-leipzig.de, www.uni-leipzig.de/~philos/meggle.htm

THOMAS MERTENS, Faculty of Law, University of Nijmegen, Netherlands, t.mertens@jur.kun.nl

SEUMAS MILLER, Centre for Applied Philosophy and Publice Ethics, Charles Sturt University, Canberra, Australia, seumas.miller@anu.edu.au

OLAF L. MÜLLER, Institut für Philosophie, Humboldt University of Berlin, Germany, MuellerO@philosophic.hu-berlin.de

ALEKSANDAR PAVKOVIC, Departement of Politics and International Relations, Macquarie University Sydney & Centre for Applied Philosophy and Public Ethics, University of Melbourne, Australia, aleksandar.pavkovic@mq.edu.au, www.pol.mq.edu.au

WALTER PFANNKUCHE, Philosophisches Institut, Technical University of Berlin, Germany, pfanrebb@mailszrz.zrz.tu-berlin.de

MIROSLAV PROKOPIJEVIC, Institute for European Studies, Belgrade & Free Market Center, Serbia, mprokop@eunet.yu

HAJO SCHMIDT, Institut Frieden und Demokratie, Fernuni Hagen, Germany, hajo.schmidt@fernuni-hagen.de, www.fernuni-hagen.de/FRIEDEN

RUDOLF SCHÜSSLER, Institut für Philosophie, University of Bayreuth,Germany, http://www.uni-bayreuth.de/departments/philosophie/deutsch/people/Rudolf/cv_d.htm

REINER STEINWEG, Außenstelle Linz des Österreichischen Studienzentrums für Frieden und Konfliktlösung (ÖSFK), Austria, reiner.steinweg@liwest.at

ULRICH STEINVORTH, Institut für Philosophie, University of Hamburg, Germany, http://www.phil-gesch.uni-hamburg.de/phil/philperson/steinvorth1.html

RALF STOECKER, Fakultät für Geschichtswissenschaft und Philosophie, University of Bielefeld, rstoecke@philosophie.uni-bielefeld.de

MICHAEL WALZER, Institute for Advanced Study, University of Princeton, New Jersey, USA, walzer@ias.edu, www.sss.ias.edu/home/walzer.html

VÉRONIQUE ZANETTI, Institut für Philosophie, University of Bielefeld, Germany, Switzerland, veronique.zanetti@t-online.de .